PROPHECY AND
THE CHURCH

PROPHECY AND THE CHURCH

AN EXAMINATION OF THE CLAIM OF DISPENSATIONALISTS
THAT THE CHRISTIAN CHURCH IS A MYSTERY PARENTHESIS
WHICH INTERRUPTS THE FULFILMENT TO ISRAEL OF
THE KINGDOM PROPHECIES OF THE OLD TESTAMENT

By

OSWALD T. ALLIS

*You, and all the prophets from Samuel and those that
follow after, as many as have spoken, have likewise
foretold of these days*

THE PRESBYTERIAN AND REFORMED
PUBLISHING COMPANY

PHILADELPHIA

1945

PREFACE

THE title, *Prophecy and the Church,* brings together two words or topics which are of great importance to every thoughtful and well-informed Christian. A very considerable part of the Old Testament is prophetic: it deals with things to come. The Christian Church is an institution whose founding and early history are clearly described in the New Testament. This Church has been in existence for centuries. The question that concerns us is as to the relation, if any, between the kingdom prophecies of the Old Testament and the New Testament Church. Until early in the last century, it was the generally accepted belief that the Christian Church is the fulfilment of the kingdom prophecies, that the glorious predictions of the prophets concerning Israel have had and are to have, at least in the main, their fulfilment in the Church. But now, for a hundred years and more, the doctrine has been taught, and is now widely accepted, that Israel and the Church are quite distinct; that the kingdom prophecies of the Old Testament refer to Israel, not to the Church; that Israel is God's earthly people, while the Church is a heavenly mystery, unknown to the prophets and first revealed to the apostle Paul; that the Church is a parenthesis in God's prophetic program for Israel, and that its presence on earth interrupts the fulfilment of that program; that the rapture of the Church may take place "at any moment" and will be followed by a Jewish age in which the kingdom prophecies concerning Israel will be literally fulfilled.

The question as to the correctness of this relatively new interpretation of prophecy is obviously a very important one. Whether the words of the prophets refer to the Church and have their fulfilment in this present gospel age, or "skip over" this dispensation completely and have

v

reference to a Jewish kingdom age which may at any moment replace it, is a question of Biblical interpretation which vitally concerns every Christian who would fain understand the world in which he is living and read aright God's purposes of grace. In fact the difference between this and the older view is so great that the new interpretation must produce of necessity, and has produced, a distinct and distinctive type of Biblical interpretation which leads to results the gravity of which can hardly be exaggerated. According to the one view, the Church is the fulfilment of prophecy; according to the other, it interrupts that fulfilment. According to the one view the Church age is the "day of salvation"; according to the other view the Church age is only an episode, even if a very important one, in that day of salvation; and the salvation of Israel and of "the enormous majority of mankind" will follow the removal of the Church. What questions should be of more concern to the Christian than these?

These questions are not only important; they are also very timely and urgent. Dispensationalism has been becoming increasingly in recent years a seriously divisive factor in evangelical circles. All who accept the Bible as the Word of God and hold it to be the only infallible rule of faith and practice should be able to stand shoulder to shoulder in their opposition to Modernism and Higher Criticism. But, unfortunately, Dispensationalism introduces, and cannot but introduce, a cleavage which tends very seriously to undermine that solidarity and harmony with which Evangelicals should face the assaults of scepticism and unbelief. Dispensationalists do not constitute a denomination, nor are they confined to any one denomination. They are to be found in practically all branches of Protestantism. They are earnest and zealous. But their beliefs as to Prophecy and the Church make co-operation difficult between them and those who do not regard their distinctive doctrines as precious "re-discovered truths," but hold them rather to be a serious departure from the historic faith of the Church as set forth in the

Scriptures. The result is a situation that is deplorable. It is more than deplorable; it is dangerous.

A further reason that this discussion is timely lies in the fact that the "Jewish question" is assuming in these days an importance that is unprecedented. The terrible Nazi persecutions of the Jews have made the question of a national home for this oppressed people a subject of earnest consideration and vigorous debate. That the Jew is a problem, a world problem, no one will deny. But why is he a problem? Is it simply because he is "out of the land," a land promised to his fathers and rightfully his? Is the solution of the problem, then, to be found in the opening of Palestine to unrestricted occupancy by the Jews, and in admitting them to a place in the family of nations? Is their presence "in the land" so important that Palestine should be regarded as belonging to them exclusively, and should they be encouraged to set up a kingdom there like that of David or Solomon? Should the Christians in all the Allied Countries use every effort to persuade their governments to insist at the coming Peace Conference that Palestine be given to the Jews? Is this the solution of the Jewish question? Or, is the reason that the Jew is a problem to be found in something quite different: in the fact that he rejected the Messiah promised to his race and was "scattered among the nations" as a punishment for his sin, that he still continues in unbelief and yet still regards himself as a "peculiar people," whose destiny is to rule the earth under a Messiah who is yet to come? And is the hope of the Jew today, as of all men, to be found in the acceptance by him of the gospel of the grace of God which the Church has been commanded to proclaim to all nations, that gospel of the Cross, which is to the Jew a *stumbling block* and to the Greek *foolishness*, but to them that are saved both Jews and Greeks, *Christ the power of God and the wisdom of God?* In other words, has the Jew a distinct and glorious future promised him independently of the Church? Is he entitled to look forward to an "earthly" kingdom which is yet to be his? Or, is his need, his supreme need, that heavenly salvation which is to be found only in the Christian Church?

These questions are timely and important because they concern both Church and State; and the Christian church-man and the Christian statesman must face them honestly and fearlessly. The answer given by the churchman will determine his conception of the duty of the Church toward the Jew, whether the Church shall offer the Jew salvation within her fold, or help him to obtain the kingdom. The answer given by Christian statesmen will determine their attitude toward Zionism and the political and national aspirations which it fosters and hopes to realize. I am quite aware, painfully so, that in my treatment of this highly controversial subject I am opposing the sincerely cherished convictions of many for whose piety and zeal I have the highest regard, and with whom I would fain co-operate most heartily in the Lord's work. It is my earnest hope that my Dispensationalist brethren will not resent this well-meant attempt to point out to them what I believe to be dangerous errors in what is often called "Dispensational truth," but will test what is here set forth by the light of Scripture under the guidance of the Holy Spirit. For I am persuaded that they share with me the profound conviction that "The Supreme Judge, by whom all controversies of religion are to be determined, and all decrees of councils, opinions of ancient writers, doctrines of men, and private spirits, are to be examined, and in whose sentence we are to rest, can be no other but the Holy Spirit speaking in the Scripture."

The literature bearing on the subject of Dispensationalism is very extensive. The Brethren were quick to discover the power of the printed page and showed themselves masters of the art of the propagandist; and their books, journals, and tracts are legion and have gone to the four corners of the world. In this as in other respects the Dispensationalists have been their apt pupils. But much of this literature is now hard to obtain; and the dearth of source-material in many or most libraries is very noticeable. The British Museum and the Municipal Library of Middlesbrough, Yorkshire, to which William Kelly bequeathed his great library, are very rich in material. A visit to England in 1936-37 made it possible for me, in connection with other work, to make considerable use of these resources. It is a pleasure to express to the Librarians of these institutions my appreciation of the courtesies extended to me there.

Among those in this country who have aided me I remember with gratitude the late John Watt of Wayne, a Plymouth Brother who, though holding *con amore* the teaching opposed in this book, assisted me in a most friendly way in my efforts to gain a correct understanding of it. Rev. Roy E. Grace, Th.M., pastor of the Beverly Hills United Presbyterian Church, Upper Darby, Pa., read the manuscript as it was nearing completion; and I am thankful to him for this and also for his comments and suggestions. Most of all I am indebted to Rev. Samuel G. Craig, D.D., president of *The Presbyterian and Reformed Publishing Co.* Dr. Craig has read the book in manuscript and proof and I am grateful to him not only for helpful suggestion and criticism, but also for aid and encouragement all along the way.

Wayne, Pa., January, 1945

A second printing of *Prophecy and the Church* has afforded the opportunity to make a few minor changes and correction, which do not affect the main positions taken. The reception which the book has received, favorable in some quarters, unfavorable in others, has served to strengthen the conviction under which it was written, that the issues it discusses are of vital and pressing interest to the Christian Church today.

Wayne, May, 1947 Oswald T. Allis.

CONTENTS

CHAPTER I

MILLENARIANISM AND DISPENSATIONALISM

"YE DO shew the Lord's death till He come" is Paul's meaningful comment on the words of institution of the Holy Supper which the Church of Christ has kept in remembrance of her crucified and risen Saviour for nigh two thousand years, and is to keep until "the kingdom of God shall come." This close connection between the Cross which was the crowning humiliation of the first advent and the coming in glory which is the blessed hope of the Church has been beautifully expressed in the words of the sacramental hymn:

> "And thus that dark betrayal night
> With the last advent we unite
> By one blest chain of loving rite
> Until He come."

But while the Church has kept the feast throughout the centuries that are past, she has not always kept it worthily. Like the Corinthian Christians she has at times and in certain communions perverted it to base ends, even making the holy sacrament a means of promoting the carnal security of those whose lives showed nothing of that sanctification of the spirit which the redemption, symbolized by the bread and the wine, so impressively demands. Likewise, though the doctrine of the coming has never entirely passed out of the thought and expectation of the Church, the hope has often burned but dimly; and earthly and carnal anticipations have marred the heavenly glory of the coming day.

Just as the meaning of the Cross has been a matter of controversy, so the meaning of the coming has been a subject of frequent debate. This is illustrated by a phrase in the verse quoted above, "with the last advent we unite." Is the advent of which the hymn-writer speaks, is the

1

coming of which the apostle speaks, the *last* advent or is it not? Will the coming of Christ terminate this present gospel age and be followed by the last judgment and the final state? Or, will it usher in another dispensation, the millennium, during which Christ will reign on earth and after which He will come to judge the world? Will the coming of Christ terminate the day of salvation for sinful men? Or, will it usher in an age during which the number of the redeemed will vastly exceed the total of those saved during the entire course of human history preceding it? Finally, if the latter view is regarded as the true one, on what basis and by what means will this vast multitude be saved? These are vitally important questions; and widely varying and conflicting answers have been given to them. According to many students of prophecy, the issue can be stated in terms of the two words, Postmillennialism and Premillennialism.[1] This would seem to make the issue very simple and clear. It would indicate that the difference is merely this: the Postmillennialist believes that the advent will follow the millennium, while the Premillennialist holds that it will precede it. But the difficulty at once emerges that in these definitions the word "millennium" is used in two more or less markedly different and even contradictory senses. It will be better, therefore, to define the issue in terms of the word "coming" or "advent."[2]

1. One Visible Coming (A- and Postmillennialism)

This is the teaching that the only visible coming of Christ to this earth which the Church is to expect will be for judgment and will be followed by the final state. It is anti-chiliastic or a-millennial, because it rejects the doctrine that there are to be two resurrections with an interval of a thousand years (the millennial reign of Christ with His saints on earth) between them. It has two main forms.

a. The Augustinian View

The view which has been most widely held by opponents of Millenarianism is associated historically with the name of Augustine. He taught that the millennium is to be interpreted spiritually as fulfilled in the Christian Church. He held that the binding of Satan took place during the earthly ministry of our Lord (Lk. x. 18), that the first resurrection is the new birth of the believer (Jn. v. 25), and that the millennium must correspond, therefore, to the inter-adventual period or Church age. This involved the interpreting of Rev. xx. 1-6 as a "recapitulation" of the preceding chapters instead of as describing a new age following chronologically on the events set forth in chap. xix. Living in the first half of the first millennium of the Church's history, Augustine naturally took the 1000 years of Rev. xx. literally; and he expected the second advent to take place at the end of that period. But since he somewhat inconsistently identified the millennium with what then remained of the sixth chiliad of human history,[3] he believed that this period might end about A. D. 650[4] with a great outburst of evil, the revolt of Gog, which would be followed by the coming of Christ in judgment. This view which discovers the millennium in the present Christian dispensation has had a number of different forms.

(1) Up to the close of the 10th century it was natural that the 1000 years should be regarded as giving, at least approximately, the actual length of the inter-adventual period.[5]

(2) When the course of history then began to make it plain that this period must be longer, perhaps much longer, than 1000 years, the advocates of this interpretation were faced with two possibilities.

(a) They could still identify the millennium with the inter-adventual period as a whole by treating the 1000 years as a symbolic number, not to be taken literally. This is the simplest solution and it has had many advocates.

(b) They could limit the millennium, as a 1000 year period, to a part only of the inter-adventual period. This view logically presents three possibilities.

(α) The millennium is past. At the time of the Reformation the view was widely held that the millennium was then past, and that the Church was in the "little season." It permitted the dating of the millennium from the time of Constantine. Now it can, of course, be regarded as commencing considerably later.[6]

(β) The millennium is now present. This requires the placing of the beginning of the millennium at a much later date. *E.g.*, Durham *(cir.* A.D. 1650), dated it at about A.D. 1560.

(γ) The millennium is still future. This view has been associated particularly with the name of Whitby (1707). It is the doctrine that the "golden age" of the Church on earth is yet to come. It differs from the other forms of the Augustinian view in one very important respect: viz., in rejecting the interpretation of the 1000 years as a recapitulation (in whole or in part) of the inter-adventual period described in the preceding chapters, and regarding it as following in chronological sequence on chap. xix.[7] Being regarded as wholly future and as perhaps belonging to a remote future, this millennium can be conceived of as very different from anything which the history of the Church has exhibited in the past, while at the same time being regarded as an integral part of the inter-adventual period: not as a different age, but as the climax and culmination of the Church age. Those who hold this view of the millennium can apply, with considerable literalness, the Old Testament kingdom prophecies regarding Israel to this glorious future of the Church on earth. Consequently, this teaching takes a decidedly optimistic view of the future of the Church. The Christian may and should expect in this present gospel age a glorious answer to the petition which his Lord has commanded him to offer, "Thy kingdom come."

It is to be noted that all forms of the Augustinian view, by which we mean, all views which discover the millennium in the inter-adventual period or in some part of it, whether that part be past, present, or future, may properly be called both *a*millennial and *post*millennial. They are amillennial in the sense that they all deny that after the present dispensation has been terminated by the resurrection and rapture of the saints, there is to be a reign of Christ on earth with the saints for 1000 years before the last judgment. But since they identify the millennium with the whole, or with some part, of the present gospel age, they may also all be called postmillennial. In this sense Augustine was a Postmillennialist. But while this is true, the word "postmillennial" has come to be so identified with the name of Whitby that as used by very many writers on prophecy it applies exclusively to that view which regards the millennium as a golden age of the Church which is wholly future, perhaps still remote, and which is to precede the second advent.

b. Kliefoth's View

About 150 years after Whitby radically modified the Augustinian doctrine by insisting that the spiritual millennium described in Rev. xx. is not a "recapitulation" of the entire Church age but follows chap. xix. chronologically and is wholly future, this interpretation was again attacked, but with a quite different result, by two German scholars, Duesterdieck (1859) and Kliefoth (1874). Kliefoth roundly declared that, from the beginning of the Church, two unwarranted and baseless views had been held: (1) the millennial or chiliastic, and (2) that view which seeks the period of the 1000 years in the present dispensation (*in dem jetzigen Weltlauf*),[8] meaning of course the Augustinian view in all its forms. In opposition to both of these ancient views, Kliefoth insisted, as did Duesterdieck, that the recapitulation theory is false, that Rev. xx. gives a vision of what immediately precedes the consummation. In this they agreed with Whitby. But, being convinced that nowhere else in the New Testament is there any reference to or any provision for a millennial reign before the advent, they concluded, as against Whitby, that this reign cannot be a period of time at all, but simply describes in terms of completeness or ecumenicity the blessed state of the saints in heaven. This view is amillennial in the strictest sense of the word. For it denies that the 1000 years has any reference to time. As compared to the various forms of the amillennial view which have been considered it is a comparatively recent one, and has not succeeded in replacing the Augustinian view which it so vigorously attacked.

The fact that the word "amillennial" is used in both a broad and a narrow sense—to cover both the view of Augustine and that of Kliefoth—has led inevitably to confusion; and statements are sometimes made that are seemingly contradictory. When Berkhof, for example, describes Amillennialism as the historic faith of the Christian Church, he is referring to the Augustinian view in general. When Chafer, Gaebelein, and others speak of it somewhat contemptuously as a new and almost unheard-of teaching, they apparently have in mind the view of Kliefoth.[9]

One point is especially to be stressed in this connection, for the reason that it is of fundamental importance to the problems to be discussed in this volume. All Amillennialists of today, whether they hold with Augustine or with Kliefoth, are in a position to maintain that the coming of the Lord is "imminent";[10] and some of them take that pessimistic view of the future of the Church on earth— that the love of many will grow cold, and that evil men will grow worse and worse—which is characteristic of the premillennial view. The great exception is the Whitbyans, whom in accordance with customary usage we shall call Postmillenarians.

2. *The Doctrine of Two Advents (Premillennialism)*

The premillennial view may be stated very briefly in the words of Nathanael West. "Christian Chiliasm, or Pre-Millennarianism, is the doctrine of the personal reign of Christ, on earth, 1,000 years after the Beast, False Prophet, and Apostate Christendom have been judged and perished in a common doom."[11] This means that a visible coming of Christ will precede the millennium. It will not be to a saved and perfected world that the Lord will come, but to a world of mingled good and evil, a world in which the evil may even largely predominate (Matt. xiii. 30; Lk. xviii. 8). "No millennium until Christ comes" is its slogan. At this coming the elect are to be caught up to meet the Lord in the air (the first resurrection and rapture) and then to return with Him to the earth for His millennial reign. This reign of Christ and His saints is to be followed by a "little season" of apostasy, when Satan will be unbound. Then will come a second or postmillennial advent, which will be followed by the last judgment and the final state. There will, therefore, be two visible comings, the one to reign, the other to judge, with a thousand year interval between them. Consequently, since it is their insistence on the first of these, a visible coming before the millennium, that is distinctive of their position, they are usually and not inaptly called Premillennialists. While this difference distinguishes their position sharply from all forms of the Augustinian view, two points of agreement may also be noted: (1) Premillennialists find in Whitby and Kliefoth support for their claim that the recapitulation theory of Augustine is untenable. (2) They have as a rule favored some form of the Historical interpretation of the Book of Revelation; and some of its ablest advocates are to be numbered among them.

Such is in broad outline the premillennial view. It was extensively held in the Early Church, how extensively is not definitely known.[12] But the stress which many of its advocates placed on earthly rewards and carnal delights aroused wide-spread opposition to it; and it was largely replaced by the "spiritual" view of Augustine. It reappeared in extravagant forms at the time of the Reformation, notably among the Anabaptists. Bengel and Mede were among the first modern scholars of distinction to advocate it. But it was not until early in the last century that it became at all widely influential in modern times. Since then it has become increasingly popular; and the claim is frequently made that most of the leaders in the Church today, who are evangelical, are Premillennialists.

3. *The Doctrine of Three Advents (Dispensationalism)*

The form of Premillennialism which is most widely accepted today, at least in this country, is often called Dispensationalism. This is due to the emphasis which is placed in this teaching upon the "dispensational" interpretation of Scripture. "Rightly dividing the word of truth" is its watchword. This is understood to mean.

dividing it according to dispensations. A dispensation is defined as "a period of time during which man is tested in respect of obedience to some *specific* revelation of the will of God."[13] Seven dispensations are usually distinguished: innocency, conscience, human government, promise, law, grace, and the kingdom. There is a marked tendency to stress the differences between these dispensations and to set them in sharp contrast to one another. This is especially true of the last four; and the dispensation of grace as representing the present Church age is distinguished from all the others as a mystery parenthesis, having no connection with the dispensation of law which preceded it or with that of the kingdom which is to follow it. In fact, so much importance is attached to the claim that this dispensation is a mystery parenthesis, that this system of interpretation should be called, not simply Dispensationalism, but Mystery-Parenthesis Dispensationalism.[14] In its distinctly prophetic aspects this Dispensational teaching may be summarized briefly as follows:

1. The millennium is that future period of human history during which Christ will reign personally and visibly with His saints on and over the earth for a thousand years.
2. A visible coming of Christ will precede it.
3. This coming will be in two stages, the rapture and the appearing, with a considerable interval of time between them, in which important events will take place.
4. The rapture may take place at "any moment," and will certainly precede the great tribulation.
5. The rapture is the "blessed hope" of the Church.
6. The Church is composed of those, and those only, who are saved between Pentecost and the rapture.
7. The Church age is a mystery period (a parenthesis dispensation unknown to prophecy) lying between the 69th and 70th weeks of the prophecy of Daniel ix.
8. Between the rapture and the appearing, the events of the last week of the prophecy of Dan. ix., of Matt. xxiv., and of Rev. iv.-xix. are to take place.
9. After the rapture a Jewish remnant will take the place

of the Church as God's agent on earth for the conversion of Israel and the Gentiles.

Of the nine points enumerated above, only the first two are entitled to be regarded as characteristic of Premillennialism historically understood. The remaining seven are distinctive of Dispensationalism.[15] The proof of this is two-fold: when these particular doctrines were announced about a century ago, they were declared to be rediscovered truths which had been lost sight of since apostolic times; and they were vigorously opposed by many Premillennialists who regarded them as dangerous innovations. Consequently, it is important to remember that Premillennialism and Dispensationalism are not synonymous terms. All Dispensationalists are Premillenarians, but it is by no means true that all Premillenarians are Dispensationalists.[16] Dispensationalists are Futurists; they are also Pretribulationists. Many or most Premillenarians are to be classed as Historicists and Post-tribulationists.

4. History of Dispensationalism

The Dispensational teaching of today, as represented, for example, by the *Scofield Reference Bible,* can be traced back directly to the Brethren Movement which arose in England and Ireland about the year 1830.[17] Its adherents are often known as Plymouth Brethren, because Plymouth was the strongest of the early centres of Brethrenism. It is also called Darbyism, after John Nelson Darby (1800-82), its most conspicuous representative.[18] The primary features of this movement were two in number. The one related to the Church. It was the result of the profound dissatisfaction felt at that time by many earnest Christians with the worldliness and temporal security of the Church of England and of many of the dissenting communions in the British Isles. The other had to do with prophecy; it represented a very marked emphasis on the coming of the Lord as a present hope and immediate expectation These two doctrines were closely connected.

a. The Parenthesis Church

The beginning of the Brethren doctrine regarding the Church is found in the claim that an ordained ministry and eldership was not necessary to the proper observance of the great central rite of the Christian Church, the Lord's Supper. It was claimed that Christian believers might meet together to break bread, without any ecclesiastical order or government whatsoever. And since the New Testament speaks quite definitely of the ordaining of elders, it was claimed that this "professing church" which is characterized by a ministry or eldership having "successive" or "derivative" authority was Jewish and Petrine, and to be sharply distinguished from the Church described by Paul as a "mystery," which is entirely unique, utterly distinct from Israel, a heavenly body having no connection with the earth. So understood, the Church age is to be regarded as a "parenthesis" between the Old Testament kingdom of the past and the Old Testament kingdom of the future, or in other words as constituting an "interruption" in the fulfilment of the kingdom promises to Israel. This distinction between the true (Pauline) Church and the professing (Petrine) church is of fundamental importance.[19]

b. The Any Moment Coming

Closely connected with the doctrine of the Church was the doctrine of the Coming. Brethrenism had its beginnings at a time when there was great interest in the doctrine of the second advent. Edward Irving had stirred London by his flaming eloquence, declaring in sermon after sermon that the Lord might come at any moment.[20] The Brethren, who were ardent Chiliasts, took the position that the Church as a heavenly body had no connection with earthly events, that such events concerned Israel and the nations, that the Church must live in constant expectancy of the coming of the Lord, that no events of any kind must be regarded as necessarily intervening between the Church and this any moment expectancy, and particularly that the rapture of the Church would certainly take place before the great tribulation.

This any moment doctrine of the coming had a natural and inevitable consequence, which is of prime importance in Dispensational teaching. It led to the discovery of a second hidden interval or parenthesis in the course of redemptive history as set forth in the Bible. If the Church has nothing to do with earthly events and may be raptured at any moment, and if the Bible clearly refers to events which are to precede the coming of Christ to the earth, the logical inference is that there must be two aspects or "stages" of the coming: one which concerns the Church only and is timeless and signless, and the other which concerns the earth and will be separated from the former by an interval during which the predicted events will take place. Consequently, instead of adhering to the view that the rapture, the catching up of the saints to meet the Lord in the air, would be immediately or speedily followed by their return with Him to reign over the earth, which was the view generally held at that time by Premillennialists, the Brethren reached the conclusion that a sharp distinction must be drawn between the coming of the Lord *for* the saints (the rapture) and His coming *with* the saints (the appearing or revelation). In between these two events, they claimed that they could recognize an important interval of time; namely the 70th week of Dan. ix., the second part of which they identified more or less exactly with the events recorded in Rev. iv.-xix. Consequently, this second parenthesis, as we may call it, between the rapture and the appearing, is both a very necessary and also a distinctive feature of Brethren teaching, almost if not quite as important as the Church parenthesis referred to above.

c. The Jewish Remnant

Closely related to this teaching regarding the Church and the Coming and indeed indispensable to it was the doctrine of the Jewish Remnant. If the Church consists only of those who have been redeemed in the interval between Pentecost and the rapture, and if the entire Church is to be raptured, then there will be no Christians on earth during the period between the rapture and the appearing. Yet during that period 144,000 in Israel and an innumerable multitude from the Gentiles (Rev. vii.) are to be saved. How is this to be brought about, if the Church has been raptured and the Holy Spirit removed from the earth? The answer to this question is found in the doctrine of the Jewish remnant. After the rapture of the Church a Jewish remnant is to proclaim the gospel of the kingdom and through the preaching of this gospel multitudes are to be saved.

These three aspects of Brethren teaching, the doctrine of the Church, the doctrine of the any moment Coming, and the doctrine of the Jewish Remnant naturally met with vigorous opposition. Since the Brethren regarded all bodies of Christians, united together on any other principles than their own, as constituting the professing church and as distinct from the Body of Christ, and called them "sects," it was only to be expected that their ecclesiastical views would arouse strenuous opposition; and their denial of the necessity or validity of the rite of ordination and their whole conception of the Church was repeatedly attacked, especially during the lifetime of Darby who was its most vigorous advocate. This Brethren Controversy, as we may call it, has now become largely a thing of the past. The Plymouth Brethren are today one of the smallest of Christian groups, and their distinctive conception of Church order and government is very largely ignored. On the other hand, the fact that many of the views of the Brethren (their conception of the Church as a heavenly mystery and their prophetic program as a whole) are fully accepted in Dispensational circles, are indeed characteristic of Dispensationalism as such, has made Dispensationalism an issue of greater or lesser importance in practically all evangelical denominations at the present time. This Dispensational controversy, as we may call it, has two aspects. On the one hand, it is a controversy between Dispensationalists, as the now most influential premillennialist group, and all anti-millenarians, whether they hold the amillennial or postmillennial view. On the other hand, the issue is between Dispensationalists and those Premillenarians who deny the last seven of the nine points stated above. The issue in this case may be broadly stated as one between Pretribulationists and Post-tribulationists.

5. Dispensationalism in America

The distinctive features of Brethrenism were fully developed and formulated before the middle of the last century. Darby made his first visit to Canada in 1859 and subsequently paid repeated visits to Canada and the United States. In 1862 James Inglis of New York began the publication of a monthly, *Waymarks in the Wilderness*, which helped to spread the teachings of the Brethren on this side of the Atlantic. One of the most influential advocates of this teaching was James H. Brookes of St. Louis, whose *Maranatha* appeared about 1870 and passed through many editions. But while Brookes' Dispensational views so closely resemble those of the Brethren that it seems clear that they were largely derived from them, Brookes gave no credit for them to Darby or any other of the Brethren. This may be due to the fact that there were associations with the name of Darby which Brookes wished to avoid.[21] But his attitude was characteristic of the movement as a whole. Dispensationalists have accepted the prophetic teachings of the Brethren, but until recently have shown themselves decidedly unwilling to disclose the source from which they derived them. Brookes was active in the summer conferences known as "Believers' Meetings for Bible Study" which were commenced in the seventies,[22] and also in the Prophetic Conferences, the first of which was held in New York in 1878.

Without attempting to trace the history of Dispensationalism in detail, it will suffice to point out that it has owed its rapid growth in no small degree to two books, *Jesus is Coming* by "W.E.B.,"[23] and the *Scofield Reference Bible*. Blackstone's *Jesus is Coming* was published in 1878. It was well received, but was not very extensively used until 1908, when a special "presentation edition" was prepared and several hundred thousand copies were distributed gratis to Christian workers throughout the world. The *Scofield Reference Bible* was published in 1909 and revised in 1917. More than two million copies have been printed.[24] It is the Bible of Dispensationalists, and has probably done as much to popularize the prophetic teachings of Darby and the Brethren as all other agencies put together. That Scofield was indebted to the Brethren for his Dispensational views cannot be questioned. He derived them first indirectly, from Brookes, and then directly from the Brethren and their writings. He held Darby's *Synopsis,* which is the standard commentary among the Brethren, in high esteem; and in the Introduction to the *Reference Bible* he acknowledged his indebtedness to the Brethren Movement without expressly mentioning it, and made special mention of the "eminent Bible teacher," Walter Scott, who was a prominent figure among the Brethren. There are today scores of Bible Schools and Institutes in this country and elsewhere, especially in Canada, where Dispensational interpretation of the Bible is stressed and the *Scofield Reference Bible* practically a textbook. And the number of books and periodicals in circulation today which represent this viewpoint is legion.

The history of Dispensationalism has not been marked by inner conflict to the same extent as has that of Brethrenism. But it is a significant fact that some of the most vigorous opponents of the movement have come out of its own ranks. More than fifty years ago Robert Cameron and Nathanael West took issue with their colleagues of the Niagara Bible Conference over the question of Pretribulationism. They were followed by others, notably by W. J. Erdman and Henry W. Frost. The cause of Posttribulationism is vigorously advocated today by the Sovereign Grace Advent Testimony (London), which represents the views of B. W. Newton, who broke with Darby about a century ago over this and related issues.[25] One of the most active opponents of Dispensationalism in recent years, Philip Mauro, is also to be numbered among those who at one time ardently advocated its teachings. Another is A. W. Pink.

6. *Ultra Dispensationalism*

While the *Scofield Reference Bible* has been largely influential in spreading and popularizing Dispensational teachings, especially in America, there is another type of teaching which has quite as much right to the name Dispensationalism as have the followers of Darby and Scofield. No one could be more emphatic than was E. W. Bullinger (1837-1913)[26] that "rightly dividing the word of truth" means to divide it dispensationally. But Bullinger carried this method to such an extreme, a logical extreme we believe, that his teachings have been roundly denounced by what we may call the Scofield party; and Bullingerism has been stigmatized as "ultra" Dispensationalism. One of the most important differences has to do, quite naturally, with the Church. Bullinger distinguished between the Pentecostal Apostolic Church of the Book of Acts and the Mystery Pauline Church of the Prison Epistles. He called the one the "bride church" and the other the "body church." He held further that the church referred to in Matt. xvi., which Jesus called "my church," is distinct from both of these and will be a Jewish remnant church of the future. Bullingerism has not attained any such widespread popularity as that enjoyed by the Darby-Scofield type of Dispensationalism. We shall concern ourselves with it only in so far as its teachings serve to illustrate the extreme positions to which Dispensationalism logically forces those who seek to carry it out to its ultimate conclusions.

CHAPTER II

IMPORTANT PRINCIPLES OF DISPENSATIONAL INTERPRETATION

THE Brethren Movement from which Dispensational-ism derived its distinctive doctrines was at first characterized by great simplicity of teaching. The Brethren denounced the historic creeds of the Church as man-made "systems" and insisted that they alone were truly "subject" and "submissive" to the Bible as the Word of God. But they very soon developed a system which was as distinctive as any of the systems which they denounced, so that their denunciation of all creeds and systems speedily came to mean no more than this, that all were false except their own; and their contempt for theology and theologians was simply due to the fact that in none of the historic creeds and theological systems known to them were the doctrines set forth which they held to be essential and which they claimed to have rediscovered, after they had been lost to view for centuries.[1] This hostility to creeds was unfortunate. Had the Brethren been willing to test their new beliefs in the light of the history of the doctrine of the Church during nearly two thousand years, they might have been saved from serious errors. Unfortunately, Dispensationalists have inherited not a little of this regrettable prejudice.[2]

I. THE INTERPRETATION OF SCRIPTURE IN GENERAL

One of the most marked features of Premillennialism in all its forms is the emphasis which it places on the literal interpretation of Scripture. It is the insistent claim of its advocates that only when interpreted literally is the Bible interpreted truly; and they denounce as "spiritualizers" or "allegorizers" those who do not interpret the Bible

16

with the same degree of literalness as they do.[3] None have made this charge more pointedly than the Dispensationalists. The question of literal versus figurative interpretation is, therefore, one which has to be faced at the very outset. And it is to be observed at once that the issue cannot be stated as a simple alternative, either literal or figurative. No literalist, however thoroughgoing, takes everything in the Bible literally. Nor do those who lean to a more figurative method of interpretation insist that everything is figurative. Both principles have their proper place and their necessary limitations.

a. Necessary Limitations to Literal Interpretation

There are at least three reasons why a thoroughly literal interpretation of Scripture is impossible:

(1) The language of the Bible often contains figures of speech. This is especially true of its poetry. In Ex. xiv. 21 Moses declares that the Lord caused the sea to go back by reason of a "strong east wind." In his Song of triumph Moses exultantly declares: "and with the blast of thy nostrils the waters were gathered together" (xv. 8). In xix. 4, on the other hand, the Lord reminds Israel through Moses: "I bare you on eagles' wings, and brought you unto myself." No one with any real reverence for Scripture or adequate understanding of its teachings as a whole, would dream of taking either of the last two statements literally.[4] In the poetry of the Psalms, in the elevated style of prophecy, and even in simple historical narration, figures of speech appear which quite obviously are not meant to be and cannot be understood literally.

(2) The great theme of the Bible is, God and His redemptive dealings with mankind. God is a Spirit; the most precious teachings of the Bible are spiritual; and these spiritual and heavenly realities are often set forth under the form of earthly objects and human relationships. When Jesus said, "Ye must be born again," He was not referring to a physical but to a spiritual birth. When He said, "Destroy this temple," He meant His body. When

He said, "He that eateth my flesh and drinketh my blood, hath everlasting life," He was speaking of a spiritual relationship in terms of an Old Testament type. Jesus' Jewish hearers, being literalists, either failed to understand or misunderstood His words.[5] Whether the figurative or "spiritual" interpretation of a given passage is justified or not depends solely upon whether it gives the true meaning.[6] If it is used to empty words of their plain and obvious meaning, to read out of them what is clearly intended by them, then allegorizing or spiritualizing is a term of reproach which is well merited. On the other hand, we should remember the saying of the apostle, that spiritual things are "spiritually discerned." And spiritual things are more real and more precious than visible, tangible, ephemeral things.[7]

(3) The fact that the Old Testament is both preliminary and preparatory to the New Testament is too obvious to require proof. In referring the Corinthian Christians by way of warning and admonition to the events of the Exodus, the apostle Paul declared that these things were "ensamples" (types). That is, they prefigured things to come. This gives to much that is in the Old Testament a special significance and importance. Thus, when Hosea and Ezekiel foretell the return of Israel to "David their king," most Christians have understood these passages to refer to the Messiah, to "great David's greater Son," and not to David the son of Jesse who is the only David mentioned in the Old Testament. Such an interpretation recognizes, in the light of the New Testament fulfilment, a deeper and far more wonderful meaning in the words of many an Old Testament passage than, taken in their Old Testament context and connection, they seem to contain.

b. Attitude of Dispensationalists to These Limitations

While Dispensationalists are ardent literalists whose canon of interpretation like that of other Premillenarians may be expressed by the words, "literal wherever possible"

(H. Bonar) or "literal unless absurd" (Govett), there are certain points which are especially to be noted.

(1) This literalistic emphasis has shown itself most plainly in their insistence that Israel means Israel: it does not mean or typify the Church. The early Brethren denounced most severely the custom, very general at that time, of applying to the Church the prophecies regarding Israel.[8] This, of course, led to literalism along other lines. In 1826 S. R. Maitland challenged the generally accepted view that the 1260 days of Daniel and Revelation are year-days. The Brethren accepted his claim that literal days are meant, *i.e.*, 1260 days or 42 months or three and a half years; and they treated them as wholly future. Consequently, Dispensationalists are definite Futurists. Many examples of this emphasis on the letter might be given. We shall confine ourselves to one which for obvious reasons is of especial interest.

In commenting on Isa. ix. 7, Scofield remarks, "The 'throne of David' is a phrase as definite, historically, as 'throne of the Caesars,' and as little admits of 'spiritualizing' (Lk. i. 32, 33)."[9] Assuming that Scofield does not refer to the material throne on which David sat, which if such a special throne ever existed was apparently replaced by Solomon's throne (described in 2 Chr. ix. 17f.), we observe that this statement completely ignores the basic difference between the "throne of David" and the "throne of the Caesars." The one was Messianic and typical, the other purely historical. The one was to have its anti-typical fulfilment in Christ and His world-wide reign (Ps. lxxii., Hos. iii. 5); the other had its day and passed away. There is, strictly speaking, no "throne of the Caesars" today; and to claim that Victor Emmanuel III. ever occupied that throne would be to use the expression in a far from literal sense. There never will be again a "throne of the Caesars," though there may be many like it. Dispensationalists look forward, indeed, to a "restored" Roman Empire. But even were it to come, which is very doubtful, it would not be identical with the "throne of the Caesars" of nearly two millenniums ago.

Along with this insistence on the letter, there early developed a tendency to seek for significant meanings in the very letter of Scripture. This led to such fanciful and even fantastic results that the word "Biblicism" as applied to it has acquired a regrettable and even sinister meaning. Thus the words "dust" (Gen. xiii. 16), "stars" (xv. 5), and "sand" (xxii. 17) are obviously used as synonymous terms to indicate that the seed of Abraham will be as countless as these familiar objects. But, if it be argued that the "stars" signify a heavenly seed and the "dust" an earthly seed,[10] then the question arises, What is the difference between dust and sand? and, why is Israel of the days of Solomon likened to the "sand" in 1 Kgs. iv. 20 and to the "dust" in 2 Chr. i. 9? and, why are the "stars" referred to in 1 Chr. xxvii. 23 in David's census of earthly Israel? "Sun of righteousness" (Mal. iv. 2) and "morning star" (Rev. xxii. 16) are beautiful figures used of the coming of Christ. But to argue that because there is an interval of time between the appearing of the morning star and the sunrise, there will therefore be an interval of time between the rapture and the appearing[11] is to make a special application of these figures in the interest of a particular doctrine which is decidedly hazardous. Such ingenious subtleties may do great harm. It is one thing to endeavor to draw out of Scripture all that is clearly there. It is quite a different thing to read into it a significant meaning for which there is no sufficient warrant. When the "doves" of Isa. lx. 8 are discovered to be airplanes, and the chariots with flaming torches of Nah. ii. 3 are made into automobiles (or tanks?) we have the *reductio ad absurdum* of literalistic interpretation.

(2) Dispensationalists recognize the importance of the spiritual values of the Bible. But they draw a distinction in this respect which is of great importance. Regarding Israel as an *earthly* people, they insist that all of the promises and prophecies which concern Israel are earthly and are to be taken literally. On the other hand, regarding the Church as a *heavenly* body having no connection with the earth, they insist that everything that concerns the Church

is heavenly. This doctrine has been expressed in the words: "The covenants and destinies of Israel are all earthly; the covenants and destinies of the Church are all heavenly."[12] This means that all the promises which concern Israel relate to an earthly people, and are to be fulfilled to this earthly people upon this earth. They do not apply to the Church; they are not types of heavenly blessings. They speak in terms of the earth and are to be literally fulfilled. To apply the prophecies that speak of Israel to the Church, to declare that heaven is the true Canaan of the Jew, is according to Dispensationalists to spiritualize or allegorize these prophecies in a way that is utterly unscriptural.[13]

(3) While Dispensationalists are extreme literalists, they are very inconsistent ones. They are literalists in interpreting prophecy. But in the interpreting of history, they carry the principle of typical interpretation to an extreme which has rarely been exceeded even by the most ardent of allegorizers. Gen. xxiv., for example, is regarded as "highly typical";[14] and the doctrine of the Trinity is found in it. Keturah, Zipporah, and many other Old Testament figures never mentioned in the New Testament are given typical significance. The character of Joseph as set forth in the historical narrative in Genesis is singularly beautiful, and has many impressive lessons for men of every age. It may seem strange that the New Testament hardly more than mentions him (Heb. xi. 22). But the Dispensationalists have taken great delight in pointing out the respects in which Joseph was a type of Christ; and as many as thirty typical features have been discovered.[15]

The Book of Esther is nowhere cited in the New Testament. As the simple record of one of the most remarkable deliverances of God's people, it is a deeply impressive record of divine providence. But these simple lessons are not regarded as sufficient by Dispensationalist interpreters. Walter Scott, whom Scofield calls "the eminent Bible teacher," gives its typical significance as the following:

"As to the typical bearing of the book Ahasuerus would represent the supreme Gentile authority, and Vashti, *beauty*, the professing church failing to show her beauty; she is then superseded by the Jewish bride, Esther, *star* (Ps. xlv.); while the wicked Haman, planning the destruction of Israel, and in the midst of his murderous purposes signally cut off, would as surely figure the conspiracy of the latter-day enemies of restored Israel (Ps. lxxxiii.); Mordecai would set forth our Lord head of His exalted people in the millennial future."[16]

Whatever else may be said of this method of interpretation, it is certainly not literal. It clearly aims to go beyond the simple letter of Scripture in order to draw forth a "deep" meaning. It may be called figurative or typical. But it does not differ essentially from the allegorical method of interpretation[17] which the Dispensationalists so warmly denounce; and it may easily be carried to dangerous extremes. There may be serious danger in attaching "typical" importance to Old Testament events and institutions which cannot be proved to have any such meaning.

Vashti's conduct has been variously appraised by commentators. The statement that the king sent for her at the end of a seven-day feast when his heart was "merry with wine" suggests that his act was of at least questionable propriety. Whether her refusal to obey the command of her royal husband was justified is perhaps doubtful. But at least it should be regarded as axiomatic that the desire to find in Vashti a type of the "professing church failing to show her beauty," must not be allowed to influence the interpretation in the slightest degree. Yet there are doubtless those who regard this, to them very attractive, interpretation as justifying or even demanding that we take an unfavorable view of Vashti's conduct. To them this "deep," "typical"—in a case such as this, we are entitled to say *allegorical*—interpretation of the story of Esther is far more impressive and instructive than the historical events which it records.

This is the reason that, in attempting to define the word "type," it is customary to say that it is a person, event, or institution which is "designed by God" and intended "to prefigure something future." The words "designed by God" mean that there must be more than a mere similarity between something in the Old Testament and something in the New Testament to constitute the one a type of the other.[18] It must enter so plainly into the scheme of redemptive history that its prefigurative meaning is clear. Scofield had this in mind when he defined a type as "a divinely purposed illustration of some truth."[19] But, unfortunately, he signally failed to observe this limitation. Where, for example, is there the slightest warrant for regarding the raven and the dove as types of the "believer's two natures"?[20]

Not only is it often difficult to determine whether an Old Testament feature has typical significance; it is also difficult to be sure just in what respect and to what extent a type is truly typical. Aaron was a type of Christ. He was a true type of Christ when on the day of atonement he offered sacrifice for the sins of the people. But in the fact that he had first to offer a sacrifice for his own sin, we see the imperfection of the type. Jesus was sinless, Aaron was a sinner. As a descendant of Levi and the founder of a succession of priests, Aaron was not a type of Christ. For our Lord came out of Judah; and Melchizedek who appears as a solitary figure in the patriarchal age, having neither father nor mother nor descendant recorded, was the type of Him whose priesthood is changeless and everlasting. The study of typology is interesting; it is important. But it is also very difficult; and it is easy to make mistakes, even serious mistakes, in dealing with it.[21]

It is a singular anomaly, which cannot fail to impress the careful student of Dispensational teaching, as represented, for example, in the *Scofield Reference Bible,* that it emphasizes and carries to such extremes these two distinct and in a sense opposite principles in interpreting Scripture. In dealing with Old Testament history its treatment is highly figurative. Indeed, we sometimes receive the impression that the events of that history have little meaning for us in themselves; it is their typical meaning, a meaning which only those "deeply taught" in Scripture are able to appreciate, that is the really important thing about them.[22] In dealing with prophecy, its treatment is marked by a literalism which refuses to recognize types and figures. Israel must mean Israel; it does not and cannot signify the Church. Canaan must mean Canaan; it does not and cannot mean heaven. Eve, Rebecca, Asenath, Zipporah, Ruth, the Shulamite, and Vashti may one and all be viewed as "types." But Israel must mean Israel and only

Israel![23] This seems strikingly inconsistent. Why is the method of interpretation which is regarded as so suitable to the Pentateuch, so utterly unsuited to Ezekiel? If Ruth can give "a foreview of the Church," if "the larger interpretation" of the Song of Solomon concerns the Church, why must the Church be absent from the glorious visions of Isaiah?

This inconsistency becomes all the more remarkable when it is remembered that Dispensationalists recognize that the Old Testament types were only feeble and imperfect representations of realities more fully revealed in the New Testament, that they foreshadowed things to come which were vastly better and more precious. Scofield undoubtedly had this in mind when he wrote his comment on Zech. vi. 9f., "The fulfilment in the BRANCH will infinitely transcend the symbol."[24] Dispensationalists cannot speak too highly of the superlative excellence and unique glory of the heavenly promises to the Church. Yet they absolutely refuse to see in the present and future glories of this heavenly Church the realization, the antitypical fulfilment, of the earthly and national promises to Israel.

The explanation of this seemingly inconsistent attitude of Dispensationalists is to be found in the very heart of their system of interpretation, their conception of the Church. If the Church is a mystery first revealed to the apostle Paul, it cannot be predicted in the prophecies of Isaiah; and if these are taken literally it is not foretold in them. Consequently, the Dispensationalist finds support for his interpretation of the prophets in his doctrine of the Church. But since the typical significance of Old Testament history, its persons, events, and institutions, was hidden from the eyes of the men of old and is only revealed by the clearer light of the New Testament, the Church can be regarded as prefigured in Old Testament history and still remain a mystery. This is the explanation of the anomaly. Having debarred themselves from finding in the prophets, which according to their basic canon of interpretation must be taken literally, any reference to the Church, they have, in what seems almost utter defiance of their canon of literal interpretation, carried the typical interpretation of Old Testament history to an unwarranted and even fantastic extreme, and try to find the Church constantly prefigured in it.

II. THE INTERPRETATION OF PROPHECY

In view of their preoccupation with the prophetic teachings of the Bible, the attitude of Dispensationalists to prophecy is of special interest and importance. For it is here that their insistence on the principle of literal interpretation is most uncompromising. This raises several questions, most important of which are: the intelligibility of prophecy, the conditional element in prophecy, the relation of the Old Testament to the New Testament, Futurism, and the basic distinction between Israel and the Church.

1. The Intelligibility of Prophecy

The claim that prophecy is to be understood literally raises the question of the intelligibility of prophecy, and bears directly on the problem of the relationship of prophecy to history. If prophecy is to be taken literally, *i.e.,* according to the letter, it would be natural to conclude that its literal meaning must be clear and obvious.

a. The usual view on this subject has been that prophecy is not intended to be fully understood before its fulfilment, that it is only when God "establishes the word of his servant and fulfils the counsel of his messengers," that the meaning and import of their words becomes fully manifest. The reason for this is to be found, as Patrick Fairbairn has so admirably pointed out, in the fact that these disclosures of things to come are made known to men by One who has made man and knows his human frailty and how much knowledge of the future is for his good.[25] Prophecy, in the words of Sir Isaac Newton, is not given to make men prophets, but as a witness to God when it is fulfilled. Prophecy is a wonderful combination of the clear and the obscure. Enough of God's purpose is revealed to act powerfully upon the heart and conscience of those to whom the heavenly message is sent, but not enough to make fatalists of them, to paralyze human effort, or to coerce the human will: enough to prove the message to have been a true word from Him to whom alone the unknown future is fully known, but not enough to enable man to foresee with certainty when and how that purpose is to be realized.

b. It is the view of Dispensationalists that prophecy is intended to be plain and fully intelligible before its fulfilment. Thus Darby tells us: "I do not admit history to be, in any sense, necessary to the understanding of prophecy." He even went so far as to say, "I do not want history to tell me Nineveh or Babylon is ruined or Jerusalem in the hands of the Gentiles."[26] This is a remarkable statement. The usual way of putting it would be this: "Since the prophets definitely foretell that Nineveh and Babylon will be ruined and Jerusalem fall into the hands of the Gentiles, I know that this is sure to take place. That it has already taken place and when and how it took place, is a matter of historical fact, which history, both sacred and profane, must make clear to me." It is to be noted, therefore, that Darby's statements are the result of the principle of literalism carried to the extreme in the interpretation of prophecy. This view received almost classic expression in the words of Brookes:

"The language in which prophecy is written is as simple and easy to understand as any other part of the Scriptures, and all that is needed in reading it is a submissive disposition, ready to take God at His word without any theory of our own to establish."[27]

This view has been more concisely stated in the words, "Prophecy is prewritten history."[28] If prophecy is written as simply and plainly as history, it should be quite as intelligible as history; and we should have no more difficulty in understanding the prophecies of Isaiah than the history recorded in the Books of the Kings. This view may seem to do great honor to the Bible by insisting that its interpretation is quite independent of the events of history. But it fails to do justice to the fact that God is quite as much the God of history as He is the God of prophecy, and that it is the historical fulfilment of a prophecy which proves that it came from God. This literal view of prophecy also makes its appeal to those who wish to exchange faith for sight, who wish to be able to read the future with clearness and to set up precise prophetical programs regarding things to come, programs which no one can conclusively disprove until the events of history have tested them. The refutation of this conception of the complete intelligibility of prophecy is to be found in the simple and inescapable fact, that it cannot be made to square with the phenomena of prophecy as they lie before us in Scripture, and in the no less obvious fact that those who insist most emphatically that prophecy is fully intelligible differ among themselves greatly at times as to its meaning. The fallacy in this claim will be clear when due weight is given to the following considerations.

(1) The use of figurative language—symbols, parables, etc.—is far more characteristic of prophecy than of historical narration. Balaam foretold the coming of a star out of Jacob. Daniel spoke of four kings or kingdoms under the figure of an image and also as four wild beasts. Ezekiel has a parable of two great eagles, of a cedar, and of a vine. These are but a few among many examples. Some of these prophecies are interpreted more or less fully in their context, which shows that they are obscure. But some are not interpreted; and those which are explained are often not fully explained. The vision of the Dry Bones in Ezek. xxxvii. clearly refers to a raising of the dead. Is it to be taken as describing a physical or a spiritual resurrection? If physical, is Israel to be utterly destroyed, and then brought back to life by supernatural means? If spiritual, is the resurrection to be regarded as spiritual, while Israel is understood as strictly literal? Ezekiel's picture of the destruction of Gog is one of complete annihilation; and this

destruction precedes the kingdom age. Yet in the Apocalypse the destruction of Gog follows the thousand years. Is Gog to be destroyed for ever, and then brought to life again to fight a last great battle against Messiah and the saints? Or, are there two Gogs? Or, are we to reverse the sequence of events in Ezekiel? or in Revelation?

It is to be remembered that the use of parabolic language serves both to reveal and conceal truth. Nathan's parable of the Ewe Lamb served and was expressly designed to serve the purpose of getting David to condemn himself, without realizing he was doing so. "The man that hath done this shall surely die" was David's verdict. "Thou art the man" was Nathan's utterly unexpected and crushing reply. Jeremiah's vision of the Seething Pot (i. 13) was misinterpreted or deliberately parodied by the leaders of the Jews, and used to support their terrible delusion that Jerusalem was impregnable, an iron pot that could not be broken into (Ezek. xi. 4), which made it necessary for Ezekiel to explain the true meaning of the symbol in words that burn and sear (chap. xxiv). The predictions that Zedekiah should "die in peace" (Jer. xxxiv. 5) and that he should not "see" the land of Babylon (Ezek. xii. 13) require for their proper understanding the brief yet terrible account given in 2 Kgs. xxv. 6f., or they might be completely misunderstood.[29] The interpretation of prophecy is not simple and easy; and it is a mistake to declare that it is.

(2) Not only is the language of prophecy often figurative and parabolic, it also differs from history in its frequent lack of precision and definiteness. While the record of history may be told in broad and general terms, it deals with recorded events and usually tells us with some definiteness when things happened. In the case of prophecy, periods and dates are only rarely defined precisely. "In that day" is one of the most frequently occurring specifications of time in the case of long-range prediction. "Day" means the Messianic age. The phrase is intentionally indefinite. The word "time" is also indefinite. The expres-

sion, "a time, and times, and half a time" (Dan. vii. 25;
cf. xii. 7, Rev. xii. 14) is frequently taken to mean "*one*
time, *two* times, and half a time." But the word "times"
may be read either as plural or dual. As plural it would be
quite indefinite. It is only the identification of this period
with the 1260 days or 42 months (Rev. xi. 2f.), assuming
this identification to be correct, which establishes the correctness of the rendering "a time, *two* times, and half a
time." The expression, "2300 evening mornings" (Dan.
viii. 14, 26), is decidedly figurative and enigmatical. If
"evening morning" is the same as "day" (cf. Gen. i. 5), the
use of the ordinary word would have made the meaning
much clearer.[30]

Even in the case of a prophecy which speaks definitely in
terms of years, as does Jeremiah's prediction of the seventy
years of captivity (xxv. 12), the time when the period of captivity will end appears to be uncertain. Daniel's words with
reference to its fulfilment: "O Lord hear; O Lord, forgive;
O Lord, hearken and do; defer not, for thine own sake, O my
God: for thy city and thy people are called by thy name"
(ix. 19), seem clearly to imply that Daniel did not regard the
restoration as something which must take place immediately
after the conclusion of the seventy years, regardless of whether
Israel had learned the lesson of the captivity, wholly regardless of whether Israel had added to its iniquity during the
captivity, but rather as a promise the fulfilment of which
might be "deferred," and which therefore might well be made
the subject of the most earnest prayer and supplication.
Daniel speaks as if he knew from what date the seventy years
were to be calculated. It would be natural to date them from
the final destruction in 589 B. C. when the temple was burned.
But the fact that the edict of Cyrus was issued in 538 B. C.
would indicate that they should be calculated from about
608 B. C., *i.e.*, from the date of the first deportation in the
reign of Jehoiakim, nearly 20 years earlier.[31] If we are to judge
of the meaning of prophecy by the facts regarding its fulfilment contained in the Bible itself, we must be prepared to
recognize that prophecy is not prewritten history. Only from
the date of Cyrus' decree can we learn that it was with
Jehoiakim's fourth year that the captivity began; and only

on the basis of this date can we determine that the fulfilment took place immediately and was not deferred because God's purpose regarding it had not been accomplished.

(3) The same principle applies to prophecies which might be regarded as perfectly simple and plain. Jacob in blessing his sons, declared regarding Simeon and Levi, "I will divide them in Jacob and scatter them in Israel." (Gen. xlix. 7.) This is the only one of the blessings which reads like a curse. It is the only one which unites two of Jacob's sons in a common destiny. The reason for this is plain. Jacob expressly alludes to their grievous sin in the matter of Shechem and refers to it as their joint act. How was this prediction fulfilled? In the case of Levi, it was fulfilled in terms of blessing. Because of the obedience of this tribe, when Israel sinned in the matter of the golden calf (Deut. xxxiii. 9, cf. Ex. xxxii. 26f.), Levi was dedicated to the service of the Lord and His sanctuary. Levi received cities in all the tribes and was supported by tithes from all of them. This was a distinction and a glory. Levi was actually divided and scattered. The prophecy was literally fulfilled. But the curse was changed into a blessing, the disgrace became an honor. In the case of Simeon, it was quite different. Simeon decreased greatly in numbers during the forty years of wandering. Simeon, alone of all the tribes, was allotted territory within the bounds of another tribe, Judah. Some members of the tribe seem to have wandered off and joined themselves to the Northern Tribes. Others of them wandered away to the South. Simeon practically disappears from Israel's history. Moses does not even mention Simeon in his Blessing of the tribes. In Simeon's case the curse remained a curse. Yet who in reading the words of Jacob regarding these two sons could have discovered in its seemingly plain and simple language the vast difference in the import of this prediction for the descendants of these two bloody-handed sons of the patriarch! The prophecy was wonderfully fulfilled; we may even say it was literally fulfilled. But only a study of history enables us to interpret it aright.[32]

(4) From a practical standpoint, the clearest indication that prophecy is not "prewritten history" consists in the fact that there is in many cases such a wide difference of opinion among commentators as to whether certain predictions have been fulfilled, and whether, if fulfilled, this fulfilment is to be regarded as complete and final or as only partial or "germinant."

There is difference of opinion even among Dispensationalists as to whether Isaiah's prophecy that Babylon should be destroyed and never again inhabited (xiii. 12f.) was fulfilled centuries ago fully and finally, or whether the destruction that is past was only a type, a germinant fulfilment, and Babylon is to be rebuilt and then again and finally destroyed in the future. Whether the Babylon of Rev. xvi. 19 is the literal Babylon on the Euphrates, or another city of which that Babylon was a type (Rome of the seven hills), depends on whether Isaiah's prophecy has been completely or only partly fulfilled. On this important question J. M. Gray took the one view, Scofield the other.[33] Certainly the language of Isa. xiii. 19f. and Jer. li. implies the total destruction of the literal Babylon, which would seem to have taken place centuries ago. But if it is inferred from this that the Babylon of Revelation cannot be the Babylon on the Euphrates but must be the city of the seven hills on the Tiber, what has become of the principle of literal interpretation of prophecy? It is only in a figurative sense that the name Babylon can be applied to Rome. Historically the two cities are entirely distinct. If Israel must be Israel and Canaan always Canaan, should not Babylon always mean Babylon and Euphrates always mean Euphrates?[34]

2. Conditional and Unconditional Elements in Prophecy

One of the arguments advanced most insistently in support of the complete intelligibility and literal fulfilment of prophecy is the claim that unconditional promises must be literally fulfilled. In making this claim Dispensationalists have the Abrahamic covenant especially in view. They insist that this covenant was "unconditional"; and they set it as such in sharp contrast and even direct antithesis to the Mosaic law.[35] The covenant was unconditional and must be fulfilled to the letter. The law was conditioned by the words, "if ye will obey my voice" (Ex. xix. 5);[36] this condition was broken immediately and repeatedly; consequently the promise attached to the keeping of this law need not be fulfilled. It is largely on this basis that it is claimed that Israel must return to the land of Canaan and possess the whole of it under the unconditional Abrahamic covenant, which we are told she has never yet done. The superior blessedness of this dispensation of promise, as viewed by Dispensationalists, is indicated by Scofield's words: "The Dispensation of Promise ended when Israel rashly accepted the law (Ex. xix. 8)."[37] The word "rashly" is startlingly significant. It implies either that Israel without due consideration forsook a more favorable for a less favorable status, or that, in accepting the more favorable one, the people did not weigh sufficiently the condition attached to it, did not realize their utter inability to perform it.[38]

Since this question of the relation of man's obedience to the fulfilment of God's covenant is a matter of great importance, we shall consider it in three aspects:

a. The Abrahamic Covenant and Obedience

(1) First of all it is to be observed that a condition may be involved in a command or promise without its being specifically stated. This is illustrated by the career of Jonah. Jonah was commanded to preach judgment, unconditioned, unqualified: "Yet forty days, and Nineveh shall be overthrown." Yet Jonah later declares, in explanation and extenuation of his disgraceful conduct, that he had assumed from the very first that God would spare the city if the people repented (even at the cost of making Jonah appear to be a false prophet); and the outcome proved the surmise to be correct. The unstated condition was presupposed in the very character of God as a God of mercy and compassion (iv. 2). The judgment on Eli's house (1 Sam. ii. 30) is a very striking illustration of this principle, which is carefully stated in Jer. xviii. 1-10 and in

Ezek. iii. 18ff., xxxiii, 13ff., where it is also made clear that the unconditional threat of judgment is intended to serve as the basis of a solemn exhortation to a repentance which will make the judgment unnecessary.

(2) It is true that, in the express terms of the covenant with Abraham, obedience is not stated as a condition. But that obedience was presupposed is clearly indicated by two facts. The one is that obedience is the precondition of blessing under all circumstances. "The rebellious dwell in a parched land" (Ps. lxviii. 6) has been true of God's people in every age. This is the general principle of God's providential and also of His gracious dealings with His children. The sin of Adam and Eve was a sin of disobedience; and it was especially heinous because they knew but "one restraint, lords of the world beside." The second fact is that in the case of Abraham the duty of obedience is particularly stressed. In Gen. xviii. 17f. it is plainly stated that, through His choice of Abraham, God proposed to bring into being, by pious nurture, a righteous seed which would "keep the way of the LORD," in order that as a result and reward of such obedience "the LORD may bring upon Abraham that which he hath spoken of him." The supreme test of Abraham's faith was when he was commanded to offer up Isaac; and after he had stood the test successfully, the covenant promise was renewed to him in fuller and more emphatic terms, closing with the words, "because thou hast obeyed my voice" (xxii. 18). When the covenant was renewed to Isaac, it concluded with what we may call the Old Testament obituary of Abraham, "because that Abraham obeyed my voice, and kept my charge, my commandments, my statutes, and my laws" (xxvi. 5). It was because of the obedience of Abraham that the promise was repeated to his son, who had himself learned on mount Moriah the extent of the obedience required of his father. The Epistle to the Hebrews magnifies the faith of Abraham; but the evidence of that faith consists in acts of obedience: "By faith Abraham . . .

obeyed" (xi. 8). Scofield speaks of faith as a condition of
this "unconditional" covenant.[39] But faith without works
is dead.

(3) That obedience was vitally connected with the Abrahamic covenant is shown with especial clearness by the
fact that there was connected with it a sign, the rite of
circumcision, to the observance of which the utmost importance was attached. Cutting off from the covenant
people was the penalty for failure to observe it. It was
truly "a seal of the righteousness of the faith which *he
had yet* being uncircumcised" (Rom. iv. 11). But the rite
was in itself an act of obedience (1 Cor. vii. 19). The cir-
cumstance that circumcision later came to be regarded as
typifying a legal righteousness, "circumcised the eighth
day, of the stock of Israel, *of* the tribe of Benjamin"
(Phil. iii. 5; cf. Rom. ii. 25, Gal. v. 3), only serves to emphasize the fact that its observance was an act of obedience to
the revealed will of God as well before the law was given
as afterwards.

(4) That those who insist that the Abrahamic covenant
was wholly unconditional, do not really so regard it is
shown also by the great importance which Dispensationalists attach to Israel's being "in the land" as the pre-
condition of blessing under this covenant.

Scofield tells us: "The descendants of Abraham had but to
abide in their own land to inherit every blessing."[40] How
important they hold this condition to be is illustrated by the
attempt made by Scofield to distinguish between the "directive" and the "permissive" will of God regarding Jacob's
going down into Egypt. The narrative tells us with great
plainness that this journey was of God: "I am God, the God
of thy father: fear not to go down into Egypt: for I will there
make of thee a great nation: I will go down with thee into
Egypt; and I will also surely bring thee up *again:* and Joseph
shall put his hand upon thine eyes" (xlvi. 3f.). What plainer
intimation could Jacob have received that it was God's will
for him to go down into Egypt? God would Himself go with
him. Should not Jacob want to go where God went? Certainly
Joseph was able to see very plainly the hand of God in his

own chequered career. He said to his brethren: "It was not you that sent me hither but God." And Joseph also understood God's purpose in it all: "God did send me before you to preserve life." The journey to Egypt was clearly God's way of preserving Jacob and his sons, and it was also a signal means of testing Jacob's faith in God and obedience to His will. It is nowhere stated that it was a punishment for sin, or an act of disbelief or disobedience. As in the case of the "good figs," who centuries later were sent into exile to escape the horrors of Nebuchadnezzar's siege (Jer. xxiv.), Jacob and his family were sent out of the land "for their good." Yet Scofield tells us that "Gen. xlvi. 3 is a touching instance of the permissive will of God. Jacob's family, broken, and in part already in Egypt, the tenderness of Jehovah would not forbid the aged patriarch to follow."[41] This explanation serves to show how deeply convinced are the Dispensationalists who profess to hold that the Abrahamic covenant was utterly unconditional, that it was really conditional, that Abraham and his descendants ought to have stayed in the land and to be now in it, that only there can they be truly blessed.[42] But Gen. xlvi. makes it plain that absence from the land, an absence of four hundred years (Gen. xv. 13), was God's *directive* will for Jacob and his sons. If God ever *directed* a man to leave his home and go to sojourn in a foreign land, He did it in the case of Jacob. If God ever prepared the way and provided the means for such a journey, He did it when He sent Joseph on before to preserve life and made him a father to Pharaoh.[43]

(5) That Dispensationalists do not regard the Abrahamic covenant as wholly unconditional is indicated also by the fact that we never hear them speak of the restoration of Esau to the land of Canaan and to full blessing under the Abrahamic covenant. This is due of course to the fact that Israel is the constant theme of Old Testament prophecy, while the burden of prophecy regarding Edom is almost wholly denunciatory. It is the New Testament which fills Amos's prediction of the subjugation of Edom (ix.12) with the glory of that gospel invitation, which is made to "the residue of men . . . and all the Gentiles" (Acts xv. 17). But if the Abrahamic covenant was uncon-

ditional, if obedience was not required until the words, "if ye will obey my voice," were uttered at Sinai, why is Esau excluded from the blessings of this covenant? He was a son of Isaac as much as Jacob was. How could his disobedience deprive his descendants of the blessings of the covenant, if the covenant did not require obedience?

(6) It is important to distinguish between the certainty of the ultimate fulfilment of the promise to the seed of Abraham and the blessedness and security of the nation or of the individual at any given time under that covenant. It is claimed by the Dispensationalists that it is because the covenant was entirely unconditional, that it is certain of fulfilment, that if obedience were a condition, sinful Israel could not confidently expect its fulfilment. This overlooks the fact that the certainty of the fulfilment of the covenant is not due to the fact that it is unconditional, nor is its fulfilment dependent upon the imperfect obedience of sinful men. The certainty of the fulfilment of the covenant and the security of the believer under it, ultimately depend wholly on the obedience of Christ. As Paul declares, Christ is in a unique sense the Seed in whom the nations are to be blessed; and it is because of His perfect obedience to the will of God that the covenanted blessings are secure to all His people (Gal. iii. 16). Obedient faith in a Saviour to come was the righteousness of Abraham quite as much as it was the righteousness of Moses, of David, of all the prophets and righteous men of the Old Testament dispensation; and the same obedient faith in a Saviour who has come is the righteousness of every saint of the present gospel age.

b. The Mosaic Law and Obedience

The distinction drawn by Dispensationalists between the dispensations of promise and of law concerns primarily the question of obedience. They declare that obedience became a condition of the covenant first at Mt. Sinai (Ex. xix. 8). It is important, therefore, to observe that no such sharp distinction is drawn in those books of the Old Testament which deal directly with these two dispensations and the transition from the one to the other. The word "law" *(torah)* appears in Gen. xxvi. 5, Ex. xii. 49, xiii. 9, xvi. 4, 28, xviii. 16, 20; and such words as "statute," "ordinance," "commandment" are already in use before Sinai is reached. They are especially prominent in Ex. xii.-xiii. Thus, the passover is to be kept as a feast "by an ordinance for ever." No uncircumcised person is to partake of it (xii. 44-48), which means that the receiving of the sign of the Abrahamic covenant is made a pre-condition to participation in this national feast. In the case of the feast of unleavened bread, failure to comply with the requirement that nothing leavened be eaten is to be punished as severely (vs. 15) as failure to comply with the condition of the covenant of circumcision (Gen. xvii. 14). When Jethro visited Moses and asked why he gave the people so much of his valuable time, Moses replied that he was making them "know the statutes of God and his laws" (Ex. xviii. 16). This statement was made before the people came to Sinai. Consequently, the people who heard the words, "if ye will obey my voice indeed and keep my covenant" (xix. 8) were not without considerable knowledge of what this condition meant. Abraham had obeyed God's voice (Gen. xxii. 18, xxvi. 5); and he knew that it was God's will that his descendants should do the same (xviii. 17f.). Pharaoh had not obeyed (Ex. v. 2) and had just been punished for his disobedience. Freedom from the plagues of Egypt had already been promised the Israelites if they would obey His voice and do His will (xv. 26). All of this before Sinai!

The difference between the law and the promise was not one of kind but of degree. The law did not demand obedience and righteousness of men to whom obedience and righteousness were quite unknown as the condition of blessedness. The Flood, which destroyed the whole human race except for one righteous man and his family, had made known the righteous judgments of God centuries before the time of Abraham. Paul tells us plainly that sin entered into the world "through the disobedience of one man," which carries us back to Adam and the Fall. The difference between the law and the promise does not, therefore, consist in this, that under the promise men were saved without obedience and under the law they are saved because of obedience. This would make the promise thoroughgoing antinomianism and the law nothing else than a covenant of works.[44] The difference lay in this, that the law made the will of God more plain by stating it in terms of definite commands, "thou shalt" and "thou shalt not"; and that by the very severity of its requirements it exposed more fully the sinfulness of man's heart and his alienation from God. Because of this the law made elaborate provision for atonement for sins done in ignorance and frailty, and by so doing pointed forward to the Cross. The great teaching of the Levitical law is that, "without the shedding of blood there is no remission" (Lev. xvii. 11; cf. Heb. ix. 22).

Scofield's attempt to prove that personal guilt was not imputed before the giving of the law makes his comment on Rom. v. 12f. self-contradictory. Paul is speaking there, as Scofield correctly points out, only of that penalty of death which passed on all men as the consequence of Adam's first transgression, irrespective of their own personal sins. But he is not denying that there was also personal guilt because of personal disobedience. In chap. ii. of this epistle he has already pointed out that there is a "law written in their hearts" which all men, whether they know the law of Moses or not, are required to obey, and that they will be rewarded or punished according as they keep it or break it. It is not true, then, that "personal guilt was not imputed" before the law. The statement, "Accordingly, from Gen. iv. 7 to Ex. xxix. 14 the sin-offering is not once mentioned" does not prove this contention. For (1) The lesson of God's dealings with Cain is clearly that *personal guilt* would be and was imputed even in his day. It is very improbable that the "sin-offering" is referred to in Gen. iv. 7. It is true, of course, that the same word is used for "sin" and "sin-offering" in Hebrew. But the natural rendering here is *sin*. However, were Scofield's interpretation correct, the mention of the "sin-offering" immediately after the Fall would prove what he is concerned to deny, that personal sins were at once imputed. (2) While the sin-offering is not mentioned elsewhere in the Pentateuch until Ex. xxix. 14, sacrifices and offerings are mentioned. Are we to hold that such sacrifices had no reference to personal guilt before the law was given at Sinai? Scofield certainly was in no position to maintain this. For he held that the Book of Job belongs to the patriarchal period before the giving of the law. It is certainly true that in it no reference is made to the law of Moses. Yet we read there that Job offered "burnt-offerings" to atone for the personal sins which his sons might have committed (i. 5). In so doing Job acted as a priest. The expiatory character of the burnt-offering appears even more plainly in xlii. 7f., where Job is commanded to offer sacrifices for his three friends, to atone for their personal guilt. While it is true that the sin-offering and the trespass-offering had special reference to sins of transgression against the law, it is also true that in all the animal sacrifices the thought is always present that without the shedding of blood there is no remission, which means that where there is sacrifice, i.e., the shedding of blood, the fact of personal guilt and the consciousness of that fact are clearly involved and implied.

c. The Law and the Gospel—Christian Obedience

The New Testament makes it clear that the Mosaic law contains and combines two elements, both of which are of the utmost importance:

(1) The law is primarily a declaration of the will of God for man's *obedience*. As such it demands and requires absolute and entire conformity. "Be ye holy, for I the LORD your God am holy"[45] states both the nature and the extent of the conformity demanded and the reason for it. So regarded, it is a covenant of works. The reward of obedience is life; the penalty for disobedience is death.

(2) The law is a declaration of the will of God for man's *salvation*. As such it manifests God's love and grace in providing a way of escape from the guilt and penalty of failure to keep the law perfectly. The priest and the altar make it possible for sinful man to obtain mercy from a

righteous God. In this respect the law is an impressive declaration of the covenant of grace. It reveals God as the One who is "merciful and gracious, slow to anger and abundant in lovingkindness and truth."

In both of these important respects the Mosaic law represented an advance upon the covenant of promise. It made the will of God for man's obedience more clear; and it made the way of salvation and the necessity for it the more evident. On the other hand, the New Testament makes it plain that the law was itself preparatory to the gospel, and that it contained some elements which were permanent and unchanging and others that were *temporary*. As a law of obedience its permanent features are set forth in the Decalogue, which was uttered by the voice of God Himself, and which Jesus summed up in terms of the two great commandments which He declared to be the perfect expression of man's duty. On the other hand, many of the statutes and ordinances of the law were clearly temporary, either because they were intended for Israel only *(e.g.,* the annual feasts, the sabbatical year, the year of jubilee) or represented a relatively low standard of morality, which was suited to a people under age *(e.g.,* the ordinances regarding slavery and the punishment of crimes of violence, Ex. xxi. 20-27) and characterized by hardness of heart *(e.g.,* polygamy and divorce, xxi. 10, Deut. xxiv. 1-4, Matt. xix. 3-12). Thus, Jesus definitely set aside the principle "an eye for an eye and a tooth for a tooth" which found expression in the law. Yet even so, the law of Moses represented so high a standard and was so inflexible in its demands that it became as Paul expresses it a "yoke of bondage," a "body of death," a standard which exposed and condemned man's inability to keep it. So regarded it directed attention especially to the law of atonement as set forth in the priestly ritual of sacrifice. And in the fulness of time, when man's utter inability to keep the law had been made perfectly clear, Christ came to fulfil both "the law and the prophets." By His perfect keeping of the law of God He both re-affirmed it in all its perfection and discarded that which was ephemeral and purely national. By His atoning death He gave to the Old Testament rites of priestly mediation their authentication as types and also proved them to be but types which having served their purpose were done away in Him. In all these respects the law was the preparation for the gospel and has its fulfilment in it.

These various aspects of the law and the relation which they hold to the gospel need to be carefully noted, especially because of the rather startling way in which the apostle Paul, the great proponent of Christian liberty, speaks of the law and of the freedom which the Christian enjoys from its curse, its yoke, its impossible demands. He even goes so far as to speak of "two covenants" and to represent the law as a covenant which "gendereth to bondage" and is to be sharply contrasted with Jerusalem which is free and stands for the covenant of promise (Gal. iv. 22f.). But that Paul is here speaking of the law only as a system of works-righteousness, which demands an obedience that it is unable to provide (iii. 21), is evident from the way in which he speaks of circumcision (v. 2f.). No one knew better than Paul that circumcision was the sign of the Abrahamic covenant (Rom. iv. 9-12), that covenant under which faith was reckoned to Abraham for righteousness. Yet here in Galatians Paul treats circumcision, which is scarcely mentioned in the law (Lev. xii. 3), except in a figurative or derivative sense, as the very symbol of what it had come to represent to the self-righteous Jews of his day, a works-righteousness which was the very antithesis of the faith-righteousness which he had preached in Galatia. Paul honors the law as the revelation of the will of God; he approves it and recognizes its perpetual obligation (Rom. vii. 12, 16). He delights in it as did the Old Testament saints (vs. 22; Ps. xix. and cxix.). Yet he is conscious of the heaviness of the yoke which it places on the neck of all those who seek to obtain righteousness through obedience to its commands. It is a yoke of bondage because of sin; and only those who have died to sin are free from that bondage (vi. 7). Yet those who have been made free from sin have been freed only that they may become bondservants of righteousness (vs. 18), whose duty it is to bring every thought into captivity to the obedience of Christ. For the gospel age in which we are living is that day foretold by the prophets when the law of God shall be written in the hearts of men (Jer. xxxi. 33) and when the Spirit of God abiding in their hearts will enable them to keep it (Ezek. xi. 19, xxxvi. 26f.). The gospel age is the age of the new covenant; and it is not marked by freedom from the law, by return to a dispensation of promise which knew nothing of obedience as a condition. Rather is it pre-eminently the age when the law of God, the revealed will of God, is and will be kept as never before—not as the means of salvation, but as the fruit of a life that is hid with Christ in God!

The reason that the Brethren and their Dispensational followers have insisted so strongly upon the unconditional character of the Abrahamic covenant is two-fold. As regards the Old Testament they are concerned to make it unconditional because they hold that being unconditional it must be literally fulfilled to the Jews, the literal seed of Abraham. As regards the New Testament they are concerned to make the promise unconditional, with a view to proving that obedience was a condition of the Mosaic age only, and that obedience is as little a condition under the dispensation of grace as it was under the dispensation of promise. This distinction was not made in the interest of a liberty which would savor of lawlessness or libertinism, but rather with a view to securing for the believer a perfect assurance of salvation.[46] The teaching of the Brethren as to the heavenly character of the Church has tended to foster a spirituality and other-worldliness which is highly to be commended.[47] But this erroneous conception of the relation in which the promise, the law, and the gospel stand to one another could not but have serious consequences. The most important of these is the failure to apprehend correctly the close and intimate relation which exists between justification and sanctification.

(1) This is shown by the tendency to distinguish sharply between the *standing* of a Christian and his *state*.[48] The teaching is this. The instant a man accepts Christ Jesus as his Saviour, his standing is that of a saved sinner. He has passed from death unto life. In Christ he is holy and blameless and an heir of eternal life. This is a precious truth. Saving faith is "the gift of God"; and no man can truly say that Jesus is Lord but by the Holy Spirit. However conscious the Christian may have been at his conversion and may continue to be of the "body of death" that is in him, he should at all times be able to say, "I know whom I have believed and am persuaded that he is able to keep that which I have committed unto him against that day." This is the precious doctrine of the perseverance of the saints and of their assurance of salvation. But it is to be carefully remembered that, if this doctrine is held without due regard to the *state* of the believer, it may easily lead to carnal security and a disregard of Biblical exhortations to holiness of life. It is quite true that a Christian should never rely upon his goodness of heart or holiness of conversation as proof that he is saved. That may easily become Pharisaic self-righteousness. But it is also true that "faith without works is dead" (Jas. ii. 26). In saying this James could appeal to the words of Christ, "By their fruits ye shall know them," and he may have had in mind the parable of the Barren Fig-tree and the cursing of the fig-tree which had leaves but no figs. Standing and state are distinct, but they are also vitally related. Justification has sanctification as its goal. Christ came to save men from sin, not to save them in sin. Justification which does not result in sanctification cannot be genuine.

(2) A further consequence of this doctrine that the Abrahamic covenant (in fact, all dispensations but those of the law and the kingdom) is unconditional is the attempt to draw a sharp distinction between the "old man" and the

"new man." Stated bluntly this amounts to saying that the Christian has a dual personality. He has an old nature, the old man, which can do nothing but sin, and a new nature, the new man, which cannot sin. Scofield tells us in commenting on Eph. iv. 24 that "the new man is the regenerate man as distinguished from the old man," and "in no sense the old man made over or improved."[49] This is a dangerous misstatement of a precious truth. The new man *is not* the old man improved. He *is* the old man made over. The Christian is "renewed in the whole man after the image of God." That renewing, that gradual change of the old man into the new man, is progressive sanctification, which is the work of the Spirit of God. As the new man grows stronger, the old man must grow weaker. For Paul refers "not to two distinct natures properly so-called, but to two distinct conditions of one and the same nature."[50] Were this not the case, the distinction between the old man and the new would practically amount to saying that Saul the Pharisee and Paul the apostle were two distinct persons, and that Christ did not save Saul but rather substituted Paul for Saul and left Saul (the old nature) to perish in his iniquity. But Paul was acutely conscious that he was the very Saul who had persecuted the Church and had been met and conquered by Christ on the way to Damascus. And every Christian, even the most saintly, knows that he is the very same lost sinner whom Jesus sought and saved.

(3) Psalm li. has an important bearing upon this question. In vs. 11, we read the petition of David, "Take not thy holy Spirit from me." The comments of Darby and of Scofield on these words are very significant. Darby wrote in the *Synopsis*:

"An intelligent saint now could not say what is said in this psalm (ver. 11); he knows God will not take His Spirit from him. He might indeed perhaps in anguish say it, and with a true heart, and be heard; but not intelligently."[51]

Scofield's statement is to the same effect although the form of expression is somewhat different:

"No believer of this dispensation aware of the promise of His abiding (John xiv, 16) should pray, 'take not thy Holy Spirit from me' (Eph. iv. 30); but while Christian *position* is not found here, Christian *experience* in essence is."52

Every one will admit that a Christian ought not to live in constant dread that God will take away His Holy Spirit whose presence in the heart of the Christian is indispensable. But these words were uttered by one who had been an adulterer and murderer and who had lived in carnal security with his sin unconfessed for perhaps a year. When Nathan said to David, "Thou art the man," may he not well have felt that God must remove utterly His Spirit from one who had fallen into such grievous sin? David may have been in terror that God would forsake him as He had forsaken Saul, despite the assurance of Nathan that he should not die. Every Christian who realizes at all adequately how often he grieves the Holy Spirit and how utterly he is dependent on His abiding presence may well cry, "Take not thy Holy Spirit from me." Even the holiest Christian may offer this petition. For, it is to be remembered that the Christian is not restricted in his praying to things which he is afraid God will not give unless he asks for them. But he is exhorted to pray for the things which he knows it is the will of God that he should have. The petition, "Give us this day our daily bread," should not be inspired by the fear that God will not give us our daily bread but by the certainty that He will. It does not imply lack of faith in God's ability and willingness to supply our physical needs. Rather it recognizes that the supplying of them is the unfailing proof of God's goodness and love. So understood the prayer, "Take not thy Holy Spirit from me," need not be the expression of fear, but rather of confident faith in the mercy of God and in His faithfulness, a faith which finds abundant illustration in this most precious of all the Penitential Psalms. The fact that the most spiritual of Christians have been able to make this entire psalm their own is a proof that this verse does not have the meaning Dispensationalists give to it.

(4) Another illustration of the application of the Dispensational doctrine that the dispensations of promise and of grace are unconditional is found in their attitude toward the Lord's Prayer and especially to the petition, "Forgive us our debts, as we forgive our debtors." The prayer, being embedded in the Sermon on the Mount, must, they tell us, be intended for the kingdom age, primarily if not exclusively; and the petition rests, according to Scofield, on "legal ground," for the reason that, "Under law forgiveness is conditioned upon a like spirit in us; under grace, we are forgiven for Christ's sake, and exhorted to forgive because we have been forgiven."[53] This is to misinterpret the petition. The meaning is not that if we forgive others we may expect, as a kind of *quid pro quo*, that God will forgive us. But rather the emphasis is on the fact, brought out so impressively in the parable of the Unmerciful Servant (Mt. xviii. 23f.), that those who have been forgiven much must themselves be ready to forgive. Those who harbor an unforgiving spirit toward their fellowmen show plainly that they do not realize that they themselves owe everything to the infinite compassion and forgiving mercy of God. Our Lord gave this prayer to His disciples as a model for prayer with the words, "After this manner therefore pray ye."[54] But thousands of Dispensationalists refuse to repeat it, mainly because of the words, "as we forgive our debtors," which they regard as implying a condition and therefore as "legal ground."

(5) The clearest illustration of the desire of Dispensationalists to eliminate everything that savors of obedience from the dispensations of promise and of grace and to confine it to the dispensation of law, is found in their insistence that the Decalogue is not intended for the Church. There was a time when it was quite customary for the Ten Commandments to be read or recited at least once a Sunday as a part of congregational worship.[55] But in many churches today they are never used. The thunders of Sinai are not heard. The love of God is emphasized

and it is forgotten that in the New Testament as well as in the Old Testament it is declared that God is a "consuming fire." The Ten Commandments are an important part of all the great Protestant catechisms. But Dispensationalists insist that they are not intended for this dispensation. This leads to, and indeed necessitates, the claim that the sabbath is exclusively Jewish. Commenting on Neh. ix. 14, Scofield remarks: "This important passage fixes beyond all cavil the time when the sabbath, God's rest (Gen. ii. 1-3) was given to man. Cf. Ex. xx. 9-11."[56] Scofield misunderstood this passage as his comment clearly indicates. What Neh. ix. 14 deals with is the time when the sabbath law as the Fourth Commandment was imposed on *Israel* at mount Sinai. It says nothing as to when it was imposed on *man*. Scofield's laborious effort to set the Lord's day (the first day of the week) in sharp contrast with the sabbath as Jewish, as a day of legal observance instead of worship, is very regrettable.[57] The statement that God rested on the seventh day, blessed and hallowed it (Gen. ii. 1-3), would lose much of its meaning and most of its importance for the Christian, if it had to be regarded as nothing more than the basis for one of the requirements of an exclusively Jewish decalogue. And the obligation to keep holy the first day of the week is greatly weakened if the connection with the Old Testament sabbath is all but completely destroyed.[58]

The reason for devoting so much time to this doctrine of the "unconditional" covenant is that in it the radical tendencies of Dispensational teaching appear so very clearly. Darby was the uncompromising foe of the Covenant or Federal Theology which he found most clearly expressed in the *Westminster Confession of Faith*. He says of the doctrines "Of God's Covenant with Man" and "Of the Law of God" as set forth in this Confession: "All this is a fable and a mischievous fable. And I notice it because it is the foundation of the whole religious system to which it belongs." He speaks of "the nonsense of this system which Presbyterians accept by tradition," insisting that it is "a grave and fundamental error," and one that is not confined to Presbyterianism. He even goes so far as to assert that "The basis of the entire system of moral relationship with God in Presbyterianism is false; and it has tainted the whole Evangelical system everywhere."[59] Nowhere does Darby's aversion to important doctrines of the "Evangelical system" appear more clearly than in his rejection of the doctrine of obedience as set forth in the Covenant Theology. Those who are disposed to accept the Dispensational doctrine that the Abrahamic covenant was "unconditional" will do well to consider this fact and also to remember that they share this doctrine with the Russellites, who likewise insist that the Abrahamic covenant was "unconditional."[60]

3. Emphasis on the Old Testament

A further important result of the claim of Dispensationalists that prophecy must be interpreted literally, that so understood it is perfectly intelligible and if unconditional must be literally fulfilled, is the tendency to exalt the Old Testament at the expense of the New Testament, to insist that its predictions stand, we may say, in their own right, and are in no sense dependent upon the New Testament for amplification, illumination, or interpretation. This doctrine has been stated succinctly and drastically by Brookes as follows: "The New Testament cannot be in conflict with the Old Testament."[61] To the same effect Scofield declares, that the New Testament "in no way abrogates or modifies either the Davidic covenant or its prophetic interpretation."[62] The assumption that underlies these statements is that anything but *literal* fulfilment would be tantamount to abrogation or modification.

For an illustration of this insistence on the literal fulfilment of Old Testament prophecy we may turn to Scofield's comment on Jesus' statements regarding John the Baptist. On the authority of Mal. iii. 1f., iv. 5f. the Jews were expecting the Tishbite to return to the earth before the coming of the Messiah. This gave rise to the question, How could Jesus be the

Messiah since Elijah had not yet appeared in person (Matt. xvii. 10; cf. Jn. i. 21)? Jesus gave two answers to this question. First, "Elias truly cometh and shall restore all things." This might seem to imply that Elijah's coming was still future and would precede the parousia. But it may refer only to the relative order of events: Elijah comes first (and he has come), and the call to repentance which he has uttered will restore all things, *i.e.*, when heeded it will bring Israel back to her God. This interpretation is favored by the second answer to the question, which is given in these startling words: "But I say unto you that Elias is come already, and they knew him not, but have done unto him whatsoever they listed." This can hardly be regarded as anything else than a definite declaration that Malachi's prophecies regarding the coming of Elijah were fulfilled in the ministry of John the Baptist, that Elijah was the type of the Forerunner. Scofield holds on the contrary that John's coming was only a type of the future literal coming of Elijah: "But John the Baptist had come already, and with a ministry so completely in the spirit and power of Elijah's future ministry (Lk. i. 17) that in an adumbrative and typical sense it could be said: 'Elijah is come already.' "[63] This amounts to saying, that Jesus' words (Matt. xi. 14, xvii. 12; Mk. ix. 13) must be interpreted *figuratively*, in order that the words of the prophet Malachi may be fulfilled *literally*.

The doctrine of the Christian Church, as generally accepted, has always been that the New Testament takes precedence over the Old, that Christ and His apostles are the authoritative interpreters of the Old Testament, that its types and shadows are to be interpreted in the light of the clearer gospel revelation. As Augustine expressed it so aptly: "In the Old Testament the New is concealed *(latet)*; in the New Testament the Old is revealed *(patet)*." This does not mean that the New Testament conflicts with the Old Testament, but rather that it explains it and that its explanation is to be accepted as authoritative.[64] But what is meant by the assertion that the New Testament cannot conflict with the Old Testament is that the literal interpretation of the Old Testament prophecies must be insisted on regardless of the New Testament.

Thus, Paul's repeated declaration that the gospel knows no distinction of race, nation, class, or condition, that all are one in Christ Jesus, must not be allowed to have any bearing on the interpretation of Ezek. xl.-xlviii. The promises to Israel must be regarded as strictly literal. And since they have not been fulfilled and cannot be fulfilled to Israel during this present gospel age, they must be literally fulfilled in a future dispensation. This amounts to saying that the Church age must be regarded as temporary, and is to be followed by a Jewish age, when the "weak and beggarly elements" will again be given all the importance which was attached to them under the Old Dispensation.[65] In short, Paul's words must be interpreted in such a way as not to conflict with the hopes and claims of the Zionists! The present glorious age of the preaching of the gospel of the grace of God to every creature must be regarded as a merely temporary interruption in the Old Testament program for the glorification of Israel. This is a claim the seriousness of which can hardly be exaggerated.

4. Futurism

Another of the necessary results of the literal interpretation of prophecy is Futurism. In proof of this it will suffice to call attention to the radical change introduced by the Brethren in the interpretation of the Book of Revelation.[66] At the time of the rise of Brethrenism, it was the generally accepted view among Protestants that the Book of Revelation gives a prophetic picture of the history of the Church from apostolic times to the final consummation.[67] The "Protestant" interpretation, as it has often been called, found much of the book fulfilled in Pagan and Papal Rome. But the more literally its language is construed, the more difficult does it become to connect its scenes with events that have already taken place. Consequently, Dispensationalists regard all except the first three chapters as unfulfilled prophecy, while the Ultra-Dispensationalists regard the entire book as dealing with still future events. This may not seem very serious to many, since the interpretation of this book is generally admitted to be difficult and more or less uncertain. But Dispensationalists do not stop with Revelation. They tell us that all of the kingdom prophecies regarding the glorious future of Israel are to be taken literally. They must, therefore, be regarded as still unfulfilled and to be fulfilled literally to Israel in a future dispensation. As numerous examples of this tendency will be cited later on in the discussion, it is not necessary to give further examples in this connection.

5. Hairsplitting Distinctions and Arbitrary Assertions

The writings of Dispensationalists furnish many examples of hairsplitting distinctions and of arbitrary assertions which have little if any basis in fact or rest upon a partial and inadequate induction of the available facts.

a. Hairsplitting Distinctions

Many examples might be given of the way in which relative or minor differences are so magnified as to lead to assertions which are positively erroneous and dangerous.

(1) The sharp distinction drawn by Scofield between holiness under the law and under the gospel is a good illustration of this antithetic method of interpreting Scripture. Scofield says of holiness in the Old Testament: "Only when used of God himself (*e.g.,* Lev. xi. 45) or of the holy angels (*e.g.,* Dan. iv. 13) is any inward moral quality *necessarily* implied."[68] Yet Lev. xix. 2 declares, "Ye shall be holy: for I the LORD your God am holy." God's holiness is a moral holiness and the Decalogue was the expression of His holy will for His people. Hence the psalmist declares, "Holiness becometh thine house, O LORD, for ever" (Ps. xciii. 5). The conduct of Hophni and Phineas was particularly heinous because, while *set apart* to the service of a *holy* God, their *unholy* conduct made Israel blaspheme His holy name. It is not true that holiness "as the experience of an inner detachment from evil" is "distinctively of the New Testament, not of the Old Testament" If such were the case, the use of the word "holy" to render both the

Hebrew word and its Greek equivalent would be unwarrant-
ably confusing. It is to be recognized, of course, that in the
Old Testament the emphasis is more on objective or ceremonial holiness, in the New Testament on subjective holiness.
But Ps. li. and Isa. vi. and liii. suffice to show how truly it can
be said that the precious doctrines fully unfolded in the New
Testament are already present and operative in the Old Testament.

(2) Among other examples of hairsplitting and antithetical
interpretation is the familiar distinction between "the kingdom of heaven" and "the kingdom of God," which necessitates
a further distinction between "the kingdom of heaven" and
"the mysteries of the kingdom of heaven" or, as it is incor-
rectly called, "the kingdom of heaven in mystery." Similarly,
distinctions are drawn between, the coming *with* and the
coming *for* the saints, between "the day of the Lord" and
"the day of Christ," between the "wife" and the "bride" as
used, the one of Israel, the other of the Church. These will
all come up for consideration in the subsequent discussion.

b. Arbitrary and Sweeping Assertions frequently made
by Dispensationalists

(1) An impressive illustration of arbitrary interpretation
is Anstey's claim that the prophecy of the Seventy Weeks must
date from the edict of Cyrus. The language of Dan. ix. 25
is quite indefinite, "from the going forth of a word [not, 'the
commandment'] to restore and build Jerusalem"; and a number of different starting-points have been proposed.[69] Yet
Anstey insists that the edict of Cyrus is "unquestionably"
the right one. This makes it necessary for him to assert that
the generally accepted (Ptolemaic) chronology for this period
is *82 years too long.* So he makes the necessary deduction and
maintains this amazing and even appalling theory, *Athanasius
contra mundum,* on what he holds to be the express teachings of the Bible.[70] Unfortunately he has found a good many
followers, Scofield among them.

(2) Perhaps the most striking example of a statement based
on inadequate data in the *Scofield Reference Bible,* is the
comment on the word "evil" (Isa. xlv. 7). It reads as follows:
"Heb. *ra,* translated 'sorrow,' 'wretchedness,' 'adversity,' 'afflictions,' 'calamities,' but never translated *sin.* God created evil

only in the sense that He made sorrow, wretchedness, etc., to be the sure fruits of sin."[71] The facts are these: *Ra* is rendered in the AV by "sorrow" (once), "wretchedness" (once), "adversity" (4 times), "affliction" (6 times), "calamities" (once); it is not rendered by "sin." So far Scofield's statement is correct. But it accounts for only 13 of the occurrences of this frequently used word. *Ra* is also rendered in the AV by "wicked" (31 times), "wickedness" (54 times), "evil" (as noun, adjective, or verb, 444 times); and in many of the cases where it is rendered "evil," moral evil or *sin* is plainly referred to (*e.g.*, Deut. xxx. 15). Consequently, the comment is not only incorrect, but utterly misleading. It is true that the word "evil" does not always or necessarily mean *sin*. But it so often does have that meaning that this comment tends to give the reader an utterly false impression regarding the use of this important word.

The great danger in this method of interpreting Scripture is that it so often fails to distinguish between the clear teachings of the Bible and doubtful interpretations of it; and it tends to be dogmatic, even piously so, where caution and reserve are obviously needed. The great temptation to which the interpreter of the Word is constantly exposed is to invest his own interpretations of Scripture with the authority of Scripture itself, and to assert that those who do not accept his interpretation of God's Word reject God's holy Word itself.[72] This temptation is especially great in dealing with the subject of prophecy. The dogmatism with which many writers on unfulfilled prophecy express themselves regarding things to come is deplorable. The facility with which they ignore the views of all who differ from them is inexcusable. And the finality with which they put forth their prophetic programs has a tendency to discredit the whole subject of prophecy in the eyes of thoughtful and judicious students of the Bible. We need to remind ourselves constantly that while the Word of the Lord standeth sure, our own understanding of that Word may be faulty and imperfect. We need to remember that we are not prophets, but only interpreters of prophecy and that, "The subject of prophecy is one that peculiarly demands, for its successful treatment, a spirit of careful discrimination. From the very nature of the subject, the want of such a spirit must inevitably lead to mistaken views, and even to dangerous results."[73]

6. The Distinction between Israel and the Church

The topics which have been discussed in this chapter lead up to and have their focus in a sharply drawn antithesis between Israel and the Church. The parenthesis view of the Church is the inevitable result of the doctrine that Old Testament prophecy must be fulfilled literally to Israel and that the Church is a mystery first revealed to the apostle Paul. The Church thus becomes a parenthesis between the historical kingdom of David and his successors which is long past and the Davidic kingdom of the future which is to constitute the literal fulfilment of the kingdom prophecies regarding Israel in an age which will be introduced after the Church has been removed. This, as we have seen, is a distinguishing feature of Dispensationalism; not that there are dispensations in Biblical history—no one denies that—but that the Church is a parenthetical dispensation which delays or interrupts[74] the fulfilment of God's promises to Israel.[75] And since this parenthesis is, according to Dispensationalists, of quite indeterminate length and may be terminated at any moment by the rapture, the Dispensational doctrine of the Church is most intimately related to the doctrine of the second coming. We shall proceed, therefore, to consider the problem of the Parenthesis Church as the first of the three fundamentals of Modern Dispensationalism with which we are to deal.

Chapter III

THE KINGDOM AND THE CHURCH

DOES the Christian Church fulfil, or does it interrupt the fulfilment of the Old Testament predictions concerning Israel? Is the Church age a mystery period unknown to the prophets, or did they foresee and predict it? This is the vital issue which confronts every student of Dispensationalism. It is presented to us in very definite form when we turn to such a passage as Titus ii. 14 where Paul, in a context which deals with the second coming, briefly states the purpose of the first coming as follows: "who gave himself for us, that he might redeem us from all iniquity, and purify unto himself a peculiar people [ARV, 'a people for his own possession'], zealous of good works." The expression, "a people for his own possession," which Paul uses here is taken from the Old Testament (Ex. xix. 5, Deut. vii. 6, xiv. 2, xxvi. 18); and Paul uses a similar expression in Eph. i. 14, as does Peter in 1 Pet. ii. 9. That this use of, or reference to, the language of the Pentateuch is intentional can hardly be questioned. Consequently, the question is this, Do Paul and Peter use this expression for the purpose of calling attention to the close and vital connection which exists between Old Testament Israel and the New Testament Church? Or, do they expect us to understand that there are two "peculiar peoples," which are to be carefully distinguished? Does the God of Israel have one peculiar people? and does the Lord Jesus Christ have another peculiar people? Or, has Jehovah-Jesus, who is the "only redeemer of God's elect," one and only one peculiar people, which is made up of Old Testament saints and of New Testament saints without distinction?

I. The Teaching of the Old Testament

The first intimation of God's redemptive purpose regarding sinful man, speaks in the most general terms of the "seed" of the woman (Gen. iii. 15), and might be taken to refer to the triumph of mankind in general over the enemy that had caused its enslavement to sin. But we know that only a part of mankind has succeeded in winning this victory, and that it is won for them through the Second Adam who is the pre-eminent and unique Seed, as Paul makes plain in his comment on the promise to Abraham (Gal. iii. 16). In the Blessing of Noah, the emergence of a peculiar people is intimated by the reference to Jehovah as "the God of Shem" (Gen. ix. 26), and the contrasted statements which accompany it. But the beginning of the particularism of the Old Testament first appears clearly in the Abrahamic covenant.

1. The Covenant with Abraham

a. The Scope of the Covenant

This covenant is recorded first in Gen. xii. 2-3. That it is not unconditional, has been already pointed out. This fact appears in connection with its announcement. For the words of blessing are definitely connected with the command, "Get thee out of thy land" (vs. 1), and with the fulfilment of that command by Abram (vs. 4). This covenant promise is repeated several times: with especial fulness and emphasis after Abraham's faith and obedience had sustained the supreme test on mount Moriah (xxii). It had three main features: the promise regarding the seed, the land, the nations. Each of these needs careful consideration:

(1) The Seed. The promise is first stated in personal terms. Abram himself is to become a "great nation," the source of blessing to all the families of the earth (or, land). The reference to the seed and the land is at first implicit. In vs. 7 it is made explicit. In xiii. 15f. the seed is promised

the possession of the land, and it is declared that it shall be as numberless as "the dust of the earth." In xv. 2f. the seed is stated to be Abram's own son, and the figure of the "stars" of heaven is used to describe his descendants. According to xvii. 15, it is Sarai herself who is to bear the son; and nations and kings of peoples are to be descended from her. According to xxii. 17, Abraham's seed is to be as numerous as the stars and as the sand by the seashore; and the promise to the seed is confirmed to Isaac after his father's death (xxvi. 3-5).

(2) The Land. When Abram reached Shechem, the Lord promised to give his seed "this land" (xii. 7). In xiii. 15 it is made more precise: "For all the land which thou seest, to thee will I give it, and to thy seed for ever." The extent of the land is described in xv. 18f. as "from the river of Egypt unto the great river, the river Euphrates," and ten nations are declared to be then in possession of it. In xvii. 8, it is briefly described as "all the land of Canaan."

(3) The Nations. The wide sweep of the promise to Abraham appears especially in the frequent references to the blessing of the nations. The words of the first announcement, "all the families of the earth (or, land)," (xii. 3, cf. xxviii. 14) might be taken in quite a restricted sense. But "nations" (xviii. 18, xxii. 18, xxvi. 4) may have the most ample scope. The word "earth" may embrace the entire habitation of man (Ps. lxxii.); and Paul describes Abraham as "the heir of the world" (Rom. iv. 13).

b. The Fulfilment of the Abrahamic Covenant

The question naturally arises whether or to what extent the Abrahamic covenant has been fulfilled. It is the claim of Dispensationalists that it has not yet been fulfilled, and that, being unconditional, it must be fulfilled and fulfilled literally. We have seen that the claim that it is unconditional is not true. Has it been fulfilled? Here we must distinguish between what the words of the covenant require and what they permit: (1) As to the *seed*, it is to be observed that the very words which appear in the covenant (Gen. xiii. 16, xv. 5, xxii. 17) are used of the nation of Israel in the time of Solomon; "sand" (1 Kgs. iv. 20), "stars" (1 Chr. xxvii. 23) and "dust" (2 Chr. i. 9) are the standards of comparison. This would indicate that the promise was regarded as fulfilled in this respect in the golden age of the Monarchy. That it was so fulfilled is confirmed by the words of Heb. xi. 12. (2) As to the *land,* the dominion of David and of Solomon extended from the Euphrates to the River of Egypt (1 Kgs. iv. 21), which also reflects the terms of the covenant. Israel did come into possession of the land promised to the patriarchs.[1] She possessed it, but not "for ever." Her possession of the land was forfeited by disobedience, both before and after the days of David and Solomon.[2] (3) As regards the *nations,* it can hardly be said that the fulfilment had more than begun. The note of world-wide blessing is sounded prophetically in the Old Testament. Actually it hardly appears in the pages of Old Testament history. Consequently, we may say that, in the respects in which the Abrahamic covenant particularly concerned Israel, it can be regarded as having been fulfilled centuries before the first advent, while in its universal aspect, in which it concerned all the nations of the earth, it was scarcely fulfilled at all during the Old Testament period.

2. *The Mosaic Law*

a. Closely Related to the Abrahamic Covenant

The proclamation of the law at mount Sinai marked the climax of the deliverance of Israel from Egyptian bondage. This deliverance is expressly declared to be due to the fact that God "remembered his covenant with Abraham, with Isaac, and with Jacob" (Ex. ii. 24). The God who sends Moses to deliver Israel describes Himself as the God of Abraham. At Sinai Moses is directed to say to the people in the name of God: "Now therefore, if ye will obey my voice indeed and keep my covenant, then ye shall be mine own possession from among all peoples" (Ex. xix. 5). The use of the word "covenant" is particularly significant here. It is to be noted that in the Old Testament this word is always in the singular, never plural.[3] The natural explanation is that all of God's covenants with His people (cf. *e.g.*, Deut. xxix. 1f.) are in reality one and the same covenant, whether made with Abraham, with Moses, or with David. The form and details may vary: the covenant is essentially the same.[4] Consequently, the words, "if ye will obey my voice and keep my covenant," simply make explicit that requirement of obedience which is so prominent a feature in the life of Abraham, to whom the promise was first made.

b. The Law Required Obedience

That the Mosaic law required obedience is self-evident. The condition of blessedness under it is to observe and do all God's commandments (Deut. xxviii. 1); and the penalty for its breach is stated emphatically in the words, "Cursed be he that confirmeth not the words of this law to do them" (xxvii. 26, quoted by Paul in Gal. iii. 10). It consisted of a "law of commandments *contained* in ordinances" (Eph. ii. 15). As the one through whom this law was revealed, Moses was the great type of the Prophet who was to come (Deut. xviii. 15f.). As the administrator of a law on the observance of which life and death depended, Moses exercised the office of a king: he represented the invisible King (Deut. xxxiii. 5); and he passed on to Joshua, to the judges, and to the kings, the duty of enforcing this law (Deut. xvii. 18f.).

c. The Law and the System of Sacrifice

Closely associated with Moses was his brother Aaron. As Moses represented the law, so Aaron represented the altar. He had charge of the tabernacle where God dwelt and of its worship, especially of the whole ritual of sacrifice, which was the appointed means by which the people were to secure the remission of sins against that law which had been given them at Sinai. The necessity of blood atonement is the clearest teaching of these sacrifices (Lev. xvii. 11). The special emphasis on obedience made the necessity of provision for the expiation of sin increasingly apparent (Rom. iii. 20, v. 20).

3. The Davidic Kingdom

Since the kingship is hinted at in the promises to Abraham and is definitely provided for in the Mosaic law, it is significant that the people in asking Samuel to give them a king appealed only to a temporary situation, the unworthiness of Samuel's sons, and to the fact that other nations had kings, but made no appeal to the covenant (Gen. xvii. 6, 16) or to the law (Deut. xvii. 14f., cf. 1 Sam. ii. 10). This made their demand an act of unbelief and disloyalty. They failed to appreciate the privilege of having Jehovah as their king, and their demand amounted to rejection of Him (1 Sam. viii. 7). Saul, their first king, showed the same spirit of self-will which marked their demand for a king. It is important, therefore, to observe that the true theocratic kingship was to be governed according to the law of Moses (Deut. xvii. 18f.). The Davidic kingship had as its charter the great promise in 2 Sam. vii. The occasion was David's expression of desire to build a house for the Lord; and the prophecy concerns the house which the Lord would build for David. Both in the prophecy itself and in David's words of thanksgiving, the emphasis is on the words *for ever*. It concerns the "sure mercies of David." The deliverance from Egypt is referred to, but no express mention of the Abrahamic covenant or of the law is made in connection with it.

A very valuable commentary on 2 Sam. vii. is given to us in the four great Royal Psalms (ii., xlv., lxxii., cx.). In reading them we are at once impressed with the vastness of outlook and extent which they assign to the Davidic kingship. The king is seated upon "my holy hill of Zion" (Ps. ii. 6, cf. cx. 2), but his dominion is world-wide: nations and peoples will rejoice to own his peaceful rule or will be subdued or crushed. Israel is scarcely mentioned (lxxii. 18). The universalism of the Abrahamic covenant burst forth, we may say, in these psalms into a fulness of bloom which is in striking contrast to that particularism which is so marked a feature of the Old Testament as a whole. Two features are especially remarkable. One is the way in which the two aspects of the Messianic rule are stressed: the coming King is both Conqueror and Prince of Peace. The other is the fact that to this King is given the office of Priest, and that this priesthood is not Aaronic, but "after the order of Melchizedek," and "for ever." Still more striking are the words, "Thy throne, O God, is for ever and ever," which declare that this universal and everlasting kingship will also be a divine kingship (Heb. i. 8).

4. The Kingdom Foretold by the Prophets

The Royal Messianic Psalms have an important bearing on the question of the nature of the kingship, because they show so clearly the lofty conception of that sovereignty centred in David's line, which was given to David and his son Solomon.[5] The golden age of prophecy did not begin, however, until the 8th century B. C. when the meaning of the words, "if he commit iniquity" (2 Sam. vii. 14), which cast an ominous shadow across the bright prospect of the Davidic covenant, had found full and ample illustration in the conduct and fortunes of David's successors. It was when the kingdom had been divided, when Israel was tottering to its fall or had already fallen, when Judah needed the most solemn admonitions and warnings, that Amos and Hosea, Joel, Micah, Isaiah, and those that followed them heard the word of the Lord and declared it to His disobedient people. It was only natural that the threatened downfall of the house of David should be the occasion of definite assurances from the God of Israel that His purpose regarding David had not failed but would surely be fulfilled. The Abrahamic covenant is not forgotten (Mic. vii. 20). But the more specific promises to David's house are naturally in the foreground. These prophecies are of two kinds.

a. Prophecies in Terms of the Mosaic Economy

With regard to these prophecies, it is to be noted that most of them are definitely promises to Israel and speak in terms of the Old Dispensation. Thus, Hos. iii. 5 concerns the "children of Israel" and declares that they shall "return and seek the LORD their God and David their king." Amos ix. 11 predicts the raising up of the fallen "booth" of David, to be followed by the conquest of Edom, which had first been accomplished by David. Not merely are these prophecies addressed to Israel; they are expressed in terms of the Mosaic dispensation. Jer. xvii. 19ff. is a striking illustration of this. The glory of David's house is conditioned on the strict observance of the sabbath; to the temple at Jerusalem where the Davidic king is enthroned the offerings required by the law are to be brought up from all parts of the land; and the Levitical ritual is to be as permanent as the kingship (xxxiii. 17f.). Similarly, Ezekiel declares that under David, their prince, they are to dwell for ever "in the land that I have given unto Jacob my servant, wherein your fathers have dwelt" (xxxvii. 25); and this land is carefully re-distributed among the tribes (chap. xlviii.). Many other prophecies might be mentioned. But these are sufficient to prove that these prophets foresaw a Davidic kingdom of the future that would follow the pattern of the kingdom of the past, aside from its failures, follies and sins.

b. Prophecies which Transcend the Mosaic Law

On the other hand, it is to be noted that we find these same prophets speaking of the future in a way which clearly implies that they expected the kingdom of the future to be different in some, and even very important, respects from the Mosaic pattern. Thus, Jeremiah who seems to expect a full revival of the Levitical system of sacrifice (xvii. 26) has already declared definitely that the time will come when the ark, whose presence in the temple would seem to be absolutely indispensable to the proper performance of its ritual, would be as completely forgotten as if it had never existed (iii. 16). Such a statement sounds like sacrilege. But the reason Jeremiah gives supplies the clue to his meaning. The ark was the symbol of God's presence. Between the cherubim, above the mercy-seat, in the holy of holies which none might enter, save only the high priest—there the God of Israel sat enthroned, in the midst of Israel, but unapproachable in holiness. Jeremiah foresees a time when Jerusalem shall be called "the throne of the Lord," a day when as Zechariah declares "every pot in Jerusalem and in Judah shall be holiness unto the LORD of hosts." In other words, the holy city shall in very truth become a holy of holies. And the apostle John in his vision of the city of God seems to be developing this thought when he declares that the city shall be four-square, the length and the breadth and the height all equal. That is, it shall be a holy of holies on a vast scale; and all its inhabitants shall be holy. No wonder that the ark will then be forgotten! This is not the only indication that the worship of the future will differ from that of the past. Isaiah declares that there will be an altar in Egypt (xix. 19); and Malachi approves the offering of incense and a pure offering in "every place," which according to the context means "from the rising of the sun even unto the going down of the same" (i. 11). While Isaiah in one of his most startling prophecies (lxvi.) denounces the idea of the rebuilding of the temple and restoration of its ritual sacrifices in the strongest possible terms.

c. The Note of Universalism

Especially noteworthy is the universalism which appears here and there in the words of the prophets. Joel declares that God will pour out His spirit upon "all flesh" (cf. Isa. xl. 5, lxvi. 23, Ps. lxv. 2, cxlv. 21). Isaiah in one of the most remarkable utterances in his prophecies declares: "In that day shall Israel be the third with Egypt and with Assyria, *even* a blessing in the midst of the land: whom the LORD of hosts shall bless, saying, Blessed *be* Egypt my people, and Assyria the work of my hands, and Israel mine inheritance" (xix. 24f.). Centuries before, the Lord had said to haughty Pharaoh, "Let my people go"; and the Lord had punished Pharaoh and the Egyptians for mistreating His people Israel and refusing to let them go. But the time is coming when Egypt will be called "my people"; and ruthless Assyria which had been the rod of the Lord's anger will be called "the work of my hands." Israel will be the third in this amazing trio. In this passage the universalism of the Abrahamic covenant reaches a fulness of expression which prepares us for the words of Paul, "all are one in Christ Jesus." Zechariah declares that the remnant of the Philistines shall be "like a chieftain in Judah" (ix. 7). The glad invitation, "Ho, every one that thirsteth," of Isa. lv. 1 begins with the individual and then goes on to speak of "nations" in language similar to that of Isa. ii. 2f. Isaiah, the "evangelical" prophet as he has been called, is pre-eminently the prophet of blessing for the Gentiles; and he declares that the Servant of the Lord will be "a light to lighten the Gentiles" (xlix. 6).

d. Prophets did not Introduce Changes

It thus appears that in dealing with the messages of the prophets, we must be careful to distinguish between the picture of the future which they saw, and their demands upon the men of their own day. It is significant that almost the last word of the last of the Old Testament prophets is this: "Remember ye the law of Moses my servant, which I commanded unto him in Horeb for all Israel, with the statutes and judgments" (Mal. iv. 4). The prophets foresaw great changes in the administration of the covenant promise; but they recognized that it was not their task to introduce them. Their duty was to enforce the law of Moses. Not only this. They themselves belonged to that dispensation and most of their utterances were in terms of it. But here and there they give us a clear intimation that they were able to see that something better and richer lay before them.

e. Church and State under the Theocracy

A word should be said in this connection with regard to the relation between church and state under the Old Testament economy. Aside from such comprehensive expressions as "the children of Israel" and "the (or, my) people," there are three words which are usually rendered in the AV by "congregation." For one of these *(edah)* the ARV has retained the rendering "congregation." It was this congregation which was numbered at Sinai and consisted of every male from twenty years old and upward. This word occurs nearly 150 times and is almost always rendered in the LXX version by "synagogue" *(sunagōgē)*. Another word *(qahal)* which occurs nearly as frequently is rendered by "assembly" in ARV. The LXX renders it 70 times by "church" *(ekklesia)* and less frequently by "synagogue." The third word *(moed)* occurs usually in the expression "tabernacle of the congregation" (ARV, "tent of meeting") and is rendered differently in the LXX. As far as usage is concerned there is little difference between the words. They are equally comprehensive. The important thing to notice is that the LXX version supplied Greek-speaking Jews with two words ("church" *i.e., ekklesia,* and "synagogue") to describe the Israelites as a corporate body, whether viewed collectively or as gathered together for worship or for the transaction of important business. In this respect the Old Testament knew no difference between church and state. Every Israelite was a member of the congregation or assembly. That a distinction was made between the civil and ecclesiastical is illustrated by the diverse functions of king and judge, priest and Levite. But the theocratic principle pervaded the entire life of Israel as governed by the law of Moses.

II. THE TEACHING OF THE NEW TESTAMENT

As in the Old Testament the song of Hannah prepares us for the establishing of the kingship in Israel, so in the New Testament the announcements to Zacharias and to Mary and their hymns of praise herald the coming of the promised Messiah. He is to be a king and to receive the throne of his father David and sit on it for ever (Lk. i. 32f., 69). This is declared to be the fulfilment of ancient prophecies which go back to Abraham, "the oath which he sware to Abraham our father" (vss. 55, 73). And the universal sweep of this covenant finds expression already in the song of the angels, "Glory to God in the highest and on earth peace, among men of good pleasure" (ii. 14), and in the words of Simeon, quoting the prophecy of Isaiah, "a light to lighten the Gentiles and the glory of thy people Israel" (vs. 32).

1. "The kingdom of heaven is at hand"

The beginning of the ministry of John the Baptist was one of the most momentous events in the history of Israel. For nearly half a millennium the voice of prophecy had been silent. Now at last that silence was broken by a voice crying in the wilderness. According to all four evangelists this was in fulfilment of Isa. xl. 3f.; and it is significant that Luke who quotes the prophecy most fully concludes with the words, "and all flesh shall see the salvation of God." The preaching of John is best summarized in his own words: "Repent ye; for the kingdom of heaven is at hand" (Mt. iii. 2). This same proclamation was made by Jesus after John was put in prison (iv. 17). What it implied must have been clear, at least in part, to every Jew. It was the announcement of the kingdom of Messiah, David's Son. What they did not understand was the real nature of that kingdom, and the way it was to be introduced.

2. The "kingdom of heaven" and the "kingdom of God"

Both of these expressions occur a number of times in

the New Testament. The one is confined to Matthew; the other is used rarely by him, but is found repeatedly in the other Gospels and elsewhere in the New Testament. The view generally held is that these expressions are practically synonymous, and are used interchangeably.[6] It would be natural that they should be. The thought of the kingdom is prominent in the Old Testament; and the passage which naturally suggests itself is Dan. ii. 44 where we read: "And in the days of those kings shall the God of heaven set up a kingdom which shall never be destroyed." This will be "the kingdom of the God of heaven." Consequently, it is quite as proper to abbreviate it to "the kingdom of heaven" and the "kingdom of God," as it is that "the ark of the covenant of the LORD" should be called "the ark of the covenant" and "the ark of the LORD" (e.g., Josh. vi. 6-8). That the two expressions are equivalent is indicated especially clearly by the fact that they are used in synonymous parallelism in Matt. xix. 23f.,[7] and also because three of the parables which appear in Matt. xiii. as parables of the kingdom of heaven (the Sower, the Mustard Seed, and the Leaven) appear in Mark or Luke as parables of the kingdom of God.[8] Unfortunately, the fact that both of these designations of the kingdom are used in the New Testament has been made the occasion for the most hairsplitting distinctions. Dispensationalists are obliged to admit that "the two have almost all things in common."[9] But intricate and involved distinctions were nevertheless drawn by Darby as early as 1834;[10] and he has been followed in the main by all Dispensationalists. The attempt to distinguish between these expressions is based mainly on the fact that most of the parables of the kingdom which are recorded in Matt. xiii. do not appear in either Mark or Luke. Thus, Scofield points out that the parable of the Tares and of the Net "are not spoken of the kingdom of God," i.e., do not occur in Mark or Luke. From this he concludes that, "In that kingdom there are neither tares nor bad fish." But the parable of the Leaven is told both of the kingdom of heaven (Matt.) and of the kingdom of God (Lk.), as to which he remarks, "But the parable of the leaven (Matt. xiii. 33) is spoken of the kingdom of God also, for, alas, even the true doctrines of the kingdom are leavened with the errors of which the Pharisees, Sadducees, and the Herodians were the representatives." This leads to the amazing conclusion that the kingdom of God in which there are "neither tares nor bad fish" is to be completely leavened ("till it was all leavened") by the "teaching of the Pharisees, Sadducees, and the Herodians." It is hard to see how a distinction which leads to such obvious absurdities can be true. But it is one which the Dispensationalists are most insistent upon.[11]

The distinction which Dispensationalists draw between these two expressions is broadly speaking the following. According to Scofield the kingdom of heaven is Jewish, Messianic, Davidic.[12] It is the kingdom promised to David, which promise he tells us enters the New Testament "absolutely unchanged."[13] It was announced as "at hand" from the beginning of the ministry of John the Baptist (Matt. iii. 2) to "the virtual rejection of the King." Then it was "postponed"; and the prophetic, i.e., future form of this kingdom will be Messianic and millennial: "the kingdom to be set up after the return of the King in glory." This definition seems clear and unambiguous: it means that the kingdom of heaven belongs to the past and also to the future. During the present age it is postponed or withdrawn: it is "in abeyance." The kingdom of God, on the other hand, Scofield defines as "universal, including all moral intelligences willingly subject to the will of God, whether angels, the Church, or saints of past or future dispensations."[14] This definition also seems clear and precise: it means that all dispensations of human history may properly be called dispensations of the kingdom of God. The present Church age is, therefore, a dispensation of the kingdom of God; but it is not a dispensation of the kingdom of heaven. This would account, supposing the distinction to be correctly drawn, for the fact that after the ascension the disciples preached the "kingdom of God"

as the "gospel" for the present age. It would not account
for the failure of all the rest of the New Testament to
refer to the future proclamation of the "kingdom of
heaven." Darby speaks of Matthew as the "gospel of dispensation." But the prophetic teachings of the New
Testament are not confined to it. Yet nowhere else in
the New Testament is the kingdom of heaven referred
to. Acts i. 3 tells us that during the ministry of the
forty days Jesus spoke to the disciples "of the things
pertaining to the kingdom of God." This statement causes
no surprise to the reader of Luke's Gospel, where the
expression "kingdom of God" is repeatedly used. But it
stands in striking contrast with Matthew, where the words
"kingdom of heaven" have appeared almost as uniformly.
If Matthew had given us a fuller account of the period of
the forty days, we might be in a position to tell whether
he would have described Jesus' ministry during that period
as treating of "the things pertaining to the kingdom of
God" or would have used his customary expression "kingdom of heaven." But Matthew did not do this, unless
we can infer it from the words, "teaching them to observe
all things whatsoever I have commanded you," which
would naturally be understood to refer to that teaching
regarding the kingdom of heaven which is the great theme
of this Gospel. The most serious difficulties connected with
this attempt of Dispensationalists to draw a distinction
between these two equivalent expressions emerge in connection with the interpretation of Matt. xiii. and xvi. 16f.,
both of which passages will come up for consideration
a little later.

3. *The Kingdom—Its Nature*

Since it is clear that the thought of the coming kingdom
was prominent at the time when the gospel story opens,
and since John the Baptist and Jesus both refer to it, the
most important question before us is this. What was the
nature of the kingdom which they announced? When
we turn back to the infancy narratives in Luke, the answer

may seem to be given very simply in the words of the angel Gabriel to Mary (Lk. i. 31f.). Mary's Child is David's Son; He is to sit on David's throne; He is to reign over the house of Jacob for ever; and of His kingdom there is to be no end. It is with reference to this passage that Scofield declares that "The promise of the kingdom to David and his seed . . . enters the New Testament absolutely unchanged." And it is the claim of all Dispensationalists that the kingdom offered the Jews by John and by Jesus was an earthly kingdom similar to that of David the son of Jesse; and since such a kingdom was not set up at the time of the earthly ministry of Jesus, they insist that it was rejected by the Jews and has been postponed to a time still future. As to this teaching there are several comments to be made.

a. The Kingdom was to be Spiritual

The kingdom announced by John and by Jesus was primarily and essentially a moral and spiritual kingdom. It was to be prepared for by repentance. "Repent ye, for the kingdom of heaven is at hand." Childlikeness, humility, forgiveness, poverty, meekness, unselfishness were characteristic of it, as described in the Sermon on the Mount. It was to be entered by a new birth (Jn. iii. 3, 5). The scribe who understood the real meaning of the law was not far from it (Mk. xii. 34). To prove his Messiahship Jesus did not appeal to the kingdom prophecies,[15] but rather to His works of mercy and healing. He allowed Himself to be called Jesus of Nazareth, despite the fact that the Messiah was according to prophecy to be born at Bethlehem; and He made no effort to correct the mistaken inference drawn by the Jews from this title (Jn. vii. 42). He accepted the title "Son of David," but never, as far as we know, used it Himself.[16] He refused the efforts of the Jews to make Him a king or to involve Him in conflict with the Roman rulers. He declared to Pilate, "My kingdom is not of this world" (Jn. xviii. 36). Had Jesus come to set up such a kingdom as Dispensationalists describe,

He could not have made this reply to Pilate. Or, at least, His words would have to be taken as meaning, "My kingdom is not *now* of this world." For according to the Dispensational view it was a worldly kingdom, a kingdom which would involve the forcible overthrow of Rome that Jesus had offered the Jews, and would have given them (even as recently as the triumphal entry?) had they been willing to receive it.

b. The Kingdom was to be Universal

While in a sense Jewish and Davidic, the kingdom which Jesus announced was also to be world-wide. The clearest proof of this is to be found in the account of the early Judaean ministry of Jesus as given us by John (i. 19–iv. 45). In His conversation with Nicodemus, Jesus uttered those most familiar and most precious words: "For God so loved the world that he gave his only begotten Son that whosoever believeth in him should not perish, but have everlasting life." And He made the scope of these words perfectly plain by conversing with the Samaritan woman at Sychar, and declaring to her that the time was already come when men might worship the Father anywhere, if only they did it in spirit and in truth (iv. 23). In His first sermon at Nazareth (Lk. iv. 16f.), He applied the words of Isa. lxi. 1f. so pointedly to the Gentiles as to give grievous offense to the nationalistic expectations of His hearers, who sought to kill Him, just as years later the Jews at Jerusalem tried to kill Paul for the same reason (Acts xxii. 21f.). Such passages as the above indicate with unmistakable plainness that from the very outset Jesus not merely gave no encouragement to, but quite definitely opposed, the expectation of the Jews that an earthly, Jewish kingdom of glory, such as David had established centuries before, was about to be set up.[17]

c. The Cross Prominent from the Beginning

It is also to be noted that just as Jesus at the very outset opposed the idea that He was come to set up a national

and earthly kingdom, so John the Baptist emphasized that
truth, which Jesus Himself after His resurrection declared
to be taught by Moses and all the prophets, that the Christ
must suffer (Lk. xxiv. 26f.; cf. xviii. 31f.). John did this
by twice pointing out Jesus to his own disciples as "the
Lamb of God" (Jn. i. 29, 35), a title which he explained
by the words, "that taketh away the sin of the world."
John, the herald of the coming kingdom, hailed its king
as "the Lamb of God," pointing back, not to Nathan's
words regarding David's royal Son, but to Isaiah's description of the Suffering Servant (chap. liii.), to the passover,
and to the altar of sacrifice. Jesus Himself declared to
Nicodemus that He the Son of man must suffer, when He
said, "As Moses lifted up the serpent in the wilderness
even so must the Son of man be lifted up, that whosoever
believeth in him should not perish but have eternal life."
The necessity of the Cross was present in the mind of
Jesus from the very beginning of His ministry. Both John
and Jesus declared this definitely and emphatically. It cannot be too strongly emphasized that the best way to gain
a correct understanding of those words which appear so
abruptly, as it seems, in Matt. iii. 2 and Mk. i. 15, "the
kingdom of heaven (God) is at hand" (cf. Lk. iv. 43) is a
careful reading of the first four chapters of John's Gospel.
Those who so confidently assert that the Baptist and Jesus
were announcing an earthly kingdom which was to be definitely Jewish can hardly have given them careful consideration.

4. "At hand"

The last words of this great announcement are of particular interest because of the construction placed on them
by Dispensationalists. All Bible students will agree that
they clearly imply the nearness of the kingdom. But
Dispensationalists give them a special meaning. According
to Scofield, " 'At hand' is never a positive affirmation that
the person or thing said to be 'at hand' will immediately
appear, but only that no known or predicted event must

intervene."[18] Since it is claimed that the kingdom referred to was one of earthly glory, the kingdom promised to David "absolutely unchanged," this must be understood to mean that divine revelation as it then stood knew of nothing which must intervene before the "setting up of the Davidic kingdom." As to this claim we observe:

a. Used also of Second Advent

This understanding of the words "at hand" is the logical result of the "any moment" view of the second advent, which will be discussed later. Since the same expression is used in speaking of both events (compare Matt. iii. 2 with Jas. v. 8), it is natural, if not inevitable, that it should be taken in the same sense in both cases. Consequently, our study of its use in speaking of the first advent will help us to understand its meaning when used of the second.

b. Does not mean "proximate"

The expression "at hand" need not and does not have the meaning assigned to it by Scofield. The word in the Greek means to be "near";[19] and it is to be remembered that while nearness suggests proximity, it also implies separation. A traveler may be near a place, very near. But the fact that he is near it proves that he has not reached it. Whether he knows how far he is from it will depend upon whether he has been there before or has acquired definite information in advance as to its exact location.

The New Testament recognizes this quite plainly. The fact that the feast of tabernacles was "at hand" (Jn. vii. 2) made Jesus' brethren eager that He should go up to Jerusalem and show Himself. This would involve a journey of several days. The last passover was "at hand" (Jn. xi. 55) at least six days (xii. 1) before it was celebrated; and reference is made to the rites of purification which might precede it.[20] It was when the passover was near or "at hand" that Jesus sent two of His disciples to prepare for its celebration (Mt. xxvi. 17f.). It was "at hand." But they knew exactly the number of hours which must elapse before it could be celebrated; and they had definite duties to perform in the meantime. Similarly, when Stephen in sketching briefly the course of Israel's history comes to speak of the sojourn in Egypt, he begins with the words: "But when the time of the promise drew near" (or, "was drawing near," Acts vii. 17). Then he goes on to refer to a whole series of events, all of which took place before the promise was fulfilled. More than a century was covered by these events. But Stephen spoke of them in terms of nearness. Especially is it to be noted that in the Old Testament the word "near" or "at hand" is used of the "day of the Lord." Isaiah speaks of the "day of the Lord" on Babylon as "at hand" (xiii. 6) and mentions the Medes as an agent in a destruction which was not to be fully accomplished for some 400 years. Joel, centuries before the first advent, uses the expression repeatedly (i. 15; ii. 1; iii. 14). And in the familiar passage quoted in Acts ii. 17f. a number of things are mentioned which are to take place "before the day of the Lord come, that great and notable *day*." Clearly the "nearness" of an event is quite compatible with the knowledge of necessarily intervening events.

c. The Kingdom and the Cross

The correct understanding of the expression "near" or "at hand" is important because of the nature of the kingdom which is said to be "at hand." Jesus said to the woman at the well, "the hour cometh and now is." By this He meant that the spiritual kingdom which He declared to be "at hand" was already present, already "come" for all who were prepared to receive it. But if this kingdom is regarded as an earthly and Israelitish kingdom, then the claim that "at hand" means that no known or predicted event must precede acquires the utmost importance. For it raises at once this important question, Where does the Cross come in? We have seen that John the Baptist pointed Jesus out to his own disciples as the Lamb of God. If, when he said, "the kingdom of heaven is at hand," John meant to imply that "the next thing, in the order of revelation as it then stood, should have been the setting up of the Davidic kingship," why did he hail Jesus as "the Lamb of God" instead of as "the Messiah, the Son

.of David"? Was he adding something to these prophecies? Or, did he find in them something which Dispensationalist interpreters show a tendency to ignore? We believe the latter alternative to be the correct one. There are Old Testament prophecies which refer plainly to the priestly office of the Messiah, to the Suffering Servant. Can it then be affirmed that the establishment of the kingdom was quite independent of the sacrifice of the Cross?[21] Can it be asserted that the order might have been, first the kingdom, then the Cross, when the risen Christ so clearly declares that the burden of prophecy gives the opposite order: "Behooved it not the Christ to suffer these things and to enter into his glory?" (Lk. xxiv. 26; Acts xxvi. 23; 1 Pet. i. 11). Finally, if the sequence could have been, first the kingdom, then the Cross, and if the kingdom is to be "without end," where can the Cross come in? In other words, if the Jews had accepted the kingdom would there have been any place, any necessity for the Cross? To the Christian who realizes the meaning of the Cross, who knows that he has been redeemed by the precious blood of Christ, the question raised by the Dispensational interpretation of the words "at hand" is of the greatest moment. It amounts to this, Could men have been saved without the Cross?

d. Dispensational Teaching regarding the Kingdom and the Cross

The answers which Dispensationalists give to this question illustrate the difficult situation in which their understanding of the nature of the promised "kingdom" and the meaning of the words "at hand" necessarily lands them.

(1) This is illustrated by two brief quotations from Darby. On the one hand Darby tells us: "From Adam to the end of time no one was or will be saved but by the redemption and the work of the Spirit."[22] No evangelical Christian will deny this. Elsewhere Darby says: "Supposing for a moment that Christ had not been rejected, the kingdom would have been set up on earth. It could not be so, no doubt, but it shows

the difference between the kingdom and the Church."[23] What is the inference to be drawn from this statement if not this, that the difference between the kingdom and the Church is that the latter required the Cross, while the former did not?

(2) This implication is certainly stated by Scofield with sufficient clearness when he tells us: "The kingdom was promised to the Jews. Gentiles could be blessed only through Christ crucified and risen. Cf. John xii. 20-24."[24] The position to which the advocates of this teaching are practically driven is this, that if the Jews had not rejected Christ and caused Him to be put to death, His death would not have been necessary for their salvation. Or, to put it somewhat differently, it was the crucifixion which made the Cross necessary. If man had stopped short of the utmost enormity of shedding the blood of the Son of God, the blood of beasts would have sufficed for the Jew of the promised kingdom age as for the Jew of Old Testament times. Why not then also for the Gentile (Gen. xx. 18)?

(3) This conclusion, which we find more or less obscurely stated by Brethren and Dispensational writers, has been clearly drawn by S. D. Gordon, the author of the "Quiet Talks" books.[25] Gordon took the position that the sacrifices required by the Mosaic law were redemptive in themselves. He tells us: "It can be said at once that His dying was not God's own plan. It was a plan conceived somewhere else and yielded to by God. God had a plan of atonement by which men who were willing could be saved from sin and its effects." This plan was the Jewish system of sacrifice. The death of Christ was Roman. God did not intend the death of Christ. But when the hate of men brought about the death of His Son, God by a "master-stroke" made His death the atonement for the sin of man. Gordon cannot of course deny that God foresaw the death of Christ. He admits that it runs "like a lower minor strain" through the Old Testament. But he insists that it was not God's plan. And God's master-stroke was that He turned the death of Christ which had been brought about by the hate of man into an "enrichment" of His plan. For the death of Christ prepared the way for the mystery of the Church which is founded on the Cross. But this enrichment, he tells us, is only temporary. For, "The Church goes up and out. The kingdom comes in and down."

All this serves to show the terrible difficulty in which Dispensationalists become involved when, in the face of plain statements to the contrary, they insist that Christ came to set up a visible earthly kingdom and reign over Israel. Such statements as the following cannot be reconciled with the Dispensational scheme. "The Son of man came not to be ministered unto but to minister and to give his life a ransom for many" (Mk. x. 45); "him being delivered up by the determinate counsel and foreknowledge of God, ye by the hands of lawless men did crucify and slay" (Acts ii. 23); "For it is impossible that the blood of bulls and of goats should take away sins" (Heb. x. 4).

5. The Postponement Theory

If it be admitted that a visible earthly kingdom was promised to the Jews and announced as "at hand" by John and by Jesus, some explanation must be found of the fact that such a kingdom was not set up, especially since it is asserted that "at hand" means that no predicted events need occur before its establishment. The explanation which is given by Dispensationalists is covered by the two words "rejection" and "postponement." The kingdom was *rejected* by the Jews and *postponed* by God; and in its place the Church was introduced. That the Jews rejected Jesus as their Messiah and finally crucified Him is clearly stated in the New Testament. But when did this rejection take place, and when was the kingdom offer withdrawn or postponed? As to this, different answers are given. Scofield tells us in commenting on Matt. xi. 20f., that the kingdom of heaven has been *"morally* rejected"; and that Jesus then began to preach a new message, "not the *kingdom,* but *rest* and *service* to such in the nation as are conscious of need."[26] Yet he tells us that the "final official rejection is later (Matt. xxvii. 31-37)."[27] On the other hand there are those who insist that the final rejection does not come until Acts xxviii., when Paul having invited the leaders of the Jews at Rome to come to him, and having "expounded and testified the kingdom of God" to them "from morning till evening," pronounced upon them the woe contained in Isa. vi., because they believed not. Two questions arise in this connection which are closely related.

a. Was the Kingdom Postponed?

The claim that the kingdom was postponed because of the rejection of their King by the Jews, is the natural inference from the assertion that an earthly Davidic kingdom was promised to the Jews and that this promise must be literally fulfilled.[28] But the New Testament speaks in quite different terms. Jesus declared to the Jews that the kingdom should "be taken from" them (Matt. xxi. 41f.). The children of the kingdom (the natural and lawful heirs) are to be "cast out" (viii. 11f.). None of those "bidden" are to taste of the marriage supper (Lk. xiv. 24). The vineyard is to be given to "other husbandmen"; to "a nation bringing forth the fruits thereof"; men are to come from the "highways," from "the east and west and north and south," to partake with Abraham, Isaac, and Jacob of the marriage supper. The language of these passages is parabolic and should not be taken too literally. But it is entirely in accord with the words of John iii. 16 which were uttered near the beginning of the Lord's earthly ministry and of Matt. xxviii. 18f. and Acts i. 8 which belong to its close. They imply clearly that the period of Jewish particularism was ended; and they do not lend any support to the view that it was ended only for a time and is to be restored after the proclamation by the Church, during the present age, of the "every creature," "whosoever believeth" evangel has been concluded.

b. When did this Postponement Take Place?

In view of what has just been said, the question should be asked in this form, When was the offer of the kingdom withdrawn? A good way to answer this question is by turning to Matt. xxi. Scofield gives this chapter the head-

ing, "The King's public offer of himself as King." These
words would seem to imply that despite the fact that the
Jews had morally rejected the kingdom much earlier,
Jesus offered Himself to them again as King on the occasion of His triumphal entry into Jerusalem. But Jesus
had repeatedly declared to His disciples that He was going
up to Jerusalem to suffer and to die (Matt. xvi. 21, xx. 18).
He entered His royal city *as its King* definitely fulfilling
Zechariah's prophecy. But He entered it thus, not to set
up an earthly kingdom, but that as Israel's King He might
be rejected and die. He said definitely to Pilate, "My
kingdom is not of this world. If my kingdom were of this
world, then would my servants fight." He did not come
to reign but to die. And His rejection by Jerusalem, when
He entered it as her King, meant the rejection of Jerusalem, "Behold your house is left unto you desolate" (Mt.
xxiii. 37f.). It was not as King but as Priest-King that
Jesus entered Jerusalem. He came to die that He might
reign; not over Israel only, but that He "might gather
together into one the children of God that were scattered
abroad" (Jn. xi. 52).

6. *The Kingdom and the Church*

It is a significant fact that while the "kingdom of
heaven" (or, of God) is mentioned about 100 times in
the Gospels (of these about half are in Matthew and only
two in John), the "church" is referred to only in two
passages, both of which are in Matthew. The chapter in
which the kingdom is most often mentioned is Matt. xiii.
And while the language is parabolic, the fact that it deals,
in seven different illustrations, with the "mysteries" of
the kingdom, *i.e.*, with essential features of it which only
those who have ears to hear can understand and they,
only when these secret things are revealed to them, makes
this chapter of great importance for the understanding
of the nature of the kingdom. And since it is also in
Matthew that the Church is referred to, we shall proceed
to examine these passages with a view to determining

what difference if any there is between these two conceptions.

a. Matt. xiii. The Mysteries of the Kingdom of Heaven

Scofield introduces his comments on this chapter with a statement which we quote in full:

"The seven parables of Matt. xiii., called by our Lord 'mysteries of the kingdom of heaven' (vs. 11), taken together, describe the result of the presence of the Gospel in the world during the present age, that is, the time of seed-sowing which began with our Lord's personal ministry, and ends with the 'harvest' (vss. 40-43). Briefly, that result is the mingled tares and wheat, good fish and bad, in the sphere of Christian profession. It is Christendom."29

Leaving aside, for the moment, the distinctly Dispensational features of this statement, we observe that Scofield tells us definitely that these parables "describe the result of the presence of the Gospel in the world during the present age." This is so obviously true that it should not need to be stressed. Consequently, we find so careful and discriminating a student of words as Trench using the words "kingdom" and "church" practically interchangeably in his lengthy discussion of these parables.30 That they have eschatological implications and emphasis is quite obvious, especially in the case of the Tares and the Net. But this does not obscure the fact that they are parables of the present dispensation, the gospel or Church age. They serve to illustrate the familiar words of the Lord's Prayer, "Thy kingdom come. Thy will be done in earth, as *it is* in heaven." It is only in the measure that the will of God is done in the hearts and lives of individual men and so makes itself felt in the affairs of the world, that the kingdom can be said to be realized, to be "come." And since those and only those, who accept the gospel and profess their faith in Christ, are entitled to be called members of His Church, the connection between the kingdom and the Church must obviously be quite close.

b. Matt. xvi. 16f. The Office and Task of Simon Peter

In response to Peter's declaration, "Thou art the Christ,

the Son of the living God," Jesus blessed Peter and said unto him: "Thou art Peter and upon this rock I will build my church; and the gates of hell [Hades] shall not prevail against it. (And) I will give unto thee the keys of the kingdom of heaven: and whatsoever thou shalt bind on earth shall be bound in heaven: and whatsoever thou shalt loose on earth shall be loosed in heaven." Two expressions in this passage are especially to be noted.

(1) "I will build my church." We need not pause to consider the papal claim that Peter is the rock and that as such he was the first Pope, the head of the visible Church, Christ's vicegerent on earth. Protestants recognize that it was Peter in his representative capacity as a professor of belief in the Deity of Christ who was the rock, or that the rock was the profession itself. This helps us to understand the meaning of the words "my church." The organization which Christ will build is founded on faith in His Messiahship. As such it is definitely connected with the Old Testament economy, with Israel: it is a congregation, a church.[31] But it is also distinct from the Old Testament Church; Christ calls it "my church"; and it belongs to the future, "I will build." This implies that it will come into being after the redemptive work of Christ on which it rests has been accomplished. Consequently, the word "church" does not appear again until after Pentecost. Then, both in the Acts and the Epistles we read of the "church" as consisting of the body of Christian believers brought into being through the preaching of the gospel, especially by Peter and Paul. That the Church was built upon Peter in the sense that he was one of the first to confess the Deity of Christ and the first to profess the crucified and risen Lord before men is evident from the statements of the Book of Acts. The body which came into being through the preaching of Peter at Pentecost, is called the "church" in Acts v. 11, where Peter's summary judgment on Ananias and Sapphira is described as causing great fear to the "church,"[32] and again in viii. 1 where we are told that the "church" was scattered abroad,

except the apostles. And when, after the lapse of years, Paul and Barnabas went up from Antioch to Jerusalem to lay before "the church" the thorny question of the status of the Gentiles, Peter took a leading part in the discussion, and his testimony was explicitly cited by James in rendering his judgment. Certainly, Peter must have seen in all this a fulfilment of Jesus' words, "on this rock I will build my church." What church was it in the building of which Peter was actively engaged, if not the one of which Jesus had spoken? While Peter does not use the word "church" in any of his discourses as recorded in Acts or in either of his Epistles, the cordial way in which he refers to "our beloved brother Paul" (2 Pet. iii. 15) indicates that they were laboring in the same cause, to the same end, the building up of the Church of Christ. Unless we are prepared to deny that the Church of the Book of Acts is the Church foretold by Christ, we can hardly deny that Peter's activities in it were a fulfilment of Jesus' words to him.

(2) "And I will give unto thee the keys of the kingdom of heaven." It is significant that Jesus, after speaking of His Church and using to describe it a word which has Old Testament associations, proceeds at once to refer to another institution which has its roots far in the past and to which, unlike the Church, He has often referred. On Peter the first "Christian," as we may say, Christ will build His *Church*. To this same Peter He will give the keys of the *kingdom of heaven*. That Jesus refers to the Church and the kingdom in almost the same sentence may properly be regarded as implying that there is a close connection between them. It is conceivable, of course, that the connection might consist simply in the fact that Peter is to figure conspicuously in both, although the two spheres are quite distinct. But the usual and the more natural view is that the two are mentioned together because, and for the very purpose of showing that, they are very closely related, that they are two aspects of the same institution which Jesus will "build."

c. Matt. xviii. 15f. Discipline in the Church

This passage deals with the subject of discipline as it concerns the disciples of Christ. Jesus is laying down a great principle which is to govern the conduct of His followers in days to come. It has its occasion, quite obviously, in the rivalries and jealousies which had been aroused partly by Jesus' special intimacy with Peter and James and John (Matt. xvii. 1) and more especially by the selfish ambition of James and John which is brought out more clearly a little later (Matt. xx. 20-28). Here in speaking to His immediate followers and in dealing with a situation which was then actually present and was certain to arise many times and in many forms in days to come, Jesus says, "Tell it to the church." These words are clearly to be connected with the "my church" of xvi. 16, and while they might at first suggest to the disciples the then existing ecclesiastical organization, the synagogue, they help us to understand how the word "church" rather than "synagogue" came to be applied to the body of Christ's disciples, the Christian Church. At all events the implication is plain that those who accepted the preaching of the gospel of the kingdom would be members of Christ's Church and therefore subject to its government and discipline. The exercise of proper discipline will, therefore, be one of the marks of the true Church.

d. "Kingdom of heaven" and "church"

Such facts as the above are quite in accord with the view that the expressions "kingdom of heaven" and "church" are in most respects at least equivalent, and that the two institutions are co-existent and largely co-extensive. The relation between them has been succinctly stated by Candlish as follows:

"Both the Church and the kingdom of God are represented in the New Testament as having a two-fold aspect, external and internal, visible and invisible. . . . the Church describes the disciples of Christ in their character as a religious society, the kingdom of God as a moral society. The special functions of the Church are the exercise of worship, and have to do with the relation of men to God; those of the kingdom of God are the fulfilment of the law of love, the doing of the will of God in all departments of human life."[33]

But the very distinction which is stated here serves to bring out the intimate relationship which subsists between them. It is not the sole function of the Church to worship God: the Church has a very plain duty to man. He that loves God should love his brother also. And if the law of the kingdom requires "the doing of God's will in all departments of human life," this would certainly include worship of God as the first duty of man. But it serves to make clear the fact that the kingdom is a broader conception than the Church. Thus, the Church is not as such concerned with politics. But the members of the Church are as Christian citizens vitally concerned that the government of the land shall be conducted on Christian principles.[34] But what we are concerned with here is the fact that the kingdom and the Church are institutions which are both present in the world today; and they are so closely related, so nearly identical, that it is impossible to be in the one and not in the other.

e. The Dispensational Interpretation of Matt. xiii., xvi. 16f., xviii. 15f.

The explanation of the three important passages in Matthew which has just been given and which aims to bring out the very close relation between the ideas, "kingdom of heaven," "mysteries of the kingdom of heaven," and "church" cannot of course be acceptable to Dispensationalists whose aim is to magnify as much as possible the differences between them. It is important to notice, therefore, that the attempt to magnify these differences leads to confusion and to very serious complications.

(1) Matthew xiii

The fact that the explanation of this chapter given above was introduced by a quotation with which substantial agreement was expressed may have surprised the reader, because of the source of the quotation and the point of agreement found with it. Scofield tells us there that these kingdom parables describe "the result of the presence of the Gospel in the world during the present age." This statement is so obviously true that the only thing striking about it is that it should be quoted from Scofield. For according to Scofield the "kingdom of heaven" was rejected by the Jews[35] and postponed until the future *parousia*. If such be the case, how can these parables describe the situation during the present age, this parenthesis period when the kingdom is said to be "in abeyance"? The kingdom of heaven is according to Scofield a Jewish, Messianic kingdom, which is both of the past and of the future; it is *not* present. How then can these parables of the kingdom apply to the present age? This would seem to be a serious difficulty. Dispensationalists solve it by giving an utterly unwarranted twist to the expression "mysteries of the kingdom." We have seen that the word "mystery" properly has to do with the true character, the inwardness of this kingdom. Dispensationalists give it a quite different meaning, expressed by the words "the kingdom in mystery" or "the mystery form of the kingdom"; and they tell us that it describes a present form or phase of the kingdom of heaven. This kingdom of heaven in mystery they call Christendom, or the professing church. This means that the words "kingdom of heaven" ("mysteries of the kingdom of heaven"[36] is used only once, while "kingdom of heaven" occurs seven times in this chapter) can be used in two senses: a strict sense, which applies only to the past and the future, but not to the present, and a special sense which applies only to the present.[37] This is confusing, to say the least; it tends to obliterate the very distinction which Dispensationalists are so eager to maintain; and it is remarkable that this special usage should appear in Matthew which we are told is a "dispensational" and Jewish gospel, whose great theme is the establishment of the Jewish Messianic kingdom. We should, therefore, certainly not expect to find anything about Christendom or the professing church of this age in Matthew's Gospel!

A still more important point is to be noted. It is the way in which Dispensationalists interpret these kingdom parables in order to apply them to the present age. The parables describe it quite plainly as an age characterized by mingled good and evil. This is brought out clearly in the parables of the Sower, the Tares, and the Net, which tell us plainly that evil will be present in the world up to the time of the consummation.[38] But Dispensationalists are not content with claiming, in common with all Premillenarians, that evil will continue to be present in the world up to the coming of Christ. They insist that it will be triumphant, that Christendom, the professing church, will be completely apostate when Christ comes, that this apostasy will be a sure sign of His coming, that the destiny of this apostate church is utter destruction. They find the clearest proof of this in the parable of the Leaven. Regarding the leaven as "the principle of evil working subtly,"[39] they insist that the words "until the whole be leavened" mean that the whole professing church is to be corrupted irremediably: "The whole of the three measures would be leavened."[40] According to Darby this parable represents the kingdom ". . . as a system of doctrine, which would diffuse itself—a profession, which would enclose all it reached within its sphere of influence." He goes on to say: "It is not faith properly so called, nor is it life. It is a religion; it is Christendom. A profession of doctrine, in hearts which will bear neither the truth nor God, connects itself always with corruption in the doctrine itself." Now since Jesus said of the Church, "The gates of hell [Hades] shall not prevail against it," if Christendom or the professing church is to be completely leavened by false doctrine and utterly corrupted by it, Christendom cannot be the church to which Jesus referred. The Church and the professing church must be totally distinct. So argue the Dispensationalists. But if their explanation is correct, we are faced with the unanswerable question, How could Jesus who represented this kingdom as so supremely desirable have said, "The kingdom of heaven is like leaven," if by this he meant "The kingdom of heaven is like an evil principle working subtly, which shall irremediably corrupt the hearts of all who receive it"? Could Jesus have used the words "kingdom of heaven" so confusingly: of a blessed kingdom into which all should wish to enter and also of a mere travesty or counterfeit of that kingdom, a kingdom of hypocrisy, falsehood and evil which all should seek to shun? Could He have done this without involving His hearers in utter and inextricable confusion?

In interpreting the parable of the Leaven, Scofield declares that the leaven is "the principle of corruption working subtly"; and he tells us that this is "the unvarying symbolical meaning of leaven." This is an overstatement, to say the least. It is quite true that leaven is sometimes so employed (*e.g.*, Matt. xvi. 6f.). But it is not always so used. We find it referred to in passages where no such idea is suggested. Ex. xii. 39 gives, as the reason that the Israelites ate unleavened bread at the time of the Exodus, the haste and unpreparedness with which they left Egypt (cf. Gen. xix. 3 and xviii. 6, where this obviously is the sole reason).[41] The feast of unleavened bread, like the passover, was primarily a historical reminder and commemoration of this momentous event. The fact that leaven, being used to cause fermentation, was regarded as a principle of corruption is doubtless the reason that it was not to be used with sacrifices and offerings for the altar. But it was in daily use by the people. And it is difficult to believe that this fact has any religious or ethical significance whatsoever.[42] Consequently, Jamieson's comment on the use of leaven at the feast of Pentecost in connection with the offering of the first fruits seems a natural and appropriate one: "The loaves used at the Passover were unleavened; those presented at Pentecost were leavened—a difference which is thus accounted for, that the one was a memorial of the bread hastily prepared at their departure, while the other was a tribute of gratitude to God for their daily food which was leavened."[43] Yet Scofield insists that in both Lev. vii. 13 and xxiii. 17 the use of leaven means that there is "still evil" in the believer and in the Church. Such an interpretation can be defended only on the assumption that leaven can mean only one thing, that it must always have an evil sense. And it is only on the same assumption that the interpretation of the parable insisted on by Dispensationalists can be justified. Otherwise, it would be obvious to every reader of the parable that an interpretation which amounts to saying, "The kingdom of heaven is like unto an evil principle working subtly" cannot be the true one. The usual interpretation, that the reference is here to leaven as illustrating the all-penetrating and all-assimilating power of the gospel, is the only natural one.[44]

(2) Matt. xvi. 16f.

Both Darby and Scofield recognize that the church referred to here is the true Church. "It is," says Darby, "on that which the Father hath revealed to thee [Peter] that I am going to build My assembly . . ." Christ will build it, not Peter. But Peter will have "the place of a *stone (Peter)* in connection with this living temple." Consequently Peter, it would seem, may be one of the twelve foundations of the true Church. Yet, according to Darby, this Church was a mystery, unknown to prophecy, a mystery to be revealed not to Peter but to Paul, a mystery which did not have any proper place in a discourse addressed to "Jewish" disciples and recorded in a "Jewish" gospel. On dispensational principles, the mention of the Church in this passage is very difficult to explain. But this is only part of the difficulty.

In line with their interpretation of Matt. xiii, Dispensationalists tell us that the keys of the kingdom of heaven which were given to Peter were the keys of the professing church: "not the keys of the church, but of the kingdom of heaven in the sense of Matt. xiii, *i.e.,* the sphere of Christian profession." This can only mean that the same special and peculiar meaning which is given to Matt. xiii by which the kingdom of heaven is identified with the professing church must be applied to the office of Peter. Instead of his use of the keys being postponed to the future, in view of the postponement of the kingdom of heaven, he is given the keys of the professing church of the present dispensation, a church which is characterized by formalism and hypocrisy, a church which is a counterfeit of the true Church, a church which was corrupted from the very beginning, is to become irremediably corrupt and is destined for destruction. Dispensationalists admit that the true Church was founded at Pentecost, that Peter "opened the door of Christian opportunity to Israel on the day of Pentecost (Acts ii. 38-42), and to the Gentiles in the house of Cornelius (Acts x. 34-46)."[45] They can hardly avoid admitting that within the sphere of Christian profession, which included Ananias and Sapphira (Acts v. 1-11), there was the true Church to which Barnabas belonged (Acts iv. 36, xi. 24). Yet the whole trend of their interpretation and of their argument in its support is to make Peter the founder of a professing church, a church in which there are only tares and bad fish, a church which is to be completely leavened by false doctrine and become completely apostate;[46] and to make Paul the sole apostle of the true Church, the mystery parenthesis Church, which was founded by Peter some five years before Paul's conversion, a church in which there are neither tares nor bad fish nor any corrupting leaven. This brings us to the question whether there is any warrant for drawing such a sharp antithesis between the functions of these two men who were both so signally honored by their Lord, a distinction which is dishonoring to Peter to exactly the degree that it is honoring to his "beloved brother Paul."

(3) Matt. xviii. 15f.

This passage simply makes more difficult the problem dealt with in Matt. xvi. 16f. If the Church is a mystery in the sense that Dispensationalists hold it to be, it becomes still more remarkable that such a subject as the matter of discipline in this mystery Church should have been dealt with by our Lord and the record of it given to us in this Gospel which is declared to be "dispensational" and "Jewish," to be particularly concerned with the "kingdom" and to have nothing to do with the Church.

Chapter IV

PAUL'S DOCTRINE OF THE CHURCH

WE HAVE seen that very early in the history of Brethrenism, the claim was made that the Christian Church is quite distinct from Israel, that it is a mystery parenthesis, the existence of which was entirely unknown to the Old Testament prophets, only obscurely prefigured in the Old Testament types, and first revealed to the apostle Paul. Was the Church a mystery in this sense?

The word "mystery" occurs 29 times in the New Testament, most of which are in Paul's epistles, 6 being in Ephesians. It is important, therefore, to observe how the word is used, especially by Paul. Paul speaks of several mysteries: "the mystery of God and of the Father and of Christ" (Col. ii. 2), "of Christ" (Col. iv. 3), "of the gospel" (Eph. vi. 19), "of his will" (Eph. i. 9), "of the faith" (1 Tim. iii. 9), "of godliness" (1 Tim. iii. 16), "of iniquity" (2 Thess. ii. 7). These passages show that to describe a person or subject as a mystery, does not necessarily imply that he or it was entirely unknown. It might be known, yet still be a mystery because not fully known. God was known in Israel—that was Israel's pre-eminence. To know God was Israel's duty. Yet Paul speaks of "the mystery of God." Christ was God "manifested in the flesh." He had been on earth and the facts of His earthly life were known. Yet Paul speaks of the "mystery of Christ." Especially noteworthy is 1 Tim. iii. 16 where Paul speaks of the "mystery of godliness" and then refers to events in the earthly life of Christ which were known to and had been witnessed by Christians who were in Christ before him. Consequently, according to Paul, a mystery may be a truth which can only be understood by believers or a truth only partly known to them, but not necessarily something entirely new or utterly unknown. Was the Church a mystery in the latter sense?

I. THE PAULINE DOCTRINE AS SET FORTH IN EPHESIANS III. 1-6

A careful examination of this passage, taken together with others which bear upon it, should give us a correct understanding of Paul's meaning when he uses the word "mystery" in speaking of the Church.

> "For this cause I Paul, the prisoner of Christ Jesus in behalf of you Gentiles,—if so be that ye have heard of the dispensation of the grace of God which was given me to you-ward; how that by revelation was made known unto me the mystery, as I wrote before in few words, whereby, when ye read, ye can perceive my understanding in the mystery of Christ; which in other generations was not made known unto the sons of men, as it hath now been revealed unto his holy apostles and prophets in the Spirit; that the Gentiles are fellow-heirs, and fellow-members of the body, and fellow-partakers of the promise in Christ Jesus through the gospel. . . ."

In this passage Paul describes himself as "the prisoner of Christ Jesus in behalf of you Gentiles." This indicates the closeness of the relationship in which he regarded himself as standing to Gentile Christians. Then he speaks of a "dispensation" or ministration of the grace of God which he had received concerning them, and he connects this directly with the "revelation" to him of the "mystery" to which he has already briefly referred[1] and as to which he expects them to be more or less fully informed. Then Paul proceeds to make several very important statements regarding this mystery. He describes it first of all as something which "in other generations was not made known to the sons of men."[2] This declaration taken by itself would seem to imply that it was absolutely new. So we must note that it is at once qualified by three supplementary and limiting statements: (1) "as it hath now been revealed," (2) "unto his holy apostles and prophets in the Spirit," (3) "that the Gentiles are fellow-heirs, and fellow-members of the body, and fellow-partakers of the promise in Christ Jesus through the gospel." After making these three important qualifications, Paul concludes by reaffirming that he is a minister of this mystery and that this is a singular honor and privilege. With a view to understanding the general statement, we shall do well to examine these three limiting clauses very carefully, and we shall do this in inverse order.

1. The Nature of the Mystery

It is significant that Paul never uses the expression, "the mystery of the Church." He does not tell us that the Church is a mystery. What he is concerned to tell us is, that something about the Church is a mystery. This he states with great plainness and very emphatically. The mystery is, that the Gentiles are to enjoy, actually do enjoy, a status of *complete* equality with the Jews in the Christian Church. They are "fellow-heirs, fellow-members of the body, and fellow-partakers of the promise in Christ Jesus through the gospel." The word rendered "fellow" is the preposition "with" ("with-heirs," etc.), which indicates close association or identification. They are co-heirs with the Jews; they belong to the same body; they share equally with the Jews in "the promise in Christ Jesus through the gospel." This is a doctrine which Paul preached with great earnestness (*e.g.*, Rom. i. 14, iii. 22, x. 12; 1 Cor. xii. 13; Gal. iii. 28f.; Eph. ii. 12f.). This important feature of the Christian Church was the mystery. But it was not a mystery in the sense that no inkling of it had ever been given. For by insisting that the Abrahamic covenant included all who were of a like faith with Abraham (Rom. iv.) Paul had already made it clear that the rights of the Gentiles for which he was contending were theirs by virtue of that covenant. It was a mystery in the sense that, like other teachings which are spoken of as such, it was not fully revealed in the Old Testament and was completely hidden from the carnal minded. A doctrine which was so hated by Jews that they were ready to kill those who preached it (Lk. iv. 16f., Acts xxii. 21f.) and which was unknown to Gentiles, might well be called a mystery. But, we repeat, it was not the Church itself, but this doctrine regarding the Church which was the mystery.

2. *Paul was not the exclusive Apostle of this Mystery*

This is indicated quite clearly by the words, "unto his holy apostles and prophets in the Spirit." This language cannot be regarded as equivalent to the editorial "we." It shows that Paul recognized that, however unique the manner in which he had been made acquainted with the mystery, it was not revealed exclusively to him. This conclusion is favored by two considerations.

(1) Jesus had sought to make clear to His disciples both by precept and example the nature of the Church which He would build. In His words to Nicodemus, in His conversation with the Samaritan woman at Sychar, in His sermon at Nazareth—all at the beginning of His ministry--and in His eulogy of the Roman centurion (Matt. viii. 5-13, Lk. vii. 1-10), in His words when Greeks sought Him at the feast (Jn. xii. 32), and in the Great Commission (Matt. xxviii. 19, Acts i. 8), Jesus had made it clear to all who had eyes to see and ears to hear that the body of believers which He called "my church" (Matt. xvi. 18) would not be strictly or distinctively Jewish.

(2) This Church, the Christian Church, was founded at Pentecost only a few weeks after the crucifixion. This momentous event was signalized by the outpouring of the Spirit upon the 120 believers who were assembled in the upper room. It was followed immediately by Peter's sermon. In this sermon Peter quoted the words of Joel, who had predicted the outpouring of the Spirit "upon all flesh"; and he declared to his hearers, who were Jews and proselytes, "For to you is the promise and to your children, and to all that are afar off, *even* as many as the Lord our God shall call." Peter was preaching to Jews and it seems quite clear that neither he nor his hearers appreciated the broad application of his words. But they certainly opened wide the door of entrance into the Christian Church to the Jews and proselytes who heard him. A little later we find Peter and John going to Samaria, as Jesus Himself had done (Jn. iv.), to complete the work begun by Philip: "Then they laid *their* hands on them, and they received the Holy Spirit" (viii. 17). That these converts were

Samaritans is practically certain. Yet for centuries the Jews
had had no dealings with the Samaritans. The door was
beginning to open! It opened still wider when Peter was sent
to preach the gospel to Cornelius. The vision of the sheet, repeated thrice that there might be no mistake, convinced Peter
that he should "call no man common or unclean" (x. 28).
He baptized Cornelius and his household; and he defended
this act on his return to Jerusalem, when it was challenged
by those that were "of the circumcision." The fact that nearly
two chapters in Acts are devoted to this incident shows the
importance attached to it by the writer. When the so-called
Council of Jerusalem was held perhaps a decade later (chap.
xv.), it was apparently Peter's appeal to this unforgettable
experience at Joppa and Caesarea, rather than the testimony
of Barnabas and Saul which caused James to declare the
Gentiles to be free from the yoke of ceremonialism. Peter's
words on this occasion are especially significant: "But we
believe that we [Jews] shall be saved through the grace of the
Lord Jesus, in like manner as they [the Gentiles]" (xv. 11).
What an amazing statement for a Jew to make! To put the
Jews on the same footing as the Gentiles! In all this Peter
says not a word about Paul, or about a special revelation made
to Paul. Peter appeals to his own experience, an experience
which for him was almost as revolutionary as Paul's on the
Damascus road. Furthermore, it is not without significance
that it was John, the beloved disciple, who accompanied Peter
to Samaria to follow up the work of Philip, for we find in his
Gospel and Epistles no mention of the distinctive privileges
of the Jews. On the contrary, John's message may be summed
up in the words, "God so loved the world," and the only
allusions which he makes to the kingdom stress its spiritual
character (iii. 3f., xviii. 36).

3. The Mystery not Entirely New

The first of the three statements, which follow the words
"which in other generations was not made known to the
sons of men," is especially noteworthy: "as it hath now been
revealed." For it at once changes an absolute into a relative statement. If the words, "which in other generations
was not made known to the sons of men," imply that the
mystery was utterly unknown in the past, the words, "as it

hath now been revealed," definitely deny that such was
the case and as definitely assert that it was previously
known, only not with the same clearness and fulness. That
this qualification or limitation was necessary becomes apparent as soon as we remind ourselves what the mystery
was. It was, as we have seen, the complete equality of
Gentiles with Jews in the new or gospel dispensation.
This was in a sense a new doctrine. For centuries the Jews
had looked upon themselves as in a unique sense the
people of God; and nothing gave them more grievous
offence than the teaching that sinners, unbelieving "dogs,"
of the Gentiles, were to share with them in the blessings
of Messiah's kingdom, especially the idea that they would
be in any sense their equals in it. But this was also, as we
have seen, an old truth which was taught at least in germ
in the Abrahamic covenant. The blessing of the nations
is one of the prominent features in that covenant. All that
was intended or involved in that blessing was not at once
made clear. The law was given to Israel. The kingship was
Davidic. The Messiah was to come of David's line. Yet
in the Psalms and in the Prophets, especially Isaiah, we
are given occasional glimpses of the world-wide scope of
this promise to the fathers. A Jew must have had his eyes
holden by Jewish prejudice who could not learn from
Isa. xix. 23-25 that the future had wonderful things in
store for the Gentiles, even for those nations at whose
hands Israel had suffered the most. Yet there were other
prophecies which seemed to declare with equal clearness
that the pre-eminence of the Jews was to continue world
without end. Consequently, the statements of the prophets
might be regarded as ambiguous, and the carnally minded
Jews would naturally interpret them all in terms of their
selfish, nationalistic desires and expectations. Clearly, the
equality of Gentile with Jew was predicted in the Old
Testament. But it was not there made known, "as it hath
now been revealed" to the apostles and prophets of the
Lord.

4. In what sense "Hidden"

It is especially important to keep clearly in mind the very carefully guarded way in which Paul speaks of the mystery, because of the fact that he several times speaks of the mystery as "hidden" (1 Cor. ii. 7, Eph. iii. 9, Col. i. 26), or as "kept in silence" (Rom. xvi. 25). With regard to the word "hid" it is to be noted, that to say a thing is "hid" does not imply that it does not exist, and need not mean that its existence is unknown, but rather that it does exist but is inaccessible, either because it is out of sight or because men do not have eyes to see. The meaning of some of Jesus' parables was "hidden" from the disciples (Lk. xviii. 34, cf. ix. 45). Similarly Paul tells us that the gospel which had been fully revealed is "hid" to those that are "lost" (2 Cor. iv. 3). That Paul is speaking in relative terms is indicated especially clearly by his words before Agrippa: "Having therefore obtained the help that is from God, I stand unto this day testifying both to small and great, saying nothing but what the prophets and Moses did say should come, how that the Christ must suffer, *and* how that he first by the resurrection of the dead should proclaim light both to the people [Jews] and to the Gentiles" (Acts xxvi. 22f.). "And to the Gentiles"—these words with which Paul concluded his defense before Agrippa, remind us of that other defense made by the apostle more than two years before while standing on the stairs of the castle at Jerusalem, when he had declared that Jesus had said to him, "Depart; for I will send thee forth far hence unto the Gentiles" (xxii. 21). At that point he had been shouted down with the words, "Away with such a fellow from the earth: for it is not fit that he should live." Here Paul categorically affirms that his mission to the Gentiles was the fulfilment of what the prophets and Moses had foretold. Consequently, it is natural to infer that Paul's knowledge of the mystery which he had received by "revelation" (Eph. iii. 4) was not nearly so much the revelation of new truth as what is meant by the words, "Then opened he their understanding that they might understand the scriptures" (Lk. xxiv. 45). By "scriptures" Jesus certainly meant the Old Testament; as did Paul when he declared that the mystery which was "kept secret" since the world began was now "manifested" and by the "scriptures of the prophets" or "prophetical scriptures" made known to all nations (Rom. xvi. 26).[3] Such passages as these strongly corroborate Paul's assertion that the "mystery" was not wholly new and that he shared the full understanding of it with the other apostles. But an even clearer proof that such is actually the case consists, as will be shown in the next two chapters, in the evidence to be found in the Old Testament itself and particularly in those passages in it which are appealed to and expounded in the New Testament.

Having now seen what the mystery was, that Paul shared it with others of the apostles, and that it was new and unknown in a relative sense only, being in its essentials an important theme of prophecy from the time of Abraham, we are now in a position to appreciate the danger of taking Paul's first statement as complete and ignoring the carefully formulated modifications and exceptions which are at once added to it. Were we to read verses 3-5 omitting the parenthesis and stopping with the word "men" ("How that by revelation was made known to me the mystery . . . which in other generations was not made known to the sons of men . . ."), we might easily conclude that Paul's doctrine of the Church was in such a sense a mystery that it was completely unknown until he received it by special, direct revelation from the ascended Christ. Paul goes on at once to point out that such was not the case. Yet this conclusion which Paul is so careful to guard against is exactly the doctrine upon which Dispensationalists insist most emphatically.

II. The Dispensational Doctrine That the Church Is a Mystery Parenthesis

It is the claim of Dispensationalists that the Christian

Church is a mystery so completely unknown that it was not the theme of Old Testament prophecy, being only obscurely prefigured in its historical types; that the Church was a mystery known only to the apostle Paul; and that the Church itself was the mystery, and not simply that feature of it which is so clearly stated by Paul, the absolute equality in it of Gentiles with Jews. Thus, Scofield tells us: "The Church, corporately, is not in the vision of the O. T. prophet (Eph. iii. 1-6)."[4] In saying this, he means to *assert* that the burden of prophecy is the kingdom, a kingdom which is Israelitish and Davidic, and to *deny,* as "a mere theological concept," that "the Church is the true Israel, and that the Old Testament foreview of the kingdom is fulfilled in the Church."[5] The kingdom and the Church he holds to be quite distinct, the one clearly revealed, the other a hidden mystery first revealed to Paul. At the risk of repetition, we shall examine this claim in the light of Paul's own words, as contained in the three statements which have been discussed above.

1. "That the Gentiles are fellow-heirs"

It is upon this statement especially that Dispensationalists base their claim that the Church is a mystery. They tell us that the Old Testament prophecies regarding the coming kingdom are so completely different from the New Testament conception of the Church, that the two bodies must be quite distinct. The promises to Israel are to an earthly people and concern the earth; and the glorious Davidic kingdom promised by the prophets will be one in which the Jews shall dwell in their own land under a king of David's line, and be pre-eminent among all nations. The promises to the Church are to a heavenly people; and the Church knows no difference between Jew and Gentile: all are one in Christ Jesus. And since the present age is the period of the preaching of this "whosoever will" gospel, the gospel of the grace of God, they insist that the restoration of the kingdom to Israel must have been postponed. Scofield speaks as follows:

"That the Gentiles were to be *saved* was no mystery (Rom. ix. 24-33; x. 19-21). The mystery 'hid in God' was the divine purpose to make of Jew and Gentile a wholly new thing—'the church, which is his [Christ's] body,' formed by the baptism with the Holy Spirit (1 Cor. xii. 12, 13) and in which the earthly distinction of Jew and Gentile disappears (Eph. ii. 14, 15; Col. iii. 10, 11)."[6]

The issue between Dispensationalists and their opponents is brought out clearly in the statement just quoted. Dispensationalists admit that the salvation of the Gentiles was not a mystery. They insist that their equality with the Jews in the Christian Church was a mystery. So they infer that the Church in which this equality is to be found must be itself a mystery, "a wholly new thing." The answer to this claim is two-fold, being derived partly from the Old Testament and partly from the New. The Old Testament itself contains very definite statements to the effect that it would be only through Israel and Israel's Messiah that the Gentiles would be saved. All nations should "flow" to the mountain of the Lord's house. The Gentiles would come to her (Israel's) light. The Old Testament also intimates, while the New Testament makes clear, the nature and the extent of the rights and privileges which the Gentiles would enjoy through the acceptance of Israel's God. That these rights were to be so extensive that "the earthly distinction of Jew and Gentile" would disappear—this was the mystery. But it is nowhere stated that, in order that such might be the case, "a wholly new thing" must come into being. This conception of the mystery is entirely due to the insistence of Dispensationalists that the kingdom promises to Israel must be literally fulfilled, and therefore that the complete equality of Jew with Gentile in the Church is utterly at variance with the Old Testament and necessitates the view that the Church age is quite distinct from the kingdom age.

This claim brings us back to the all-important question, already discussed, of the real meaning of the kingdom promises. It is significant that practically all the texts upon which the claim is based that the Jews are to return to their own land and enjoy special privileges, are taken from the Old Testament.[7] Even more significant is the fact that while Paul devotes a considerable part of Romans (chaps. ix.-xi.) to the discussion of the future of the Jews, he has nothing to say about their restoration to their own land or of their enjoying special rights and privileges. He longs most intensely for their conversion, for their re-engrafting into the olive tree. But he does not connect this with restoration to the land of Canaan. This fact is especially noteworthy, because this passage in Romans would seem to be exactly the place for Paul to point out the difference between the heavenly mystery and the earthly promises to Israel, and to explain, if such was really the case, that the fulfilment of these kingdom promises to Israel was to take place literally, after the rapture of the Church. But Paul, who was a profound student of the Old Testament, has nothing to say on this subject,[8] which Zionists and Dispensationalists regard as so vitally important. The reason for this reticence on Paul's part may be found in the fact that the basic problem which is involved is made the great theme of the Epistle to the Hebrews. If this epistle is by Paul, as Darby, Kelly, Scofield and probably most Dispensationalists believe, we may turn to it for the solution of this vexing question. When we do this we note that the great aim of the writer is to prove and illustrate the fact that the institutions and history of the Old Testament period were typical. His main concern is to prove this as regards the sacrificial system set forth in the Mosaic law. The blood of bulls and of goats was only a feeble type of the precious blood of Christ. Aaron was a sinful and imperfect priest, very different from the One whose atoning work he foreshewed. Christ was the Mediator of a better covenant. The law had a shadow of good things to come, things infinitely higher and better than the shadows which prefigured them.[9] Obviously the writer of Hebrews regarded these things as "weak and beggarly elements." And it is to be observed that while he clearly represents them as done away in Christ—the imperfect being done away because the perfect is come—he nowhere suggests that this change is only temporary, that a new age may be ushered in at any moment when the old order will be revived and restored.

In Hebrews as in Romans, we find nothing about a return to the land of Canaan. On the contrary, the writer stresses the *heavenly* character of the hope which the patriarchs cherished. It was not an earthly *land,* but a home (xi. 14, a "country of their own" [*patris*]) which is not earthly, but heavenly (vs. 16), a *city* "whose maker and builder is God" (vs. 10). The whole emphasis in this great faith chapter in Hebrews is that the faith of the Old Testament worthies was not earthly but heavenly. When we take this in connection with these three facts, (1) that the main aim of the book is to show that the Old Testament covenant foreshadowed better things to come, (2) that it is definitely asserted that the new has made the other old and abolished it, (3) that no hint is given of a future restoration of the old, it seems evident that the writer regarded it as so obvious that the promises regarding the land of Canaan were types of a better and heavenly country that he did not think it necessary to speak more plainly on this subject. His closing words in vs. 40, "That they without us should not be made perfect" show very clearly that the hopes of Israel are most intimately connected with those of the Church. Such a concluding statement would be preposterous if the writer really believed and taught elsewhere that the hope of Israel is quite different from and entirely independent of the Church.[10]

This does not necessitate the inference that Israel will not return to and possess the land of Canaan. When two such ardent opponents of the doctrine that "Jewish peculiarities" will be restored as David Brown and Patrick Fairbairn took opposite sides of this question, we may well hesitate to speak too positively. This much however may be said. By ignoring this subject as completely as they do, the writers of the New Testament indicate at the very least its relative unimportance. What the writer of Hebrews is concerned to prove is that the whole ceremonial law, with its rites and sites, has been fulfilled in Christ. Whether, if this main thesis be granted, any importance attaches to the possession of the land of Canaan is a matter which he does not discuss and with which the Christian need not greatly concern himself.

2. *"Unto his holy apostles and prophets in the Spirit"*

As we have seen, the tendency of Dispensationalists is to assign to Paul a pre-eminent place in their doctrine of the Church. They regard the true Church of the New Testament as distinctively and we may say uniquely Pauline. They do this despite the fact that in the words, "unto his holy apostles and prophets," Paul so plainly declares that his knowledge of the mystery was shared by others.

a. Paul and Peter

Despite the fact that they date the Church from Pentecost, Dispensationalists insist that it was a mystery first revealed to Paul some twenty to thirty years later. Despite the fact that Peter and the other apostles were the instruments used by God for the establishing of the Church, they insist that "the kingdom of heaven" of which Peter was given the keys is not the Church which Jesus said He would build, that it is not the millennial kingdom of the future, that it is not the true Church which was revealed to Paul, but that it is "the kingdom in mystery," *i.e.*, the "sphere of Christian profession during this age," or "the professing church," or "Christendom," "the sphere of a profession which may be true or false." And they proceed to draw a sharp distinction between the Pauline mystery Church and the Petrine professing church. Yet Paul declares that the true Church is built upon "the foundation of the apostles and prophets, Jesus Christ Himself being the chief cornerstone" (Eph. ii. 20), which should certainly include Peter with Paul. Is it not tragic to think that, according to Dispensationalists, of the two most prominent of the apostles, the one (Paul) was made the founder of a Church which is to have a unique pre-eminence over every other body of believers, is to be raptured and to reign with Christ, while the other (Peter) was made the founder of a church regarding which we are told, "I will spew thee out of my mouth," a church which Dispensationalists have called a "Satanic counterfeit" of the true Church? Is it credible that when Jesus said to Peter, "I will give unto thee the keys of the kingdom of heaven," He was speaking of such a church, a church which would prove the direct antithesis of the one which He had just declared that He would build?

The use made by Dispensationalists of the expression "professing church" is an unfortunate and misleading one. For it uses only in a bad sense a word which should and often does have a good sense. "Profess" is used in the AV in both senses. It is the duty of every believer to witness a good "profession." A believer must be a professor (or confessor). Consequently, the true Church is pre-eminently a *professing* church. The fact that in some cases the profession is false is evidence that there are tares among the wheat, not that there are tares only. The whole point of the parable of the Tares is that the tares resemble the wheat, may resemble it so closely and become so intimately identified with it, that there is danger of rooting up wheat if the attempt is made to remove the tares. This does not mean that noxious weeds (heresy and profligacy) should be tolerated in the visible Church. Such things are not compatible with professed acceptance of Christ as Saviour and Lord; and the Church should not tolerate them. If it does, the Church may become a synagogue of Satan. But unless we are to hold that the officers of the Church are given supernatural power to discern the thoughts and intents of the heart, we must recognize that there will always be the danger of the presence of tares even in a congregation which seems to be singularly faithful and devout.[11] But while this is sadly true, it would seem to be self-evident that since it is the duty of all Christians to profess Christ before men, and since Christians are exhorted not to forsake the assembling of themselves together, the members of the true Church will all be found, except under very unusual circumstances, in one or other of the professing churches, or as they are often called "denominations," of Christendom.

When we compare the epistles of Paul with those of Peter, we do not find any essential difference in their conception of the Church. The church at Philippi was founded by Paul. Yet he felt constrained to warn it most earnestly against evils which are characteristic of the "professing church" (Phil. ii. 17-20). The church at Corinth was one to which he had devoted much precious time. Yet the conditions in that church, which Paul so severely and yet so affectionately admonished, suggest a professing church, which needed the same admonitions as we find in Peter's Second Epistle. If the letters to the Seven Churches (Rev. ii-iii) are addressed to the seven literal churches of apostolic times, as well as to the entire professing church in various phases and stages of its history, then Ephesus where Paul labored so earnestly was from the beginning, or soon became, according to John, a professing church which was in danger of becoming apostate. Paul spoke of "grievous wolves" who would enter in among them (Acts xx. 29) and Peter warned against "false teachers" (2 Pet. ii. 1). Yet Peter, writing to "the sojourners of the dispersion in Pontus, Galatia, Cappadocia, Asia, and Bithynia," uses the word "elect," which we find in several of Paul's epistles, addressing them as "elect according to the foreknowledge of God the Father, through sanctification of the Spirit, unto obedience and sprinkling of the blood of Jesus Christ." What is the difference between Paul and Peter? Did not both alike have in mind the true believers in a visible Church made up of men and women whose profession might be true or false? And is not the same true of John who did not receive the keys of the kingdom of heaven, who says nothing of a mystery being specifically revealed to him, but who as an apostle was a part of the "foundation" of the Church and whose epistles to the Seven Churches show exactly the same conception of the Church as we find in those of Peter and Paul? The attempt to make the true Church exclusively Pauline must lead logically to the conclusion that the apostolic (Petrine) church is false, worldly and Satanic, a professing church in which there is no wheat, which will not be owned by Christ, but spewed out of His mouth. This is to make one of the chief apostles the founder of a church which is destined to destruction.

b. Paul's Disobedience

The attempt to make Paul the exclusive recipient and

custodian of what is called "church truth" has another serious consequence. It tends to make the apostle to the Gentiles an apostle to the Gentiles exclusively. There is no warrant for this. The first explanation of the Lord's words to Paul on the Damascus road, "It shall be told thee what thou must do" (ix. 6), is given in the words of the Lord to Ananias: "he is a chosen vessel unto me, to bear my name before the Gentiles and kings, and the children of Israel" (vs. 15). That Paul did not regard his mission as restricted to the Gentiles is shown by the fact that on his missionary journeys he made it a rule to preach first to the Jews. His procedure at Pisidian Antioch is a sufficient illustration of this. Not merely did Paul go to the synagogue on the sabbath and preach there; he addressed himself to the Jews as Jews, calling them his brethren. A week later when the Jews opposed him, he said, "It was necessary that the word of God should first be spoken to you" (xiii. 46). It was only when they rejected it that he turned to the Gentiles. This was during the first missionary journey. Years later when Paul came to Rome as a prisoner, his first act was to appeal directly to the Jews (xxviii. 17f.), with precisely the same result. To offer salvation to the Jews was a part of his commission of the Lord. It was also the expression of that "heart's desire" for the salvation of his "brethren after the flesh" which finds such intense expression in Rom. ix.-xi. It was quite natural, then, that Paul should wish to keep in close touch with the church at Jerusalem. The Council at Jerusalem (Acts xv.) came between the first and second missionary journeys. After his second journey he went up to Jerusalem from Caesarea before returning to Antioch; and he wished to conclude the third there also, if possible at the time of the feast of Pentecost. Of this journey and its consequences the Dispensationalists take a most unfavorable view. They argue that Paul, being the apostle of the Gentiles, had no business to go to Jerusalem and that the Holy Spirit "forbad" him to go there (Acts xxi. 4).[12] Consequently, they hold that Paul was "disobedient," and that the afflictions

which befell him and his imprisonments at Caesarea and
Rome were designed to chasten him for his disobedience,
even though this chastisement prevented his carrying out
his true mission to the Gentiles.[13]

This is a serious charge. The best answer to it is found in
the fact that it is psychologically impossible to accept it as a
true explanation of Paul's conduct. Here is a man who had
been singularly devoted to the work of the Lord. He had suffered persecutions and afflictions of every kind. He knew that
"bonds and imprisonment" (xx. 23) awaited him. Yet he declared that he was "ready not only to be bound, but also to
die at Jerusalem for the name of the Lord Jesus" (xxi. 13).
And when these afflictions came upon him, he never admitted
or intimated that he had done wrong, that he should not
have gone to Jerusalem. To "resist the Spirit" Paul regarded
as a heinous sin. But he did not acknowledge that he had
committed it. After he had spent more than two years as a
prisoner at Caesarea, he was permitted to plead his cause
before Agrippa. Could he have said, "Wherefore, O king
Agrippa, I was not disobedient unto the heavenly vision"
(Acts xxvi. 19), if for two years he had been suffering the
consequences of disobedience? He described himself as "the
prisoner" of the Lord (Eph. iii. 1) on behalf of the Gentiles;
as bound with chains "for the hope of Israel" (Acts xxviii. 20).
He declared that his imprisonment at Rome had turned out
for "the furtherance of the gospel" (Phil. i. 12). It is hard, in
fact it is impossible, to believe that one whose conscience was
as tender as was Paul's could have been conscious that his
sufferings, which seemed such a grievous handicap, were due
to an act of stubborn disobedience, and at the same time refer
to them as he does. It is equally difficult to believe that Paul
could have failed to realize what the Dispensationalists see
so clearly, that his determination to go to Jerusalem was an
act of disobedience to the Spirit of God if such was actually
the case. On a previous occasion Paul had carefully heeded
the admonition of the Holy Spirit regarding a course of action
which he was disposed to follow (Acts xvi. 6-8) and regarding
which no personal suffering as a consequence of "disobedience" was mentioned. Should not this be decisive in determining our interpretation of his conduct here, unless we are

willing to hold that under two very similar situations his attitude and conduct were totally different? The reason Dispensationalists are so ready to denounce Paul for disobedience is because they are so firmly convinced that Paul, the apostle of the mystery Church, had an entirely distinct mission from that of the other apostles. But such was clearly not the case.

3. *"As it hath now been revealed"*

Of the three statements made by Paul regarding the mystery, this is the most important and for a very obvious reason. Dispensationalists tell us that the Church is something new, unique, *sui generis,* entirely unknown to the prophets. In order to make this assertion, it is necessary for them to ignore these words of Paul, "as it hath now been revealed." The extent to which they ignore them is illustrated by such facts as the following. In the section on "The Mystery" in *Jesus Is Coming,* Eph. iii. 3-6 is the second passage appealed to and it is quoted as follows: "The mystery . . . which in other ages was not made known unto the sons of men." [14] Vs. 5[b] is omitted from the quotation and ignored in the discussion. Scofield, likewise, has no comment on vs. 5 in the *Reference Bible.* In *What Do the Prophets Say?,* Scofield quotes Eph. iii. 5-6 in full five times as a Scriptural reference, but nowhere does he interpret vs. 5. In commenting on vs. 6, he makes the statement: "The revelation of this mystery, which was foretold but not explained by Christ (Mt. xvi. 18), was committed to Paul. In his writings alone we find the doctrine, position, walk, and destiny of the church."[15] Here Scofield endeavors to reconcile the Dispensational doctrine that the mystery was unknown before it was revealed to Paul with Mt. xvi. 18, by asserting that Jesus *foretold* but did not *explain* the mystery of the Church. Had he done full justice to Paul's words "as it hath now been revealed," he would not have drawn the distinction between *foretold* and *explained* so sharply. Scofield practically admits this when he tells us elsewhere that all of Paul's distinctive doctrines regarding the Church and the Christian believer "were latent in the teachings of Jesus Christ."[16] This is a very significant admission. For Jesus said almost nothing about the Church, but a great deal about the kingdom. If Paul's teachings regarding the Church were latent in Jesus' teachings, this can only mean that they were latent in His teachings regarding the kingdom. This justifies the conclusion that in His proclamation of a spiritual, universal kingdom, which would be quite different from the earthly and glorious kingdom which the Jews were expecting, Jesus was really describing the Church which He would build through the labors of His apostles and other believers upon the foundation of His finished work of redemption. Scofield was certainly right in finding Paul's teachings latent in those of Jesus—they are more than latent! But this admission tends to destroy that doctrine of the mystery which is so central in Dispensational teaching, and in consequence of which the Dispensationalists have discovered that the Lord's Prayer, the Sermon on the Mount, the Kingdom Parables, the Great Tribulation, are "Jewish" and "legal" and do not concern the Church.

III. The Olive Tree

Before we pass on to consider the evidence which supports the view that the Pauline doctrine of the Church was "latent," *i.e.*, foretold but not explained, in the teachings of the prophets as well as in the teachings of Jesus, there is one passage which requires especial attention. It is Paul's familiar illustration of the olive tree in Rom. xi. 17-24. For in it the apostle gives us a very clear presentation of the relation which exists between the Church and that Old Testament economy in which he had grown up and the true nature of which he had so completely misunderstood that he had persecuted the "church of God."

There is, Paul tells us, one good olive tree. Some of the branches are broken off. Branches from a wild olive are grafted in among the branches which remain, that they "may partake of the root and fatness of the olive tree." The new branches represent Gentile Christians. It would be difficult to state more clearly that the Gentiles in entering the Christian Church become members of a body, a church or theocracy, which has its roots in the Abrahamic covenant and to which all true descendants of Abraham belong. The tree represents the true Israel. Faith is the bond of union. Some of the *natural* branches have been broken off because of unbelief. Branches of a *wild* olive are grafted in among them (*i.e.*, among the good branches that are left) on the basis of faith. From this Paul draws two important and weighty inferences. The first is that, since unbelief caused the breaking off of some of the natural branches, the branches of the new graft owe their present status, their participation in the root and fatness of the olive tree, solely to faith. If they become unbelieving, they will be cut off. This is a solemn warning to the Gentiles against presumption and carnal security. The second inference is the one which bears most directly on Paul's argument. Since the Gentiles owe their present blessed condition to grace alone, it is only to be expected that the same grace which has spared them, who in a sense have no title to the blessings they enjoy, will also restore the natural branches which should by right enjoy these blessings, by means of that same faith on the basis of which alone Jew or Gentile can be in and remain in the olive tree, *i.e.*, can enjoy the blessings of the covenant through membership in the household of faith. In short, what Paul is saying here is simply by way of illustration and application of his argument in chap. iv., that Abraham is "the father of all them that believe" (vs. 11), whether Jew or Gentile, circumcision or uncircumcision. They are the true "Israel of God" (Gal. vi. 16).

It is only to be expected that such a passage as this would cause Dispensationalists great difficulty. Their easiest course is to ignore it. But this is hardly possible. Darby's explanation as given in the *Synopsis* is obscure.[17] If we understand him correctly, the olive tree represents the blessings of the Abrahamic covenant. These are earthly and, therefore, cannot concern the Church, all of whose blessings are heavenly. The tree is the "tree of promise," and it "remains on the earth." The natural branches are broken off. Gentiles are grafted in that they may enjoy these earthly blessings. They become unfaithful (Darby speaks of this as hypothetical, but he clearly regards it as certain to take place); and then the natural branches, the Jews, are to be grafted in again. Darby does not refer specifically to the "professing church." But since he denies that the true Church (the assembly) is referred to here, by Gentiles he must mean the professing church. Consequently, according to Darby, we have here a parable of the Jews, the professing church, and the future Jewish remnant—all earthly—and of the earthly promises which concern them, but not a word about the true Church, which is heavenly. The inadequacy of this interpretation is so obvious as to make detailed discussion of it unnecessary.

Scofield has very little to say about this important passage. He tries to avoid the difficulties in which Darby involved himself, by interpreting the good olive tree as representing Christ; and, like Darby, he directs attention to the difference between the promises to Israel and those to the Church, despite the fact that the whole aim of Paul's illustration is to show that the Gentiles are to partake of the "root and fatness" of the olive tree, *i.e.*, are to enjoy with the Jews all that is of real and lasting worth in the blessings promised to the true seed of Abraham.

How determined Dispensationalists are to insist upon a distinction which Paul ignores, is shown by the way in which Darby and Scofield in dealing with Rom. ix.-xi. stress the earthly blessings promised to Israel in order to force the conclusion that the Church and Israel are quite distinct, despite the fact that in this elaborate discussion Paul has nothing to say about earthly blessings and aims to show that the spiritual blessings promised to Israel are to be secured only by faith, and are the common possession of all believers, both Jew and Gentile. Paul's concern for Israel was not that they might inherit the land of Canaan, but that they might be saved (Rom. x. 1, cf. vs. 9). And in his proclamation of the gospel Paul made no distinction between Jew and Gentile (vs. 12).

CHAPTER V

OLD TESTAMENT PROPHECIES CONCERNING THE KINGDOM

THE effect produced on the interpretation of prophecy by the "parenthesis" doctrine of the Church as set forth by Dispensationalists is one of the clearest proofs of the novelty of that doctrine as well as of its revolutionary nature. In 1835 an article appeared in the *Christian Witness*,[1] the earliest organ of the Brethren, in which the claim was made that all of the prophecies of Daniel are still unfulfilled, that they do not relate to the Church age but are to be fulfilled in the future kingdom age. At the time this article was written the view was generally held[2] that the Christian Church or dispensation was the great theme of Old Testament prophecy.[3] Today in Dispensational circles it is regarded as axiomatic that the Church is completely ignored by the prophets. Consequently, the prophets have a very important role in deciding the issues raised by Dispensationalism. And since the Dispensational doctrine that the Church was unknown to them was first applied to the Book of Daniel, we shall confine ourselves largely to it in testing the correctness of this method of interpreting the prophecies of the Old Testament.

I. THE PROPHECIES OF DANIEL

1. Daniel ix. 24-27

The importance of the prophecy of the Seventy Weeks in Dispensational teaching can hardly be exaggerated. It is often appealed to as the conspicuous proof that the entire Church age is a parenthesis in the prophetic program which is to be discovered between vss. 26 and 27

of Dan. ix. Walter Scott, "the eminent Bible teacher," refers to it thus:

"This, then, is a parenthetic period of great importance and which has already lasted nigh 2,000 years. If the parenthesis between these periods (verse 26) is not seen, the prophetic future will be wrapped in confusion, and the student will find himself involved in inextricable difficulty; admit the parenthesis, and all becomes clear."[4]

Since Dispensationalists hold that the prophecy of the Seventy Weeks is directly Messianic, it is not necessary for us to discuss the various anti-Messianic interpretations that have been proposed. Our concern is to defend that form of the Messianic interpretation which has been called the "traditional" one because it has been so widely accepted,[5] and to show its superiority over this "parenthesis" interpretation, the discovery of which has furnished, so Dispensationalists tell us, the key to the interpretation of prophecy. Before considering the differences between these two views, the points of agreement are to be carefully noted. The most important are:

(1) The seventy weeks represent weeks of years, a total of 490 years.
(2) Only one period of weeks is described, as is proved by the fact that the subdivisions $(7+62+1)$ when added together give a total of 70.
(3) The "anointed one, the prince" (vs. 25) and the "anointed one" (vs. 26) are the same person, the Messiah.
(4) The first 69 weeks or 483 years had their terminus in the period of the first advent; their fulfilment is long past.

These points of agreement are substantial and important. The points of difference are also important: they centre about two questions:

(1) Have the great events described in vs. 24 been fulfilled, or is their accomplishment still future?
(2) Is the 70th week past, or is it still to come?

On both of these questions Dispensationalists take the futurist position in opposition to the "traditional" view.

a. The "Traditional" Interpretation of the Seventy Weeks.

(1) According to this view, all of the great transactions referred to in vs. 24 are to be regarded as having been fulfilled at the first advent and, more specifically, in what is to be regarded as the climactic event of the prophecy, the redemption at Calvary, which is referred to literally in vs. 26 and figuratively in vs. 27. Thus the words, "to finish transgression and to make an end of (or seal up) sins and to make reconciliation for iniquity," are to be regarded as referring to that atonement for sin which was accomplished, fully and completely, once for all, on the cross. This interpretation is quite in accord with many New Testament statements *(e.g.,* Heb. x. 12-14). Thus, Paul says that Jesus has "abolished death" (2 Tim. i. 10). Death was a very real thing to Paul. He was living under its shadow, when he wrote these words to Timothy. But the fear of death and the power of death had been destroyed, because Christ had brought life and immortality to light through the gospel. For Paul, death was indeed "abolished." Sin is, likewise, very much alive; it is very active in the world. But sin was finally dealt with ("made an end of")[6] and reconciliation brought about through the death of Christ, His passive obedience as a sufferer for sin. It only remains that the benefits of that finished work be applied to all those for whom it was performed. The same applies to the three other matters referred to in this verse. An "everlasting righteousness" was provided for all the redeemed through the active obedience of Christ, His perfect keeping of the law of God. Prophecy was "sealed," *i.e.,* authenticated in a unique way by the life and death and resurrection and ascension of Christ; and prophetic gifts ceased in the Christian Church with the close of the apostolic age. The "anointing of a most holy" may refer either to a person or to a place. If to a person, the reference may be to the descent of the Holy Spirit on Jesus to

fit Him for His Messianic work (Lk. iii. 22, iv. 18); if to a place, it may refer to the entrance of the risen Christ into heaven itself, when "through his own blood he entered once for all into the holy place, having obtained eternal redemption" (Heb. ix. 12) for all His elect. In a word, we have in vs. 24 the prophecy of the "satisfaction of Christ," of His obedience and sufferings, by virtue of which the sinner obtains forgiveness and acceptance with God.

(2) According to this view, the 69th week ended with the beginning of the ministry of John the Baptist and the baptism of Jesus; and the 70th week followed immediately upon it. Consequently, the "cutting off" of the Anointed One which occurred "after the threescore and two weeks" must be regarded as having taken place in the 70th week; and a reference to it is to be found in the words, "in the midst [half] of the week, he [the Messiah] shall cause the sacrifice and the oblation to cease." That Christ by His death put an end to the Jewish ritual of sacrifice, substituting for bulls and goats "a sacrifice of nobler name and richer blood than they," is the great argument of the Epistle to the Hebrews. So interpreted, it is the Messiah who makes firm or confirms the covenant for the one (the 70th) week; and the crucifixion which takes place in the midst of it is the great event of that week and may be regarded as the climax of the entire prophecy.

A difficulty with this interpretation is to be found in the fact that it does not clearly define the terminus of the 70th week. Unless the view is taken that "in the midst of the week" means "in the second half" of it, and even at the end of that half, the end is not definitely fixed.[7] It seems very unlikely that if "in the midst" really meant "at the end," it would have been described in this way. On the other hand if "in the midst" is taken in its natural sense, a half-week, or three and a half years, remains to be accounted for after the crucifixion. Many interpreters regard this as referring to the period of the founding of the Church and the preaching of the gospel exclusively to the Jews, a period ending with or about the time of the martyrdom of Stephen. Others hold that the period of three and a half years was graciously extended to some 35 years, to the date of the destruction of Jerusalem by Titus, a reference to which is found in vs. 26. Both of these explanations may be regarded as possible.

With regard to the claim that the prophecy extends to the date of the destruction of Jerusalem in A. D. 70 it is to be noted that while the language of vs. 26 may seem to favor this, it does not require it. Vs. 26 speaks of events which will come "after the threescore and two weeks." Of these events it mentions first the cutting off of Messiah which vs. 27 describes as taking place in the midst of the week. Then it speaks of the destruction of the city and sanctuary and finally of an "end" or an "end of war," which is a very indefinite expression. Vs. 27 declares that a covenant is to be made firm for "one week," that "in the midst of the week" someone will cause sacrifice and oblation to cease. Then it goes on to speak of the coming of a "desolator" and of a "full end." None of the predictions of desolation and vengeance contained in these verses can be regarded as so definitely included in the program outlined in vs. 24 that we can assert with confidence that they must be regarded as fulfilled within the compass of the 70 weeks. They are consequences of the cutting off, they may be regarded as involved in it, but their accomplishment may extend, and if this interpretation is correct, clearly does extend beyond the strict limits of the 70 weeks, since the destruction of Jerusalem was much more than three and a half years after the crucifixion. But, in either case, the great climactic event of the last week was the crucifixion which took place "in the midst" of that week. So interpreted there can be no interval between the 69th and the 70th weeks.

b. The Dispensational Interpretation of the Prophecy of the Seventy Weeks

This interpretation differs, as we have seen, from the one just outlined in two important respects: it regards vss. 24 and 27 as both referring to events which are still entirely future. Since this affects the details of interpretation very materially, several important features of it must be considered.

(1) The Events of Verse 24 still Future

According to the "traditional" interpretation of this prophecy there is, as we have seen, good warrant for the view that all the events described in vs. 24 have been fulfilled. The claim to the contrary is based largely on that literalistic method of interpretation which is insisted upon by Dispensationalists. If, for example, "to make an end of sins" means to eliminate moral evil completely from this world, then it is quite obvious that the accomplishment of the prophecy must lie in the future.[8] But the expression need not mean this; and the emphasis placed in vss. 26f. on the atonement may properly be regarded as indicating that the reference is to it. The special reason that Dispensationalists must insist that vs. 24 refers to the future is quite clear. If the fulfilment of the prophecy is still incomplete, and if the predictions relating to the 69 weeks had their fulfilment centuries ago, then the 70th week must be still future. Hence there must be an interval between the end of the 69th week and the beginning of the 70th week; and the entire Church age can be regarded as forming a parenthesis at this point.

(2) The 69th Week ends with the Triumphal Entry

According to Dispensationalists the 69th week ends with the triumphal entry of Jesus into Jerusalem a few days before His death. The only basis for this claim is the expression "unto the anointed one, the prince." But the word "prince" (nagid) is far too indefinite an expression to warrant such an inference. For that matter, the words of the annunciation to Mary (Lk. i. 32) would justify us in regarding these words as referring to the birth of "the Son of the Highest," who was acclaimed by the angel as "Christ the Lord"; or they might refer to the baptism, at which He was declared to be God's "beloved Son."[9]

Some years ago Sir Robert Anderson endeavored by an elaborate mathematical calculation to prove that there are exactly 483 years between the 14th of March 445 B. C. and the 6th of April A. D. 32, which he regarded as the date of the triumphal entry. But there are several weaknesses in this mathematical demonstration which Anderson and many others have regarded as flawless:

(a) Even if it be granted that the "commandment" referred to in vs. 25 was issued in 445 B. C. (the 20th year of Artaxerxes), not a word is said in Neh. ii. 1 as to the day of the month on which it was issued. All that we are told is that it was "in the month Nisan." Consequently, accuracy "to the very day" is impossible. The date, 14th of March (1st of Nisan), is arrived at simply by calculating backward 483 prophetic years from April 6th of A. D. 32. The meticulous accuracy of fulfilment, to the very day, is an inference for which there is no basis in fact.

(b) Anderson regarded the 69 weeks as representing 483 prophetic years of 360 days each. This total is about 7 years less than the total in terms of *solar* years of 365¼ days. That Scripture sometimes uses a "prophetic" year of 360 days seems probable (cf. Rev. xi. 2-3). But to make such a year, which may be regarded as a round number, corresponds neither to the lunar nor the solar year, and makes no provision for the intercalating of "leap" days or months to bring it into harmony with the solar year, the basis of a minute mathematical calculation is decidedly hazardous. Denny[10] and Kelly, both of them leaders among the Brethren, based their calculations on *solar* years and arrived at dates for the beginning and ending of this period markedly different from those reached by Anderson.[11]

(3) The Cutting-off of Messiah not in the 70th Week

The question whether the "cutting off" of the Anointed One is to be regarded as taking place in the last week depends entirely upon whether the 70th week follows immediately on the 69th or not. That it would do so, is a natural and proper inference from the statement that 70 weeks are included in the scope of the prophecy. Dispensationalists have become so accustomed to the idea of hidden intervals or parentheses in prophecy and have found them so helpful in solving the problems which beset the path of the literalist interpreter that it is easy for them to overlook the difficulty which confronts them at this point. It is a very serious difficulty. Is it credible that this prophecy, which speaks so definitely of 70 weeks and then subdivides the 70 into 7 and 62 and 1, should require for its correct interpretation that an interval be discovered between the last two of the weeks far longer than the entire period covered by the prophecy itself? If the 69 weeks are exactly 483 consecutive years, exact to the very day, and if the 1 week is to be exactly 7 consecutive years, is it credible that an interval which is already more than 1900 years, nearly four times as long as the period covered by the prophecy, is to be introduced into it and allowed to interrupt its fulfilment? It would seem to be obvious that the more definite and precise the chronology of the weeks is held to be, the more difficult must it become to regard the insertion of a quite indefinite and timeless interval into it as permissible or possible. $483+7$ is 490, no more and no less. $483+x+7$ is a very different total, especially if x is an "unknown," already proved to represent more than 1900. Furthermore, the fact that the 62 weeks are regarded as following directly on the 7 would indicate that the last week is to follow immediately on the 62.

(4) "Jewish" Time—The Ticking Clock

Dispensationalists are fond of the illustration of a clock. The ticking clock, they tell us, represents "Jewish" time. The mystery parenthesis is "time out." God only counts time in dealing with Israel, when the people are in the land. Some add to this the further specification, when "they are governed by God." Neither of these requirements is met by the interval which they find here in the prophecy of the Seventy Weeks. Consequently, the clock ceased to tick at the time of the triumphal entry. It will not tick again until that moment, still future, when God resumes His direct dealings with Israel. This will be when the people are once more in their own land. It will follow the rapture and be marked by the appearance of the Roman prince. There are at least two serious objections to this view.

(a) If it is claimed that it is necessary for Israel to be restored to and in their land in order for the clock to resume ticking, it is to be remembered that Israel was still in the land for nearly 40 years (to A. D. 70) after the clock stopped ticking, quite as much in the land as during the entire earthly life of Jesus preceding the triumphal entry and for several centuries before it. So it must be admitted that Israel could still be in the land after the clock stopped ticking.[12]

(b) On the other hand, if the clock could only tick when Israel was "governed by God," was this condition really fulfilled at any time during the period of the 69 weeks? The last theocratic king of the House of David had lost his throne full 50 years before the edict of Cyrus and nearly 150 years before the decree of Artaxerxes. "The times of the Gentiles" are regarded by Dispensationalists as beginning with Nebuchadnezzar's destruction of Jerusalem. Hence this entire period was distinctly not a period when Israel was "governed by God." If the clock represents "Jewish" time, with Israel in the land and governed by God, how then could it tick at all during the entire period from 445 B. C. to A. D. 30? If they are logical, Dispensationalists must admit that the parenthesis which they discover between the 69th and 70th weeks is really a parenthesis (the Church age, broadly speaking) within a parenthesis (the times of the Gentiles).[13] And what we maintain is, that on Dispensational principles the one parenthesis is no more entitled to be called Jewish time than is the other. If the clock could tick during part of the times of the Gentiles, it could tick during the whole of it. If it stops at A. D. 30 or 33 instead of at A. D. 70, it does so quite arbitrarily. For Israel continued to be in the land and under foreign rulers during these forty years, quite as much as from 445 or 538 B. C. to A. D. 30. In short, the clock does not run on Jewish time or on Gentile time. It stops at the triumphal entry and resumes ticking at the rapture simply because the exigencies of the Dispensational theory require it, because room must be found for the entire Church age, which began at Pentecost, between the 69th and 70th weeks of a prophecy regarding which we are told that it covers only 70 weeks.

(5) Calvary Overshadowed by the Triumphal Entry

Whatever view is taken regarding the purpose of the triumphal entry the fact remains that it was speedily followed by Calvary. Jesus declared that He went up to Jerusalem to die; and He did die. The shouts of "Hosanna to the Son of David" were soon drowned by the cries of "Crucify him. . . . We have no king but Caesar." Jesus wept over the city because He knew that the acclaims of the multitude would be followed by the journey to Golgotha, and that then there would come upon the rejoicing city days of vengeance such as had not been since the beginning of the creation. The triumphal entry illustrated the fact that the "goodness" of the Chosen People was "as a morning cloud, and as the early dew it goeth away" (Hos. vi. 4). It was not to Palm Sunday but to Calvary (and Olivet) that Jesus referred when He said, "And I, if I be lifted up from the earth, will draw all *men* unto me." Yet Dispensationalists make the former event the climax of this prophecy in so far as fulfilled; and they declare that the crucifixion is not within the compass of the weeks at all. It occurred "after" the sixty and two weeks; but how long after, they cannot tell us, except as a fact of history. The definiteness of the reference to the one event is in striking contrast to the indefiniteness with which the other is referred to.

It is to be noted, therefore, that the shortness of the interval between the triumphal entry and Calvary (less than a week), as this has been proved to be by the fulfilment, makes the emphasis placed on the former event all the more remarkable. The interval is almost negligible. Anderson reckoned 173,880 days to the triumphal entry. To the crucifixion would be only five days more, 173,885 days. Consequently, it is not surprising that Dispensationalists sometimes speak, inaccurately of course (even Anderson himself does so), of the 69 weeks as ending with the crucifixion.[14] But such a statement is inexcusable, according to their interpretation. For they are most emphatic that the cutting-off was *after* the 69th week, after it and not in it. Yet this very fact that the two events lay so close together makes the choice of the former to be the climactic event all the more significant; while the fact that the latter can be spoken of as the climax of the 69th week only inaccurately and by ignoring the express language of the prophecy itself becomes all the more noteworthy. The Dispensational interpretation of the prophecy minimizes the Cross! The traditional interpretation magnifies it!

(6) Who Confirms the Covenant?

Vitally connected with the question whether the Cross is referred to in vs. 27 is the further question whether the one who confirms or makes firm a covenant is Christ or Antichrist. For it is only natural to suppose that the confirming of the covenant and the abolishing of sacrifice is performed by the same person. Who is it, then, that confirms the covenant? According to the Dispensational view, it is the "prince who shall come"; and it is argued that "prince" is the subject of the verb "confirm" because it is nearer to it than is the word "anointed (one)." But this argument is more than offset by the fact that the subject of the verb "destroy" is not "prince" but "people" ("and the people of the prince, the coming one, shall destroy"). If the nearest subject must be regarded as the subject of the verb "confirm," it should be "people" not "prince." On the other hand, there are many instances in the Bible where the subject which is to be supplied to a verb is not the one which immediately or closely precedes it but another that is more remote. Furthermore, the statement regarding the people of the prince is that they shall destroy the city. Dispensationalists admit that this refers to the destruction of Jerusalem by the Romans under Titus. It should follow then, according to their view, that the subject of the verb "confirm" must be Titus himself. But if vs. 27 refers exclusively to the time of the end, it must be *Titus redivivus* or another Roman king of whom he was a type.[15] We have already seen that the interpretation of the words, "and he shall cause the sacrifice and the oblation to cease," find a very appropriate fulfilment in the atoning work of Christ on the cross. The same applies to the words, "and he shall confirm [or, cause to be strong, or, to prevail] covenant [or, a covenant] for many (for) one week." It is a mistake to say that these words speak of the making of a seven-year covenant, and to infer that the maker of it cannot be the Messiah whose covenant is an everlasting covenant. The natural meaning is "cause to prevail." [16] This may properly be taken to mean that during the brief period of His earthly ministry Jesus fulfilled the terms of the ancient covenant made with the seed of Abraham (cf. Rom. xv. 8), that He secured its benefits to "many," that is "to the believers in Israel," for the period up to the stoning of Stephen, or perhaps, in mercy, until the time of the destruction of Jerusalem, at which time the "new covenant," which was in fact only the full unfolding of the old covenant and made no distinction between Jew and Gentile, went fully into effect through the destruction of the temple and of Jewish national existence. According to Dispensationalists, the head of the "restored" Roman Empire is yet to make a covenant for seven years with the Jews and permit them to return to their own land, rebuild the temple, and restore the Mosaic ritual of sacrifice; and then, in the midst of the week, he will break the covenant, abolish the temple worship and inaugurate that reign of terror which is commonly called the great tribulation.

Since, according to the Dispensational interpretation of vss. 24 and 27, the fulfilment is still wholly future, only the future can pass final judgment upon it. But the superiority of the older interpretation of this prophecy is clearly indicated by the arguments in its favor stated above. They may be summarized as follows:

(a) The view that Messiah is the subject of the verb "make firm" regards the 70th week as following immediately on the 69th week. It does not destroy the chronological sequence and value of the prophecy by inserting between a predicted period of exactly 483 years, which is completely past, and a period of exactly 7 years, which it regards as wholly future, an indefinite period of time which is already more than 1900 years (*i.e.*, almost four times the length of time covered by the prophecy) and which may even now be very far from ended.

(*b*) It gives to the death of Christ its proper and climactic place as central in the last week; it does not place it outside the compass of the weeks altogether and make it of minor importance as compared with a far less important event, the triumphal entry.

(*c*) It does not involve the inconsistency of declaring that the "coming prince" will "make firm" a covenant for a week and declaring also that he will break it (by causing sacrifice and oblation to cease) in the midst of the week.

(*d*) It recognizes that the abolishing of sacrifice and oblation took place at Calvary, as Hebrews tells us so plainly was the case. It does not involve and require the future restoration of "Jewish" ordinances by the Roman Prince, in order that they may then be speedily abolished by him.

(*e*) It seeks to explain and does explain the events of the last week as actual events of history. It does not refer them to a future, the course of which is dark and mysterious.

So interpreted Daniel ix. does not skip over the Church age as a hidden parenthesis between the 69th and 70th weeks of the prophecy. On the contrary, it finds in the 70th week the prediction of that great climactic event upon which the Christian Church is founded, the atoning death of the Messiah as the fulfilment and authentication of the types and prophecies of the Old Testament.

2. *Daniel ii. 44*

"And in the days of those kings shall the God of heaven set up a kingdom, which shall never be destroyed." At the time of the rise of Dispensational teaching it was the generally accepted view that the kingdom foretold in this passage is the kingdom of Messiah, that this kingdom was set up 1900 years ago in the days of the Caesars by Jesus and His apostles, and has been growing and spreading ever since. In favor of this view is the fact that, at the time of

the first advent, the Jews were expecting the coming of
Messiah and that both John and Jesus announced the
kingdom of heaven (or, of God) as at hand. We have seen
that the expression "kingdom of heaven" or "kingdom of
God" is most naturally derived from this prophecy. If then
the kingdom which Jesus announced as at hand was not
an earthly kingdom of worldly splendor and glory, but a
moral and spiritual kingdom, it is natural and proper to
interpret the dream of Nebuchadnezzar in harmony with
the spiritual nature of the kingdom. The smiting stone
will then represent the irresistible spiritual might of this
kingdom. This found expression first in the resurrection
and ascension of Christ. The terror of the Roman guard
at the tomb (Matt. xxviii. 4) showed in a striking manner
the impotence of Imperial Rome. The Great Commission
had back of it the "all power" conferred on the risen
Christ. At Pentecost that power was bestowed upon the
Christian Church. The stone began to become the mountain. One of its signal triumphs was the overthrow of Pagan
Rome three centuries later. This kingdom has not passed
and will not pass to another people. Its task is to subdue
and overthrow all other kingdoms and it shall itself endure
for ever. Thus interpreted, we have here a prophecy of
the kingdom of Christ with primary reference to its establishment and growth. If this be correct, the words "in the
days of those kings" would refer most naturally to the four
kingdoms or kings represented by the image. This interpretation is clearly involved in the symbolism of the image
(vs. 45) and is permissible because, while distinct, these
four kingdoms were also in a sense one. Medo-Persia conquered and incorporated Babylon. Greece did the same to
Medo-Persia. And while Rome never conquered all of
Alexander's empire, she did conquer much of it and the
extent of the Roman Empire was far greater and more
world-wide than any of the others. It was while the image
was still standing that the blow was struck.[17] So we may
say that it was in the period of those four empires as to-

gether representing Gentile world dominion but in the days of the last of the four that the kingdom of Messiah was set up.

The Dispensational interpretation of this prophecy is quite different. According to it, the blow is described as not only shattering but sudden; and the kingdom to be set up is an earthly and glorious Jewish kingdom, which will violently overthrow and crush the Gentile world power (Ps. ii.). Consequently, Dispensationalists insist that the fulfilment is wholly future. They hold that by "those kings," the toes of the image are meant, and they identify them with the ten horns of the fourth beast of Dan. vii. which they regard as representing ten kingdoms which are yet to arise out of the "restored" Roman Empire.[18] But while the dream of Dan. ii. and the vision of Dan. vii. are identical as regards their main divisions and similar in some of the details, it is hazardous to connect them too closely. The only kings or kingdoms mentioned in chap. ii. are the four of which the image is composed. It is nowhere stated in Dan. ii. that there are *ten* toes. This is only an inference from the fact that the image has the form of a man.[19] Nor are the toes referred to or interpreted as meaning kings or kingdoms. They are only mentioned in connection with the feet as illustrating the weakness of the image due to the fact that feet and toes are of iron mingled with clay. Finally, it is not on the toes but on the feet that the image is struck. A blow struck on the toes would do only slight damage to the massive image. That this identification is not warranted appears more clearly when we turn to Dan. vii.

3. Daniel vii. 23-27

That the four beasts here described correspond to the four parts of the image of Dan. ii., is generally recognized. If the legs and feet of the image represent Rome, the fourth beast will do so likewise. This general resemblance is important. But the differences are almost if not quite as

important. While it is only an inference that the image
has *ten* toes, we are told definitely that the beast has *ten*
horns. Since no beast known in Daniel's day or today had
or has *ten* horns we must conclude that the number *ten* is
significant, because it is arbitrary.[20] We are told that later
on a little horn comes up which uproots three of the original ten. There is nothing in Dan. ii. to correspond with
this little horn.[21] Two interpretations of it especially concern us. The one finds the fulfilment in the present Church
age. It identifies the "little horn" with the "man of sin"
referred to by Paul (2 Thess. ii. 3), the last and greatest
of the many antichrists. Many Protestant interpreters have
applied it directly to the Papacy; and it has been called the
"Protestant" interpretation. But what here concerns us is
the fact that, whatever its application, the prophecy concerns the Church age. Premillennialists, as well as Post-
and Amilliennialists, have so understood it. The other interpretation is that of the Dispensationalists, according to
whom all of this is future. The little horn of Dan. vii. is the
future king of the "restored" Roman Empire who is to be
revealed after the rapture of the Church. So interpreted
this prophecy must, of course, skip over the Church age
entirely.[22]

The interpretation of this prophecy is especially important because vii. 18 declares that the "saints of the most
High" shall take the kingdom and possess it for ever
(cf. vss. 22, 25, 27). Whether these saints are Church saints
or Jewish remnant saints will depend entirely upon
whether the parenthesis theory of the Dispensationalists
is correct. If the "kingdom" of the "God of heaven" was
set up in the days of the Caesars, these saints will naturally
be Church saints, *i.e.*, Christians. If the entire Church age
is a parenthesis which all of Daniel's prophecies "skip
over," then they cannot be Church saints; they must be
Jews, a Jewish remnant on earth after the rapture of the
Church. This question occasions Dispensationalists some
embarrassment. They regard the doctrine that the Church

saints will reign with Christ as clearly taught in the New Testament. So Scofield in the first edition of his *Reference Bible* declared that the saints of Dan. vii. are Church saints. But this was so gross a violation of the parenthesis theory that it could not be allowed to stand. So he changed the note to read as follows: "That church saints will also share in the rule seems clear from Acts xvi. 17; Rom. viii. 17; 2 Tim. ii. 10-12; 1 Pet. ii. 9; Rev. i. 6; iii. 21; v. 10; xx. 4-6." But if the saints of Dan. vii. cannot be Church saints, vs. 18 is certainly a strange place for a note declaring that they will "share" in the reign. Is it not better to hold that Scofield's first note was correct, and that the saints of Dan. vii. are Church saints? Since this kingdom which the saints are to receive is an "everlasting kingdom" it is a matter of no small interest to Christians whether these saints are Christians or a Jewish remnant of the end-time.

4. Daniel iv

The extremes to which many Dispensationalists are prepared to carry their method of interpretation is illustrated by their explanation of this chapter. On the face of it this prophecy, as interpreted by Daniel, concerned Nebuchadnezzar directly and exclusively and was completely fulfilled in the strange and tragic experience through which he personally and individually was obliged to pass. Vs. 25 gives the reason he was to pass through the "seven times"; vs. 34 declares that he did so, and that he learned the lesson they were meant to teach him. There is nothing to indicate that the prophecy was not completely fulfilled within the reign of this Chaldean king more than 500 years before the Christian era. It is quite obvious that this amazing experience of one of the greatest kings of ancient times has important lessons for men and especially rulers in every age. But this is a very different thing from saying, as Dispensationalists are disposed to do, that it is an unfulfilled prophecy.[23] They see in the "tree" the type of Gentile domination, and in the cutting down of the tree the judg-

ment of the apostate professing church at the end of this
age, after the rapture of the true Church. The "seven
times" become the seven year interval between the rapture
and the appearing; and Nebuchadnezzar's changed attitude is regarded as foreshadowing the millennium. So interpreted, Daniel iv. skips over the Church age.

5. *Daniel viii*

The same method of interpretation is applied to all the
other prophecies in Daniel. We shall consider only chap.
viii. In view of the brevity with which the prophecies in
chap. ii. and in chap. vii. dismiss the second and third
kingdoms, it is only natural that in this chapter these two
kingdoms should be particularly dealt with. We are told
expressly that they represent Medo-Persia and Greece. The
time of the fulfilment is also defined with some definiteness. It is to be "in the latter time of their kingdom" (vs.
23), *i.e.,* of the four which stand up after the great horn of
the rough goat is broken, that a king of fierce countenance
is to arise.[24] It is generally agreed that the "great horn" is
Alexander the Great and that the "four notable horns"
represent the four kingdoms into which his empire was
mainly divided. It is also agreed that the "little horn," who
is referred to as "the king of the fierce countenance" is
Antiochus Epiphanes. But the claim is made that Antiochus was only a "remarkable type of the Beast" of
Revelation.[25] Consequently, if the prophecy skips from
Antiochus to the Beast, and if the Beast does not appear
until after the rapture of the Church, this prophecy also
skips over the Church age. It is on this wise, *i.e.,* by adopting a system of interpretation according to which all the
prophecies of Daniel refer to the end-time, that the Dispensationalists seek to establish their claim that the Church
age is a parenthesis of which Daniel knows nothing. The
danger of this method of interpretation becomes especially
clear when we turn to some of the prophecies outside of
Daniel.

II. Some Other Old Testament Prophets

1. Isaiah

Isaiah is quoted in the New Testament more frequently than any other prophet. Jerome called him an "evangelist and apostle," and even declared that his book was "not a prophecy but a gospel."[26] The Book of Consolation (as chaps. xl.-lxvi. are often called) contains some of the chapters in the Old Testament which are most precious to the Christian. Indicative of this is the fact that in the AV the word "Church" appears in the summaries of 12 of the last 27 chapters. This means that the translators of the 1611 version regarded these as "Christian" prophecies, i.e., as referring to the Christian Church.[27] According to Dispensationalists, this is a glaring illustration of the appropriating to the Church of promises made to the Jews. They feel this so strongly that they do not hesitate to use the word "robbery" or "theft."[28] They tell us that the Church has stolen the blessings promised to Israel and left her only the curses. For the moment we are concerned to point out that this charge is only true if these predictions really concern Israel exclusively and not the Church. If, as countless Bible students have believed, they really concern the Church, to take them away from the Church and give them to Israel is not to restore them to their rightful owners, but to rob the rightful owners of what is properly theirs.

Isaiah lv. 1 is an example in point. Most Christians have been accustomed to claim that the words, "Ho, everyone that thirsteth, come ye to the waters" is an invitation which they can claim and accept quite as much as the invitation, "Come unto me all ye that labour and are heavy laden" (Matt. xi. 28). But Scofield says regarding this entire group of chapters (xl.-lxvi.): "The great theme of this section is Jesus Christ in His sufferings, and the glory that shall follow in the Davidic kingdom."[29] Consequently, as Darby expressed it, "Chap. lv.

is full free grace, which consequently embraces the Gentiles.
For this reason it can be applied as a *principle* to the gospel.
Its accomplishment will be in the time of blessings to the
earth through the Lord's presence."[30] This means that, according to Darby, the words of Isa. lv. 1 contain the principle of
the gospel, but are not a prophecy of the Church age. Consequently, the Christian can only claim them as expressing
the principle of the gospel: he cannot claim them as a prophetic declaration of the gospel invitation itself. That must
wait for the millennium. As a prophecy chap. lv. will have its
fulfilment in the future kingdom; it does not belong to the
Church.

Isaiah x. As an illustration of the way by which the claim
that the prophets pass over the Church age is made good,
Isa. x. is especially instructive. Scofield gives vss. 5-19 the
heading, "Predicted judgment on Assyria, God's rod on
Samaria." Vss. 20-27 are described as, "The vision of the
Jewish remnant in the great tribulation," on the ground that
"The prophecy here passes from the general to the particular,
from historic and fulfilled judgments upon Assyria to the final
destruction of *all* Gentile world-power at the return of the
Lord in glory." This means that the Assyrian of vs. 24 is not
the Assyrian of vs. 5, but an enemy yet to arise; and vss. 28-34,
which give a list of cities most of which perished centuries ago,
are said to describe "The approach of the Gentile hosts to
the battle of Armageddon (Rev. xvi. 14, xix. 11).[31] There is no
sufficient warrant for distinguishing two Assyrians in this
chapter. But this interpretation is another striking illustration
of the way in which evidence is accumulated by Dispensationalists in support of their claim that the Church is a mystery
parenthesis in Old Testament prophecy.

2. *Zechariah*

Zech. xi. 11 is a striking example of the quibbling to
which the Dispensationalists are obliged to resort in order
to avoid the admission that the Church is predicted in the
Old Testament. Scofield tells us that the "poor of the
flock" are "those Jews who did not wait for the manifestation of Christ in glory, but believed on Him at His first
coming, and since."[32] In other words they are Jewish Chris-

tians or Church saints. But as this has dangerous implications, Scofield adds: "Neither the Gentiles nor the Gentile church, corporately, are in view: only the believers out of *Israel* during this age. The church, corporately, is not in O. T. prophecy (Eph. iii. 8-10)." This is a misstatement. The New Testament Church is not a "Gentile church" nor is it a "Jewish church"; it is the *Christian* Church, and the believers out of Israel are Christian believers, just as the believers from among the Gentiles are Christian believers. On Scofield's own statement this is a prophecy of the Christian Church, at least as it concerns all Jews who have believed on Jesus "at His first coming and since."[33]

3. The Psalms

The Psalter has been from the earliest times the great hymn book of the Christian Church. It is given a conspicuous place in the liturgies of all liturgical churches. In fact there are some Christians who hold that the Old Testament Psalms should be used exclusively in Church worship. The Psalter is also the great manual of private devotion. There are few if any chapters in the New Testament which are used more frequently by Christians than the most familiar of the Old Testament psalms. But according to Dispensationalists this is a very exaggerated view to take of them, not to say an actually perverted view.

Darby tells us that the Psalms "concern Judah and Israel, and the position in which those who belong to Judah and Israel are found. Their primary character is the expression of the working of the Spirit of Christ as to, or in the remnant of the Jews (or of Israel) in the last days."[34] How close a student Scofield was of Darby is indicated by his parallel statement: "The truth revealed is wrought into the emotions, desires, and sufferings of the people of God by the circumstances through which they pass. But those circumstances are such as to constitute an anticipation of analogous conditions through which Christ in His incarnation and the Jewish remnant in the tribulation (Isa. x. 21, *refs.*), should pass; so that many Psalms are prophetic of the sufferings, the faith and the victory of both."[35] The reader will note how carefully Scofield, following Darby, excludes the present gospel age from any direct claim to these Psalms. They concern Christ and the Jewish remnant. They concern Christ in His incarnation (we understand this to refer to the earthly ministry, before the founding of the Church) and the Jewish remnant of the end-time. They are "spiritually true in Christian experience also," he tells us. But they are not prophetic of the Church; they refer to a Jewish remnant. This means, for example, that the Church as such can have no portion in the fulfilment of the great Royal Messianic Psalms (ii., xlv., lxxii., cx.); they are to be fulfilled to the Jewish remnant in the end-time. It means that Ps. ii. 8, "Ask of me and I shall give *thee* the heathen for thine inheritance, and the uttermost parts of the earth for thy possession" is not being fulfilled through the missionary activities of the Church. The Church has no part in the fulfilment of Ps. lxxii.: "converted Israel" [*i.e.*, the Jewish remnant] will be the "handful of corn"; and the prophecy concerns the time after the rapture of the Church. Scofield admits that historically Ps. cx. begins with the ascension of Christ. The words, "Sit at my right hand until I make thine enemies thy footstool," certainly refer to and embrace the entire inter-adventual period, *i.e.*, the Church age, during which Christ has been giving repeated proofs of His power to save (Acts ii. 33, v. 31). And Paul connects the Church directly with this all important fact (Rom. viii. 34, Eph. i. 22, Col. iii. 1). Yet Darby finds in Ps. cx. 1 an indication "how entirely all is Jewish" in Ps. ii. and cx.

Many other passages in the Old Testament might be discussed here. But the most important will come up for consideration in the next chapter which deals with the vitally important question of the interpretation of Old Testament prophecy by the inspired writers of the New Testament. In looking back over the prophecies that have been discussed and forward to those which are still to be considered, the point to be borne constantly in mind is this. The issue we are concerned with is not one between Historicists and Futurists as such. It is not merely as to whether certain events or series of events in the prophetic program have been already fulfilled or are still wholly future. That question is an important one; and its importance is not to be minimized. But it is overshadowed in large measure by a still more vital question. Are these events which Dispensationalists regard as still future to take place in this dispensation, the present Church age? Do they directly concern the Church? Or, do they belong to a dispensation or dispensations which will follow the Church age and with which Christians of this age have no direct or immediate concern? Our contention is that, in insisting that prophecy does not have reference to the Christian Church, Dispensationalists "rob" the Church of many of the exceeding precious promises contained in the Old Testament which she is fully entitled to claim and possess.[36]

CHAPTER VI

PROPHECIES APPLIED IN THE NEW TESTAMENT TO THE CHURCH

SINCE the Book of Acts contains an account of the preaching of the gospel by the apostles, especially Peter and Paul, it should be a very important witness in deciding the question whether they regarded the institution which they were used of God to found as an innovation, something entirely unknown to Moses and the prophets, or whether they saw in it the fulfilment of ancient predictions regarding the future of the people of God. So we cannot do better than to devote our attention mainly to the principal passages in this important New Testament book which bear on this question.

I. The Old Testament in the Book of Acts

1. Acts i. 8

"But ye shall receive power, after that the Holy Spirit is come upon you: and ye shall be witnesses unto me both in Jerusalem, and in all Judaea, and in Samaria, and unto the uttermost part of the earth." These words of the risen Christ form the keynote of the Book of Acts. They show the scope of the enterprise which Jesus entrusted to His disciples. They do not expressly quote the prophets, although the words, "unto the uttermost part of the earth," are found in Isa. xlix. 6. They simply reiterate the Great Commission which is stated briefly elsewhere by Luke (Lk. xxiv. 46f.) and more fully by Matthew (Matt. xxviii. 18f.). These passages make it impossible to attach any narrow or restricted meaning to the words "uttermost part of the earth." The mission of the disciples is not Jewish or Palestinian: it is world-wide. Scofield calls it "the apos-

tolic commission."[1] The words, "and in Samaria" are both
a very pointed rebuke to the bigoted nationalism of the
Jews, and also a solemn reminder that Jesus had Himself
gone to the Samaritans and preached this world-embracing
gospel to them.

2. Acts i. 20

The impressive way (vs. 16) in which Peter appeals to
Pss. lxix. 25 and cix. 8 as bearing directly on Judas' death
and its consequences makes especially noteworthy this
application of the Psalms to the circumstances and needs
of the Church age which is about to begin.

3. Acts ii. 16-40

The summary account given us here of Peter's sermon
on the day of Pentecost is made up very largely of quotations from the Old Testament. The first of these is from
Joel (ii. 28-32) and it is one of the longest quotations in
the entire New Testament. Peter appeals to Joel as proving that the gift of tongues was "that which hath been
spoken through the prophet Joel." He not merely quotes
the first verse of the prophecy which contains the words,
"I will pour out of my Spirit upon all flesh," but he extends it to include the words: "And it shall come to pass,
that whosoever shall call on the name of the Lord shall be
saved." This passage certainly applies very definitely to
the Church age and describes its most marked characteristic. It does not enter into the details of the mystery. It
does not state in so many words that the Gentiles are
"fellow-heirs." In fact Peter concludes his sermon with an
appeal to "all the house of Israel" (vs. 36). But it does
declare emphatically that the "whosoever will" stage of
God's dealings with mankind has been reached. It took
Peter a long while and required a further special revelation before he fully understood the import of the words
which he had quoted from Joel. But the words themselves
are clearly applicable to that mystery Church in which
there is neither Jew nor Greek, the nature of which was

most fully revealed to and declared by the apostle Paul.
Darby and Scofield both admit that the Church was
"formed" at Pentecost. So Scofield says of Joel's prophecy
as cited by Peter: "A distinction must be drawn between
'the last days' when the prediction relates to Israel, and
the 'last days' when the prediction relates to the church."
This is an admission that Joel's words do concern the
Church, and amounts to a confession that the Church is
the subject of prophecy. How then are we to understand
the statement that "The church, corporately, is not in
O.T. prophecy"? What does "corporately" mean?

The same conclusion is to be drawn from Peter's quotations from Pss. xvi. and cx. For he definitely describes the
manifestation of the Holy Spirit which marked the birth
of the Church as the consequence of Jesus' resurrection,
ascension, and session at the right hand of the Father; and
he declares (vs. 33) that "having received of the Father the
promise of the Holy Spirit, he hath poured forth this,
which ye see and hear." This "promise of the Holy Spirit"
regarding which he has appealed to Joel is found also in
the prophecies of Isaiah, Jeremiah, and Ezekiel regarding
the coming age of the Spirit, and is clearly referred to in
Jn. xiv. 16ff. But it is especially noteworthy that Peter
appeals to Ps. cx. which Dispensationalists tell us refers to
the future of Israel.

In dealing with Peter's discourse at Pentecost, it is especially
important to observe the close connection between it and the
Great Commission. The words, "All power is given unto me
in heaven and on earth," are the words of the risen Lord
speaking as a king who is about to receive His kingdom, to
assume His place at the right hand of the Majesty on high.
There He is to await the time that His enemies be made His
footstool. But Peter in vs. 33 describes the outpouring of the
Spirit predicted by Joel as a demonstration of the fact that
He has already received and is now exercising that royal
authority. This can only mean that the kingdom is now
"come"; and this great inaugural event of the Church age is
to be regarded as the fulfilment of Messianic prophecy. The
King is now exercising His sovereign power (cf. iii. 16, iv. 10,

30, v. 31, xiii. 32f.), despite the fact that His enemies are not yet subdued under Him (v. 24ff.).

4. Acts iii. 12-26

Peter's discourse at the temple after the healing of the lame beggar probably followed at no great interval the one made on the day of Pentecost. It appeals to the Old Testament quite as definitely, although its quotations are briefer. Peter refers three times to the testimony of "the prophets," and also to Moses and to the Abrahamic covenant.

(1) The first appeal to the prophets (vs. 18) has reference to the death of Christ, as foretold by them.

(2) Peter's second appeal to them is in connection with his call for repentance (vss. 19-21). He urges three reasons for this: (a) "that your sins may be blotted out"; (b) "that so [ARV] there may come seasons of refreshing from the presence [face] of the Lord"; (c) "and [that] he may send the Christ who hath been appointed for you, even Jesus: whom the heaven must receive until the times of restoration of all things, whereof God spake by the mouth of his holy prophets that have been from of old."

This is a difficult passage. The main question at issue concerns the connection between these statements, especially their temporal sequence. The first of the three (a) is very closely connected with the call for repentance, being represented by a prepositional phrase: "Repent and be converted unto (pros) the blotting out of your sins." That this blessed result is to follow immediately on the act of repentance would seem to be the natural and even necessary inference. The Christian is represented in the New Testament as one whose sins have been forgiven and who is justified by faith in Him who has blotted out the handwriting of ordinances that was against him by nailing it to His cross (Col. ii. 14). The statement which follows (b) is introduced by a compound conjunction (hopōs an) which is used to express the effect or final cause, "so that (or, in order that) there may come seasons of refreshing."[2] There is nothing in the expression itself to indicate that these seasons may not be the immediate result of the blotting out of sins and refer to that joy, peace, and prosperity which accompany and flow from the acceptance of the offer of salvation. It is to be noted, however, that *(c)* is joined immediately to *(b)* by "and" and is apparently to be regarded as governed by the same conjunction. It refers to the sending of Christ. This cannot be a reference to the first advent which is past. It is unnatural to regard it as referring to an invisible coming through the Holy Spirit. It seems to refer most naturally to the second visible coming of Christ to earth. This is indicated by the words "whom the heaven must receive *(i.e.,* retain) until." It might, therefore, be taken to mean that the "seasons of refreshing" and the visible coming of Christ are closely connected or even simultaneous in time, and that if the former are imminent the coming must be no less so. Or, on the other hand, it might mean that if the coming is to be remote, the seasons of refreshing must be equally remote. But it is not necessary to hold that there can be no interval of time between these events. "And" may introduce a sequence which is remote as well as one which is temporally close. The words "whom the heaven must receive until the restoration of all things" seem clearly to imply that there may still be much in the prophetic program to be fulfilled before the advent can take place. Consequently, it seems proper to conclude that the apostle is speaking of two matters which are closely related: the immediate blessings resulting from the acceptance of the Saviour who has died for sinners and the future blessings which will follow upon His return to the earth from which He had so recently ascended. It does not seem necessary to insist either that the seasons of refreshing must wait for a coming which may be remote, or that the coming must itself be very near at hand despite the plain intimation which is given to the contrary. The seasons of refreshing may begin at once and include as an important feature in their refreshing the assured hope of the coming of the One who has made them possible. So understood Peter's words refer to the entire inter-adventual period which is to end with the advent, in other words to the entire Church age.

(3) Peter's third appeal to the prophets follows immediately on the reference to Moses, who predicted the coming of a prophet like unto himself, obedience to whom would be a matter of life or death. It was this Prophet whom the Jews had rejected and slain that Peter set before them as

the promised Saviour. So Peter clinches his appeal for immediate repentance by saying: "Yea and all the prophets from Samuel and them that followed after, as many as have spoken, they also told of these days." What does Peter mean by "these days"? The whole question at issue between the Dispensationalists and their opponents is brought to a focus in these words. By "these days" does Peter mean days that are now present, a period that has already begun, or does he refer to a future time? If the reference is to a future time, "those days" or "that day" would certainly be more natural. And the fact that he immediately appeals to his hearers as "the sons of the prophets, and of the covenant," and cites that part of the Abrahamic covenant which predicts the universal scope of the gospel, makes the inference a natural, if not a necessary one, that by "these days" Peter means the gospel age of the Great Commission.[3] The words, "unto you first" indicate that Peter, as later Paul, recognized that, until they finally rejected it, the Jews, as individuals not nationally, were entitled to be the first to hear the gospel message.[4] How far the implication of his words was clear to him can only be inferred from his subsequent conduct as a preacher of a gospel which was to bring blessing to "all the kindreds of the earth."

Dispensationalists are disposed to draw a distinction between the discourses in Acts ii. and iii. While they admit that the Church was founded or formed at Pentecost, they insist that, on the occasion described in Acts iii., Peter's appeal was not individual but national; he offered "national blessings (the millennial kingdom)" to the Jews on condition of *national* repentance.[5] According to Darby, "In a word, they are invited to return by repentance, and enjoy all the promises made to Israel." He tells us: "The return of Jesus with this object depended (and still depends) on the repentance of the Jews. Meanwhile He remains in heaven."[6] These are surprising statements to be made by Dispensationalists. If Peter offered the Jews on this occasion "all the promises made to Israel," this can only mean, according to their principles, that he offered them the earthly Davidic kingdom, "the kingdom of heaven," on exactly the same terms as John and Jesus Himself had already offered it to them: "Repent ye; for the kingdom of heaven is at hand." This involves them in serious difficulty. For if the offer of this kingdom had already been postponed for the entire Church age, what right had Peter to offer it practically at once to Jews whose hands were red with the blood of their Messiah, and on exactly the same terms as those on which it had been offered to them some three years previously? If this is the meaning of Peter's exhortation, there was really no postponement of the kingdom offer. The kingdom was just as much "at hand" when he preached this sermon as it had ever been. If this is the meaning, then Scofield's statement that the second preaching of the gospel of the kingdom is "yet future (Matt. xxiv. 14) during the great tribulation, and immediately preceding the coming of the King in glory" cannot be accepted as correct.[7] For Peter preached it shortly after Pentecost; and unless we are to hold that this offer was again withdrawn we must regard it as still in force during the entire Church age. Furthermore, if the only condition for the establishment of the earthly Davidic kingdom was the repentance of the Jewish nation, then conceivably the Church age might have been terminated practically at its very beginning by the repentance of the Jewish nation. Yet Paul tells us expressly that this conversion is dependent on something quite different; that it will not take place until "the fulness of the Gentiles be come in" (Rom. xi. 25). The only way open to Dispensationalists to avoid these difficulties would seem to be, to take the view that Peter did not preach the "kingdom of heaven," the keys of which were committed to him, but the "kingdom in mystery" (*i.e.*, the professing church) which was not the Davidic kingdom but that "gospel of the kingdom (of God)" which was appropriate to the

Church age and was applicable in a sense to both the true Church and the professing church. But, as we have seen, this gospel was not entrusted to Peter according to dispensational principles strictly construed.

All these difficulties and complexities are avoided if it be recognized that there is no essential difference between the two discourses which we have been considering. In both Peter preached repentance to the Jews and acceptance of the Messiah of whom they were the murderers. In both he offered a salvation so comprehensive that it would include others besides Jews. In the second he referred definitely to the return of Christ. But he intimated just as definitely that this event might not occur for a long time. The only warrant for finding in his reference to the "restoration of all things" the offer of the re-establishment of the earthly Davidic kingdom is to be found in the argument which has been already discussed that the kingdom promised to the Jews was such an earthly kingdom. But whatever this expression may mean it refers to a future event. And, in view of the way in which the New Testament stresses the blessings which the believer receives under the gospel, we see no sufficient reason for denying that the "times of refreshing" offered here to his hearers by Peter may refer to the period, which has already proved to be a lengthy one, between Pentecost and the second advent, that is to say, to the Church age.

5. *Acts iv. 23-31*

According to this passage the early Christians saw, in the sufferings of Christ and in the persecutions which they were being called upon to endure because of their loyalty to Him in the preaching of the gospel, a fulfilment of Ps. ii. 1-2. Since Dispensationalists admit a partial fulfilment of Joel ii. in the events of the day of Pentecost, they should be ready to recognize at least a partial fulfilment of prophecy here also. Otherwise the citation from the Psalms would be neither applicable nor appropriate.

6. Acts vii. 48

The statement, "Howbeit the Most High dwelleth not in temples made with hands," is clearly meant to be axiomatic. It suggests 1 Kgs. viii. 27, but is directly supported by appeal to Isa. lxvi. 1f., which as used by Stephen can only mean that an earthly temple has no proper place in the dispensation ushered in by the preaching of the gospel (cf. Acts vi. 14). The conclusion is unavoidable that Stephen applies Isaiah's words directly to the Church age.

7. Acts viii. 4-25

The proclamation of the gospel to the Samaritans whom the Jews particularly despised and hated is very significant, as is also the fact that the apostles sent Peter and John to investigate, as it would seem, this amazing event. Peter's hearty approval is clearly stated. In fact we are told that "they preached the gospel" in "many villages of the Samaritans" (cf. v. 42, viii. 4, 12, 25, 35). This incident reminds us that our Lord preached in Samaria apparently before He preached in Nazareth, and that the Samaritans received Him while the men of Nazareth sought to slay Him. How then could Scofield say that Acts x. 44 is "one of the pivotal points of Scripture" because "Heretofore the Gospel has been offered to Jews only"? Coming after the incidents of chap. viii. the words, "unto the Jews only" (xi. 19) suggest reproach or surprise. Prophecy is not appealed to. But the trio of Ezek. xvi. 53-55 strikingly parallels Isa. xix. 24f. One is as comprehensive as the other.

8. Acts viii. 26-40

Philip's preaching to the Ethiopian eunuch must be viewed in the light of the context. It was not merely a case of "individual work for individuals." The vast potentialities of the act, the conversion of a high official of the queen of Ethiopia, are clearly indicated; and this was brought about through the applying of Isa. liii. to those events upon which the Christian Church was founded.

9. Acts ix. 15

The Lord's words to Ananias regarding the mission of the terrible man whose sight he is to restore, "he is a chosen vessel unto me, to bear my name before the Gentiles, and kings, and the children of Israel," give us the first intimation of the special work in which Paul was to engage. The placing of the Gentiles first may indicate emphasis. The words are not a quotation from the Old Testament. But such passages as Mal. i. 11 and Isa. xlix. 6 would naturally suggest themselves to Ananias and to Saul.

10. Acts x

The story of the conversion of Cornelius shows us how slow the apostle Peter was to realize the full meaning of that universal gospel which he had declared on the day of Pentecost. We are told very plainly that he was given a remarkable vision (repeated three times, to impress him with its importance) to remove the scruples which he as a Jew would naturally entertain regarding such an errand as the one on which he was about to be sent. We are also told that to avoid the slightest possibility of misunderstanding, the Spirit applied it directly to the coming of Cornelius's messengers. Consequently, Peter quite naturally points out first the proper attitude of the devout Jew (vs. 28) and then proceeds to show how completely it has been changed by the gospel, of the true nature of which he has just received conclusive evidence by a special revelation from God. This is now strikingly confirmed by the words of Cornelius. So, after declaring the universal scope of the gospel, Peter concludes with a direct appeal to prophecy: "To him bear all the prophets witness, that through his name everyone that believeth on him shall receive remission of sins" (vs. 43). That "everyone" means Gentiles as well as Jews is obvious. The gospel is for all men everywhere; the prophets can be appealed to in proof of this; and the work and witness of the Spirit of God is the final proof (vss. 44f).

11. Acts xi. 20

"Spake unto the Greeks" is a better reading than "Grecians" (AV). "Greek" *(Hellēn)* is used 10 times in Acts, **"Grecian"** *(Hellēnistēs), i.e.,* Greek-speaking Jew only twice (vi. 1, ix. 29). The broader word "Gentile" is used 30 times in Acts in the AV, being the rendering of *ethnos* (nation, Heb. *goi*). The fact that this latter word has been used several times in the Cornelius narrative (x. 45, xi. 1, 18, cf. x. 35), which immediately precedes, makes it highly probable that here in xi. 20 the reference is to Gentiles; and the contrast with the "Jews only" of xi. 19 also favors this reading. The work at Antioch, as at Caesarea, raised the Gentile issue in definite and unmistakable form. A preaching to "Grecians" would not have done this at all (cf. vi. 1). Barnabas not only had the personal gifts and graces (vs. 24) needed to deal with the situation; but being a Levite of Cyprus he was probably in closer touch with it than were many others.

12. Acts xiii. 40-41

In his discourse in the synagogue at Pisidian Antioch, Paul quotes Ps. ii., Isa. lv., and Ps. xvi., and applies the words of Hab. i. 5, "for I work a work in your day," to the gospel age, by using it to warn the Jews of the consequences of rejecting that gospel through which remission of sins is offered to them and through which "every one that believeth" is justified, far more completely than by the provisions of the law of Moses. And when they continued in unbelief and blasphemed, Paul and Barnabas justified their turning to the Gentiles by an appeal to Isa. xlix. 6 (cf. Acts i. 8) which declares that the Servant of the Lord is to be "for salvation unto the uttermost part of the earth." The accomplishments of the first missionary journey are summed up in the words: "they rehearsed all things that God had done with them, and that He had opened a door of faith unto the Gentiles" (xiv. 27). That this involved the founding of churches is clear from Acts xv. 41.

13. Acts xv. 13f.

Opponents of Dispensationalism will be inclined to agree with Scofield when he says, "Dispensationally this is the most important passage in the N.T."[8] That is to say, they will agree that it is perhaps the best passage in the New Testament for testing the correctness of the Dispensational method of interpreting Scripture.

The reason this passage must be regarded as so important is quite obvious. Chap. xv. deals with the Council at Jerusalem. The occasion of this council was the question which had arisen at Antioch regarding the status of Gentiles in the Church and their obligation to observe the Mosaic law. In other words, it concerned the nature of the Christian Church and the relation of Gentile to Jew in it.

(1) While Paul, Barnabas and others had come up to Jerusalem for the express purpose of pleading the cause of the Gentiles, we find that the only witness whose testimony is expressly quoted is Peter who appeals directly to that unforgettable experience at Joppa and Caesarea some ten years before which had led to the conversion of Cornelius and made it necessary for him then to plead the cause of the Gentiles before the church at Jerusalem. The statement is made that "all the multitude kept silence, and gave audience to Barnabas and Paul, declaring what miracles and wonders God had wrought among the Gentiles by them." But we are told nothing of what they said. Then James, as Scofield expresses it, "declares the result." And the surprising thing is that he completely ignores Paul and Barnabas and confines himself to a brief reference to Peter and his testimony. He sums it up with the words: "Symeon hath declared how God at the first did visit the Gentiles, to take out of them a people for his name," which is the briefest possible reference to Peter's experience at Caesarea and testimony regarding it. He says nothing to suggest that Paul was uniquely qualified to speak upon the subject of the Church. Yet the question under discussion concerned the nature and essence of the

Church as a body in which Jew and Gentile were both one in Christ Jesus.

(2) The second point which we notice is that James appealed to the prophets. After summarizing Peter's testimony very briefly, he goes on to say: "And to this agree the words of the prophets; as it it written, After these things I will return, and I will build again the tabernacle of David, which is fallen, and I will build again the ruins thereof, and I will set it up: that the residue of men may seek after the Lord, and all the Gentiles, upon whom my name is called, saith the Lord, who maketh these things known from of old." This reference to the Old Testament is often spoken of as a quotation from Amos ix. 11f. But James does not mention Amos in particular: he refers to "the prophets." And his words imply that Peter's testimony as to what has happened is in accord with what the prophets foretold would happen. The language of Amos' prophecy is followed in the main; but instead of the words of Amos, "that they may possess the remnant of Edom," we read "that the residue of men may seek after the Lord." This represents, it is true, the LXX rendering of the Amos passage. But James, who certainly knew Hebrew, was doubtless aware of the fact that these were not the exact words of Amos, but that they involved a slight change in the original which made the LXX rendering a kind of paraphrase of Amos in the spirit of Isa. xi. 10, where the Gentiles of whom Edom might be regarded as the most recalcitrant are represented as seeking the Lord. This change in the LXX is justified by the fact that the words of Amos, "all the nations upon whom my name is called," clearly imply that Edom and all the Gentiles are to be incorporated with Israel as the people of the Lord. But, although it involves only a slight change in the text of Amos and has the sanction of the LXX, which the New Testament writers often quoted as sufficiently accurate for their purpose, and is in accord with the words of Isaiah, James, who perhaps knew better than we do today

the reason for this change and how it came about, is careful to say "prophets" instead of "Amos."

We observe then that James declares expressly that Peter's experience at Caesarea, which he speaks of as God's visiting "the Gentiles to take out of them a people for his name," was in accord with the burden of prophecy as a whole, and quotes freely from Amos in proof of it. Now if James' quotation refers to the Christian Church, the claim of Dispensationalists that prophecy skips over the Church age cannot be maintained: it is directly refuted by this passage. How then is this natural inference avoided? Scofield has given us the standard Dispensational interpretation. He first tells us in general that this passage "gives the divine purpose for this age and the beginning of the next." Then he makes two very striking statements. He declares in the first place that the taking out from among the Gentiles of a people for His name which is James' summary of Peter's argument is "the distinctive work of the present, or church-age." Then he comes to James' quotation from the prophets and tells us: " 'After this [viz., the outcalling] I will return.' " He ascribes these words to Amos and says of them: "The verses which follow in Amos describe the final regathering of Israel, which the other prophets invariably connect with the fulfilment of the Davidic Covenant." In other words, according to Scofield, the words which James quoted from the Old Testament had no direct bearing upon the question at issue. That question was, the status of the Gentiles in the Christian Church. James quoted passages which referred to and were to have their fulfilment after the restoration of the kingdom to Israel. That is to say, James' appeal to Scripture, which would seem to be intended to give weight and authority to his decision, had no bearing, certainly no direct bearing upon the question under debate. That this is the logic of the Dispensational interpretation is shown by the fact that Scofield applies the quotation from Amos to the future and does not have a word to say as to its bearing upon the point at issue. This is the inevitable conclusion from Dispensational premises. It is not an attractive conclusion. It is hard to believe that James would have beclouded the issue by quoting a passage from the Old Testament which had no bearing upon the question under consideration. If James was a good Dispensationalist, he should have said something like this: "Brethren, what you say may be perfectly true. I believe it is true, since the Holy Spirit has blessed and owned your labors among the Gentiles. But you must remember that the prophets have nothing to say about the Church. So we cannot appeal directly to them." And the only argument James could have used to justify a quotation from the Old Testament would have been the one used by Darby and others: viz., that there is a certain analogy between the outcalling of the Gentiles during the Church age and the ingathering of the Gentiles in the future kingdom age. But if that had been his meaning, James might have stated it far more clearly than he did.

All of the difficulties involved in the Dispensational interpretation of this important passage in Acts are avoided, if it is simply recognized that the words quoted by James apply directly and definitely to the situation under discussion, the status of the Gentiles in the Church, and that this is the reason that James appealed to them. The words, "I will raise up the tabernacle of David which is fallen" do not refer to a future Davidic kingdom. The house of David, the mighty kingdom of David and Solomon, had sunk to the level of a lowly "booth" (cf. Isa. i. 8 where the same word occurs; it has no connection with the Mosaic tabernacle).[9] When Immanuel-Jesus, the Son of David, was born in Bethlehem, He was heralded and acclaimed by angels; and the incarnation of the Second Person of the Trinity as David's Son was the beginning of the raising up of the fallen booth of David. And when David's Son rose triumphant over death and commissioned His disciples with the words: "All power is given unto me in heaven and on earth," He claimed a sovereignty far greater than David ever knew, or ever dreamed of possessing. So, when Peter and the other apostles declared that God had raised up Jesus and "exalted him with his right hand to be a Prince and a Saviour" (Acts v. 31), they were insisting that the mighty acts which they were enabled to perform were the direct exercise through them of His sovereign power.

The words "After these things I will return and build" do not refer to a time which was still future when James used them. In the Amos passage the words used are simply, "in that day," which is the most general formula used by the prophets to introduce an utterance regarding the coming Messianic age. "After these things I will return and build" is a slightly more emphatic form of statement. Viewed in the light of their context in Amos, they refer to a time subsequent to the complete destruction of the Northern Kingdom, which had ceased to exist centuries before the New Testament age in which James was living. The words "I will return and build" are simply an emphatic way of saying, "I will build again." There is no warrant for making them refer directly to the second advent.[10] They naturally refer to the first advent and to the whole of the great redemptive work of which it was the beginning and which will culminate in the second advent. The only natural interpretation of this passage is that it refers to the Church age and to the ingathering of the Gentiles during that age, as a signal proof of the world-wide sovereignty of the Son of David.

It is quite understandable that Darby and the Brethren seem to have regarded this passage as more of a liability for their parenthesis theory than an asset. They could admit only an analogy between the calling of the Gentiles in the Church age and the gathering of the Gentiles in the millennial age. But gradually it came to be regarded as of such great importance, that Scofield did not hesitate to say of it, as we have seen: "Dispensationally, this is the most important passage in the N.T." It is frequently appealed to as supplying a convincing argument for the

Dispensational doctrine of the parenthesis Church. Consequently, the fact is to be emphasized that, in order to do this, Scofield must apply James' quotation from the prophets *exclusively* to the future, and by so doing utterly destroy its pertinence and direct application to the question under debate by the council. The futility of such an evasion of the plain implications of the narrative would seem to be obvious.

14. Acts xxiv. 14

In defending himself before Felix, Paul expressed his confident belief that "the way which they call heresy," to which he belonged and for which he labored, was entirely in accord with the Old Testament. For he spoke of himself as "believing all things which are according to the law, and which are written in the prophets." If Paul really believed that the Church was a mystery parenthesis unknown to the prophets, here would have been a fine opportunity to preach Dispensational truth. He might have explained to Felix and the notables who were present just how the Church age was to be fitted in, as such a parenthesis, between the Davidic kingdom of the past and the promised kingdom of the future. It would certainly have made things much easier for him, had he been able to declare that what he was preaching, however offensive to Jewish pride, was simply a temporary interruption of the fulfilment of the kingdom promises to Israel. Why did he not do so, if he really believed this to be the case?

15. Acts xxvi. 6, 22, 27

Paul's defense before Agrippa, being more theological in character and somewhat more fully reported than the defense before Felix, answers clearly the question that has just been asked. Paul begins by asserting positively, that he is on trial "for the hope of the promise made of God unto our fathers" (vs. 6). In saying this he must refer primarily to the Abrahamic covenant, with its definite promise of blessing to the nations. He indicates here (a matter only hinted at in the defense before Felix), that his preaching to the Gentiles (vs. 20) is partly or largely responsible for the fierce hatred of the Jews (xxii. 21f.). Then he declares negatively (cf. xxiv. 14f.) that since his conversion he has, in his testimony to all men, been "saying nothing except [literally, 'outside of,' or 'beyond,' or 'in addition to'] what the prophets and Moses did say should come" (vs. 22), the death and resurrection of Christ, as a source of light to "the people (the Jews) and to the nations (Gentiles)" (cf. Isa. xlix. 6 and Lk. ii. 32). Finally, to clinch his argument, he calls on Agrippa to avow that he believes the prophets, thereby clearly implying that, if the king accepts their teachings, he must admit that what Paul says is true. Here again was a splendid opportunity to preach the mystery doctrine of the Church. Paul not merely does not do this; but he declares emphatically that he has been preaching nothing which Moses and the prophets had not foretold. What clearer illustration could be found of the need of giving heed to Paul's words, "as it hath now been revealed" (Eph. iii. 5), when he speaks of the mystery? In commenting on this passage in Acts, all Darby has to say is this: "He does not speak of the assembly [the Church]—that was a doctrine for instruction, and not a part of his history."[11] That a man of Darby's mentality should have offered so lame and arbitrary an explanation is convincing proof that Paul's words on this memorable occasion cannot be made to square with the doctrine of the Pauline mystery Church as it is held by Dispensationalists. What was Paul's whole ministry if not a ministry of instruction? What was the doctrine of Gentile salvation and equality with the Jews if it was not instruction? Was not the history of Paul's career the story of the way in which his insistence on this instruction had finally made of him a prisoner on trial before the Roman governor? Here Scofield was wiser than Darby. Instead of adopting Darby's lame defense he attempted none, leaving chap. xxvi. without footnote and vss. 22-23 almost without comment.

16. Acts xxviii. 20

"For because of the hope of Israel I am bound with this chain." When we think of Paul as the apostle to the Gentiles and recall how his statement on the stairs of the castle that he had received a commission from God to preach to the Gentiles was met with the frenzied shout of the mob, "Away with such a fellow from the earth: for it is not fit that he should live" (xxii. 22), we might almost surmise that here Paul has been misquoted, that what he really said was this, "for because of the hope of the Gentiles I am bound with this chain." But Paul has not been misquoted, as a comparison with xxvi. 6 makes unmistakably plain; and the only natural explanation of his words is that he believed the "hope of Israel" rightly understood was the hope of the world, of Jew and Gentile without distinction (Gal. vi. 16).[12] And it is upon this note of universalism that Luke closes his record of Paul's career. For, after quoting Isaiah's solemn words regarding the blinding of Israel, Paul adds, "Be it known therefore unto you, that this salvation of God is sent unto the Gentiles: they will also hear"; and the Book of Acts concludes with the statement that in accordance with this declaration Paul during two whole years received "all that went in unto him, preaching the kingdom of God, and teaching the things concerning the Lord Jesus Christ with all confidence, no man forbidding him."

The purport of the passages in the Book of Acts, that have been discussed, is clearly this: the Book of Acts describes a transitional period during which the Christian Church, founded at Pentecost, emancipated itself from the shackles of Judaism and became, in accordance with the essential nature of that gospel which was the fulfilment of the Abrahamic covenant, a universal Church which recognized no distinction between Jew and Gentile. It tells us how Peter, the apostle of the circumcision, declared this universal gospel at Pentecost, was taught its meaning at Joppa and Caesarea, and supported Paul and

Barnabas at Jerusalem, when they contended for the freedom of the Gentiles. It tells us how Saul the Pharisee became the apostle to the Gentiles, the great protagonist of
a gospel which knows no distinction of age or race or sex,
for that all are one new man in Christ Jesus. Yet it also
tells us how this same apostle became the "prisoner of
the Lord" as a direct result of his assuming responsibility
for the performance of a Jewish vow with its attendant
ceremonies in the temple at Jerusalem.

It is this transitional character of the Acts period which
makes this book in some respects a difficult one to interpret. The attitude which we find in it toward the ceremonial law and Jewish customs seems at times incompatible with the freedom of the Christian from the law
and the abolishing of the distinction between Jew and
Gentile, which is so definitely taught by Paul in his
epistles. But that this anomalous situation was only temporary, that it was not to continue indefinitely, is indicated
with especial clearness by two things, the one a matter of
doctrine, the other a fact of history: (1) the teaching of the
Epistle to the Hebrews which sets forth so fully and
clearly the typical nature of the Mosaic economy and its
fulfilment in Christ and His Church; and (2) the utter
destruction of the Jewish state with its temple worship by
Titus before the close of the apostolic age. It is difficult to
read Isa. lxvi. 1f. in the light of Hebrews without receiving
the impression that it refers to that time which, when the
Epistle was written, was almost at the door, when the
temple was to be destroyed never to be restored. It is hard
to understand how anyone can read *Hebrews* without recognizing that it speaks of the complete and final abolish-
ment of the Mosaic ritual of animal sacrifice. As long as
the temple stood and its worship was allowed to continue,
the apostles treated it with reverence. Its destruction
marked the close of the period which it represented. Then
the old order came to an end and the new entered fully
into its rights.

II. The Old Testament in Other Books of the New Testament

The verdict of the Book of Acts on the question, whether the Church, the founding of which it describes so graphically, was foretold by the prophets seems to be so clear and unmistakable that we might rest our case after citing its testimony. But it may be well to show that the testimony of Acts is fully confirmed by the use made of the Old Testament in other books of the New Testament. We shall confine ourselves to five passages which are of special interest.

1. Hebrews viii. 8-12

The Epistle to the Hebrews, because its great purpose is to show how the Old Testament types have found their fulfilment in New Testament realities, quotes frequently from the Old Testament. The longest of these quotations, one of the longest in the entire New Testament, is from Jeremiah (xxxi. 31-34). The passage speaks of the new covenant. It declares that this new covenant has been already introduced and that by virtue of the fact that it is called "new" it has made the one which it is replacing "old," and that the old is about to vanish away. It would be hard to find a clearer reference to the gospel age in the Old Testament than in these verses in Jeremiah; and the writer of Hebrews obviously appeals to it as such. Scofield, in commenting on this passage, gives a "summary" of eight covenants, and says of this one: "The New Covenant rests upon the sacrifice of Christ, and secures the eternal blessedness, under the Abrahamic Covenant (Gal. iii. 13-29), of all who believe."[13] That Scofield should appeal to a long passage in Galatians which deals with the status of the Gentiles in the Christian Church and concludes with the words: "And if ye be Christ's, then are ye Abraham's seed, and heirs according to the promise," is as clear an admission as anyone could ask of the fact that the new covenant relates to the Christian Church; and the fact that this admission is made by a leading Dispensationalist makes it all the more significant. It is difficult to read Scofield's note without finding in it a practical admission that the new covenant is fulfilled in and to the Church. It is true that he does state as the seventh point in his "summary" of the new covenant that, it "secures the perpetuity, future conversion, and blessing of Israel (Jer. xxxi. 31-40)." But few of Scofield's readers probably would take this to mean that the new covenant directly concerns Israel and Israel only. Yet such is the correct Dispensational teaching. Darby tells us expressly: "The new covenant is made also with the two houses of Israel." By "also" Darby means, like the one at Sinai. "The gospel is not a covenant, but the revelation of the salvation of God." "The new covenant will be established formally with Israel in the millennium. Meanwhile the old covenant is judged by the fact that there is a new one."[14] This is consistent Dispensationalism. If the Church is a mystery unknown to the prophets, the new covenant foretold by Jeremiah cannot concern the Church. It must concern Israel.

In his treatment of Hebrews Scofield is markedly inconsistent. He classes this epistle among the "Jewish Christian" epistles which differ in important respects from Paul's. Yet he apparently accepts the Pauline authorship as proved;[15] that is, he attributes this epistle to the apostle who knew the mystery of Church truth. Yet he tells us that this epistle is applicable only to the professing church, since "the Judaeo-Christian writers view the church as a professing body in which, during this age, the wheat and tares are mingled (Mt. xiii. 24-30)."[16] It is strange that, if Paul wrote Hebrews, he should leave the true Church completely, or almost completely, out of the picture! But this does not save the situation. For certainly, on strict Dispensational principles the professing church was as much a mystery as the true Church. Otherwise Scofield's statement, "When Christ appeared to the Jewish people, the next thing, in the order of revelation as it then stood, should have been the setting up of the Davidic kingdom,"[17] must be modified. If Scofield has stated the matter correctly, Jer. xxxi. 31f. can apply to the professing church as little as to the true Church. It is to be fulfilled to Israel in the millennium. This is the inexorable logic of Dispensational teaching.

2. *Romans ix. 25-26*

A good illustration of the light which its use in the New Testament may throw upon the latent implications of an Old Testament text is Paul's use here of Hos. ii. 23 and i. 10. In their context the words of Hosea refer to disobedient Israel. Israel was "my people" by virtue of God's choice and call. But Israel had become "not my people" through disobedience to God and consequent rejection by Him. Yet Hosea declares that Israel shall again be called "my people." So the prophecy might very naturally be regarded as referring exclusively to Israel. But Paul, under the guidance of the Holy Spirit and in the light of gospel truth, sees a deeper meaning in these words of the ancient prophet. "Not my people" may mean two things: "no longer my people" and "not yet my people." In the one sense it would refer to the Jews, in the other to the Gentiles. Just as James interprets Amos' prophecy regarding the tabernacle of David, considered in the light of prophecy as a whole, as referring to the conversion of the Gentiles in the Church age, so Paul declares that Hosea foretold the calling of "vessels of mercy . . . not from the Jews only, but also from the Gentiles." So here, as elsewhere in these chapters (*e.g.,* ix. 33, x. 11f., xi. 5), prophecy is appealed to as foretelling that very situation which is represented by the Church age.

3. *2 Corinthians vi. 2*

To impress the Christian community at Corinth with the urgency of the gospel call, Paul appeals to Isa. xlix. 8 and declares definitely that "now" is the "accepted" time (using a much more emphatic word for "accepted" than appears in his quotation from the LXX), that "now" is the "day of salvation."   Here as in Acts xv. 16f., the only natural view is that the prophecy quoted is directly applicable to the Church age.   Similarly, the "acceptable year" (Isa. lxi. 1f.), announced by Jesus early in His ministry (Lk. iv. 19) can only be that spiritual kingdom which was already "come" (Jn. iv. 23), that day of salvation in the course of which He would build His Church.   The quotation from Ps. xcv. 7-11 in Heb. iii. and the emphasis on the word "today" in the extended comment on it quite as definitely apply that passage to the Church age.

4.   1 Peter ii. 9-10

Whether this epistle is addressed to Christians in general or only to Jewish Christians has been much discussed by the commentators. This question need not concern us, however, since all will agree that Jews who have become Christians are certainly included among those to whom the epistle is addressed, even if they deny that it is intended exclusively for them. Consequently, it is significant that, according to Peter, "All the most splendid titles of the old Israel belong in a fuller sense to these Hebrews who have joined the new Israel."[18] They are "a chosen generation, a royal priesthood, a holy nation, a peculiar people." They are all of this by virtue of their acceptance of the gospel as preached by Paul (1 Pet. i. 12, 25; 2 Pet. iii. 15), in the course of his missionary journeys through Asia Minor, and by Peter himself, whether he was known by face to these converts or not. They are "now the people of God"; they "now have obtained mercy." The prophecy of Hosea has now been fulfilled in them through their acceptance of the Lord Jesus Christ as their Saviour. They have been called "out of darkness" into the "marvelous light" of the gospel. Clearly, Peter finds in their membership in the Christian Church the definite fulfilment of prophecy. The emphatic "you" of i. 10-12 makes this especially plain. Peter tells us that the prophets knew by revelation that their prophetic ministry concerned "these things which now have been announced unto you through them that preached the gospel unto you." What clearer proof do we need that the prophets foresaw and foretold the establishment of the Christian Church?

5. *John xix. 37*

The words quoted here from Zech. xii. 10, "they shall look on him whom they pierced" are a notable example of a prediction which has been fulfilled, is now being fulfilled, and which still awaits complete fulfilment. In the second of these aspects it may be described as "germinant." That the "piercing" took place when Jesus' lifeless body was hanging on the cross is clear. This is the main reason John appealed to it. This piercing was the act of the unbelieving Jewish nation which had rejected its Messiah, though the hand which held the spear was that of a Roman soldier. So far the fulfilment lies in the distant past. But the words of the prophet are, "They shall look on me whom they pierced." Who are referred to? It is natural to suppose that the fulfilment of this part of the prophecy began at once, that it has already had its fulfilment in all those who have looked to the Pierced One and found in Him their Sacrifice, their Saviour, and that its fulfilment will not be complete "Till all the ransomed Church of God, Be saved to sin no more." When Jesus said, "And I, if I be lifted up from the earth, will draw all men unto me" (Jn. xii. 32), He was certainly thinking of the Church which he had declared that He would build (Matt. xvi. 18). And if the building of that Church began at Pentecost, surely, as is held by many of the ablest commentators, the fulfilment of Zechariah's prophecy began then or even before it (Lk. xxiii. 48). That it awaits complete fulfilment in the future is equally clear (Rev. i. 7). Yet Dispensationalists are disposed to deny this progressive or germinant fulfilment during the Church age. They are emphatic that Zech. xii. 10 is a prophecy regarding the Jewish remnant and does not concern the Church. It skips, they tell us, to the end-time. It must do so, if their theory is a true one.

Conclusion

The discussion of the Dispensational interpretation of prophecy in this and the preceding chapter makes one thing abundantly clear. Teulon did not overstate matters when, more than fifty years ago, he declared that the conclusions reached by the Brethren on the subject of prophecy "involve an entire recasting of the received interpretation of a large portion of the Scriptures."[19] This fact, which is not only admitted but emphatically asserted by Dispensationalists, would be sufficiently startling in itself to justify the most searching investigation of this novel system of interpretation. But the all-important result of our investigation is the discovery of conclusive evidence that this received interpretation is not "a legacy in Protestant thought from post-apostolic and Roman Catholic theology,"[20] but the interpretation placed by the writers of the New Testament themselves on Old Testament prophecy. This is the reason, the all-sufficient reason, that it has been accepted as determinative in Protestant thought. To reject it is to reject the authoritative statements of the inspired writers of the New Testament. For they clearly believed that the New Testament Church was foretold in the Old Testament; and they appealed to it as establishing their claiming that in preaching the gospel of the grace of God to Jew and to Gentile they were announcing the fulfilment of the ancient covenant and declaring none other things than those which the prophets and Moses did say should come.

III. The Bullingerite Doctrine of the Church

The teaching that the entire period from Pentecost to the rapture is, so far as the true Church is concerned, a mystery parenthesis first revealed to the apostle Paul may seem to be relatively simple, and it has come to be regarded as practically axiomatic by most Dispensationalists. But, as we have seen, it encounters serious difficulties when the attempt is made to harmonize it with the teachings of Scripture as a whole and especially with the Book of Acts. According to Darby and Scofield this Church began at Pentecost. But it remained a "mystery" for twenty years or more until its true character was made known to Paul. Peter figured very prominently in the early history of the Church. But it is to be regarded as distinctly Pauline. This Church was unknown to the Old Testament prophets. But their writings are repeatedly appealed to as fulfilled in it. These practical difficulties are obvious and hard to overcome. It is not surprising, therefore, that some advocates of Dispensational teaching should have found in these facts clear indication of the necessity for further Dispensational distinctions. According to Bullinger and his followers, the New Testament does not speak of only one true Church, but of several, at least three, distinct churches: the Church of Matt. xvi. 18, the Church of the Book of Acts, and the mystery Church of the Prison Epistles.

1. The Church of Matthew xvi

According to Darby and Scofield the church of which Jesus was speaking when He said, "Upon this rock I will build my church" was the Christian Church, the mystery Church of Paul. This is the common belief of nearly all Christians. But from the Dispensational viewpoint it is open to serious difficulties. If Matthew's Gospel is Jewish, as Dispensationalists have been insisting for a hundred years and more, and if, when Jesus spoke to His disciples in the Olivet discourse (Matt. xxiv) about His coming, He must have been speaking to them as the representatives of a future Jewish remnant and cannot have been speaking to them as the prospective founders of the apostolic Church of the Book of Acts, is it natural, is it possible to hold that the Church of which He spoke to them was an institution which did not concern them as Jewish believers at all, but was an utter mystery to them? The word "church" as a designation of the congregation of Israel was familiar through its use in the LXX version. Consequently, the Church referred to in Matt. xvi. might well be a future Jewish remnant church. Bullinger insists that "Those who heard these words of the Lord's promise could not connect them with the Secret or Mystery which was 'hid in God' and had not yet been made known to the sons of men. But they could connect them with Hos. i. 10; and ii. 23";[21] and Bullinger appeals to Paul's use of these verses in Rom. ix. 25-27, which he of course interprets of the future Jewish remnant. This is likely to be quite disconcerting to many Dispensationalists who like other Protestants are accustomed to claim that the words "my church" refer to the Church of the present gospel age, the Church of which they are members. But can it be denied that Bullinger's teaching is consistent Dispensationalism? How can men who insist that Matthew's Gospel is Jewish and that the mystery Church was unknown until revealed to the apostle Paul maintain with any real consistency that the Church to which Jesus refers in Matthew is the true mystery Church of Paul?

2. The Church of the Book of Acts

According to Bullinger this Church is distinct both from the mystery Church of the Prison Epistles, and from the Church referred to in Matt. xvi. The period described in Acts is regarded by him as a transitional period during which the gospel of the promised kingdom was still preached by Peter and by Paul to the Jew first and also to the Gentile. The final rejection of the kingdom by the Jews would then be referred to in Acts xxviii. 25f.; yet even after that, for two whole years Paul still preached the "kingdom of God" to all who would listen. Consequently, it must have been after this that Paul began to preach the "mystery"; and "church truth" is to be looked for only in the Prison Epistles.

This distinction, radical though it is, solves some of the difficulties which are inherent in the Darby-Scofield teaching. For one thing, it makes it unnecessary to attempt to deny that the references to the Old Testament in Acts apply to, and are cited as applying to the Church whose founding and early history is described in that book.[22] If the Pentecostal and Apostolic Church of Acts is not the mystery Church but one which is to a large extent Jewish, it might well be the subject of prophecy. This teaching also meets the difficulty connected with Peter's activity in a church of the nature of which he is supposed to be in ignorance. As an apostle, Peter would naturally be active in the founding of the Apostolic Church! It also accounts for the Jewish coloring of this transitional period and for the preaching of a kingdom gospel up to its very close. But it makes a sharp line of demarcation between this Pentecostal Apostolic Jewish Kingdom Church and the Church of this present age.

3. The Pauline Mystery Church

While the distinction drawn by Bullinger between the Apostolic Church and the Mystery Church may appear to solve some of the difficulties inherent in the Dispensational doctrine of the mystery, it has difficulties of its own to contend with. It has the obvious advantage that it places the founding of the Mystery Church long after Pentecost and denies that the Church which Peter was largely instrumental in founding is the Mystery Church which was first revealed to Paul. This is a decided gain, as far as consistency is concerned, but it is secured at very serious cost. It means or should mean that neither in Acts nor in any of Paul's epistles written during the Acts period is the mystery Church referred to. This makes the portion of the New Testament which concerns the Church of the present age extremely meagre, confining it to the Prison Epistles; and the assurance that all Scripture is edifying and applicable to the Christian of today does not make up for that tremendous loss. But this is not the only difficulty. It is one thing to argue, as against Darby and Scofield, that the mystery Church was not founded by Paul until after the close of the Acts period. But the question must then be faced, whether Paul was really ignorant of the doctrine until so near the end of his life. Bullinger himself denies this. He argues that when Paul in writing to the Corinthian Christians referred to the "abundance of the revelations" which he had received "fourteen years" earlier (2 Cor. xii. 2-4), he was referring to the mystery of the Church. This amounts to saying that before he started out on his first missionary journey Paul had received the revelation of the mystery. Bullinger speaks of Acts xiii. as "the great dispensational chapter."[23] Consequently, according to Bullinger, Paul spent the greater part of his apostolic ministry laboring in the interest of the Apostolic Church, despite the fact that almost at the very outset of his active ministry he had received the revelation regarding a quite different Church of which he himself was to be the founder. That Paul should have kept this transcendent doctrine locked in his breast for twenty years seems incredible. Did he really do this? Bullinger tells us that the mystery is referred to in Rom. x. 12, 1 Cor. xii. 13, Gal. iii. 28 and Col. iii. 11.[24] Only the last of the four epistles mentioned belongs to the imprisonment period. So Paul actually did refer to the mystery at a much earlier date. Yet Bullinger did not hesitate to treat the closing verses of Romans as a postscript added at Rome, because they refer so clearly to the mystery!

Bullinger was very insistent on what he considered to be the important distinction between the words "body" and "bride" as used of the Church. He held that the "body church" is the mystery church of Paul and quite distinct from the "bride church" which is composed of "the elect Old Testament saints." To illustrate the confusion which in his opinion results from the failure to draw this distinction, he remarks: "This is why the Church of God is spoken of as 'she;' while in the [Prison] Epistles its members grow up 'unto a perfect MAN'; and are part of Him who is the Bridegroom; and in Him are made 'one new man,' and not a 'new woman.' "[25] This was to Bullinger conclusive evidence that the "body church" and the "bride church" must be distinct. To most students of Scripture such an argument will seem absurd. We have only to think of the many figures which are used to describe the Saviour in all the plenitude of His redemptive work—light, water, bread, lamb, temple, vine, shepherd, etc.— to realize how dangerous it is to base a doctrine upon a figure of speech. The distinction drawn here by Bullinger makes it necessary to place a very forced interpretation on Eph. v. 21-33, where Paul uses the relation of husband and wife as a figure of that between Christ and the Church. For Paul there combines the figures of head and body and husband and wife, insisting that there is not merely an analogy between the headship of Christ over the Church and the headship of the man over the woman, but that the man as the head should love his wife as he loves his own body; and he clinches the argument with an appeal to Genesis where it is declared that the man shall be joined to his wife and "they two shall become one flesh." It would be hard to find a better argument for the identical use of the two figures than Paul gives us here.[26]

It may also be noted that Bullinger denied that the seven churches of the Apocalypse are to be identified either with the Apostolic Church or with the Mystery Church. He interpreted them as describing "future assemblies of Jewish believers on the earth" after the rapture.

It is hardly necessary to point out to the reader that our appeal to Bullinger is purely an *ad hominem* argument. The followers of Darby and Scofield are quite justified in regarding Bullingerism as a very dangerous teaching and in attempting to expose its serious errors. The tragedy of the situation is that they are themselves in no position to refute Bullinger, because Bullinger with all his errors was a most ardent Dispensationalist and held as tenaciously as any of them do the doctrine that the Bible must be divided "dispensationally"; and this is responsible for their own most serious errors. For example, the Brethren regard the Lord's Supper as pre-eminently a "church ordinance." They observe it every Lord's day. It is the very centre of their worship. But it is to be noted that its institution is recorded in Matthew's Gospel. If Matthew is "Jewish," it is only a step to say with Bullinger that all the gospels are Jewish. Tregelles tells us that it was claimed in Brethren circles many years ago that the only warrant for the observance of the rite by Christians in this present age is to be found in the fact that it is referred to by Paul in his epistles. But it is not referred to in the Prison Epistles. Consequently, some of the Bullingerites insist that both Water Baptism and the Lord's Supper are kingdom ordinances and not to be observed by Christians today. All Bullingerites believe that this applies to Water Baptism.[27]

IV. THE DISPENSATIONAL METHOD OF INTERPRETATION PRODUCES DISCORD

It is instructive to study the logical outworkings of a system of interpretation for the purpose of testing the correctness of its basic principles. Bullingerism starts with the same fundamental teaching regarding the Church as did Darby and the Brethren.[28] It goes farther than they went and leads to greater complexities and to the recognition of more dispensational differences than they regarded as necessary. But it cannot be denied that it is consistent Dispensationalism, more consistent in some respects than the position of Darby and Scofield. When Dispensationalists try to refute Bullinger, they are in danger of refuting themselves. When Ironside, for example, in endeavoring to show the falsity of Bullinger's doctrine of the mystery, describes the words of Jesus, "Other sheep

I have which are not of this fold. Them also I must bring, and there shall be one flock and one shepherd," as "perhaps the earliest intimation of the mystery that we have," and finds here proof that John "had received the revelation of the mystery even before the apostle Paul did," he is making a statement which is irreconcilable with the Darby-Scofield position. And when he goes on to say, "Then what of the apostle Peter? We dare to say this same mystery was made known to him on the housetop of Simon's residence in Joppa," he makes it clear that he is not unconscious of the serious implications of such a statement, coming from the lips of one who was for some years connected with the Brethren and is now a leader in Dispensational circles.[29]

Bullingerism would be a blessing in disguise, if it would induce Dispensationalists who realize the seriousness of its errors to examine afresh the fundamentals of their own position. The divisive, antithetical method of interpretation which is so characteristic of Dispensationalism leads in Bulleringerism to divisions and distinctions which are unreasonable and absurd. It is the system that is at fault. What is needed is a return to that harmonistic method of interpretation which does full justice to the fact that the revelation contained in Scripture is a self-consistent whole. Darby was, as we have seen, the sworn foe of the Covenant Theology. So we quote from that well-known statement of it as set forth in the *Westminster Confession of Faith* which Darby particularly denounced:

"This covenant was differently administered in the time of the law, and in the time of the gospel: under the law it was administered by promises, prophecies, sacrifices, circumcision, the paschal lamb, and other types and ordinances delivered to the people of the Jews, all foresignifying Christ to come, which were for that time sufficient and efficacious, through the operation of the Spirit, to instruct and build up the elect in faith in the promised Messiah, by whom they had full remission of sins, and eternal salvation; and is called the Old Testament.

"Under the gospel, when Christ the substance was exhibited, the ordinances in which this covenant is dispensed are the preaching of the Word, and the administration of the Sacraments of Baptism and the Lord's Supper; which, though fewer in number, and administered with more simplicity and less outward glory, yet in them it is held forth in more fulness, evidence, and spiritual efficacy, to all nations, both Jews and Gentiles; and is called the New Testament. There are not, therefore, two covenants of grace differing in substance, but one and the same under various dispensations."30

This we believe to be in essentials the Protestant position. The common doctrine of Protestants is that there is only one true Christian Church. It is the Church which is built upon "the foundation of the apostles and prophets, Jesus Christ himself being the chief cornerstone" (Eph. ii. 20). As a visible body it may have many forms and divisions; and there may be many tares among the wheat. As an invisible body it consists of the elect, of all those who truly believe in Christ as Saviour and belong to Him. This Church was founded at Pentecost. It was originally wholly Jewish and is proved by this very fact to be the continuation and successor of the Old Testament Church. Gentiles were early received into it and soon came to constitute a majority in it; and the teaching that the middle wall of partition between the two was completely broken down was especially, but not exclusively, committed to Paul who was in a pre-eminent sense the apostle to the Gentiles. But no one emphasized more strongly than did Paul the vital oneness of the New Testament Church with the Old Testament Church. The Gentile branches were grafted into the good olive tree that they might enjoy its fatness, the fulness of the blessing promised to all the spiritual heirs of the Abrahamic covenant.

We conclude, therefore, that the Christian Church does not interrupt the literal fulfilment to Israel of the Old Testament kingdom prophecies. Far otherwise, it constitutes the fulfilment of these prophecies to both Jew and Gentile in that gospel dispensation which the prophets foresaw but saw afar off and the full and glorious meaning of which was in the fulness of time made known by the Lord "unto his holy apostles and prophets in the Spirit," especially to the apostle Paul.

Chapter VII

THE COMING OF THE LORD

IT HAS been the oft-repeated claim of Premillennialists that their doctrine of the second coming alone does justice to the Biblical injunctions that the Christian be ready for it, expect it, watch for it. If, according to the Postmillenarian or Whitbyan view, the millennium is wholly future and is to precede the advent, it is absurd, they tell us, to speak of expecting or watching for the coming of the Lord. This argument is not without weight. Amillennialists feel this objection to the Postmillenarian view quite as strongly as do Premillenarians. The fact that, according to an Act of Parliament adopted in 1752, the Episcopal *Book of Common Prayer* gives directions for calculating the feasts of the Church year as far ahead as A.D. 8500+, was not calculated to convince Darby and his associates a century ago that the bishops and other clergy of the Established Church were living in eager expectancy of the advent. It indicated rather that they regarded the Church of England as firmly established on earth and expected it to remain there almost "world without end." And what was true of the Church of England at that time was also true then and is true today of many other Christian bodies and perhaps of most of their membership. Belief in a still future spiritual millennium does undoubtedly tend to weaken the Christian's expectancy of the coming, by referring it to a remote future. But it cannot be denied that many Postmillennialists have looked for, longed for, and confidently expected the coming of the Lord, even though they believed that they themselves would not live to behold it.[1] And it is important to keep in mind that the view of those Amillennialists, who believe in a spiritual millennium which is past or nearly past, and of those Amillennialists who do not believe in any earthly millennium at all, may approximate very closely to that of Premillennialists regarding the imminence of the coming.

It is to be remembered that while Premillennialists have been insistent that, as Brookes expressed it, there can be "no millennium till Christ comes,"[2] they have not claimed, as a rule, that the advent is "imminent" in the sense that there can be no known events still to take place before it.[3] Many of them have held the Historical view of the Apocalypse, regarding it as giving a prophetic foreview of the history of the Church from the time of the apostle John to the final consummation; and they have worked out elaborate chronological charts of its fulfilment. Probably most of them have regarded the coming as quite near at hand, have even expected it in their own day (*e.g.*, E. B. Elliott, J. A. Seiss, H. Grattan Guinness); others have regarded it as more remote (*e.g.*, Bengel). But they have been prepared, as a rule, to recognize that the occurrence of certain predicted events, notably the carrying out of the Great Commission, must precede the coming of the Lord.

I. The Any Moment Theory Regarding the Second Advent

The Brethren Movement had its beginning, as we have seen, at a time when there was a great revival of interest in the doctrine of the second coming. About the year 1825, and primarily under the preaching of Edward Irving, the emphasis began to be placed on the "imminence" of that event. Irving held that the Lord might appear any day, at any hour, and that He would certainly come during the lifetime of the generation then living. The Brethren were opposed to Irvingism, but it cannot be denied that, however they came by it, they speedily became ardent advocates of what is called the "any moment" doctrine of the coming. In other words, they regarded the coming as imminent in the sense of *proximate, i.e.*, as the *next* event in the prophetic program of the Bible; and they insisted that there is nothing in that program so far as it is revealed in Scripture which *must* take place before it.[4] We have described this any moment doctrine as the second of the great fundamentals of Dispensationalism. It is of equal importance with the doctrine of the parenthesis Church and must now be discussed in some detail.

1. The Psychological Argument for the Any Moment Doctrine

This argument has been stated in various ways, all of which involve the assumption that men cannot expect and watch for the coming of Christ and be stimulated and safeguarded by the thought of it unless they can believe that it may take place "at any moment." This argument is not valid. A mother may live in the constant, ever-present hope and expectation of seeing her absent boy, even when she knows that he is on the other side of the globe. Intensity of affection disregards time and distance. Seven years was a long time for Jacob to serve for Rachel; and he had made a contract with Laban and knew that he would be held to the letter of it. Yet the years seemed to him like a "few days" (the Hebrew might be rendered "single days") for the love he had for her. Patriots have toiled, suffered, and died in the cause of freedom, knowing full well that it was not likely to come, that it was almost certain not to come, in their day. Social reformers, inventors, discoverers have devoted themselves to great projects, often without expecting to enjoy the fruit of their labors. The interest men take in an objective, the effort they are willing to make to attain it, does not depend on its nearness nearly so much as on its greatness, its desirability, and the probability or certainty of its ultimate achievement. The nearness of the goal may appeal to a man's selfishness, ambition, pride, even to his indolence. To labor in a cause knowing that others may or probably will attain the goal, reap the harvest, receive the reward, enjoy the triumph—such a cause appeals to those who can forget themselves and think unselfishly of others. Yet we are told regarding the coming of Christ:

"If the slightest hint had been given to the early disciples that the Saviour would not return for centuries, we can hardly imagine how disastrous would have been the effect upon their zeal in proclaiming the glad tidings of the gospel, and their patience amid sore persecution, and their holy contempt of earthly honors and pleasures."5

So wrote Brookes in *Maranatha*. Is this a true statement? We believe it is not. There is no mention of time in the Great Commission. Whether the generations to be evangelized be many or few, every generation since the ascension has needed or will need the gospel. The call for the "evangelization of the world in this generation," which was the ringing challenge of the Student Volunteer Movement to Christian youth a generation ago, is just as imperative today, whether the present generation is to be the last, or unnumbered generations are to follow. Christians can only be directly responsible for their own generation; and the time allotted to them to perform their share in its evangelization is short, whether other generations are to follow or not. Love of the Saviour, longing to exchange faith for sight, struggle for victory, labor for rest, may make the any moment doctrine appeal strongly to many Christians. But careful pondering of Jesus' words, "It is expedient for you that I go away" (Jn. xvi. 7), "All power is given unto me in heaven and on earth. Go ye therefore . . . lo, I am with you alway" (Matt. xxviii. 18f.), should school them in patience. The any moment doctrine is not essential to the maintaining of Christian love and devotion. It is not essential to the accomplishing of the task which the Lord has assigned His Church until He come.

That this is the case is illustrated very clearly by the fact that there is an event—death—which men everywhere may encounter literally *at any moment*. It is the sword of Damocles which is suspended by a hair over the head of every mortal; and in countless instances that sword has fallen with startling suddenness. To the Christian it means the end of his probation, of his labors, of his loneliness and absence from his Lord; it means translation into the very presence of Christ. To the unbeliever it means, "after death the judgment." Is the coming of Christ for His Church, in so far as the *individual* is concerned, so different from death, that the Christian needs to believe that both may occur at any moment in order that his love for his absent Lord and zeal in His service may not grow cold?[6] If only all true Christians could fully realize that death is the ordinary means by which *absence from the Lord* is changed into *presence with the Lord,* then their longing to be with Him would rob death of its terrors. They would be able to sing with Muhlenberg, "I would not live alway; no, welcome the tomb!" and with Malan and Bethune,

> "It is not death to die,
> To leave this weary road,
> And midst the brotherhood on high
> To be at home with God."

And they would take seriously the challenging words of Isaac Watts,

> "Why should we start and fear to die?
> What timorous worms we mortals are!
> Death is the gate of endless joy,
> And yet we dread to enter there."

For it can hardly be denied that a strong reason, a very strong reason, that the any moment rapture doctrine appeals to so many Christians is because they are encouraged by it to believe, that they, unlike the countless multitudes of Christians, even very eminent Christians, of the generations that are gone, will be ushered into the presence of Christ, not as they through the grim portal of death, but by being caught up to meet Him in the air. That expectation is of course very delectable, if Scriptural. But it is or should be a secondary question. As Christians we have the blessed assurance that whether we "wake or sleep," whether we be living or dead at His coming, we shall be for ever with the Lord. And in the light of the goal, the means by which it is attained is of minor importance.

There is another side to this question which should not be overlooked. Darby used a familiar illustration: "Suppose a wife expects her husband to return from a journey, don't you think there would be an effort to have everything ready?"[7] We reply, Of course, if she really loves him! But we would add this qualification: If "ready" were to mean, to have a meal ready to serve, as soon as he comes into the house, would she not expect, and be entitled to expect, that he would give her some idea when he would return? Suppose he said, "Expect me any moment" and then went away for days, weeks, months, even for years. Would such treatment increase her affection? Would it not rather cause her worry, deepening into anxiety, perplexity, even doubt of his affection for her, or fear that he was dead? And suppose that he knew all along that he would not return for years and when he did return explained his conduct by saying, "Had I given you the slightest hint that I would be gone for many years, you would not have been expecting me daily and hourly as I wished you to do." What would be the natural reaction to such treatment? The illustration is by no means perfect. But if the any moment doctrine was needed by the Early Church to keep it from coldness and despair in view of the centuries of waiting still to come, of which it was *ignorant,* is not this doctrine likely to discourage rather than encourage the Church of today in view of the many centuries of waiting already past of which it does *know*? Would it not be better to have some intimation that the interval might be long, especially if there were coupled with it some indication that the interval is now nearly ended? These questions would seem almost to answer themselves. Our only reason for dwelling so long on this subject is that this psychological argument is so stressed by Dispensationalists.

2. Psychological Argument not Supported by Biblical Evidence

a. "At hand" suggests Intervening Events

Basic to the discussion of the any moment theory regarding the rapture of the Church is the fact to which attention has already been directed, that the same expressions, "at hand" or "near," are used both in the kingdom announcement of John the Baptist and of that coming of the King which is still future: "Repent ye, for the kingdom of heaven is at hand" (Matt. iii. 2); "for the coming of the Lord is at hand" (Jas. v. 8), "the day is at hand" (Rom. xiii. 12), "the end of all things is at hand" (1 Pet. iv. 7). Consequently, if we have found that the any moment theory of the establishment of the kingdom at the first advent encounters serious difficulties, we have a strong presumption to begin with, that the any moment theory regarding the second advent is equally untenable. If "at hand" as used of the one event cannot mean that "no known or predicted event must intervene," it will require very convincing evidence to establish the claim that it must have this meaning in the case of the other. It is not necessary to review the evidence already given that the words "at hand" and "near" involve the notion of separation and imply or allow for intervening events, known as well as unknown. For

b. The Occurrence of Such Events is Implied in Scripture

There are definite indications in Scripture that the coming of the Lord might be much delayed, and that the Christian should be expecting to see signs of its approach. The expressions, "if he shall come in the second watch, and if in the third" (Lk. xii. 38), "went into a far country" (Lk. xix. 12, taken in connection with the reason for the parable, "they supposed that the kingdom of God was immediately to appear"), "while the bridegroom tarried" (Matt. xxv. 5), "now after a long time" (xxv. 19), all suggest the possibility or even probability of a considerable interval of waiting. The oft-repeated words, "and I will raise him up at the last day" (Jn. vi. 39, 40, 44, 54), certainly suggest that death will be the lot of most believers. Paul foresaw and referred to the condition of the churches after his death (Acts xx. 29); and when he knew that his death was "at hand,"[8] he wrote from Rome to Timothy (at Ephesus?) exhorting him to "come before winter." Paul instructed Titus to ordain elders in every city (of Crete), which suggested a certain measure of permanence and continuance of the Church on earth. Peter expected to die. These passages do not favor the any moment view. Furthermore events, which are in some cases definitely referred to as signs, are spoken of as preceding the coming. This is particularly true of Matt. xxiv. which, according to Scofield, sums them up in terms of "wars, international conflicts, famines, persecutions, and false Christs," to which is to be added "the preaching of the gospel in all the world for a witness unto all nations" (vs. 14). The believer should be able to "see the day approaching" (Heb. x. 25). It is also to be noted that the statements that the Lord or His day will come "like a thief" are in the form of a solemn warning against sloth, disobedience, carnal security, scepticism (cf., e.g., Lk. xii. 35-48). It is expressly stated that it ought not to come upon the Christian as a thief (1 Thess. v. 4). The Christian should be ready for it, joyfully ready, whenever it comes: and he should be able to interpret the signs of its approach.

One of the clearest indications that Dispensationalists do not believe that the rapture is really "without a sign, without a time note, and unrelated to other prophetic events"[9] is the fact that they cannot write a book on prophecy without devoting a considerable amount of space to "signs" that this event must be very near at hand. These signs may be wars, famines, pestilences, the political situation—they may even include tanks and airplanes. Blackstone listed eight signs. A recent writer gives fifteen.[10] That they should do this is not surprising. The Brethren were quite as confident a full century ago that the rapture must be very near in their day as are present day Dispensationalists that such is now the case. Consequently, unless they are prepared to adhere rigidly to their any moment doctrine and reject dates altogether, they are naturally concerned to show that there are reasons for believing it to be at the threshold now which were not present a century or several centuries ago. Hence, they concern themselves fully as much with signs and prophetic charts as do the members of the Historical School of interpretation. This is of course quite incompatible with their any moment doctrine. It can be justified only on the ground that these "signs" prove that the day of the Lord as a day of judgment on apostate Christendom must be very near and that therefore the rapture of the Church must be much nearer (at least 7 years earlier). But this amounts to making those events which concern Israel and Christendom and the nations a time-schedule for establishing the nearness of the rapture. Scofield does this in effect when he declares that "The 'mysteries of the kingdom of heaven' and the 'mystery' of the church (Eph. iii. 9-11) occupy, historically, the same period, i.e., this present age."[11] Darby denounced this tendency during his lifetime;[12] and Dispensationalists should recognize that the attempt to prove by signs and events that the "signless" and unheralded *any moment* rapture must be near at hand really amounts to a surrender of the *any moment* principle.

II. THE NATURE OF THE COMING—INVISIBLE AND VISIBLE

Dispensationalists often speak as if the word "coming" is used only of a visible return of Christ. That it may be used and is used of such a coming is clearly implied in Acts i. 11: "This same Jesus, which is taken up from you into heaven, shall so come in like manner as ye have seen him go into heaven." But this does not require or justify the inference, that every reference to the coming of the Lord must be to this visible event.

1. *The Old Testament*

The Old Testament uses several different words to describe the comings of the Lord: come, come down, return, visit, appear. It is not necessary to prove that these words are sometimes used of a visible appearance of the Lord, or of the Angel of the Lord, or of a visible manifestation of His presence. The point to remember is that such may not be the case. For example:

a. The words "Return, O LORD, unto the many thousands of Israel" (Num. x. 36) were the prayer of Moses whenever the ark rested and the tabernacle was set up. The pillar of cloud and fire, the Shekinah glory, symbolized and made visible the presence of God among His people; God sat enthroned above the mercy-seat and between the cherubim. But after the Exile there was no ark; and there is no indication in Ezra, that the cloud filled the second temple as it had filled the tabernacle and Solomon's temple. Yet Zechariah tells us twice (i. 16, viii. 3): "(therefore) thus saith the LORD (of hosts), I am returned unto Jerusalem."

b. "Go down" is used in Gen. xlvi. 4 of the Lord's promise to Jacob, "I will go down with thee into Egypt." This clearly promised Jacob God's providential guidance and blessing. Probably no one would maintain that the Lord went with Jacob in visible form (cf. 2 Sam. vii. 9). There was certainly nothing in this at all like the tremendous theophany of Ex. xix. 16f., xx. 12f. Yet even at Sinai, they saw no shape. They heard only a voice!

c. In Gen. xviii. 1, we read that Jehovah "appeared" unto Abraham. This appearance was clearly a theophany, for one of the three "men" was the Lord. In vs. 14, the Lord declares that He will "return" at the appointed time and Sarah shall have a son. In xxi. 1, we read that the Lord "visited" Sarah. It is unlikely that "visit" is used here in a different sense from that in Ruth i. 6, 1 Sam. ii. 21, Ps. lxv. 9.

d. In like manner, "come" is used of appearances to men in dreams (Gen. xxi. 3, xxxi. 24, cf. Num. xxii. 9, 20, also 1 Sam. iii. 10). It is used of the divine Presence in the cloudy pillar (Ex. xix. 9). It is also used of comings in the future (Ps. xl. 7,

l. 3, xcvi. 13, xcviii. 9, Isa. xix. 1, xxxv. 4, xl. 10, l. 2, lix. 20, lxvi. 15, Mal. iii. 1).

2. The New Testament

The same variety of usage is found also in the New Testament:

a. "Come" is used repeatedly of the coming of Christ. The Messiah was "the coming one" (Mt. xi. 3, xxi. 9). He has come visibly in His incarnation (Jn. i. 11). He will come again visibly (Acts i. 11). The Son of man will come in the clouds of heaven (Mt. xxvi. 64). But the word is also used in passages where such a reference is hardly admissible. After Peter's confession at Caesarea Philippi, Jesus distinctly affirmed that He, the Christ, must be rejected and suffer and rise again. In all three Synoptics, He concluded this announcement with a statement that there were some then present who should not taste of death till they should "see" the "Son of man coming in his kingdom" (Mt. xvi. 28, cf. Mk. ix. 1, Lk. ix. 27). Both Matthew and Mark use the word "come." All three declare that "some" men then living and present shall "see" Him *come.* Here there is no room for doubt as to the meaning of the expression which describes those who are to witness the coming. It concerns some of those alive and present when the words were uttered. They are to witness the coming. Consequently, we may say with positiveness that this coming must have taken place during the lifetime of the apostle John. The claim that these words of Jesus referred to the transfiguration is plainly inadequate. That event was too near at hand (about a week distant) to make the fact that some of Jesus' immediate followers would live to see it a sufficiently important matter to mention. The coming referred to seems most likely to be the destruction of Jerusalem by Titus, at which time there was so far as we know no visible appearance of Christ.

In the Apocalypse, four of the seven churches are threatened with the Lord's coming—Ephesus, Pergamus, Sardis, Philadelphia; and the final word to Laodicea is "Behold, I stand at the door and knock." The words to Ephesus, "I will come to thee and I will remove thy candlestick" (ii. 5), and to Sardis,

"Thou shalt not know what hour I will come unto thee" (iii. 3), read like warnings intended for these particular churches (as well as for all others like them). And the fact that Ephesus and Sardis (in fact nearly all of the seven cities and churches) ceased to exist centuries ago seems a clear indication that Christ's coming to them in judgment has already taken place. However much Dispensationalists may be disposed to regard the seven churches as typifying seven ages of the professing church, they should certainly be prepared to recognize a literal application as primarily intended. If so, they can hardly deny that Christ's coming in judgment on these churches lies in the distant past.

b. "Come down" or "descend" is used of the descent of the Holy Spirit on Jesus (Jn. i. 32) and repeatedly of the incarnation (*e.g.,* Jn. iii. 13). It is used of the second advent in 1 Thess. iv. 16.

c. "Return" is not a New Testament word for the coming of Christ. It occurs only in the parabolic language of Lk. xix. 12, 15, and in Acts xv. 16, where "return and build" is probably the Old Testament idiom for "build again."

d. "Visit" is used of the incarnation (Lk. i. 68, 78), of the raising of the son of the widow of Nain, which was appealed to as a proof that "God hath visited his people" (vii. 16), and in James' comment on Peter's testimony before the Council at Jerusalem: "Symeon hath declared how God at the first did visit the Gentiles, to take out of them a people for his name" (Acts xv. 14) which is a reference to Cornelius.

e. "Appear" is used of the first advent, of the post-resurrection appearances of Jesus, of the vision on the Damascus road, of the second advent. It is also used of Paul's vision of the "man from Macedonia."

A careful study of the passages cited above makes it quite clear that in the New Testament as in the Old the words which describe God's manifestations of Himself to men may be used in two senses: of a visible presence and also of an invisible presence, *i.e.,* of an exercise of divine power which manifests the presence of the invisible God. The difficulty of deciding between these possibilities is clearly shown by the different meanings attached by commentators to the allusions to Jesus' departure and coming in John xiv.—xvi. Darby recognized that the words, "I will not leave you comfortless: I come to you" (xiv. 18) refer to an invisible coming through the Holy Spirit. He said of them:

> "His presence, in spirit, here below, is the consolation of His people. They should see Him; and this is much more true than seeing Him with the eyes of flesh. Yes, more true; it is knowing Him in a much more real way, even though by grace they had believed in Him as the Christ, the Son of God. And, moreover, this spiritual sight of Christ by the heart, through the presence of the Holy Ghost, is connected with life."[13]

This statement is impressive in itself. Coming from an ardent literalist, from one of the conspicuous leaders in the whole Dispensational movement, it is doubly impressive. The words, "I come to you," certainly suggest a visible coming. Darby says that they refer to an invisible coming, to that presence of Christ in the heart of the believer which Christians have enjoyed from the day of Pentecost until now. In this interpretation Darby has the support of most if not all competent scholars. It is significant, therefore, that neither Blackstone nor Scofield made any attempt to explain this passage; and Scofield must have been forgetting his great teacher, Darby, when he made the sweeping assertion that such "alleged explanations and theories" (as the view that the coming might be through the Holy Spirit) are not found "in the books of reputable theologians of any school or denomination, nor are they maintained by a single exegete of universally recognized eminence."[14] Such unqualified words are not a reflection on the reputation and eminence of Darby alone, but of a host of others as well, among whom Calvin, Bengel, Alford, Olshausen, Godet, and Tholuck may be mentioned. All who believe Jesus' words, "Lo, I am with you alway," must be willing to admit, that there must be a very real sense in which Jesus has come and is now present with believers, even while they maintain as they should, that this coming is not the visible and glorious coming that is elsewhere referred to in Scripture. The passages we have examined make this clear. As Fairbairn has well remarked of the language of prophecy, "every-thing of moment in the dispensations of God is there con-nected with His presence and working."[15] But all of these comings, whether visible or invisible, providential or mirac-ulous, are in a sense only preliminary to and preparatory for that great final and climactic coming which will be followed by the judgment of all mankind.

In the above quotation from Darby the following words are especially noteworthy: "They should see Him; and this is much more true than seeing Him with the eyes of flesh." Dispensationalists often write and speak as if the visible presence of Christ were far more important and would be far more efficacious for salvation and sanctification than His presence through the Holy Spirit. Darby here denies, at least by implication, that such is the case; and no other interpreta-tion does justice to Jesus' words: "It is expedient for you that I go away: for if I go not away the Comforter will not come unto you." If the full force of these words of the Saviour is recognized, in the light of the explanation that He gives of the purpose of the coming of the Spirit, it will be apparent that the emphasis placed by Dispensationalists on the visible coming and visible presence of Christ is to no small degree a misplaced emphasis. The coming of the Spirit concerns sal-vation: "He will reprove the world of sin, and of righteous-ness, and of judgment." The visible coming of Christ will not be to save men. That is the work of the Holy Spirit in the present dispensation. The second coming of Christ will be to judge and to reign.

III. THE DISPENSATIONAL DOCTRINE OF TWO PREMILLENNIAL COMINGS

While Premillennialists have insisted most emphatically that the millennium must follow and not precede the second advent, they have usually been prepared to admit that the imminence of the coming does not preclude the occurrence of intervening events, but must be interpreted in harmony with the evidence cited above which makes it clear that events will precede a coming which is to be expected and regarded as at hand, and that these events will be signs of its approach. Dispensationalists argue differently. They hold that "at hand" must mean *proximate*. They insist that the occurrence of known and predicted events before the coming is incompatible with its nearness. They recognize that the occurrence of such events before the *parousia* is clearly foretold. Hence, they draw the inference, the inevitable inference from their premises, that there must be two premillennial comings spoken of in Scripture These they distinguish as Christ's coming for His saints, or the rapture, and His coming with His saints or the appearing (revelation). The former of these may take place literally "at any moment." The latter is to be preceded by events, by which is meant, all the events described in the prophetic program, which will not have already taken place before the rapture. The question we must now consider is whether there are any data in Scripture to justify this startling inference. For it would certainly be remarkable if so important a doctrine were to rest on inference alone.

1. The Words for Rapture and Revelation or Appearing

In addition to the verbs, "come," etc., which have already been discussed, three nouns are used of the second advent which must be carefully considered: "coming" *(parousia,* or presence), "revelation" (apocalypse), "appearing" (epiphany). One, two, or all of these words are used in the epistles of Paul, of James, of Peter, of John, and also in Matt. xxiv.;[16] and the question is, Do they refer to the same event or to two events definitely distinguished as to time of occurrence?

a. The New Testament Usage of these Words

(1) By Paul

(a) "Coming" *(parousia)* is used by Paul 14 times, 8 of which refer to the coming of Christ.[17] 1 Thess. iv. 15, which speaks of the catching up of living believers, clearly refers to the rapture; likewise 2 Thess. ii. 1, which speaks of our "gathering together unto him." On the other hand, 1 Thess. iii. 13

speaks of the "coming of our Lord Jesus with all his saints."
If "saints" means or includes the Church, as all Dispensationalists believe, this verse speaks quite as plainly of the
appearing. In 2 Thess. ii. 8, which clearly refers to the appearing, since it speaks of the slaying of Antichrist, the expression used is "the manifestation" (or "brightness," epiphany)
of his "coming" (parousia). Consequently, we must recognize
that Paul uses coming both of the rapture and of the appearing and even combines the two expressions in 2 Thess. ii. 8
to describe what is apparently one and the same event.

(b) "Revelation" (apocalypse) is used 13 times by Paul.[18]
In 1 Cor. i. 7 it is used of the rapture. It is what the Christian
waits for. In 2 Thess. i. 7 the reference is as plainly to the
appearing, the coming in glory.

(c) "Appearing" (epiphany). This word is used only by Paul.
In 1 Tim. vi. 14, the reference to the rapture seems unmistakable. In 2 Tim. iv. 1, 8 the allusions to judgment as in Tit. ii. 13
to glory favor the reference to the appearing. On 2 Thess. ii. 8
see above.

(2) By James
James uses only the word "coming" (parousia, v. 7f.). Since
he exhorts to patience and speaks of the coming as "at hand,"
it is natural to interpret it of the rapture. James makes no
mention of the appearing.

(3) By Peter
Peter uses only the words "coming" (2 Pet. i. 16, iii. 4, 12)
and "revelation" (1 Pet. i. 7, 13; iv. 13). "Coming" seems to
refer to the appearing. "Revelation" apparently is used of the
rapture in i. 7, 13, although in iv. 13 the word "glory" suggests the appearing.

(4) By John
John uses "coming" (parousia) in 1 Jn. ii. 28 apparently
of the rapture. "Revelation" occurs only in Rev. i. 1.

(5) In Matthew's Gospel
In Matt. xxiv. the "coming" (parousia) of the Son of man
is referred to four times (vss. 3, 27, 37, 39). These are regarded
by Dispensationalists as all referring to the appearing.

b. Significance of New Testament Usage

Reviewing the above data, we note the following important
facts: (1) Paul uses all three words and he uses them am-

biguously. Particularly clear is the fact that he uses *parousia*
both of the rapture and of the appearing. This is important
for two reasons: *(a)* We might expect Paul of all men to be
painstakingly exact in the use of these words, if he was in a
unique sense the custodian of Church truth. *(b)* In 1 Thess.
iv. 13-18, which Dispensationalists appeal to especially in
proof of their doctrine, Paul gives as his authority the Lord
Jesus Christ: "For this we say unto you by the word of the
Lord." Some commentators believe that the "word" referred
to is the discourse in Mt. xxiv., known to Paul orally. Others
insist that he refers to a special revelation made to him
personally. In either case the difference in diction is striking.
In Mt. xxiv. the word "coming" *(parousia)* is clearly used of
the glorious appearing. It would be natural then to expect
Paul to use it in this sense. That he does so sometimes is
obvious. But equally obvious is the fact that he also uses it
of the rapture. How is this to be explained, if he had been
told by the Lord that there was an important difference between these two events?

(2) In the case of Peter, it is claimed that the ambiguity of
his language is due to his ignorance of the mystery doctrine
of Paul. But his language is no more ambiguous than Paul's.
Furthermore, even if we regard Paul as the special custodian
of Church truth, Peter shows acquaintance with Paul's epistles,
especially Ephesians, and commends them (2 Pet. iii. 15f.).
Consequently, unless Peter found the difference between the
rapture and the appearing "hard to understand" and was
unable to grasp it, we might expect him to distinguish carefully between them. Yet he does not do so.

(3) James and John use only the word "coming" *(parousia)*
in speaking of the advent. Their failure to use the other
words is regarded as indicating their ignorance of the mystery
doctrine. But John probably wrote his epistles many years
after Paul's death and had had plenty of time to master Paul's
doctrine, whether the tradition which connects his later years
with Ephesus be correct or not.

c. The Dispensational Explanation

The embarrassment which the New Testament usage
of these words occasions Dispensationalists is illustrated
by the attempt made by Darby to explain it. On the one

hand he insists that "The Church's joining Christ has nothing to do with Christ's appearing or coming to earth."[19] Again and again we are assured by Dispensationalists that the great expectation and concern of the Christian is the rapture: he is to live in constant hope of it. Yet Darby also tells us: "When it is a question of the responsibility of individuals whether Christians or of the world, the New Testament speaks of the *appearing* of Jesus. For the joy and portion of the church, according to the counsel of God in grace, it is the *coming* of Christ into the air, before His revelation, that the word presents to us as the object of faith and hope."[20] The object of this statement is plain. It is an attempt to explain why the word "revelation" or "appearing" is used in such passages as 1 Cor. i. 7 and 1 Tim. vi. 14, which clearly refer to the rapture. But the explanation shows the weakness of the position defended. If the Christian is wholly concerned with the rapture, if he is not to be judged, if he is to be taken instantly unto the presence of Christ, how can it be claimed that he is to be established unblamable in holiness by the appearing which occurs a considerable time later? Why should the "rest" of the Christian be connected with the revelation (2 Thess. i. 7), if it has already taken place or begun at the rapture?

d. The Issue

The question which confronts us is this. If the distinction between the rapture and the appearing is of as great moment as Dispensationalists assert, how are we to explain Paul's failure to distinguish clearly between them? and the failure of other writers, Peter, James, and John, to do the same? Paul was a logician. He was able to draw sharp distinctions. If he had wanted, or regarded it important, to distinguish between these events, he could have done so very easily. Why did he use language which Dispensationalists must admit to be confusing? Feinberg recently made the following surprising statement regarding the three words we have been discussing: "We conclude, then,

that from a study of the Greek words themselves the distinction between the coming of the Lord for His saints and
with His saints is not to be gleaned."[21] Such an admission
raises the question whether the distinction itself is valid.
If the distinction is of importance, Paul's ambiguous language is, we say it reverently, inexcusable. If the distinction
is negligible, accuracy of statement would be quite unnecessary. We conclude, therefore, that the usage of the New
Testament and especially of Paul not merely fails to prove
the distinction insisted on by Dispensationalists but rather
by its very ambiguity indicates clearly and unmistakably
that no such distinction exists.

2. The Coming for and the Coming with the Saints

This distinction is so stressed by Dispensationalists that
it would be natural to suppose that these expressions occur
frequently in the New Testament. Such is not the case.

a. "For the saints"—This expression is not found in the
New Testament. The idea is clearly expressed in Jn. xiv. 3,
1 Cor. xv. 23 (cf. xv. 51f.), 2 Thess. ii. 1 and 1 Thess. iv.
15-17. But it is to be observed that no one of these passages
refers to a coming with the saints; and the last mentioned
is the only one which refers to a meeting with Christ
"in the air."

b. "With the saints"—This expression occurs only three
times in Scripture (Zech. xiv. 5, 1 Thess. iii. 13 and
Jude 14). Who are meant by the "saints"?

(1) "Holy ones" or "saints" (hagioi) are referred to in the
Old Testament. In some cases angels are clearly meant (e.g.,
Dt. xxxiii. 2, Dan. iv. 13, 17, 23), in others men (e.g., Dt. xxxiii.
3, Dan. vii. 18, 21ff., Ps. xvi. 3). Some passages are uncertain
(e.g., Ps. lxxxix. 5, 7).

(2) Angels are frequently mentioned in the New Testament
in connection with Christ's coming (Mt. xiii. 39-49, xvi. 27, xxiv.
31-36, xxv. 31, Mk. viii. 38, xiii. 27, Lk. ix. 26); and they are
sometimes called "holy (hagioi) angels" (Mk. viii. 38, Lk. ix. 26,
Acts x. 22, Rev. xiv. 10). Especially noteworthy is 2 Thess. i. 7
where we read of the rest to be given the afflicted saints (on

earth?) "at the revelation (apocalypse) of the Lord Jesus from heaven with angels of his power."

Nothing could be plainer than this: when the Lord Jesus Christ comes in His glory, He will be attended by the angels of heaven. The only debatable question is this. Will He be attended also by the redeemed of earth? Several facts will help us to answer this question:

(a) The "saints" are never mentioned *together with* the angels; we never read of the angels *and* the saints.[22]

(b) On the contrary, the task assigned to the angels implies that the saints, at least some of them, will be on earth. The angels are to "sever" the wicked from among the "righteous" (Mt. xiii. 49); they are to gather together Christ's "elect" (xxiv. 31) from all over the earth.

(c) Since the angels are sometimes called "holy angels" it would be quite proper to refer to them simply as "holy (ones)," *i.e.,* as "saints." In Dan. iv. 13f. heavenly beings are called "holy ones." This may be the case in Zech. xiv. 5 and Jude 14. At any rate the Dispensationalists have no right to appeal to these two passages as referring to *Church* saints since they hold that the Church was unknown to Old Testament prophecy. Consequently, on their own interpretation these three passages can no more refer to Church saints than can Dan. vii. 18.

(d) 1 Thess. iii. 13 refers to "the coming of our Lord Jesus with all his saints." There are four possible interpretations of this passage: (α) That "saints" includes only the angels. The warrant for this has been given above and need not be repeated. (β) That "saints" refers to the redeemed in heaven, the saints of both the Old Testament period and of the New. In support of this interpretation, it is argued that the New Testament nowhere else uses "saints" of the angels, but only of believers on earth (*e.g.,* Acts ix. 13, Rom. i. 7). But the fact that Paul is referring here to the coming of Christ from heaven and that the (holy) angels are constantly referred to as accompanying Him would account for his use of this word here in speaking of angels. (γ) That "saints" means only Church saints. This is opposed by the word "all," which, if it applies to the redeemed at all, must include all of them. (δ) The words "all his saints" are so comprehensive that it is difficult, in the light of the data given above, to avoid the

conclusion that both holy angels and holy men are referred
to—all the holy ones in heaven. The only exception which
the language of the passage seems to justify us in making
concerns the living believers who will be on earth at the
time of the coming. That there will be such is clearly implied
by the words, "may establish your hearts [the hearts of those
on earth] . . . at the coming of our Lord Jesus with all his
saints." When we compare this passage with iv. 14 ("so also
them that are fallen asleep in Jesus will God bring with him")
and with the words of 1 Cor. xv. 23 ("they that are Christ's
at his coming"), and note the order of events as it is given
in 1 Thess. iv. 16f., the natural meaning seems to be that
when the Lord comes from heaven He will be accompanied
by the angels and by the disembodied spirits (the souls) of all
the holy dead. While He is in the air (vs. 17), the bodies of
the holy dead will be raised and these dead will be "clothed
upon" with their resurrected and glorified bodies. Then the
living, "we that are alive that are left," will be "gathered
together" (Matt. xxiv. 31), will be "changed" (1 Cor. xv. 52)
and "caught up" to meet the Lord "in the air," and to come
with Him and all His saints to the earth (Acts i. 11). Whether
this coming to earth will follow the coming into the air
immediately or after an interval of time may be regarded as
uncertain. As to the purpose of this coming, it is to be noted
that according to Millenarians it will be for the setting
up of the millennial kingdom, while anti-Chiliasts hold that it
will be for the Last Judgment and the Consummation.[23]

This interpretation will account, if it is correct, for the
seeming ambiguity of the language used in describing it. It
will be both a *coming for* and a *coming with*: a *coming with*
the saints already in heaven *for* the redemption of their
bodies, a *coming for* the saints then on earth who are to be
changed and caught up; and this *coming with* and *for* the
saints *into the air* will be followed by a *coming with* the saints
to the earth. If these events are all practically contemporaneous, or if the intervals between them, whether short or long,
are of relatively minor importance, the language used in the
New Testament to describe them, the confusing use of such
words as coming and appearing, is sufficiently accounted for.

(*e*) Colossians iii. 4. Darby regarded the words, "When
Christ *who is* our life shall be manifested, then shall ye also

be manifested with him in glory," as proving, when taken in connection with the passages in Thessalonians, that the distinction drawn by Dispensationalists between the rapture and the revelation is a matter of "express revelation."[24] He held it to be axiomatic, apparently, that the saints must first be with Christ (the rapture) before they can be manifested with Him in glory (the appearing). But the most that can be claimed is that if the doctrine is established by other passages, this one can be interpreted in harmony with it. The word "manifested" is a general expression which is used of the first advent and of events connected with it; and all that we are told is that when Christ comes in glory, His people shall share in that glory. They shall be manifested with Him. Nothing is said about a *coming with* which implies a previous *coming for*. On the contrary, if the manifestation of Christ which is referred to is to take place on the earth, all that is stated is that the saints will share in His manifested glory there.

3. *The Day of the Lord and the Day of Christ*

The difficulty of drawing a sharp distinction in time between the "coming for" and the "coming with," is illustrated by the other distinctions which are appealed to in support of it. Dispensationalists assert that "the day of the Lord" refers to the latter of these events, the coming of Christ with His saints to set up His kingdom. Their reasons for this are mainly two: (1) They recognize that this day is to be preceded by events. This is made especially clear by 2 Thess. ii. 2, where "day of the Lord" is a better reading than "day of Christ." But we have seen that in the Old Testament the expression used regarding the day of the Lord is that it is "near," exactly the phrase used in the New Testament of the coming of Christ (*e.g.,* Jas. v. 8). Consequently, it must be recognized that the fact that events are to precede this day (Scofield gives seven signs of its approach)[25] is not at all incompatible with its nearness. (2) It is argued that the day of the Lord is a day of terror and because of this cannot be the blessed hope of the Christian. But this argument completely ignores the fact that for the righteous and the wicked, the

same event may and must have totally different meanings.
This is made especially clear by Mal. iv. 1f., where it is
declared that "the day" shall burn like an oven and all
the wicked shall be as stubble. "But, unto you that fear
my name shall the sun of righteousness arise with healing
in its wings." The day begins with the sunrise. So the
very beginning of this day will bring blessing to God's
saints. There are not two days, but only one.

Scofield has attempted to draw a distinction between the
"day of Christ" and the "day of the Lord," making the one
refer to the rapture, the other to the revelation.[26] But the
words used by Paul to refer to it seem to indicate quite
clearly that no such difference exists. Paul would hardly
put the two words together, "day of our Lord Jesus
(Christ)" as he does in 1 Cor. i. 8, 2 Cor. i. 14 (cf. 1 Cor. v
5), if there were an important difference between the "day
of the Lord" and "the day of Christ" (Phil. i. 10, ii. 16)
or "of Jesus Christ" (Phil. i. 6). Darby apparently drew
no distinction between the two. If there were an important difference, the words "as ye see the day approaching"
(Heb. x. 25) would be dangerously ambiguous. They
clearly suggest that there will be signs of its approach.
Yet the writer does not say "the day of the Lord" or
"the day of Christ" but simply "the day," as if there were
only one day which could be called "the day."[27]

In view of the claim that the day of the Lord is a day of
judgment on the nations and is to be preceded by events or
signs, it is important to remember that according to Scripture,
it is precisely this "day of the Lord" which is declared to be
near or *at hand*. This is stressed in Joel, as we have seen.
Especially significant is Ezek. xxx. 3 which declares emphatically that a day of the Lord is "near" (*qarob*), a day which
shall be "the time of the heathen." In commenting on this
passage,[28] Scofield declares that "the mention of the day of
Jehovah (Ezek. xxx. 3) makes it evident that a fulfilment in
a final sense is still future." Here the very word is used which
is rendered by "at hand" in the New Testament and made
the basis of the any moment doctrine of the rapture. Yet

Scofield finds in it a reference to a day of the Lord upon the heathen, which is still future, which is to be preceded by events, and which is to be sharply distinguished from the any moment rapture. Both are spoken of as at hand. Yet Scofield insists that the one (the rapture) is at hand, while the other (the appearing, or day of the Lord) is not at hand. This is clearly an attempt to draw a distinction which is not drawn in Scripture.

4. The Secret Rapture

In considering the claim of Dispensationalists that the rapture must be regarded as preceding the appearing by a period of years, it is not to be overlooked that this question is further complicated by difference of opinion among them as to the manner of the rapture. All are agreed that the Church saints are to be caught up to meet the Lord in the air. The Lord is not to come directly to the earth. Consequently, many hold that this coming for the saints will not be an earthly event at all. The rapture will be a secret rapture. The fact of its having taken place will be known on earth only through the sudden and unaccountable disappearance of all true Christians. Such a doctrine lends itself readily to very dramatic and even terrifying presentation.[29] A worldly man in New York, or San Francisco, or London awakes one morning to find that his wife, or his daughter, or his son has suddenly disappeared. He makes inquiries and finds that many devout Christians of his acquaintance have disappeared. In other respects his world is just as it was. But the day of opportunity is gone, the reign of Antichrist on earth begins, the great tribulation is coming, and he must pass through it. The doctrine is calculated to startle and terrify the unsaved and the worldly Christian. But the question is, Is it true? The clearest description of the rapture is given in 1 Thess. iv. 16. There we are told, "For the Lord himself shall descend from heaven, with a shout, with the voice of the archangel, and with the trump of God: and the dead in Christ shall rise first." That these mighty

sounds and voices should be unheard by, or utterly mean-
ingless to all except the saints (dead and living) seems
very unlikely.[30] Furthermore, this doctrine seems strangely
inconsistent. It is singular, to say the least, that those
who insist so strongly on a visible coming of Christ before
the millennium, and who are equally insistent that this
visible premillennial coming has two "stages" should be
willing to admit that the first, and for the Church the
more important, of these stages is a secret and invisible
one.[31] There has been much difference of opinion among
Dispensationalists regarding the question of secrecy. Darby
did not commit himself on this point. Brookes accepted it.
Scofield definitely rejected it. It is not an essential part
of the rapture doctrine. Its significance lies rather in the
fact that it illustrates the extremes to which many Dispensationalists are prepared to go to escape, or explain away,
what seems to be the obvious meaning of a passage of
Scripture when a strained or unnatural one is more in
accord with their conception of things to come.[32]

CHAPTER VIII

THE SECOND ADVENT PARENTHESIS AND PRETRIBULATIONISM

IF IT be admitted that the way in which the New Testament writers refer to the rapture and the appearing does not favor the view that there is an important difference between them but rather opposes it, the question naturally arises why Dispensationalists attach so much importance to this alleged difference. The answer is, as we have already seen, a simple one. Dispensationalists are literalists and being literalists they must be Futurists in the interpretation of prophecy. Consequently, they must hold that there are a number of predicted events, many of which interpreters of the Historical School believe to have already taken place, that must occur before the coming of the Lord in glory. On the other hand, they are equally insistent that the rapture may take place "at any moment," that "no known or predicted event must intervene." Put these two together and the conclusion is inevitable that there must be a considerable interval between the rapture and the appearing, during which events that have not occurred before the rapture and are to occur before the appearing will take place.[1] If it can be shown that the events in question must be placed between the rapture and the appearing, it may be regarded as proved that there will be an important interval between them, however difficult it may be to explain the failure of the New Testament writers to describe it definitely. Consequently, we must examine the events which Dispensationalists assign to this parenthesis period.

I. Predicted Events Which Dispensationalists Place Between the Rapture and the Appearing

1. Matthew xxiv.

Few if any chapters in the Bible have occasioned inter-preters of prophecy greater difficulty than this one. Some have applied it entirely to the destruction of Jerusalem by Titus. Many regard it as referring to that event and also to the second advent. Dispensationalists regard it as concerning only the professing church and the future Jewish remnant[2] and as referring especially to events which will follow the rapture, *i.e.,* to the period between the rapture and the appearing. The point which especially concerns us is that this interpretation requires that a peculiar meaning be given to vs. 14. Scofield tells us: "Verse 14 has specific reference to the proclamation of the good news that the kingdom is again 'at hand' by the Jewish remnant."[3] This means that, the preaching of the "gospel of the grace of God" having been terminated by the rapture of the Church, the proclamation of the "gospel of the kingdom," which was "postponed" because of the refusal of the Jews to accept their Messiah at His first advent, is to be resumed by a Jewish remnant which will be on earth after the rapture. This Jewish remnant and their converts of the tribulation period constitute therefore the "elect" who are to be gathered together by the angels. This view is open to objection along several lines.

a. So interpreted this chapter is completely silent about the Church. It says nothing about a coming *for* the Church saints, or about a coming *with* them. It speaks only of a coming of Christ accompanied by His angels and of the gathering to-gether of the Jewish remnant and their converts. If the Church saints come with Christ and the angels, this must be read into the narrative. Only those who regard the "elect" as Christian believers who will be on earth when the Lord comes in glory can find here any express mention of the Church or any allusion to it, or any mention or hint of the rapture of the Church.

b. Since elsewhere in the New Testament (by Paul, Peter, John) the word "elect" is used of Church saints, if the word is used in this chapter of a Jewish remnant of the future, we have here a further difference between Paul and Matt. xxiv. For Paul not merely uses the word "coming" of both the rapture and the appearing; he also uses "elect" of Christian believers (both Jew and Gentile) of the present age.[4]

c. In this chapter Jesus uses the "you" and "ye" of intimate address nearly 20 times. We must hold either that He expected His auditors to be still alive at His coming, or that He was speaking to them in a representative capacity. Similarly in 1 Thess. iv. 15 the "we which are alive and remain" must be either the Christians of Paul's day, or those same Christians as representing the believers who will be on earth at the time of the rapture. The "coming with the saints" did not take place within the lifetime of those who heard the discourse of Matt. xxiv.; and the "coming for the saints" did not take place during the lifetime of the Thessalonian Christians who received Paul's letter. Both groups have been dead for centuries. Consequently, we must regard them as representative of those who will be alive when the events referred to will transpire. The question, then, which must be answered is this. Who did these two groups respectively represent? As regards the Thessalonian Christians the answer is simple. They were Christians; and Paul addressed them as representative of all the Christians who will be living on earth at the rapture. As to Matt. xxiv. Dispensationalists hold the answer to be equally simple. Jesus' auditors were godly Jews. So they must be regarded as representative of the godly Jewish remnant of the future. But the problem is not so simple as this. For these believing Jews included all the apostles and disciples who had believed on Jesus during His earthly ministry and were faithful to Him; and they were to be in a few days, or rather weeks, the founders and first members of the Christian Church, that institution which Jesus had called "my church." Is it conceivable then that these men who were to devote their lives to the preaching of the gospel of the grace of God, the gospel for the Church age, are here addressed as the representatives of a future Jewish remnant which will come into being after the Church age is ended and preach the gospel of the kingdom? Such an inference seems absurd.

Surely we can only determine whom and what these men represented by taking into account the position which they were to occupy and the task which they were to perform during the remainder of their life on earth. If we do this, we will see in them the founders and first members of the Christian Church.

  d. An especially impressive feature of this prophecy is the startling way in which it stresses the *suddenness* of the coming of Christ. It is to be preceded by events. Christians are expected to know when it is "near," when it is "even at the doors." But the day and the hour is unknown. It is to come like lightning, like the flood for which men were utterly unprepared. It will make an instant separation between the "elect" and the rest of humanity.[5] The fact that two persons are in the same place and doing exactly the same thing will not prevent this sudden and final separation: "one shall be taken the other left."[6] There is no passage in the New Testament which speaks more vividly of the suddenness of the advent or of the unreadiness of the world to receive her King. It would seem as if this should be a passage to which above almost all others Dispensationalists would appeal to support their doctrine of an "any moment" rapture, even of a secret rapture. But the description of preceding events makes it quite impossible for them to do this. We have here a striking proof of the fact that the coming of Christ can be and will be both sudden and unexpected and at the same time preceded by known, because predicted, events.

2. 2 Thessalonians ii. 1-10

The futurist emphasis of Dispensationalists appears nowhere more clearly than in their interpretation of this passage. Here Paul tells his recent converts at Thessalonica that the "day of the Lord" (not, "day of Christ," as in AV) will be preceded by certain events, notably the falling away, the revelation of the man of sin, the removal of the one that restraineth, the revelation of the wicked one whom the Lord will destroy with the brightness *(epiphany)* of His coming *(parousia)*. To the same effect but less specifically 1 Tim. iv. 1-3 speaks of the coming apostasy. That these events are almost wholly future (vs. 7) from the viewpoint of the writer and that they are referred to as proving the day of the Lord to be still future—whether that future be remote or near at hand—so much is quite clear. The day of the Lord cannot be "at hand" in the sense of proximate or "now present,"[7] if these events must precede it. They are still future; and the day of the Lord lies beyond them. Such being the case, the only question at issue is as to when these events are to occur. The two interpretations which demand our attention are the Historical and the Dispensational or Futurist. The essential difference between them is that, according to the one, this apostasy is to reach its climax during the Church age, whether that climax be regarded as lying in the past, the present, or as still future, while, according to the other view, this climax will not take place until after the Church has been raptured. Advocates of the Historical view have often identified the Antichrist with the Pope as "Vicar of Christ." Advocates of the Futurist interpretation insist that the manifestation of Antichrist will not take place during the Church age, that it will follow the rapture. Consequently, those of them who comparatively recently rather confidently referred to Mussolini as a likely candidate for this awful role, were careful to insist that he could not be definitely affirmed to be the Antichrist because the rapture had not yet taken place, but that he might speedily be manifested as such, since the rapture must be near at hand and might take place at any moment.

That there are difficulties connected with the Historical interpretation is of course to be admitted.[8] But to solve them by treating the whole as still future and as belonging to an age quite distinct from the Church age is a very radical step. It may seem to be a simple and easy way of solving the problem, for then there are no facts of history to reckon with. But this does not establish its correctness. The reason Dispensationalists must insist on the futuristic interpretation of this passage is simply that their any moment theory of the rapture requires it; and their desire to escape the great tribulation which is to follow very speedily makes it necessary.

It seems quite probable that the immature converts at Thessalonica were troubled by the thought that the persecutions they were suffering were but the precursors of the day of the Lord which they very likely envisaged as a time of suffering and terror (Joel ii. 2, Amos v. 18).[9] Consequently, if they were in terror of the impending tribulation, we might expect that Paul would have reassured them by distinguishing very carefully between the rapture and the day of the Lord, if he really made this distinction, and would have told them that the day of the Lord did not concern them at all, because they might be raptured at any moment and would certainly be raptured before that day and the great tribulation which it would bring with it. But Paul says not a word about the any moment rapture. What he does say is, that the day (drawing no distinction between rapture and revelation) has not yet come, that it is not proximate, but that ominous events are to precede it. Yet surely, if these disciples were afraid the rapture had already taken place and they were left behind, because the day of the Lord which was to follow it had already begun, here was the place of all places to assure them that the rapture could not have taken place because *all* believers would be raptured together (which had not happened to them or to Paul himself), and because the rapture must occur before the day of the Lord. Certainly, if Paul held the any moment rapture doctrine, it is passing strange that he did not expound it here.

3. *Revelation iv.-xix*

According to the Historical method of interpreting the Book of Revelation, the events described in these chapters have already been fulfilled to a very considerable extent. In *The Signs of the Times* (1845) Edward Bickersteth referred to what he called the singular unanimity of interpreters in holding that the sixth trumpet (ix. 13f.) referred to the Turks; and he named over a hundred who advocated this view. Historicists differ much as to details, the Continuists being more, the Synchronists being less insistent on precise dates and events. But according to Dispensationalists, this entire series of chapters is not only wholly future but concerns the period between the rapture and the appearing, having reference especially to the second half of the 70th week of Dan. ix., which they place between these two important stages of the coming. Here then, if anywhere it would seem, we might expect to find the rapture and the appearing carefully described and clearly distinguished.

a. The Rapture is not described in Revelation iv

If, as Dispensationalists tell us, chaps. ii.-iii. of this book describe the Church on earth and with the beginning of chap. iv. the entire Church[10] is in heaven, it is certainly remarkable that no mention at all is made of that unique event, the rapture of the Church, through which this wonderful change will have been brought about. It must be assumed to have taken place. What proof is there of the correctness of this assumption?

(1) The words, "Behold I come quickly" (iii. 11), are thought to imply that the rapture is near at hand. But we find similar statements in chap. i. (vss. 1, 3), which precedes and introduces chaps. ii. and iii. Furthermore, these words are addressed to the church of Philadelphia, not to that of Laodicea which follows it.

(2) The words, "I will spew thee out of my mouth" (iii. 16), are regarded as proving that the judgment of the professing church must be at hand; and this must, according to Dispensationalists, follow the rapture of the true Church.

(3) With iv. 1 the scene shifts, it is claimed, to heaven; and the fact that the Church is not mentioned by name in chaps. iv.-xix. or referred to as being on earth is adduced as proof that the rapture is to be assumed to have taken place. According to Scofield, the call "Come up hither" (iv. 1) "seems clearly to indicate the fulfilment of 1 Thess. iv. 14-17."[11] And it is assumed that, if the Church has been raptured, it is of course

in heaven. Yet the statement is not that the saints meet the Lord in heaven but "in the air." Scofield goes on to say: "The word 'church' does not again occur in the Revelation till all is fulfilled." This seems intended to imply that since the Church was on earth in chaps. ii.-iii. and is not mentioned as being still on earth in chaps. iv.-xix., it may safely be assumed that it is in heaven. But the more natural inference would seem to be that since the Church is clearly on earth prior to chap. iv. and is not expressly referred to as being in heaven during the events of chaps. iv.-xix. it is to be assumed that it (the Church Militant) is still on earth during these events.

What proof is there that the Church is in heaven? Since the word "church" is not used in chaps. iv.-xix., in what way is it referred to? With which of the several groups mentioned in these chapters is it to be identified? We find mention of 4 living creatures,[12] 24 elders, 144,000 sealed ones out of the 12 tribes (of Israel), individual angels of whom the greatest number mentioned is 7, and of a woman and her son (xii. 1-5). We also find references to saints (holy ones), servants of God, angels (as very numerous, v. 11; called "holy angels," xiv. 10), an innumerable multitude (vii. 9, cf. xix. 1, 6), the armies of heaven (xix. 14), the souls of the martyrs (vi. 9, xx. 4). With which of these is the Church to be identified? or, by which is it represented? Scofield does not tell us expressly in his comments on Revelation in the *Reference Bible*. But elsewhere he has asserted positively that the 24 elders are or represent the raptured Church.[13] This was the view of Darby and the Brethren. But it is open to serious objection:

(1) It is a view which is quite inconsistent with the Brethren position. They hold that "eldership" is Jewish, that the "successive authority" which it represents was characteristic of the professing (Petrine) church, but inconsistent with that expectancy of any moment rapture which is distinctive of the Pauline mystery Church. Furthermore, if the word "elder" is Jewish, the number "24" is also Jewish. Darby and Scofield

connect it with the 24 courses of the priests as established by
David. This would mean that the mystery Church which is
held to be quite distinct from the Old Testament Church
is designated in Rev. iv.-xix. by a figure which is distinctly
Jewish. Scofield seeks to justify this interpretation by pointing
out that the Church is called a priesthood in Rev. i. 6. He
appeals also to 1 Pet. ii. 5-9. But this passage is clearly based
on Ex. xix. 6 which makes no reference to the Levitical priesthood, which was instituted by Moses and further organized
by David, but refers to Israel the nation as a kingdom of
priests, *i.e.*, as a people to be set apart for the service of God.
If this prediction is taken literally, it refers to Israel. If it is
regarded as applying to and fulfilled in the Church, we have
an example of an Old Testament prophecy regarding Israel
fulfilled in the New Testament Church. How Dispensationalists can with any show of consistency find the raptured
Church in the 24 elders it is certainly very difficult to see.

(2) A second objection to the identifying of the 24 elders
with the Church, as a body distinct from the other groups
referred to in these chapters, is that little or nothing is said
about them which is distinctive of the Church. Unless the
AV rendering of v. 9f. ("redeemed us . . . made us") is retained in preference to the better and more generally accepted
rendering of RV ("didst purchase . . . madest them"), we
cannot even be sure that the elders represent *redeemed* persons. They praise God and the Lamb for the work of redemption. But they do not clearly represent themselves as of the
number of the redeemed. This is especially noteworthy when
we read what one of these elders has to say about the "multitude" described in chap. vii.: "they have washed their robes
and made them white in the blood of the Lamb."[14]

(3) The fact that the number 24 is mentioned so often (5 or
6 times) seems to suggest that the number itself is significant.
Unless this is to be regarded as solely due to the desire to
connect them with the 24 courses of Levitical priests, which
stresses the connection of the New Testament Church with
the Old Testament church—a fact which Dispensationalists
are at pains to ignore—the number 24 contrasts so markedly
with the 144,000 and the multitude that no man could number of chap. vii., as to suggest that the Church will form a
very small proportion of the redeemed. They may be an elite

body (the elders were men of distinction in Israel); but they will be relatively few in number. This implication is a serious one. If, on the other hand, the view is taken that the "multitude" of chap. vii. are Church saints (either martyr saints or all the redeemed) which is the view of those who do not hold the rapture doctrine of Darby and Scofield, the 24 elders can be regarded as simply representing the redeemed of all ages; and the number 24 is then most naturally to be taken as standing for the 12 tribal patriarchs of Israel and the 12 apostles of the Lamb.[15]

(4) Since it is not stated that the 24 elders ever were on earth or how they have come to be in heaven, the attempt to find in them the raptured Church is one of the clearest indications that the attempt to find any evidence of the rapture of the Church in these chapters is a difficult if not impossible one.

(5) How hard pressed Dispensationalists are in their effort to prove that the Church is in heaven during the events of this period is illustrated very strikingly by Darby's treatment of chap. xii. According to both Darby and Scofield, the woman who is with child is Israel, the child is Christ.[16] Vs. 5 tells us that this child "was caught up unto God and unto his throne." Darby's comment is, "But the child, Christ, and the assembly [the Church] with Christ, is caught away to God and to His throne." In saying this Darby reads into this passage something which is not there, but which must be assumed to be implied, if his interpretation of this group of chapters is correct. A more flagrant example of biased interpretation, it would be difficult to find!

We conclude, therefore, that chapter iv. is completely silent regarding the rapture of the Church, that there is no conclusive proof that the 24 elders symbolize the Church, but that if they do, it is as representatives, not of a mystery parenthesis church, but of the Church of all the ages, Old Testament and New Testament alike, a church which may be regarded as still on earth, while ideally, representatively, and in large measure actually in heaven, in the heavenlies, in the presence of Christ and of God.

b. The Appearing according to Revelation xix

All Premillennialists are agreed that vss. 11-16 of this chapter describe the coming forth of Christ to conquer His enemies and to set up His millennial kingdom. Those who do not accept the view that a millennium, in the sense of a visible reign of Christ on the earth, is described in chap. xx. find here a symbolical description of the triumph of the cause of Christ through the proclamation of the gospel; and they find support for this explanation in the fact that the Rider on the white horse is called the "Word of God" and that the sharp two-edged sword proceeds out of His mouth, which suggests that the battle in which He is engaged, despite the martial and even gory imagery, is to be fought in the realm of moral and spiritual ideas and not with carnal weapons. What especially concerns us in this connection is the question, Who accompany this warrior on his victorious way? The answer is of course, the armies of heaven. But who are meant by this? Dispensationalists find here a description of the coming of the Lord with the saints; and think first of all of the raptured Church. Is there any express warrant for this conclusion?

(1) "Armies of heaven" most naturally suggest a host of heavenly beings, especially the angels. "Armies" is used again in this chapter of the army of the Rider and of that of His enemies (vs. 19). Elsewhere in Revelation it is used of the locust plague (ix. 16). A passage in Matthew naturally suggests itself (xxii. 7). If this prophecy was fulfilled in the destruction of Jerusalem, the armies would be the Roman legions of Titus as used by God for purposes of vengeance, or the unseen spiritual forces which made them invincible. In Lk. ii. 13 the angels who sang their alleluias at Bethlehem are called "the multitude of the heavenly host [army of heaven]." In the Old Testament, the title "Jehovah of hosts" is of frequent occurrence from the time of the Judges onward. It is a comprehensive expression which may be used of Jehovah in His relation to the whole of the creation, to heavenly beings or objects, and to His earthly people. The expression "host of heaven" is also an Old Testament expression, though

of much less frequent occurrence. It is sufficiently comprehensive to include any or all of the inhabitants of the heavenly world. That the angels are or form a part of the armies of heaven referred to in xix. 14 is made clear by the following considerations:

(a) Angels are frequently mentioned in this book. In v. 11 they are described as exceedingly numerous. They would constitute an army or armies.

(b) One of their duties is to engage in warfare, to execute vengeance (xii. 7). This task is specifically assigned to them in Matt. xiii. 41; and Matt. xxiv. 31 speaks of the sending forth of the angels to gather together the elect. No mention is made there of any others as coming with them.

(c) These armies ride on white horses and are clothed in fine linen white and clean. White is the symbol of purity and holiness. The raiment of the angels at the tomb was white (Matt. xxviii. 3, Mk. xvi. 5, Jn. xx. 12, cf. Acts i. 10); and according to Matt. xvii. 2, Mk. ix. 3, Lk. ix. 29 the vesture of the transfigured Christ became white and shining. Such passages show clearly that the white raiment mentioned here may represent the inherent righteousness of Christ and of the holy angels.[17] But it would be equally appropriate as a description of the imputed righteousness of the redeemed in heaven.

(2) Do or may the words "armies of heaven" include others besides the angels? We have already seen that various groups are referred to in Revelation. Chap. xix. begins with adoration, the great voice of a great multitude in heaven (the words used are the same as in vii. 9) celebrating the destruction of Babylon. The 24 elders and the 4 living creatures join in this adoration. Then a voice is heard from the throne calling on all God's servants to praise Him. And this is followed by the voice of the multitude again raised in adoration, and for the special reason that "the marriage of the Lamb is come and his wife hath made herself ready" (vs. 7). This is the first mention of the wife (*gunē*) unless the view is taken that she is already referred to in chap. xii. It seems rather singular that the word *wife* is used here rather than *bride,* despite the fact that the marriage is spoken of as about to be celebrated.[18] The fact that she is here referred to as the *wife* and in xxi. 9 described as "the bride the Lamb's wife," would make it easy to conclude that the reason "wife" is used here is to suggest

to the reader that the bride of the Lamb is the wife of Jehovah; *i.e.*, that the Old Testament Church and the New Testament Church are essentially one and the same.[19] But what concerns us especially is the question, Where is the bride? There is not the slightest intimation that the wife or bride is to be identified with the 24 elders. Were such the case the transition would be quite abrupt; and the statement that it was granted to her to be arrayed in fine linen, clean and white, would be superfluous. For the 24 elders are already described as so appareled. Furthermore, is it at all clear that the bride is to be found among the armies of heaven? Would it not be more natural to suppose that the Rider is going forth to conquer the earth and that his bride is on the earth and is awaiting him there? Certainly the fact that the destruction of Babylon has just been described and celebrated in song might seem to favor this. Babylon is on the earth; and the Church may be there also. If we may compare chap. xii., we observe the remarkable fact that while the sign or wonder is in heaven (vss. 1 and 2) the woman is clearly on the earth. It is definitely stated that the earth helped her (vs. 16); and she escapes to the "wilderness" (vss. 6, 14), a word which would hardly be used of heaven or any part of it. It is used elsewhere in Revelation only in xvii. 3 as the place whither the seer is taken that he may view the great harlot. If the destruction of Babylon which is foretold in xiv. 8 and described in xvii.- xviii. does not actually take place until after xix. 11f., it may well be that the marriage of the Lamb which is referred to in xix. 7 is not to take place until after the triumph described in the latter part of the chapter. If the bride is on earth, she cannot be included in the armies of heaven that issue forth with the Rider. Dispensationalists and their opponents are of course agreed that the Church cannot be said to be wholly on earth. According to most interpreters the Church Triumphant is in heaven, the Church Militant is still on earth; there has been no rapture of the Church Militant. According to Dispensationalists the entire Church, *i.e.*, the mystery Church of Paul, is in heaven. On the one view, the Church cannot be said, except ideally or representatively, to be in heaven; nor is it on earth: it is in both places. According to the other, the entire Church is in heaven. Consequently, according to the older view as held by Premillenarians, we have here a coming of Christ both with and also for the saints: with the saints who are in heaven for the saints who are on earth. According to Dispensationalists, it must be a coming with the saints, or the Church would be left behind, since the entire Church is already in heaven.

In dealing with such high mysteries, especially where the language of Scripture is not explicit, it behooves us to be cautious and to refrain from unwarranted dogmatism. But certainly there is good warrant for the view that if, as all Millenarians believe, Rev. xix. 11f. describes a visible Premillennial coming of Christ, this passage should be interpreted by and in connection with 1 Thess. iv. 15f.[20] This would mean that the rapture is not to be *assumed* to have taken place before the beginning of chap. iv., but is to be connected with the appearing described in chap. xix., and therefore that the Church is to be regarded as still on earth up to that time. According to the A- and Postmillennial views the connection of 1 Thess. iv. 15f. will not be with Rev. xix. 11f. but with xx. 11f. From the standpoint of Dispensationalists the greatest objections to the connecting of 1 Thess. iv. 15f. with Rev. xix. 11f. are that the rapture must then be regarded as preceded by events, and especially that it will not then precede but follow the great tribulation. The first of these objections has been already sufficiently discussed. The other will be considered presently.

c. The Church is on Earth during Rev. iv.-xix. 10

This is the natural inference if the rapture described in 1 Thess. iv. does not take place until Rev. xix. 11f. It is not merely an inference, even though a very cogent one. It finds definite support in these chapters themselves, in statements that are made regarding the saints who are on earth. That these saints are Christian believers is undeniable. The great harlot is described as "drunken with the blood of the saints, and with the blood of the martyrs of Jesus" (xvii. 6). It is quite natural and proper to regard these martyrs as Church saints. The description fits them perfectly. The same is true of xii. 17, xiii. 7, 8, 10, 15, xiv. 13. Even the 144,000 who are "sealed out of every tribe of the children of Israel" are proved by xiv. 1-5 to be Christian believers (whether as representing the Church Universal or only part of it, Jewish believers, does not concern us). If these saints are not Church saints, it can only be because the Church is no longer on earth. But this is the very assumption which Dispensationalists must first prove to be correct, before they can assert with any degree of plausibility that these saints are Jewish remnant and tribulation saints who are to be sharply distinguished from Church saints.

II. Pretribulationism

We have purposely reserved the consideration of Rev. iv.-xix. to the end of our discussion of the alleged interval between the rapture and the appearing because it brings us directly to one of the most important matters connected with the whole subject of Dispensationalism. This is Pretribulationism. Since the Brethren were ardent literalists and futurists and equally ardent believers in the any moment doctrine of the coming, it was inevitable that the question whether the Church will pass through the great tribulation (Rev. vii. 14) would early be raised. The question was this, "Were they to warn their disciples of an impending trial, far more terrible than the worst that the blood-stained annals of the Church record, or were they to comfort them with the assurance of total immunity from it?"[21] Darby and his followers answered the question as follows: "Let us remember one thing; it is, that we Christians are sheltered from the approaching storm."[22] This means two things: the Church *may* be raptured at any moment; it *will* and *must* be raptured before the great tribulation. Consequently, Dispensationalists are double Pre's: they are *Pre*tribulation-*Pre*millennialists. And the vigorous controversy which they have waged against all Premillenarians who are Posttribulationists shows the immense importance which they attach to this distinction.

1. Pretribulationism Appeals to Unworthy Motives

a. Before examining the evidence brought forward in support of this doctrine, it may be well to notice how singularly calculated it is to appeal to those selfish and unworthy impulses from which no Christian is wholly immune. We have seen that Jesus said to His disciples: "In the world ye shall have tribulation" (Jn. xvi. 33). Paul speaks of the afflictions which the Christians are to suffer before the coming of Christ (2 Thess. i. 4f.). Peter speaks of the "fiery trial" (1 Pet. iv. 12). John speaks of the "tribulation" which he shares with other Christians (Rev. i. 9) and of the "tribulation" of the church of Smyrna (Rev. ii. 9, 10). Yet the Dispensationalists assure us that the Church will certainly be raptured before the "great" tribulation which is still to come. Consequently, Christians who hold this doctrine are encouraged to view the present evil state of the world with a composure which savors not a little of complacency. For if the present gloomy world situation means that the great tribulation is near at hand, it means, according to their doctrine, that the rapture is still nearer, a rapture which will snatch them away from the far worse evils which are speedily to come upon the earth. Hence, they are in a position to say, and many do say in effect, even if not in so many words: "The world situation is getting worse and worse. This is a sign that the revelation of the man of sin is near, and that the great tribulation cannot be far distant. But this does not concern us. We can even rejoice in it, because it proves that the rapture must be very near indeed. The great tribulation will come very soon. But we won't be here, when it comes." This doctrine may, it is true, stimulate some earnest Christians to redoubled efforts to save lost souls from the wrath to come. But there is a danger lest this wrath be pictured, not as that eternal punishment in hell which awaits the wicked, but as the great tribulation on the earth which is at hand: "Repent now, be saved now; and escape by rapture from the great tribulation." In so far as the "any moment" doctrine of the coming owes its popularity to a desire to escape the evils which are to come upon all the earth, it is by no means a commendable doctrine. It makes its appeal to the human frailty of the Christian, instead of challenging him to face the worst of earth's ills courageously, because strengthened by the assurance that Christ has overcome the world and will enable His people to overcome, and to face them sympathetically because he knows that he may himself be called upon to suffer these very afflictions.

b. The Biblical Basis of Pretribulationism

We may dismiss at once two arguments which are advanced in support of the view that the Church will not pass through the tribulation. The one is, that the coming of Christ could not be the blessed hope and joyous expectation of the Church, if it must be preceded by the great tribulation. This argument is almost an insult to the true Christian who loves his Lord. The other is that the great tribulation is for the punishment of the wicked, and that the Christian has nothing to do with punishment. As to this, it is to be remembered that throughout the whole age-long history of the Church on earth the good have suffered again and again with and at the hands of the wicked. For them it has not been punishment but chastening. Yet this chastening has caused many of them to "climb the steep ascent of heaven through peril, toil and pain." When the world is suffering, it sees to it that the Church suffers with it. And the more zealous the Church is in proclaiming the gospel, the more certain is she to suffer persecution at the hands of those who will not accept it. There is nothing said about the great tribulation which indicates that the Christian, who through much tribulation is to enter the kingdom of God, will be exempt from it.

(1) Darby's Four Proof-texts

According to Darby there are four passages (Jer. xxx. 7,
Dan. xii. 1, Matt. xxiv. 21 and Mk. xiii. 19) which speak of
the "unequalled tribulation"; and he declares that they "apply
it distinctively to Jacob, Jerusalem, and Judea and the Jews."
And he adds, "It is entirely another order and sphere of things
from the church and profoundly so."[23] This means that Jews,
Gentiles and the professing church (Christendom), will pass
through this tribulation, but the Church will be exempt
from it.

(a) Jeremiah xxx. 7 speaks of a day which is called "the
time of Jacob's trouble." It is described as "great," so that
there is "none like it." It is difficult to see in this verse any
definite reference to the great tribulation. "Great" may be
used in the sense of "long" (great in length); and this is favored
by the word "time" which follows. This prophecy was probably uttered before the destruction of Jerusalem by Nebuchadnezzar. There is no reason for believing that it refers exclusively to a brief period of three and a half years which
are still wholly future. The time of Jacob's trouble, or affliction, if reckoned, as it may well be, from that destruction of
Jerusalem which took place in Jeremiah's day, has been
incomparably long; it still continues; and the end is not yet.
The times of the Gentiles have been, and will continue to be
until their close, a time of trouble for Jacob.[24]

(b) Daniel xii. 1 speaks of a "time of trouble such as never
was since there was a nation even to that time," at which time
"thy people shall be delivered." It has been variously interpreted. The "wilful king" (xi. 36) has been regarded as
Antiochus Epiphanes, as Herod the Great, as the Pope or
Papacy. If it be admitted that this king is the Antichrist,
that the time is wholly future and is to be identified with
the period variously described as 1260 days, 42 months, a time,
times and a half a time, it would be possible to refer it to
a future great tribulation. What here concerns us is the phrase
"thy people." From the Old Testament standpoint this passage like Jeremiah's might be regarded as referring exclusively
to Israel. But we have seen that the New Testament gives a
larger meaning and scope to Old Testament prophecies which
seem to be restricted to Israel; and the reference to the resur-

rection in vs. 2 has been regarded by many scholars as justifying or demanding a much broader application.

(c) Matthew xxiv. 21f. Darby naturally uses this passage as
a proof-text for Pretribulationism because according to his
interpretation of it the Church cannot be referred to here,
but having been already raptured will not be on earth when
the tribulation which it describes takes place. But if the objections to this interpretation that have been already stated
are valid, if the "elect" are the Church saints who are still on
earth, this passage is one of the clearest proofs that Church
saints will pass through the tribulation. It is expressly for
their sakes that it will be *shortened* (vs. 22). If Christians,
Church saints, are not referred to here, if the precious word
"elect," which is used everywhere else of Christian believers,
does not here apply to them, then it is safe to say that the
Church is not and cannot be referred to anywhere else in
Matthew; not in xvi. 16—here Bullinger is far more consistent
than Darby and Scofield; and not in xxviii. 19. If the "ye" of
chap. xxiv. does not refer to Christian disciples, the "ye" of the
Great Commission cannot be addressed to them. The Dispensational interpretation may and does insure the Christian
against the terrible and terrifying prospect of passing through
the great tribulation. But it obliges him to pay a tremendous
price for such immunity from suffering. Christians who fully
appreciate that cost will certainly regard it as greater than
they are willing to pay.

(d) Mark xiii. 19f. is the last of the four principal passages
referred to by Darby as proving a pretribulation rapture. It
does not need separate consideration. If Matt. xxiv. is regarded
as "Jewish" and interpreted of a Jewish remnant, then in this
passage also the disciples addressed must represent, and the
elect must constitute, a Jewish remnant quite distinct from
the Christian Church.

(2) Darby's More General Passages

In addition to the four passages just considered, Darby
referred to two passages in Revelation (iii. 10, vii. 14) as
"more general passages." That he did not regard them as
primary witnesses is not to be wondered at. The Book of
Revelation is a hard book to interpret; and we do not
hesitate to affirm that the Dispensationalists have not been

very successful in solving its difficulties. This statement
will startle some of our readers. For the interpretation of
this book advocated by most Dispensationalists seems at
first glance to be a very simple one. The key is found, they
tell us, in i. 19: "The things thou sawest" are the vision
of the glorified Christ (chap. i); "the things that are,"
are contained in the letters to the seven churches (chaps.
ii.-iii.); "the things which shall come to pass hereafter,"
are found in the rest of the Book, of which chaps. iv.-xix.
cover the period between the rapture and the appearing,
and chaps. xx.-xxii. the millennium, the little season, and
the final consummation. This is a simple analysis, but
when we examine it we find that it is complicated, arbitrary, and inconsistent. This is shown by the two passages
now to be examined.

(1) Rev. iii. 10. This verse refers to an "hour of trial," which
is to take place in the time of the church of Philadelphia.
Since Philadelphia was an important city of the Roman
province of Asia in the lifetime of the apostle John, we would
expect the Dispensationalists, as literalists, to interpret this
promise as made to this ancient church; and they do this. But
most of these seven churches passed out of existence centuries
ago, which would indicate that the trial of this particular
church must lie in the past. So they add to the literal meaning
a figurative or allegorical one. Scofield, for example, finds four
different meanings of the epistles to these churches. According to the last of the four, these messages "present an exact
foreview of the *spiritual* history of the church, and in this
precise order."[25] *E.g.*, Thyatira represents the Papacy of the
Middle Ages. This is not only a flagrant violation of the principle of literal interpretation, but it involves its advocates in
serious difficulties. There are according to Scofield *seven* ages
represented in "precise order." If the tribulation is referred to
at all, it should be in the seventh. But Philadelphia is only
the sixth. Consequently, if iii. 10 refers to the tribulation,
Philadelphia and Laodicea must be at least in part contemporaneous. In other words, the Philadelphia period must over-
lap the whole of Laodicea. Scofield makes it do this. Some
advocates of this interpretation go so far as to assert that

the last four of the seven church ages all run parallel with one another.[26] This is practically the *reductio ad absurdum* of the theory of a "precise order." But unless the "great tribulation" into which the Jezebel which persecutes the church of Thyatira is cast (ii. 22) is a different tribulation from that described in iii. 10 and in Mt. xxiv. 21, this conclusion is inevitable.

But there is an even more serious difficulty connected with this interpretation. According to Dispensational teaching, "at hand" means that the Lord may come "at any moment," and therefore that there are no known or predicted events which must precede it. If then the epistles in Rev. ii.-iii. were written in the apostolic age and "present an exact foreview of the spiritual history of the church," how can it be asserted that there are no predicted events, and that the rapture is "without a sign, without a time note, and unrelated to other prophetic events"?[27] Scofield tells us, "It is incredible that in a prophecy covering the church period there should be no such foreview."[28] But Scofield's own words regarding the rapture make it incredible that there should be. If the Church has nothing to do with events, how can the events of its history be given?

There are apparently only two possible answers to this very natural and proper question; and both have been given by leading Dispensationalists. On the one hand, it is alleged that it is only now, when the end of the Church age is supposed to have been all but reached, that the full meaning of these prophecies is being made clear. It is admitted that the conspicuous events or distinguishing features of what is now a period of nearly two thousand years of Church history are set forth in these chapters. The prophetic program is there. But it is only now, when this long period is assumed to be almost ended, that this prophetic program is intelligible. The difficulty with this explanation is that it is quite irreconcilable with the claim of Dispensationalists that the meaning of prophecy is simple and clear, should be readily understood by the spiritually discerning, does not need the light of history to interpret it, and supplies the necessary data for the preparation of elaborate and detailed prophetic charts. Either this passage must be regarded as an important exception to this principle, or the principle itself must be greatly modified, if this explanation is to be accepted as valid.

The other explanation is, that these chapters do not give the prophetic history of the true Church, but of the professing church which is to remain on earth after the rapture. This explanation also is faced with serious difficulties: *(a)* Granted that these seven churches are professing churches, it is the true believers in them who constitute the true Church, the overcomers, those that have ears to hear, who are addressed in them. Consequently, the true Church, at least in part, must be on earth during this entire period. Otherwise the promise in iii. 10 could have no bearing on the question of a pretribulation rapture of the Church. *(b)* The only argument that can be appealed to as proof that the rapture, as an "any moment" event, is any more likely now to occur in the *near* future, than it was likely to occur a century ago in the then *near* future when this doctrine first became popular, must be found in the claim that the Laodicean period of the professing church is nearly ended. Scofield speaks of the present gospel age as the period "during which the two great divine secrets—the out-calling of the church and the mysteries of the kingdom of heaven [the professing church], run their course. Both seem well-nigh completed. If this is true, the seventieth week of Daniel is upon the very horizon."[29] What does this mean if not that the earthly existence of the true Church runs parallel with the *history* of the professing church, and that the rapture of the true Church will come at the close of the Laodicean period of the professing church? If so, the conclusion is in-escapable that the predicted events in the history of the professing church must be signs of the approach of the rapture of the true Church. If so, the rapture of the true Church cannot be "sign-less."

It is not to be overlooked that while Pretribulationists are quite positive that the Church will not pass through the great tribulation, they are no less positive that the Jews will do so. This involves a somewhat arbitrary interpretation of the word "from" as it is used in the relevant passages. Jer. xxx. 7 de-clares, "but he shall be saved out of it" (literally, "from it"). Dan. xii. 1 says only, "thy people shall be delivered." In Rev. iii. 10 we read, "I also will keep thee from *(ek)* the hour of trial." In chap. vii. 14 we are told of those "who have come out of *(ek)* the great tribulation." Matt. xxiv. 22 by speaking of the shortening of the days of the tribulation clearly implies that the elect will pass through it. John xvii. 15 illustrates the ambiguity of the preposition "from" *(ek)*: "I pray not that thou shouldest take them from *(ek* in the sense of 'out of,' 'away from') the world, but that thou shouldest keep them from *(ek)* the evil." The purpose of the sealing of the servants of God before the pouring out of the plagues (vii. 3), favors the view that they are to pass unscathed through them. Why should not the same apply to Rev. iii. 10? It seems rather inconsistent to insist that "from" in Jer. xxx. 7 must mean that Israel will pass through the tribulation, but that "from" in Rev. iii. 10 must mean that the church of Philadelphia, and by implication the entire Church then on earth, will not pass through it but be delivered from it by rapture.

(2) Rev. vii. 14. While Darby regarded this passage as of secondary importance as a proof of the pretribulation doctrine, it is worthy of careful consideration. Chapter vii. is divided into two scenes, the first of which is on earth (vss. 1-8), the second in heaven (vss. 9-17). The former describes the sealing of the 144,000 "out of every tribe of the children of Israel," before the hurting of the earth. That this total is not to be taken literally is indicated by the fact that 12,000 are sealed from each tribe, which is quite out of accord with the history of the tribes as set forth in Biblical history, and from the further fact that the tribe of Dan is not included. The reason for this we do not know.[30] Suffice it to say that we are told expressly that these sealed ones represent "every tribe of the children of Israel."

That the second scene is in heaven seems clear because the multitude of which it speaks are "standing before the throne and before the Lamb." This throne is the one described in chap. iv.; and it is surrounded by the angels, the living creatures, and the elders. That the multitude is standing on earth before the heavenly throne would be a very arbitrary view. Hardly less arbitrary would it be to hold that the throne has been transferred to earth. Two things are told us about this multitude. The first is that it is so "great" that "no man could number" it, and that it is taken "out of every nation and of *all* tribes and peoples and tongues."[31] This is one of the most emphatic statements of the comprehensive, world-wide mission of the Christian Church to be found anywhere in Scripture. In the second place, it is stated that they are "arrayed in white robes" and, we are told more specifically, that "they washed their robes and made them white in the blood of the Lamb." This also is a sweeping and comprehensive statement, which is applicable to all the redeemed of every age and race. But it is said also that they "come out of the great tribulation." Dispensationalists tell us that this great tribulation is a wholly future period, a brief period of only three and a half years but one of intense trial. But we have already seen that the New Testament represents tribulation as the lot of all true Christians. Since it is quite clear that the word rendered "great" can be understood extensively as well as intensively, it is quite as arbitrary to insist that it must have reference to a period which is almost negligible in extent and which is entirely future, when we think of the terrible and extended persecutions which the Church has already passed through, as it is to insist that this must be the meaning of Jer. xxx. 7. If it is to be the lot of Christians generally that through "many tribulations" they are to enter into the kingdom, it is quite appropriate to refer to this entire period as "the great tribulation." And such an interpretation is favored by the language used to describe those who shall have passed through it. To restrict language which is perfectly applicable to believers, at least to many believers, of all ages, to a special group living in a restricted period is arbitrary. To say that the redeemed (or at least the martyrs) of nearly two millenniums, the Church saints, are not included among them seems so improbable that it would require to justify it far more conclusive evidence than any which Pretribulationists have been able to produce. The vision seems clearly to describe the heavenly felicity of all the redeemed of every age and of every race.

Since Rev. vii. gives us such a glorious picture of the world-embracing character of the Church of Christ, it is to be carefully noted that it is nowhere stated or even hinted in this chapter that the "multitude" owe their salvation to the missionary activities of the "144,000." Scofield does not in the headings and notes appended to this chapter assert that they do; but in his notes on Matt. x. 23 and xxiv. 14 he makes it quite clear that he holds this to be the case. The evangelizing of the "cities of Israel" and of the "world," described in these chapters, is to be the work of the Jewish remnant "immediately preceding the return of Christ in glory." He declares that

"The scope of verses 16-23 [of Matt. x] reaches beyond the present ministry of the twelve, covering in a general sense the sphere of service during the present age," and that vs. 23 has in view the preaching of the remnant in the tribulation period. Here we have one of the tragic results of the Dispensational doctrine of the Church and of the coming: Rev. vii., instead of giving us a glorious picture of the result of the proclamation of the gospel by the Church in obedience to the Great Commission, is taken away from the Church completely and becomes instead a vision of the wonderful success of a Jewish remnant in preaching the Jewish gospel of the kingdom after the termination of the present Church age.[32]

This, as has already been pointed out, is a tremendous price for the Christian to pay for exemption from the sufferings of the great tribulation which the Dispensationalist regards as so near at hand. Far more commendable is the attitude expressed by Bickersteth in the following noble words:

"How impressive, how elevating, and yet how solemn, are the things to come, as set before us in the word! There is the great tribulation, that we may be prepared and ready for trials; and yet that tribulation is the sure mark of our Lord's speedy coming, that we may be comforted and filled with joy even when the trials have arrived: knowing how short the time is before His full return in glory and our full redemption."[33]

How prominently and even disastrously Pretribulationism has figured as an issue in the history of Dispensationalism has been recently pointed out by Gaebelein,[34] who makes it clear that disagreement on this question was largely responsible for the discontinuance of the "Niagara" Bible conferences in 1898. The death of J. H. Brookes and of A. J. Gordon[35] may have contributed. But the rejection of this essential feature of Dispensationalism by Robert Cameron, Nathanael West, Wm. J. Erdman and others was far more important and came near to wrecking the Dispensational cause in this country. Gaebelein gives Scofield the credit of having saved the day for Dispensationalism.

It is remarkable that Scofield, who at this crisis stepped forth as the protagonist of Pretribulationism, sought and secured the co-operation and support in the preparation of his *Reference Bible* of two men with whom he differed radically on an issue which like Blackstone he apparently regarded as "infinitely important."[36] For the names of two prominent Post-tribulationists appear among the seven Consulting Editors of the *Reference Bible*, Wm. J. Erdman and W. G. Moorehead. In the case of Erdman this was partly due to personal friendship, but especially to the fact that Erdman was a conspicuous figure among Premillennialists in this country and had been for twenty years the secretary of the "Niagara" Conference. But the fact that he had held the Pretribulation view and then changed to that of Post-tribulationism must have been a severe strain upon this friendship. It is worthy of note that in the *Reference Bible* Scofield has used Erdman's analysis of the Book of Revelation, but has stated it in terms of Pretribulationism. He tells us, "It is noteworthy that the church is not mentioned in chapters v.-xviii." and he insists that the Church is in heaven during the entire period covered by chaps. iv.-xix. 10. The first episode or interlude (vii. 1-17) he calls: "The Jewish remnant and the tribulation saints." Erdman simply entitles it: "The sealed and the saved." Of them he says: "Unless the contrary can be proved, it is a fair inference from many facts that by the 'saints' seen as future by Daniel and by John are meant 'the Church' which consists of Jews and Gentiles."[37] As this is irreconcilable with the Pretribulation view advocated in the *Reference Bible* it is easy to understand why Scofield felt obliged to state, in expressing his sense of indebtedness to his Consulting Editors for their "valuable suggestions and co-operation," that "the Editor alone is responsible for the final form of notes and definitions." But the reader of the *Reference Bible,* unless he has some knowledge of its history, would hardly infer from such a statement that it applies to so radical a difference of interpretation as the one we have been considering.

CHAPTER IX

THE JEWISH REMNANT

LIKE the two fundamental doctrines of Dispensationalism which have now been examined, the doctrine of
the Jewish Remnant stands in definite relation to the
situation in Great Britain and Ireland more than a century
ago, when the Brethren Movement had its beginning.
Many whose ideas on the history of the Jewish question
are largely derived from Shakespeare's Shylock or Scott's
Isaac of York, which they think of as belonging to ancient
history, and who have had it brought home to them as a
present-day problem in all its tragic seriousness only by
the terrible Nazi persecution of the Jews today, are not
aware that in England the First Emancipation Bill of
1830 was defeated in Parliament, and that full parlia-
mentary rights were not secured to the Jews until thirty
years later. "The Society for Promoting Christianity
amongst the Jews" was organized in London in 1809; and
in 1820 "The American Society for Ameliorating the
Condition of the Jews" was incorporated in New York.
In 1839 the Church of Scotland sent out a committee to
investigate the condition of the Jews in Syria, Palestine,
and Eastern Europe.[1] Writing some years later E. B. Elliott
pointed out that there had been "a very general abandon-
ment by modern commentators of the decided *anti-Jewish*
view of the predicted blessedness held by the ancient
Fathers."[2]

This situation naturally affected the Brethren Movement. Carrying to an almost unprecedented extreme that
literalism which is characteristic of Millenarianism, they
insisted that Israel must mean Israel, and that the kingdom promises in the Old Testament concern Israel and
are to be fulfilled to Israel literally. This means, as Sco-

field has phrased it, that "The Church corporately is not in the vision of the O.T. prophet."[3] Accusing the Christians of having stolen these prophecies from the Jews, they proceeded to give them back to the Jews, to give them all back. And since it is the remnant, the pious, believing, persecuted, remnant, that figures largely in those prophecies, this remnant naturally assumes a place of great importance in the Dispensational system. When we turn to the New Testament we find that the great theme of the Gospels is the kingdom. If the kingdom is Jewish, it is putting it mildly to say that we must expect "a strong legal and Jewish coloring up to the cross"; or, to put it more strongly, that "All Scripture, up to the Gospel accounts of the crucifixion . . . has primarily in view Israel, and the blessing of the earth through the Messianic kingdom";[4] and that it is only in the Epistles of Paul that we are given "the doctrine of the Church." This means, broadly speaking, that, except for the Pauline Epistles, Israel, and more particularly the pious remnant in Israel, is the great theme of the Bible and especially of its prophetic portions. This is a long step in the direction of Judaizing the Bible. Yet we find Scofield making the decidedly naïve confession: "Doubtless the whole subject has been made an offense to many sincere and well-meaning students of the Bible by the too exclusively Jewish conception of the 'age to come' in controversies over it."[5] For in saying this he has placed his finger on the sore point in Dispensational teaching, the exaltation of the Jew *per se*. In their glorification of the Jew and the rosy future they assign to him, Dispensationalists vie with Zionists. The future belongs to the Jew!

It is to be remembered, however, that this glorifying of the Jew is not with Dispensationalists an end in itself. It is in a sense only the foil for the greater glorification of the Church. The zeal of the Dispensationalist is primarily for the heavenly glory of the Parenthesis Church. All the earthly promises are given to earthly Israel, that the heavenly glory of the Church may be rendered distinctive. Times and seasons, human history and its happenings, are given to Israel, or rather to Israel and the professing church, that the expectancy of any moment rapture may be cherished by the Church without the intrusion of any hampering or hindering events. For, if the earthly promises are to be taken literally and the heavenly nature and destiny of the Church is to be safeguarded, these earthly promises must be given to an earthly people. If the rapture is to take place at any moment, predicted events must concern this earthly people. Hence, the interval between the rapture and the appearing, being a time when predicted events will happen on earth, must concern only the Jew and the nations, the Jew and the professing church. Because of the unique position given in it to the Jew, this interval may, therefore, properly be called a Jewish remnant parenthesis. The rapture of the Church, its complete absence from the earth during this important interval, makes this inevitable. And if the Jew is to have all the earthly blessings, it may be held to be only right, at any rate it is inevitable, that the horrors of the great tribulation, an earthly event, should be borne by them. This is the logic of Dispensationalism, or as we have called it, *Pre*tribulation-*Pre*millenarianism.

In view of the importance which this Jewish remnant doctrine assumes through its vital relation to the two even more important doctrines of the Church and the Coming which have already been considered, it has been referred to repeatedly in connection with them. But three questions remain which must now be discussed in some detail. How does the Jewish remnant come into existence? What is its nature? What is the task assigned to it?

I. THE JEWISH REMNANT OF THE POST-RAPTURE PERIOD

Since the Jewish remnant doctrine is closely related to the doctrine of the rapture of the Church, it is to be noted that this latter doctrine has appeared historically in two main forms, the partial and the total rapture doctrines

1. The Partial Rapture Doctrine

According to the partial theory, a distinction is to be drawn between devout Christians who are looking for the coming of the Lord and worldly Christians who are neither ready for nor expecting the call of the Bridegroom.[6] It is only the former who will be raptured; the rest will be left on earth to pass through the great tribulation. Some even hold, as did Bengel, that there will or may be a series of raptures, that as they become ready groups of living believers will be caught up to meet the Lord. The great objection to this doctrine is that it is contrary to the plain teachings of Scripture. The Bible teaches the great doctrine of justification by faith. Those who truly believe are saved; those who do not believe are lost. The saved have "washed their robes and made them white in the blood of the Lamb." The teaching that some Christians need to pass through a period of tribulation on earth in order to be made fit for heaven is the same in principle as the Romish doctrine of purgatory. The only difference is that these imperfect Christians are to have their purgatory while alive on earth, in passing through the great tribulation, instead of after death. Furthermore, the doctrine of a partial rapture practically necessitates the acceptance of the Romish doctrine of purgatory. For it must be admitted that many Christians have died, to all appearances, in that imperfect state which we are told will characterize those who at the rapture are left on earth to be purified by the great tribulation. So, unless it is to be held that in the very article of death they have or will have endured purifying or chastening sufferings equivalent to those which will be endured by those who are left behind at the time of the rapture, the argument that these latter need to pass through the tribulation falls to the ground, unless the doctrine of purgatory is accepted. There is no warrant for such teachings. The dying thief was in all probability a very imperfect and a very ignorant believer.

But the Lord said to him, "Today thou shalt be with me in paradise." That there will be differences in blessedness and in rewards in heaven is clearly indicated in the Bible. But there is nothing to indicate that when Paul says to the Thessalonian Christians, "we that are alive, that are left, shall be caught up together with them in the clouds to meet the Lord in the air," he means to limit the "we" to an elite body of Christians. The "we" are clearly contrasted with "the dead in Christ." Unless it is held that only a choice group from the dead in Christ will be raptured, there would be no basis for arguing that only a choice group from among those who may be called "the living in Christ" will be raptured. This doctrine of a partial rapture can be stated in a less offensive form by saying that it refers only to rewards, not to salvation: pretribulation rapture will be a special reward for extraordinary devotion and faithfulness. But even when stated in this modified form, the doctrine finds no warrant in Scripture.

2. *The Total Rapture Doctrine*

The doctrine of a total rapture could not be more emphatically stated than has been done by the Brethren and their Dispensationalist followers. It is stated by Andrew Miller as follows:

"Before a seal of judgment is broken, a trumpet blown, or a vial poured out, the saints are gone, all gone, gone to glory, gone to be with the Lord for ever! What a thought, what an event! Not a particle of the redeemed dust of God's children left in the grave; and not a believer left on the face of the whole earth."[7]

This we believe to be, as regards the completeness of the rapture, a correct statement of the doctrine of Scripture. It is in accord with the words used elsewhere by Paul, "afterward they that are Christ's at his coming," "them also that sleep in Jesus." These words are clearly intended to include all believers, all the redeemed. They will all be raptured: not just a superior grade of believers, dead and living, but all whom Christ Jesus has purchased with

His precious blood. No believer is worthy of this, nor is he entitled to it because of his works, even though he have given his body to be burned. But every true believer may claim and expect it because of the infinite merit of the Saviour who died that he might live.

At this point we encounter a question of the utmost importance. If every believer will be caught up at the rapture, what will be the state of the earth after the rapture? For the Postmillenarian, and the Amillenarian, this question is not an important one. They hold that after meeting the Lord in the air, all the saints will return with Him to earth for the last judgment, which will be followed by the final state, the new heavens and the new earth. Hence, the day of salvation will be ended, the number of the elect will be complete, at the rapture. For the Premillennialist, the question is far more important. He believes in a reign of Christ and His saints on or over the earth. This reign will follow the rapture immediately or speedily, and will last for a thousand years before the final judgment. Such being the case, he must deal with the question whether this considerable period, the millennium, will be a "day of salvation"; and if so, the further question arises as to the nature of the means by which this salvation will be brought about. How will the visible reign of Christ and the binding of Satan affect the means of grace now operative in the world? Will they no longer be needed? For Dispensationalists this problem becomes especially important and also especially difficult. According to them, the rapture will remove from the earth "every believer." There will not be a single true Christian left on earth after the rapture. The entire Church will be in heaven, or "in the air." Yet after the rapture and during the (7 year) period before the return of Christ with the saints, i.e., in the important interval between the rapture and the appearing, while the Church is absent and after the Holy Spirit has been removed, a great work of salvation will take place on earth. There will be the sealing of the 144,000 of the tribes of Israel.

There will be the assembling of "a multitude which no man could number," who have washed their robes and made them white in the blood of the Lamb. These are described by Scofield as "the saved of the tribulation period." The difficult question raised by this Dispensational doctrine is obviously this, How does this great body, or, to be more exact, How do these two great bodies of redeemed ones come into being? According to Darby and Scofield the entire Church has then been raptured, the Holy Spirit, whom they hold to be the one "that restraineth" (2 Thess. ii. 6), has been taken away.[8] How then will the saints of the tribulation period be saved?

3. The Total Rapture and the Jewish Remnant

The answer to the question that has just been asked is found by Dispensationalists in their doctrine of the Jewish Remnant. This remnant is to be identified, they tell us, with the 144,000 who are sealed on earth before that hurting of the earth which they understand to refer to the great tribulation. But this answer at once raises the question, How does this remnant come into being? The fact that they are sealed by an angel, apparently with a view to their passing unscathed through the tribulation, would imply that they are believers who are now on earth after the rapture of the Church has taken place. How can this be? If they were believers in Christ at the time of the rapture, why were they not caught up with the (other) Church saints? It is regarded as distinctive of the Church age that during it Jew and Gentile are both one in Christ Jesus. Already in the course of this gospel age many thousands of Jews have become Christians. None of these believing Jews could be left behind unless we are to disregard utterly Paul's declaration that the middle wall of partition has been broken down, making all one in Christ Jesus. There seem to be only two ways of accounting for the presence of this remnant upon earth after the rapture of the Church has taken place and every Christian believer has been removed from the earth.

a. Remnant will Come into Being After the Rapture

It appears to be Scofield's view that the Jewish remnant will come into being after the Church age. "During the church-age," he tells us, "the remnant is composed of believing Jews (Rom. xi. 4, 5) . . . During the great tribulation a remnant out of all Israel will turn to Jesus as Messiah, and will become His witnesses after the removal of the church (Rev. vii. 3-8)."[9] This remnant he tells us "will have returned to Palestine in unbelief."[10] If this be so, the rapture will be a unique event. It will make a complete and utter break in the continuity of the body of believers on earth. When the Flood came, a "few that is eight souls" were saved. The call of Abraham did not come to a heathen, but to a believer who was to separate himself from a heathen environment (Gen. xii. 1; Josh. xxiv. 14f.); and when Abram came to Canaan, Melchizedek was king of Salem and "priest of the most high God." When the Israelites refused to go up to possess Canaan, Caleb and Joshua were faithful. When the Northern Kingdom was destroyed there were some faithful ones who responded to the exhortations of the pious kings Hezekiah and Josiah and came up to Jerusalem to worship. When the Kingdom of Judah was carried away captive, a considerable remnant returned under Zerubbabel or later under Ezra. When the Jews rejected and crucified their Messiah, a believing remnant became the nucleus of the Christian Church. Viewing human history as a whole, we may say that God has never left Himself without a witness. There has always been a remnant, however small, to keep the torch of faith burning upon the earth. But, according to the doctrine which we are considering, this will not be the case when the Church is raptured. Not a believer will be left on earth. Every saint, every truly saved person will have been raptured. Yet, shortly after this unparalleled event and within an incredibly short time (less than seven years), 144,000 Jews and an innumerable multitude of non-Jews will be saved. Is this probable? We do not say, Is it possible? But, is it in harmony with what we know to have been God's dealings with mankind throughout the whole long course of human history? Is such an absolute break in the continuity of the history of redemption likely to occur? The least that can be said is that it is quite contrary to the analogy of Scripture.

b. The Remnant will be in Existence at the Rapture

The alternative position is that there will be a believing remnant of Jews on earth at the time of the rapture, which will remain there after the removal of the Church. Darby affirms this quite definitely: "That there will be a Jewish remnant at the close, delivered and blessed by the Lord at His coming, blessed on earth, is, beyond all controversy, the doctrine of Scripture."[11] Darby is quite correct in holding that there will be a future Jewish remnant. The doctrine of the remnant is one of the important teachings of the Bible. It is especially prominent in prophecy. No matter how dark the picture of woe and destruction which the prophets set before their sinful and apostate people, they always teach expressly or impliedly that a remnant of grace shall be saved. The prophets see in this remnant the hope of Israel; and while often speaking of it as extremely small, they hold out the hope that it may become large. So what concerns us especially is what Darby has to say about this remnant. He speaks of this remnant as "blessed." Yet he goes on at once to say, "This remnant has neither the church's blessings nor the church's hope." Such a remnant could of course be on earth both before the rapture and after it. If it will not be a "Christian" remnant, if it will not be a part of the Church, it will not share the Church's blessed and heavenly hope. Its hopes and blessings will be earthly. It will belong on earth and remain on earth after the rapture.

The reason Darby gives for insisting so strongly that the difference between the hopes and blessings of the Church (as heavenly) and the hopes and blessings of Israel (as earthly) be clearly recognized is a very important one. Not

to make this distinction is, he tells us, to bring the heavenly
hopes of the Church down to the level of the earthly hopes
of Israel. To accomplish this is, he insists, the great aim of
"the enemy" (Satan).[12] But what we are contending for is
not the lowering of the hopes of the Church to an earthly
level, but the raising of the hopes of Israel to the heavenly
level. All that this involves and requires is the recognition
of the essentially spiritual and heavenly character of the
hopes of Israel as set forth in the Old Testament and as
more fully expounded in the New Testament. It was their
insistence on the literal interpretation of prophecy, and
this alone, which prevented Darby and his followers from
accepting this alternative view, which avoids so many of
the perils and pitfalls of their position.

II. The Character of the Jewish Remnant

The statement last quoted from Darby raises an issue
of great importance. Unless we have utterly misunderstood
Darby and Scofield and other expounders of Dispensational doctrine, they all declare that for and during the
Church age the middle wall of partition has been done
away, that Jew and Gentile are saved, if saved at all, on
exactly the same basis. The gospel to be preached during
this age is the "gospel of the grace of God." Paul preached
it to Jews most earnestly; and when they refused it he
turned to the Gentiles and preached the same gospel to
them. Paul did not have one gospel for the Jew and another for the Greek. He had only one gospel which was
for all men, for Jew and Gentile alike and without distinction or difference. The gospel which Paul preached to
the Jews at Rome concerned the "kingdom of God" (Acts
xxviii. 23); and, when they rejected it, he continued
preaching "the kingdom of God" to "all that came in unto
him" (vss. 30f.). This must mean that he preached it to the
Gentile as well as to the Jew, which shows that this "gospel of the kingdom of God" was the same as the "gospel
of the grace of God."[13] Now the all-important question is
this: Could any Jews be described as "pious" and "godly"

—these adjectives are constantly applied to the Jewish remnant by Dispensationalists—who refused or failed to accept the preaching of the gospel of the grace of God as proclaimed by Peter and Paul? Could these adjectives apply to men whom Paul denounced as "despisers" (Acts xiii. 41) or upon whom he pronounced the woe of Isa. vi. 9f. (Acts xxviii. 25f.)? Scofield, as we have seen, describes the "poor of the flock" as "those Jews who did not wait for the manifestation of Christ in glory, but believed on Him at His first coming, and since."[14] Apparently Scofield recognized two classes of believing Jews: those who were determined to wait for the Messiah to appear as King, and those who accepted Jesus as their Saviour. So the question to be answered is this. Can a remnant of Jews who refuse to accept Jesus as Saviour, but are waiting for Him as King, be called "pious" or "godly"? Can they be blessed by Christ?

The New Testament makes it quite clear that the Jews were expecting a Messiah who would free them from the yoke of Rome and set up a glorious earthly kingdom. Jesus' failure and positive refusal to do this aroused the opposition of the leaders of the Jews; and His teaching concerning His death gave grievous offense even to His most loyal disciples (Mt. xvi. 22). Yet Jesus called Peter "Satan," when he resented and repudiated what seemed to him a monstrous doctrine, that the Christ must suffer. Paul declared the preaching of the cross to be a "stumbling-block" (1 Cor. i. 23) to the Jews. And it is undeniable that the teaching that "the Christ should suffer" is to the unregenerate Jew the most offensive doctrine of the Christian faith. How then could a Jewish remnant which rejected the Crucified be pious and blessed? How could a remnant which believed on the Saviour fail to participate in the rapture? Here is the dilemma which total-rapture Pre-tribulationism must solve.

If the Church is to escape the great tribulation, the "elect" referred to in Matt. xxiv. cannot, as we have seen, be Church-saints; they must be a Jewish remnant which will be on earth after the rapture of the Church. And this remnant is clearly a "godly" remnant. This interpretation of Matt. xxiv. was adopted by Darby at least as early as 1837. Almost immediately he began the publication in *The Christian Witness* of a series of articles entitled, "Heads of the Psalms." The principal aim of these articles was to develop the doctrine of the Jewish remnant. Some years later he summed up the teaching of the Psalms as follows:

"The Spirit of Christ working and developing itself in the remnant of Israel in the latter day; only therewith shewing the personal part He has taken, whether to lay the ground for them, or to exercise sympathy with them, continuing on up to the border of the millennium, but not entering into it except prophetically. They are divided into five books."[15]

It is especially to the Psalms, therefore, that we must look for the doctrine of the "godly" remnant.

It is perfectly true that in the Psalms we frequently find the Lord's people, either individually or collectively, asserting their righteousness and appealing to God for deliverance from their enemies and for the fulfilment of His promises. But it is important to remember that the righteousness or godliness which these Jews profess is not to be understood as amounting to sinless perfection. Such assertions are to be taken in connection with, and to be explained by, the frequent declarations of Scripture that man is sinful and needs, that even the very best of men need, forgiveness and mercy. Solomon declared that "there is no man that sinneth not" (1 Kgs. viii. 46). Jeremiah said, "The heart is deceitful above all things and desperately wicked" (xvii. 9). Paul roundly declares that "All have sinned and come short" (Rom. iii. 23). It is quite possible for a man to assert most emphatically his innocence and righteousness relatively to his fellowmen and the charges which they bring against him unjustly and the wrongs which he suffers at their hands, while at the same time being deeply conscious that in his relation to God he must cry with the publican, "God be merciful to me a sinner." The whole Mosaic ritual of sacrifice was designed to emphasize the fact that as Paul also declares on the authority of the Old Testament, "there is none righteous, no, not one" (Rom. iii. 10), and to press home the further fact that "without shedding of blood there is no remission" (Heb. ix. 22). So, unless we are to regard this remnant in Israel as claiming that Pharisaic righteousness which Jesus so severely condemned, we must recognize that it is "godly" only in the sense that it loves God, accepts and rejoices in His salvation, and tries to do His will, but not "godly" in the sense that it does not stand in need of the redemption purchased by Christ.

This point is of the utmost importance, because this doctrine of the "godly" remnant, as taught by Darby, gave rise to one of the most serious of the many controversies which have marred the history of Brethrenism, and also because it has a direct bearing on Dispensationalism. It concerned what were called the "third class" sufferings of Christ. On the basis especially of certain passages in the Psalms, Darby declared that Jesus in many of His earthly sufferings identified Himself non-atoningly with the godly Jewish remnant; and that it was only in the "forsaking," *i.e.*, during the last three hours on the cross, that He suffered as the sin-bearer. Now it is obvious that Jesus could identify Himself with sinners only as Sinbearer and Saviour. Only with sinless beings could He identify Himself non-atoningly. Hence, this claim that Jesus identified Himself non-atoningly with the Jewish remnant makes the inference a very natural one that for "godly" Jews the sacrifice of the Cross was unnecessary.[16]

We have seen that the most serious objection to the claim of Dispensationalists, that the declaration that "the kingdom of heaven is at hand" meant that it could be set up "at any moment," was the fact that this involved the ignoring of the definite teaching of Jesus that the "Christ must suffer and enter into his glory." It made the Cross unnecessary by implying that the glorious kingdom of Messiah could be set up immediately. It left no room for the Cross since Messiah's kingdom was to be without end. It led to the conclusion that had Israel accepted Jesus as

Messiah, the Old Testament ritual of sacrifice would have sufficed for sin, that it was only the enormity of the crucifixion which made the Cross necessary. Darby, as we have seen, tells us quite definitely:

"Supposing for a moment that Christ had not been rejected, the kingdom would have been set up on earth. It could not have been so, no doubt, but it shows the difference between the kingdom and the church."[17]

The only conclusion which can be drawn from such a statement is this, that the Church required the Cross while the kingdom did not, that the gospel of the kingdom did not include the Cross, while the gospel of the grace of God did include it.

Here we are again concerned with the question of the setting up of the kingdom, only with this difference that it now relates to the second advent instead of to the first. So the problem is somewhat altered, although basically the same. It is not merely the question whether the kingdom could have been set up without the Cross. Now, it is the question whether, the Cross and the Church age having intervened the kingdom and the gospel of the kingdom presuppose and require the Cross; or, to state the question somewhat differently, whether the "godly" Jewish remnant of the end-time will accept the Cross and preach the Cross or not. We have seen that if a "godly" Jew believes the "gospel of the grace of God" during the Church age, he becomes a Christian, a member of the body of Christ. As such a believer, he will be caught up with all the rest of the Church saints at the rapture. If then there is to be a "godly" Jewish remnant which has neither the Church's blessings nor the Church's hopes, this must mean that this "godly" remnant will have refused to accept the gospel of the grace of God while waiting for the proclamation of the gospel of the kingdom and for the coming of the King. This we believe to be the inevitable result of Darby's doctrine of the remnant; and we hold it to be utterly irreconcilable with the teaching of the Bible, that "the word of the cross is to them that perish foolishness; but unto us who are saved it is the power of God." No Jew who in this gospel age during which Christ is preached as Saviour rejects the Saviour while waiting for the King can be called "godly" or "pious" or be "blessed" of God. Christ has died on the cross. To reject Him as Saviour is for the Jew as well as for the Gentile to spurn the offer of salvation and merit the wrath and curse of God.

III. THE MISSION OF THE JEWISH REMNANT

The question as to the nature of the gospel which this Jewish remnant (assuming it to exist at, or to have come into being after the rapture) is to preach, must now be considered. It is an important one because "the Jew . . . will then be the missionary, and to the very 'nations' now called Christian!" [18] It is to be "the gospel of the kingdom." Scofield defines this gospel as follows:

"This is the good news that God purposes to set up on the earth, in fulfilment of the Davidic Covenant (2 Sam. vii. 16, and refs.), a kingdom, political, spiritual, Israelitish, universal, over which God's Son, David's heir, shall be King, and which shall be. for one thousand years, the manifestation of the righteousness of God in human affairs."[19]

Scofield also clearly distinguishes "two preachings" of this gospel:

". . . one past, beginning with the ministry of John the Baptist, continued by our Lord and His disciples, and ending with the Jewish rejection of the King. The other is yet future (Mt. xxiv. 14), during the great tribulation, and immediately preceding the coming of the King in glory."

It is to be carefully noted that this "gospel of the kingdom" is stated by Scofield in terms of kingship only, and also that the kingdom is to be established by power, not persuasion.[20] In this respect it stands in marked contrast with the "gospel of the grace of God" regarding which he tells us:

"This is the good news that Jesus Christ, the rejected King, has died on the cross for the sins of the world, that He was raised from the dead for our justification, and that by Him all that believe are justified from all things."

This contrast is further illustrated and accentuated by the claim that the Sermon on the Mount is not to be regarded as setting the ideal standard for living in this present age but as the "constitution" for that kingdom of heaven which was offered to the Jews nearly two millenniums ago, and, being rejected by them and postponed, is to be established in the millennial age. It is "pure law"; and this is explained to mean that "There is not a ray of grace in it, nor a drop of blood." [21]

The "gospel of the grace of God" according to Scofield is the gospel for the Church age. The "gospel of the kingdom" was preached before the Cross, before the Church age during which the gospel of the Cross is to be preached; and its preaching is to be resumed, apparently without change or addition, after the Church age. The natural inference is that, if it did not involve the Cross when it was preached at the first advent, it will not include it when it is preached after the rapture. Such a conclusion is all the more necessary, if it is to be preached by a Jewish remnant which remained on earth at the rapture because it was expecting the kingdom and had refused to accept the gospel preached by the Church. We are told that this remnant will number 144,000 and that through its proclamation of the gospel of the kingdom the "great multitude which no man could number" will be saved, and that, apparently during this period and the millennium which immediately follows it, "the enormous majority of earth's inhabitants will be saved." But it is not stated in Rev. vii. that the multitude owe their salvation to the preaching of the 144,000. More important still, it is expressly declared that this multitude that are arrayed in white robes "have washed their robes and made them white in the blood of the Lamb" (vii. 14). This can only mean that they have accepted, not that "gospel of the kingdom" which, as defined by Scofield, makes no mention of the Cross, but "the gospel of the grace of God" which is "the good news that Jesus Christ . . . has died on the Cross for the sins of the world." It will have been the preaching of the Cross, whether by a Jewish remnant or by Church saints, to which they will owe their salvation.

IV. Where Does the Cross Come In?

It cannot be too strongly emphasized that if the Dispensational doctrine regarding the *nature* of the promised kingdom and the *meaning* of the words "at hand" is accepted, it leads logically to the view that the Cross, as an atoning sacrifice for sin, concerns the Church age and the Church saints only. As preached at the first advent it did not include or involve the Cross; as preached at the second advent it will not include or presuppose the Cross. It was the rejection of Jesus by the Jews which made the Cross necessary; and it was this rejection which made the Church age possible. So it is for the Church age and for it alone that the Cross is of supreme importance. Only Church saints can say, "Who loved me and gave Himself for me." This we maintain is logical, thoroughgoing Dispensationalism. We feel obliged to point it out, not because Dispensationalists are thoroughly logical and draw these disastrous conclusions fully and clearly, but because we believe that a doctrine which leads to such conclusions cannot be true. Scofield's words already quoted: "The kingdom was promised to the Jews. Gentiles could be blessed only through Christ crucified and risen," [22] state the difference as sharply as any opponent of Dispensationalism could desire. Yet Scofield undoubtedly held with Darby that "From Adam to the end of time no one was or will be saved but by the redemption and the work of the Spirit." Dispensationalists do not reject the Cross or minimize its importance: they glory in it. The unfortunate thing is that they insist on an any moment view of the setting up of the kingdom at the first advent and an any moment view of the coming of Christ (for the Church) at His second advent which makes it possible for them to glory in the Cross only as regards the Church age and lands them in such difficulties and absurdities as we have been considering, unless they shut their eyes to the logical implications which are involved in their all-important any moment doctrine. When we read the statements made by

Darby and Scofield, we cannot help being amazed that realizing as they must have done, at least to some extent, the serious implications of their any moment doctrine, they did not re-examine it in the light of Bible teaching as a whole, instead of allowing it to force them into a position where they must make contradictory statements which come very near to denying, if they do not actually deny, doctrines which in common with all evangelical Christians they regarded as supremely precious.

Chapter X

THE FUTURE OF ISRAEL AND THE MILLENNIUM

IT WAS pointed out at the outset of this study of Dispensationalism that an issue of the greatest importance is involved in the Millenarian question. It is this, Is there to be a period before the final consummation during which salvation will be on a different basis from that of the present gospel age? This question has already been answered as far as Dispensationalists are concerned in their doctrine of the Jewish-remnant interval or parenthesis between the rapture and the appearing. This interval will be relatively short, as compared with the millennial age which will immediately follow it. But it will be an era which will witness the greatest and most successful missionary movement of human history. The Jewish remnant will make vastly more converts during this brief period through the preaching of the gospel of the kingdom, than the Church will have made in the nearly or more than 2000 years since Pentecost through her preaching of the gospel of the grace of God, though this preaching has been attended with the presence and gracious influence of the Holy Spirit.

Coming now to the question of the millennium we observe that the issue is here obscured by the fact that there is so much difference of opinion as to just what the word millennium means. What may be called the popular and naïve idea of a millennium is derived largely from such a passage as Isa. xi. It is to be a golden age, when "the wolf shall dwell with the lamb," when none shall "hurt or destroy," when the earth shall be "full of the knowledge of the LORD as the waters cover the sea." So regarded the millennium is a kind of foretaste of heaven; it is a happy and blessed condition in which sin and suffering will alike be unknown. It will be paradise regained. Scofield tells us: "The *moral* characteristics of the kingdom are to be righteousness and peace. . . . It is impossible to conceive to what heights of spiritual, intellectual, and physical perfection humanity will attain in this, its coming age of righteousness and peace (Isa. xi. 4-9; Ps. lxxii. 1-10)."[1] Such a picture of an ideal age raises only one serious difficulty. It is whether the Bible and especially the New Testament predicts or allows for such a period of blessedness before the eternal state is ushered in, or whether the picture given to us by Isaiah is a description of that eternal state itself under earthly forms and images. This question is a moot point between Postmillennialists and Amillennialists. The former believe there will be such a golden age before the final consummation. It will be the golden age of the *Church:* Satan will be bound. It will be Christianity triumphant and supreme. The latter deny that either in the Gospels or in the Epistles is there provision for such a millennium. They may take an optimistic view of the future of the Church on earth, or they may agree with Premillennialists that evil will be at work in the world, even increasingly active, up to the very time of Christ's coming. But they agree with the Postmillennialists in denying that Rev. xx. 1-6 describes a period in the world's history in which salvation, should salvation be needed when so wonderful a state of society is attained, will be on any other basis than that on which it has rested throughout the entire Church age until now. Whether it be to a world of mingled good and evil, or to a world evangelized and saved, that Christ comes, His coming will *terminate* the day of salvation and usher in the last judgment and the final consummation of all things.

The millenarian doctrine, as held by Premillennialists and by Dispensationalists, involves two important and closely related assumptions: (1) the identifying of the millennium of Rev. xx. 1-6 with the future kingdom age foretold by the Old Testament prophets, and, therefore, (2) the finding of the description of this millennium in these same prophets. This is the case because the millennium as a period of 1000 years is referred to only in Rev. xx. without any description of it being given there, and because the Old Testament prophecies if literally interpreted cannot be regarded as having been yet fulfilled or as being capable of fulfilment in this present age. It is consequently assumed that they will be so fulfilled during the millennium when Satan will be bound and the saints will reign with Christ. In other words, Rev. xx. 1-6 is to be regarded as providing the New Testament frame for the Old Testament picture of the future kingdom of God on earth. Each of these assumptions raises difficulties which must be carefully considered.

I. THE KINGDOM AND THE MILLENNIUM

Before we identify these two important conceptions several matters demand attention.

1. The Kingdom Endless, the Millennium a Limited Period

This is a significant difference. When we read such chapters as Isa. lx. and lxv.-lxvi., we receive the definite impression that the prophet is picturing the ultimate and final state of God's people: the troubles of Israel will then be ended for ever. This impression is strengthened when we turn to Ezekiel and find that chapters xl.-xlviii. give us a picture of Israel's peaceful possession of the land after all of her enemies have been utterly destroyed. Daniel declares emphatically that the kingdom which God will establish "shall stand for ever" (ii. 44), that "the saints of the most High shall take the kingdom and possess the kingdom for ever, even for ever and ever" (vii. 18). Jeremiah gives us the same impression. The "new covenant" will be as permanent as the ordinances of heaven: the walls of Jerusalem will be extended and shall "not be plucked up nor thrown down any more for ever" (xxxi. 33-40). It is nowhere suggested in these passages that this glorious age will be, in a sense, as transitory and ephemeral as was the age of David

and Solomon.[2] Israel need have no more anxious fore-
bodings: the days of her mourning will be ended, never to
return. Such a picture corresponds with that given us in
Rev. xxi.-xxii. We cannot read xxi. 23-27 without being
reminded of Isa. lx. 19-22, while xxi. 22 reminds us of Isa.
lxvi. 1ff. Even Scofield admits that Isa. lxv. 17 "looks
beyond the kingdom-age to the new heavens and the new
earth."[3]

2. *The Kingdom Age Follows the Final Triumph: the Millennium Precedes It*

The second difference between the millennium and the
kingdom age foretold by the prophets is also an important
one. Not only will it be a limited period, during which
Satan will be bound, but it will be followed by an episode
called the "little season" which will be both the last and
apparently the greatest of all man's efforts, instigated by
Satan, to set aside and overthrow the rule of Messiah. It is
a very significant fact that in this respect as little as in the
other does the New Testament framework and setting suit
the Old Testament picture. Premillennialists insist that
the establishing of the millennium is to follow God's judgments upon evil. One of the signal proofs of this to which
they appeal is the fact that the overthrow of Gog and
Magog described in Ezek. xxxviii.-xxxix. immediately precedes the description of the establishment of a kingdom
which apparently is to have no end. Yet in Rev. xx. the
millennium is followed by a world-wide revolt of which
Gog is definitely declared to be a leader. This difficulty has
been already referred to as a crux of literal interpretation.[4]
It is responsible for a decidedly unpleasant feature of the
millennium to which we must now give some attention.

3. *The Problem of Evil in the Millennium*

The question as to where Gog, whose armies according
to Ezekiel were utterly destroyed before the kingdom age,
is to raise up a multitude "the number of whom is as the
sand of the sea," with which to attack "the camp of the

saints and the beloved city," has been a stumbling-block
to Premillennialists, as David Brown pointed out many
years ago.[5] Dispensationalists can answer it, as it would
seem, only in one or other of three ways: by holding that
a race of evil men will come into existence after the millennium, by restricting the extent of the millennial kingdom
to a comparatively small part of the earth, or by concluding
that the millennial age will to no small degree resemble
the present dispensation as an age during which good and
evil will both be present and contending for the mastery,
so that evil both within the realm of Messiah and outside
of it will be kept in subjection only by the rod-of-iron rule
of the King who sits on David's throne.

Those who are accustomed to think of the millennium
in terms of the naïve conception referred to above, as a
golden age of righteousness and peace, will be surprised
to find how different is the view of it held by Dispensationalists. Two brief descriptions of it will serve to illustrate this fact rather impressively. Darby tells us:

"*Now* there are a faithful few, Satan being the prince and god of this
world, going against the stream. *Then* Christ will be the prince of this
world, and Satan bound, and obedience will be paid to Christ's manifested
power even when men are not converted. When this obedience is not
paid, excision takes place, so that all is peaceful and happy. It is a perfect
government of the earth made good everywhere. When Satan is let loose
and temptation comes again, those not kept by grace follow him. I have
an impression that piety will decline in the millennium; but it is founded
on a figure (Numb. xxviii., xxix.), so that I do not insist on it; but the
rest of what I have said is revealed. That men should fall when tempted,
however sad, is nothing but what is very simple. It is the last effort of
Satan."[6]

Brookes gives us an even darker picture in his *Maranatha:*

" 'That which is born of the flesh is flesh' and though restrained during
the Millennium it will manifest its inherent pravity at the first favorable
opportunity, like a tiger long caged and curbed that will bound back to
its native jungle with unquenchable thirst for blood when the iron bars
are removed."[7]

The picture of the millennium given in the above quotations is not an attractive one. It is not pleasing to think

of the Messianic King, the Prince of Peace, sitting enthroned as it were on a smouldering volcano; of a reign of
Messiah, peaceful on the surface but seething with hate
and muttered rebellion; of people yielding outward obedience because "excision" is the inevitable consequence of
disobedience and opposition, since a rod-of-iron rule can
only mean the "dashing in pieces" of the rebellious like
a potter's vessel. When we read that "the wolf shall dwell
with the lamb," we do not take this to mean that the wolf
will be as eager as ever to devour the lamb and be restrained from doing so only by fear of the consequences.
We naturally understand it to imply a change of nature;
the ravening beast, whether the words be taken literally
or figuratively, will no longer *desire* to devour the lamb.
"They shall not hurt nor destroy" in all God's holy mountain, for the reason that they will not want to, not because
they will be restrained by *force majeure* from doing what
they will want to do.

Dispensationalists find warrant for this decidedly unat-
tractive picture of the millennium especially in the fact that
in the Psalms which they regard as prophetic of the millennial
age, we find many allusions to "enemies." In fact they claim
that they have found the correct solution of the problem of
the Imprecatory Psalms. These psalms are, they tell us, "unsuited to the church." But they will be quite appropriate on
the lips of the Jewish remnant in the coming age, when Israel
will be justified in demanding vengeance on all her enemies.
That there will be enemies and that these will submit feignedly
or hypocritically to the rod-of-iron rule of Messiah (Ps. ii.),
they infer especially from Ps. lxvi. 3, "Through the greatness
of thy power shall thine enemies submit themselves unto
thee." Open resistance to the rule of the Davidic King would
be folly. The word rendered "submit" means to "pretend,
deceive, *make a shew of obedience*." The enemies of Messiah
will make a show of obedience to a rule which they hate. So
we may say that, according to this view, the millennium
will surpass all others as the age of hypocrisy and hypocrites.
Men, many men, will submit only because they must; and
these tiger-men will be waiting with ever growing impatience

for the moment when defiance and resistance may offer at least the semblance of a successful issue.

Of less importance, but not to be overlooked, is the fact that according to this method of interpretation this future age will resemble the present in that it will be acquainted with birth and death, those two events which are so characteristic of the present age. The voice of the bridegroom and the voice of the bride will be heard in the streets of the millennial city (Jer. xxxiii. 11). Life may be greatly prolonged, but death will not be unknown (Isa. lxv. 20). In short, this millennial age will not differ essentially from our own as far as the basic facts of human life are concerned. Evil will be curbed, but not eradicated; its effects will be controlled, but not removed.

In view of these and other difficulties which result from the attempt to find in Rev. xx. 1-6 the fulfilment of the kingdom promises, the problem would, we repeat, be made much simpler for the interpreter of prophecy, were it admitted that the golden age foretold by the prophets is not to be identified with the millennium of Rev. xx. 1-6 but with the glorious picture of the eternal state in the chapters which follow. But even then there would remain some difficulties which the literalist would have trouble in solving.

II. The Millennial Age Essentially Jewish

Even more important than the questions just considered, weighty as they unquestionably are, is the second of the basic propositions involved in the millenarian doctrine, the fact that, if the millennium represents the future kingdom age, the entire picture of that age must be obtained from the Old Testament.[8] This obvious fact makes the question of the interpretation of these kingdom prophecies a matter of the utmost importance. For the more literally these prophecies are construed, the more thoroughly and pervasively Jewish will be the millennium to which the Millenarian will look forward with keen anticipation.

Since all Premillenarians believe that there will be a visible reign of Christ on or over the earth for a thousand years before the last judgment, and since they find glowing pictures of this blessed state in the Old Testament, it is to be carefully remembered that we have at least two conceptions of this millennium given to us by them. We may distinguish them broadly speaking as the Christian and the Jewish; or, to speak more exactly, we should say that the one is essentially or predominantly Christian, the other essentially or predominantly Jewish. These two conceptions are respectively the Premillennial and the Dispensational doctrines of the millennium. In view of the data given above, this statement should not surprise our readers; and no further proof of it should be needed than has been already given. While it is true that there has always been a tendency on the part of Premillennialists to stress the earthly and sensuous in their descriptions of the millennium, the best and worthiest representatives of this school of interpretation have opposed this tendency or endeavored to restrict it. They have insisted that the millennium will be the glorious age of the *Church*, when Church saints will reign with Christ and when the gospel will have such sway in the world as never before. It is true that the Old Testament predictions of the restoration of the temple and of the Mosaic ceremonial law have occasioned them no little embarrassment, and sometimes led them to assign Israel a position in the coming age hardly compatible with Paul's teaching that "all are one in Christ Jesus." But, generally speaking, Premillennialists have held that as Bickersteth, who was one of their chief spokesmen a century ago, expressed it:

"Jerusalem, Zion, and in fact the whole Mosaic Dispensation, were in some important respects types of the spiritual church of Christ, and we may be well assured that the promises and prophecies which concern the types have a yet more important reference to the antitype."

And Bickersteth tells us still more definitely:

"There are many prophecies that have been fulfilled in the state of the Christian church since the coming of Christ, and that are now manifestly fulfilling. We may refer to Bishop Newton on the Prophecies, in proof of this. A considerable part of the book of Revelation has, in this way, been made sufficiently clear by the event."9

Bickersteth was a Post-tribulationist. He believed that the "little horn" of Dan. vii. was the "Papal kingdom," that the Papacy was Antichrist, and that much of the Book of Revelation had already been fulfilled in the history of the Christian Church. He opposed the extreme literalism and futurism of many Premillennialists.

Literal interpretation has always been a marked feature of Premillennialism; in Dispensationalism it has been carried to an extreme. We have seen that this literalism found its most thoroughgoing expression in the claim that Israel must mean Israel, that it cannot mean the Church, that the Old Testament prophecies regarding Israel concern the earthly Israel, and that the Church was a mystery, unknown to the prophets and first made known to the apostle Paul. Now if the principle of interpretation is adopted that Israel always means Israel, that it does not mean the Church, then it follows of necessity that practically all of our information regarding the millennium will concern a Jewish or Israelitish age. The prophetic descriptions appealed to are found in the Psalms and in the Prophets, which speak largely in terms of the Mosaic dispensation and economy. According to Dispensationalists the Psalms have as their central theme, Christ and the Jewish remnant in the millennial age. Isaiah's Book of Consolation (chaps. xl.-lxvi.), we are told, has as its great theme, "Jesus Christ in His sufferings, and the glory that shall follow in the Davidic kingdom." Similarly, the general theme of Ezekiel xl.-xlviii. is declared to be "Israel in the land during the kingdom-age."

The implications of this teaching as it concerns the millennium are, briefly stated, the following:

1. The Millennial Kingdom will be a Jewish kingdom

What this means is illustrated very clearly by such a verse as Isa. lx. 21, "Thy people also shall be all righteous."

Thousands of Christians of every age of the Church have claimed this promise. They have regarded these words as including themselves. They have held that "thy people" means God's people, His elect of every age and race and condition. They have regarded it as a prophecy of the Church. But according to Dispensationalists "thy people" means Israel; and in the millennium "the kingdom will be restored to Israel." The Jews will be again pre-eminent among the nations; they will again be God's people in a unique sense. The nations will be held in subjection by the rod-of-iron rule of Messiah. This conception of the future can be reconciled with the teachings of Paul that all distinctions between Jew and Gentile have been broken down by the Gospel, if indeed the word reconciled can be used at all in such a connection, only by recognizing that the millennial age will follow the Church age and be quite distinct from it. In a word, the earthly Davidic kingdom which entered the New Testament "absolutely unchanged," which was offered to the Jews and rejected by them, will at the second advent be given to them "absolutely unchanged." The millennium will be a Jewish age![10]

2. Jewish Peculiarities will be Revived

Since the pictures of the millennium are found by Dispensationalists in the Old Testament kingdom prophecies and are, consequently, markedly Jewish in character, it follows that the question of the re-establishment of the Mosaic economy, its institutions and ordinances, must be faced by them. We have seen that the picture of the future kingdom given by the prophets is in a sense ambiguous. On the one hand they speak in terms of the Mosaic law and of Mosaic institutions and demand their observance; on the other hand they foresee and predict important changes. If the New Testament is allowed to testify, if the words of Jesus and of Paul regarding the true nature of the kingdom of God are accepted as normative, then the words of the prophets which predict important changes will be stressed, and the typical nature of these institutions will be recognized. But if the view is taken that the promised Davidic kingdom enters the New Testament "absolutely unchanged," that an earthly kingdom was promised to the Jews, was offered to them at the first advent and will be given to them at the second advent, and that the New Testament must not be allowed to be "in conflict" with or as we should rather say, to *interpret* the Old Testament prophecies at any point, then the question of "Jewish peculiarities" becomes a burning one. Isaiah and Jeremiah in certain passages speak of the observance of the ceremonial law as obligatory in the kingdom age. Ezekiel demands it most emphatically. A single example will suffice to illustrate this. According to Zech. xiv. 16-19 the nations that survive the futile attempt to destroy Jerusalem must come up yearly to "worship the King, the LORD of hosts, and to keep the feast of tabernacles." If Egypt, for example, fails to do this, she will be smitten with the plague—a reminder of the plagues of the time of the Exodus, when Egyptians felt the might of the strong and out-stretched arm of Jehovah the God of Israel.[11]

3. *Animal Sacrifices will again be Offered*

The crux of the whole question is undoubtedly the restoration of the Levitical ritual of sacrifice. This is referred to or implied a number of times. In Ezek. xlvi. burnt offerings and sin offerings are mentioned. The bullock, the he-goat, the ram are to be offered. The blood is to be sprinkled on the altar. The priests, who are Levites of the seed of Zadok, are to officiate. Literally interpreted, this means the restoration of the Aaronic priesthood and of the Mosaic ritual of sacrifices essentially unchanged. Yet Paul speaks of these things as "weak and beggarly elements" which have been abolished; and the great theme of Hebrews is the fulfilment of the Old Testament typical system of expiation in the high priestly atonement and mediation of the Lord Jesus Christ. We are told there expressly, "For it is not possible that the blood of bulls and of goats should take away sins" (Heb. x. 4). The author of the Epistle warns his readers most earnestly against returning to this system which has been done away; and he nowhere even hints that a time is "at hand" when it will be fully restored and its observance required of all "Hebrews."

Scofield has endeavored to solve the difficulty by saying:

"Doubtless these offerings will be memorial, looking back to the cross, as the offerings under the old covenant were anticipatory, looking forward to the cross."[12]

But this does not meet the situation at all. There is not the slightest hint in Ezekiel's description of these sacrifices that they will be simply memorial. They must be expiatory in exactly the same sense as the sacrifices described in Leviticus were expiatory. To take any other view of them is to surrender that principle of literal interpretation of prophecy which is fundamental to Dispensationalism and to admit that the Old Testament kingdom prophecies do not enter the New Testament "absolutely unchanged." It is true that they are only "weak and beggarly elements" when viewed in the light of the Cross from which they derive their entire efficacy. But they were not memorial but efficacious in the days of Moses and of David; and in the millennium they must be equally efficacious if the Dispensational system of interpretation is a true one. And this they cannot be unless the teaching of the Epistle to the Hebrews is completely disregarded.[13] To make use of the "beggarly elements" before the reality had come, and to do this when directly commanded to do so, was one thing. To return to them after the reality has come and when expressly commanded not to do so, would be quite another thing. There is only one memorial feast for believers, since the Cross showed so plainly the inadequacy of the blood of bulls and goats, and that is the Holy Supper of the body and blood of Christ, which the Church has observed for centuries and is to keep "until He come." The thought is abhorrent that after He comes, the memory of His atoning work will be kept alive in the hearts of believers by a return to the animal sacrifices of the Mosaic law, the performance of which is so emphatically condemned in passages which speak with unmistakable plainness on this very subject. Here is unquestionably the Achilles' heel of the Dispensational system of interpretation. Its literalistic and Old Testament emphasis leads almost inevitably, if not inevitably, to a doctrine of the millennium which makes it definitely Jewish and represents a turning back from the glory of the gospel to those typical rites and ceremonies which prepared the way for it, and having served that necessary purpose have lost for ever their validity and propriety.[14]

4. The Problem of Salvation in the Millennium

Since, according to Dispensationalists, the kingdom which is to be set up in the millennial age is essentially the same as the kingdom which was declared to be "at hand" by Jesus and by John, it is not altogether strange although decidedly significant that, as we have seen, Scofield places his clearest and most significant statement regarding the "four forms" of the gospel in his notes on the Book of Revelation. While mentioning four, he distinguishes most emphatically between *two* forms of the gospel: the "gospel of the kingdom" and the "gospel of the grace of God"; and between two "preachings" of the former. We have seen that the definition of the "gospel of the kingdom" makes no mention of the Cross. It is "to be established by power, not persuasion." It is to be the period of the visible reign of the King, as distinct from the present period of the preaching of the Cross of the ascended Saviour. It is to be proclaimed by a Jewish remnant who have a "right Jewish" faith. Yet "the multitude that no man could number," converted through the preaching of this remnant, is described as made up of those who have "washed their robes and made them white in the blood of the Lamb." This is the anomaly which results from this attempt to distinguish between the gospel of the kingdom and the gospel of the grace of God.

While Dispensationalists must hold, to be consistent, that the Old Testament ritual of sacrifice will be restored in the millennium, many, perhaps most of them, would insist with Scofield that it will be simply memorial pointing back to the Cross as the event of which they were typical and from which all their efficacy was derived. This raises the question as to the warrant for the assumption that the sole efficacy of the Cross will be recognized in the millennium even if these typical sacrifices are re-established. Two passages especially require attention, Zech. xii. 10 and Isa. liii. The former tells us that "they shall look on me whom they pierced." If this prophecy refers to the death of the Messiah, and if it also refers to the future conversion of Israel, it clearly implies that the Jews will most earnestly mourn and repent of the monstrous crime of slaying their Messiah, their promised King, their true Shepherd (cf. Acts ii. 23). But looked at from the Old Testament standpoint which, according to Dispensationalists, is the only proper one, it says nothing as to any realization on their part of the vicarious significance of His death, that He was the Lamb of God. To interpret it in that sense is to read into it something that is not there, however plainly we may regard it as involved and implied in the light of New Testament truth.[15] Isa. liii. is decidedly different. It speaks unmistakably of vicarious suffering; and in it John the Baptist, who belonged to the Old Testament dispensation, saw, as did other believing Jews, the doctrine of the suffering Servant of the Lord. But the any moment doctrine regarding the setting-up of the kingdom at the first advent (and of the coming at the second advent) makes it impossible for Dispensationalists, with any show of consistency, to claim this prophecy as a kingdom prophecy. For if it is emphasized, the falsity of the claim that "the next thing in the order of revelation as it then stood, should have been the setting up of the Davidic kingdom" is at once apparent. The consequence is, therefore, the tendency to restrict the Cross to the Church age. And if Dispensationalists so minimize or ignore the typical nature of the Mosaic sacrifices as to insist that these sacrifices must be restored in the millennial age, and so ignore Isa. liii. as to assert that the setting up of an earthly kingdom at the time of the first advent was the next step in the prophetic program, the natural tendency will be to regard these animal sacrifices as being quite as sufficient for the Jews during the millennium which is to come as they were during the Old Testament period which is long past. It is impossible, we maintain, for the consistent Dispensationalist to do full justice to the Cross except as it concerns the Church age.

This is further illustrated by Zech. xiii. 1: "In that day there shall be a fountain opened . . . for sin and for uncleanness." Scofield entitles the chapter, "The repentant remnant pointed to the cross"; and Cowper's familiar hymn, "There is a fountain filled with blood," owes its beautiful though painful imagery to this verse. But this is a strictly Christian interpretation (1 Jn. i. 7). Comparing Zech. xiv. 8 and Ezek. xlvii. 1-12, we see that the thought in xiii. 1 is of water, as the symbol of cleansing and purification (Ezek xxxvi. 25), not at all of blood. The laver may be suggested, but not the altar of sacrifice. So we find Darby making this statement: "Here it is practical cleansing with water." This is consistent Dispensationalism. But when he goes on to say: "Faith in Him whom they had pierced was already in their hearts," if his thought is that expressed in Jn. xiii. 10, then Darby has interpreted Zech. xii. 10 in a sense which his system does not warrant, but rather forbids. Consequently, when Savage interprets the opening up of the "fountain" as meaning that "Then Jehovah graciously comes in, and provides full deliverance by cleansing them from all their uncleanness, through the application to their hearts and consciences of the blood of Christ, and through the washing of water by the Word," he is giving a thoroughly evangelical exposition, but one which on Dispensational principles is quite inadmissible. It is the same difficulty which is raised by Rev. vii. 14. How can it be said of those who shall have been converted during the Jewish remnant parenthesis, through the preaching of the "gospel of the kingdom" which does not mention the Cross, that "they have washed their robes and made them white in the blood of the Lamb"?

This Judaizing tendency, which results from failure to do justice to the typical character of the Old Testament economy and its fulfilment in the Christian Church, has always been the weakness and the bane of Millenarianism. It finds its fullest expression in Dispensationalism. It is quite true that Dispensationalism does not Judaize the Christian Church. Dispensationalists are perfectly justified in asserting this. For they draw a very sharp distinction between Christianity and Judaism. They regard the Church as *sui generis,* unique, an entirely new thing, utterly distinct from Israel. But this distinctiveness is not secured by recognizing that the Church is the fruition of the Old Testament economy, as identical with it and also as different from it as the butterfly which comes out of the chrysalis differs from the caterpillar which formed it. This distinctiveness is secured by making the Church a mystery parenthesis, an interruption, in the course of Israel's history. There has been an *"ad interim* disannulling of Judaism" for the period of the Church age. After that age has run its course, there is to be "the regathering of Israel and the restoration of Judaism."[16] Mark well the words, "the restoration of Judaism"! Whatever else this restoration of Judaism may involve, it must certainly include the restoration of the temple worship, of those animal sacrifices the inadequacy of which is so fully exposed in Hebrews. The glorious earthly, Davidic, Messianic, world-dominating kingdom promised to the Jews is to be given to them; and this earthly kingdom is to endure for ever. Dispensationalists vie with those of the circumcision in proclaiming the greatness and glory that is in store for the Jews as an earthly people on this earth. And salvation for all the inhabitants of the earth for all ages to come will literally be "of the Jews." This Judaizes human history to an appalling degree. And in so doing it sadly disparages the Christian Church.

The charge that Dispensationalism disparages the Church will be indignantly repudiated by all Dispensationalists. They tell us that the Church enjoys a unique and heavenly glory as the body and bride of Christ. They describe the heavenly blessings and glories of the Church as so great that it becomes impossible for them to deny that

in and through the Christian Church the literal seed of
Abraham who accept the gospel enjoy far greater blessings
than the earthly ones which they regard as so definitely
promised in the Abrahamic covenant. All this is true. But it
does not affect the main issue. Dispensationalists make of
the Church an elect, we may say a very select, or elite body.
The Church consists of those only who are saved in the
interval between Pentecost and the rapture. "The taking
out from among the Gentiles of a people for His name"
is affirmed to be "the distinctive work of the present or
church-age." And this is explained as meaning that "The
Gospel has never anywhere converted all, but everywhere
has called out *some.*" But in the kingdom age, after the
rapture of the Church, "the enormous majority of earth's
inhabitants will be saved." This can mean nothing else
than that as a soul-saving agency, the Church is to be
regarded as, to say the least, a relative failure. During the
Church age *some* are being saved. After the Church age,
during the great tribulation and the millennium which is
to follow it, and through the preaching of a Jewish gospel
by a Jewish remnant, the *enormous majority* of earth's
inhabitants will be saved. What could disparage the
Church more than this? A Jewish remnant, whose Christianity will be, to say the least, highly questionable, will,
in a brief interval of time, far surpass the Church in
performing what has been for centuries the one supreme
task of the Church, the saving of souls. The only way of
escaping this singularly damaging inference would be to
declare that the souls of Church saints are qualitatively
and intrinsically so much more precious than those of
Jewish-remnant saints and their Gentile converts, that a
few Christians plucked as brands from the burning now
are of more value than a multitude of Jews and Jewish
proselytes however numerous who are to be saved after
the rapture. Are Dispensationalists, however much they
may magnify the Church, really prepared to assert this?

We cannot state the issue more clearly than by referring

to the message sent by Dr. Scofield to the Prophetic Conference in session at Philadelphia May 28-30, 1918:

"To the Philadelphia Conference on the Return of our Lord. Greeting:

I pray that God may guide all your proceedings, especially in the putting forth of a fearless warning that we are in the awful end of the Times of the Gentiles, with no hope for humanity except in the personal return of the Lord in glory; and also a statement of the fundamentals of Christian belief, which may form a clear basis for Christian fellowship in a day of apostasy."[17]

The words to which we would direct particular attention are these, "with no hope for humanity except in the personal return of the Lord in glory." This is a thoroughly mistaken statement.[18] But it was a perfectly logical one for Dr. Scofield to make. The hope of humanity lies today, as since the day of Pentecost, in the faithful proclamation of the gospel of the grace of God, throughout the whole world, to every creature, to Jew and Gentile, to the wise and to the unwise. That has been the task of the Church for 1900 years. It is a glorious task. And the Church has had and has today the promise of Omnipotence in performing it. "All power is given unto me in heaven and on earth. Go ye therefore and make disciples of all nations . . . and, Lo I am with you alway even unto the end of the world." The idea that the Church is bankrupt, that the Church is inadequate to the task assigned her, that the presence of the Church on earth interferes with the realization of God's purpose to save humanity, is as false as it is dangerous. The Church has every reason to lament in dust and ashes her failure to fulfil the Great Commission of her ascended and all-powerful Lord, her failure to use the power He has promised her for the performance of the task He has assigned her. But to declare that this is not the task of the Church, or that the Church cannot perform it is unscriptural and dangerously so. The great weakness of the Dispensational viewpoint is its pessimism and defeatism. It is expecting the Lord to accomplish after His coming the task which He has assigned His

Church to perform in anticipation of His coming. It is expecting Him to accomplish through a Jewish remnant and by His visible presence what He has declared that He will accomplish through His Church by the power of His Holy Spirit.

The worst thing about this doctrine is, we repeat, that in effect it assigns to a Jewish remnant of the end-time the task which it tells us the Church is unable to accomplish: it assigns to a Jewish remnant the carrying out of the Great Commission. According to Ironside this is one of the major errors of the Bullingerites. He tells us:

"According to the Bullingeristic interpretation of this passage, we should have to paraphrase it somewhat as follows: 'Then the eleven disciples went away into Galilee, into a mountain where Jesus had appointed them. And when they saw Him, they worshipped Him; but some doubted. And Jesus came and spake unto them saying, All power is given unto me in heaven and earth, and after two entire dispensations have rolled by, I command that the remnant of Israel who shall be living two thousand or more years later shall go out and teach the nations, baptizing them in the name of the Father and of the Son and of the Holy Ghost, teaching them to observe all things whatsoever I have commanded you, but from which I absolve all believers between the present hour and that coming age, and lo, I will be with that remnant until the close of Daniel's seventieth week.'"19

Ironside concludes this indictment of the Ultra-Dispensationalist view with these words: "Can anything be more absurd, more grotesque—and I might add, more wicked—than thus to twist and misuse the words of our Lord Jesus Christ?"

We heartily agree with this brother whose praise in the gospel is in all the churches in his condemnation of this Jewish-remnant-izing of the Great Commission by the Bullingerites. It is unscriptural and it is "wicked." But what surprises us is that Dr. Ironside and the many other followers of Darby and Scofield seem to overlook the fact that the view which he so severely denounces is the logical and inevitable result of those very teachings upon which Dispensationalists have been insisting for years. They have been telling us that Matthew's Gospel is a "Jewish" gospel. They have assured us that the disciples to whom Jesus spoke in the discourse recorded in Matt. xxiv., whom He addressed as "ye" and whom He certainly included in the company called "my elect," did not represent the Church which He had already declared that He would build, but represented a Jewish remnant of the end-time, which will be on earth after the rapture of the Church. But, if the discourse of Matt. xxiv. was addressed to a Jewish remnant of the future, it is certainly logical, inescapably logical, to regard the Great Commission of Matt. xxviii. as addressed to that same remnant. As proof that this is so, we have only to refer our Dispensationalist brethren to that Commentary, which is the great treasure-house of Dispensational teaching, Darby's *Synopsis*. Darby tells us regarding the Great Commission: "It links the testimony to the nations with a remnant in Israel owning Jesus as Messiah but now risen from the dead, as He has said, but not to a Christ known as ascended on high."[20] If this is not in all essentials the doctrine which Ironside so severely denounces when affirmed by Bullinger, the difference is so slight as to be negligible. The Great Commission, according to Darby the apostle of Dispensationalism, is for a Jewish remnant and the gospel it is to preach is not the good news of a Christ who has ascended on high, but of a Christ who was, and is to be again, on earth, because the Jewish gospel concerns the earth, while the covenants and promises to the Church are heavenly.

Dispensationalists cannot shift to the shoulders of the Ultra-Dispensationalists the onus of taking away the Great Commission from the Church of this present Gospel age and making it the marching orders of a Jewish remnant of the future. For either they teach this doctrine themselves or they insist on principles of interpretation which lead inevitably to it. Surely, it is not too much to ask that if they denounce as heretical the conclusions, they should be willing to reexamine carefully the validity of the principles on which they rest.

CONCLUSION

SINCE the examination of Dispensationalism upon which we have been engaged has been somewhat lengthy and has involved the detailed consideration of many topics, it may be well to sum up briefly the course and results of our investigation.

The primary aim has been to show that Dispensationalism has its source in a faulty and unscriptural literalism which, in the important field of prophecy, ignores the typical and preparatory character of the Old Testament dispensation. The assertion that "Israel always means Israel" and that the kingdom prophecies regarding Israel enter the New Testament "absolutely unchanged" leads at once and inevitably to the conclusion that the "kingdom of heaven" which John the Baptist announced as "at hand" was an earthly, political, national kingdom of the Jews. Since neither Jesus nor His apostles made any effort to introduce such a kingdom, it must then be held that this kingdom offer was rejected by the Jews and the establishing of it postponed by God. This prepares the way for the claim that this postponement made possible the introduction of an entirely new thing, the Church, which is held to be a "mystery" unknown to the prophets, a "parenthesis" between the Old Testament kingdom of the past and the Old Testament kingdom of the future, an "interruption" of the prophetic program for the glorification of Israel.

Closely related to this literalistic and anti-typical conception of the kingdom is the claim that the words "at hand" mean that "no known or predicted event must intervene" before it could be introduced. This definition cannot be defended as "literal": it is a purely arbitrary assumption that "at hand" means *proximate,* that the coming may take place "at any moment." Yet this arbitrary definition involves very serious conclusions: as regards the first advent, that this Jewish kingdom could have been set up at once, that the Cross played no part in its establishment; as regards the second advent, that the Church can have no predicted history in the New Testament, as it is claimed that it has none in the Old, that the Church is to look for and expect but one event, the "any moment" rapture. This definition of "at hand" also requires that a distinction be made between this any moment coming "for the saints" and a subsequent coming "with the saints." In between these two comings many predicted events, notably the great tribulation, find a place.

The rapture of the Church, as a heavenly body, prepares the way, according to this teaching, for the literal fulfilment of the kingdom prophecies to the Jews, as an earthly people. The distinction between Jew and Gentile was, we are told, only broken down temporarily, for the period of the Church age; it will be re-established during the parenthesis between the rapture and the appearing; and this interval and the millennium which follows it will witness the "restoration of Judaism." This new age, which may be ushered in at any moment by the rapture of the Church, will be pre-eminently the day of salvation, of mass salvation; and the "enormous majority of earth's inhabitants will be saved." The gospel which will then be preached will be a kingdom gospel which will involve the re-establishment of the Mosaic law and the observance of the Levitical sacrifices and feasts as "memorials." How the Cross, which could form no part of the kingdom gospel as preached at the first advent, can enter into the kingdom gospel as preached by the Jewish remnant after the rapture is not clear. The Church is founded on the Cross. But the Jewish remnant will have a right Jewish faith and can have neither "the Church's blessings nor the Church's hope." Otherwise it would have been, must have been, raptured with the Church. Yet after the rapture the Jewish remnant "will then be the missionary, and to the very 'nations' now called 'Christian'!" Thus the kingdom will be restored to Israel. The future belongs to the Jew!

This Dispensational system of interpreting Scripture is very popular today. The reasons are not far to seek. Literal interpretation seems to make Bible study easy. It also seems reverent. It argues on this wise: "God must have said just what He means, and must mean just what He has said; and what He has said is to be taken just as He said it, *i.e., literally.*" But the New Testament makes it plain that literal interpretation was a stumbling block to the Jews. It concealed from them the most precious truths of Scripture. The temple and its worship were typical of the high priestly work of Christ (Jn. ii. 19). But the Jews failed to understand His application of it to Himself, and used His words to encompass His destruction (Matt. xxvi. 61). Moses, Aaron, and David were types of Christ as Prophet, Priest, and King. He came to fulfil the law and the prophets. But the fulfilment which He offered the Jews was so different from their literal and carnal desires and expectations that they sent their King to Calvary. The kingdom which He preached and which He declared to be "at hand," to be already "come," corresponds to that spiritual Church which He said that He would build; and the gospel of the kingdom as proclaimed by His followers led to the founding of Christian churches throughout the length and breadth of the Roman world.

The Church is not a mystery in the sense that it is an unexpected and temporary interruption of the prophetic program for Israel. It does not interrupt: it unfolds and fulfils that program. The Great Commission is not reserved for a Jewish remnant of the end-time. It has been the marching orders of the Church for nigh two thousand years. It authorizes and requires the offering of salvation to all men. The wall of separation between Jew and Gentile has been broken down. The limitations and peculiarities of Judaism have been done away. They have been done away not for the time being only, but for ever.

They are never to be restored. There is a great and glorious future for the Jews. But that future is to be found in and through the Christian Church. For there is but one true olive tree. All the true seed of Abraham (both Jew and Gentile) are or will be in it and partake of its fatness. Unbelieving Israelites were cast off; believing Gentiles were grafted in; they will remain in it unless they fall away through unbelief; and finally "all Israel" will be saved by being grafted back into the one and only true olive tree. There is no distinctively Jewish age for the Jew to look forward to. Salvation is of the Jews. But the blessing of Abraham is now fully come; and the Gentiles are "blessed with faithful Abraham." Old things are become new; and the old are passed away for ever. Whether the Jews are to return to the earthly Canaan is a matter of relatively little importance. That they may become citizens of the holy city, the New Jerusalem, is the only thing that really matters.

The Church is a heavenly body, with a high and heavenly calling and destiny. But the Church Militant is still on earth, she has a work to do on earth, and earthly events concern her greatly. She is to look and long for the coming of her Lord; and her love for Him will make her patient, vigilant, and faithful in the doing of His will. Whether He comes "at even, or at midnight, or at the cock-crowing, or in the morning," she will be ready to welcome Him. But the Christian must not allow his natural shrinking from death or his dread of tribulation to lead him to attach a meaning to the words "at hand" which is thoroughly unscriptural and leads to interpretations which endanger some of the cardinal doctrines of the faith. The intense interest which Dispensationalists themselves show in the discovery of signs of the nearness of the rapture furnishes of itself convincing proof of the fallacy of their *any moment* doctrine.

Finally, and most important of all, the rapture of the Church, whether it comes today or tomorrow or not

within the lifetime of this generation or of many generations yet unborn, will not prepare the way for the salvation of "humanity": it will close the door of hope to the
unsaved of "humanity." "Now is the accepted time; now
is the day of salvation." The presence of the Church on
earth does not prevent a more inclusive work of redemption; her taking away from the earth will not prepare the
way for the more successful prosecution of the missionary
enterprise. The task is her task, committed to her by her
ascended and almighty Lord. Not until that task is accomplished may she confidently expect Him to come to
reckon with His servants. Whether the number of the
redeemed is now nearly complete or yet greater tasks await
her in the coming years, the Church should show her longing for His coming by her zeal in hastening the completion of her task. As to this all Christians, be they Millenarians or anti-Millenarians should be of one mind and
heart, that all who love His appearing should show it by
their zeal in carrying the glad tidings of His great salvation to the ends of the earth. For it is only when her task
is accomplished that

> "The great Church victorious
> Shall be the Church at rest."

It is indeed strange, passing strange, that a teaching
which holds out as the hope of the world the removal of
the Church from the world and the world-wide and glo-
riously successful proclamation of a Jewish gospel by a
Jewish remnant should have gained credence with and en-
thusiastic support from very many earnest Christians, and
that it should have been doing this increasingly for a
century. The doctrine of the Church and the doctrine of
the Coming are very precious and important. It is to
their credit that Dispensationalists have emphasized certain aspects of these doctrines which have often been neglected. But it is distressing to find these doctrines so
taught by them, that they are brought into serious con-

flict with some of the clearest and most precious doctrines of the Christian faith, as that faith is set forth in the
Word of God. There are many things regarding the future which are by no means plain. One thing we believe
to be clearly revealed. The task of saving sinners and
edifying saints is to be accomplished through the proclamation of the gospel of the grace of God, which concerns
the kingdom of God. This glorious task has been committed to the Church. It must be accomplished by the
Church. It is not to pass *at any moment* to a *Jewish
remnant* which will preach *another* gospel which is not
another *gospel*. The hope of the world is not in the
restoration of Judaism. The hope of the world is in the
world-wide proclamation of that gospel of the Cross of
Christ which is "unto Jews a stumbling block and unto
Gentiles foolishness; but unto them which are called, both
Jews and Greeks, Christ the power of God and the wisdom
of God."

This is the great issue in the millennial problem. A
millennium, which will be a thousand-year reign of Christ
on earth over a *redeemed* humanity, would be in a very
real sense only a foretaste of that eternal state of blessedness which God has prepared for them that love Him.
Such a dispensation would be indeed a golden age compared with this vale of tears, this scene of conflict and
trial, of suffering and sorrow, of faith and hope deferred,
in which God's people have lived for unnumbered generations. But it would be only as the dawning which
would soon pass into the perfect day. Whether there is
to be such a millennium is a question which must be
decided in the light of Scripture. It does not seem to
involve any issue sufficiently serious to warrant its being
a divisive factor among those that are of the household of
faith. If the millennium is to be the golden age of the
Church and is wholly future, it presents the difficulty, a
somewhat serious one, that it makes it difficult, to say
the least, for any Christian living before the millennium
really to "watch for" a coming of Christ which is to fol-

low it. The issue becomes far more serious when the millennium is regarded not only as future but as quite distinct from the Church age, yet as being, like the Church age, a "day of salvation." It becomes an issue of the utmost importance, a most pressing and practical question, when this new dispensation is regarded as pre-eminently *the day of salvation*, the day which will witness, not "the calling out of *some*," but the saving of "the vast majority of mankind," a glorious task to be accomplished, not through the Church, but by a Jewish remnant after the Church has been removed. For then it tends necessarily and inevitably to weaken and even to nullify the solemn and urgent proclamation of the Church, "Behold, now is the accepted time; behold, now is the day of salvation," by declaring that a *more acceptable time,* a *far greater day of salvation* is "at hand" and may be ushered in "at any moment," that the presence of the Church on earth delays its coming, and that Christians should earnestly pray for the rapture of the Church in order that this better day for humanity may come. To expose the danger in this teaching regarding things to come which is a cardinal doctrine of Dispensationalism and to prove it to be unscriptural has been the principal aim in this discussion of *Prophecy and the Church.*

APPENDIX

PRESIDENT CHAFER ON MATTHEW XVIII. 8f.

THE interpretation of this passage recently given by President Chafer of the Dallas Theological Seminary is a striking example of extreme literalism and is specially pertinent because it bears upon that distinction between Israel and the Church which is drawn so sharply by the advocates of the Dispensational method of interpreting Scripture. In a context in which he is discussing the difference between the conception of eternal life as it concerns the Jew and the Christian, Dr. Chafer appeals to six passages, of which this is the last, as proving this distinction:

"(f) Matthew xviii. 8, 9, which passage presents the alternative of entering life—a future experience—maimed or halt, or entering 'everlasting fire' or 'hell fire.' That a Christian, already possessing eternal life and perfected as he is in Christ, could not enter heaven maimed or halt when his body is to be like unto Christ's glorious body, or into hell fire after Christ has said that he shall not come into judgment and that he shall never perish, is obvious indeed."[1]

The distinction drawn here by Dr. Chafer makes it quite clear that he takes the language of Matt. xviii. 8f. with entire literalness. If we understand the argument, it is this. For the Jew who is expecting the ushering in of the Messianic kingdom, self-mutilation may be necessary for the avoiding of offences. If so, it should be resorted to, although it will mean mutilation not only for time but for eternity. By the Christian, who is a member of the body of Christ, such mutilation may not be practiced; he must keep his body physically perfect, since his resurrection body is to be perfect like Christ's resurrection body. Consequently, we have here, according to Dr. Chafer, convincing proof of the wide difference which there is between the Jew and the Christian both in time and in eternity.

It would be hard to find an example that illustrates more clearly the great importance of the issues that may be involved in literal interpretation and the extremes to which this principle is often carried by Dispensationalists. Consequently the fact that the literal interpretation of this passage and its implications are stated for us by one of the leaders of contemporary Dispensationalism makes this statement worthy of the most careful consideration. The question involved is a complicated one.

First of all, there is this important question: Does the principle laid down by Dr. Chafer mean that all physical defects and injuries must appear in the resurrection body? If such were the case, and if the resurrection bodies of all Christians are to be perfect, then it would follow that the Church on earth can be composed of the physically perfect only. Not only is Jacob excluded from the Church as a Jew of the OT period; he is also excluded because he limped away from the Jabbok and continued to limp until he died; and poor Jacob is to limp through all eternity! If so, then, by parity of reasoning, John Milton and George Matheson, and Fanny Crosby cannot have been Christians; and their blindness was not merely for time but for eternity. This is a very drastic and even monstrous conclusion to draw. Who will venture to draw it?

Does this principle, then, apply only to *self*-mutilations? Is it only such defects which would appear in the resurrection body? This would make the problem somewhat less difficult. But even then the difference would have no basis historically. We have no data to show that the Jews who were looking for the establishment of the kingdom 2000 years ago, have been looking for it ever since, and are still looking for it, ever practiced self-mutilation as a means of securing entrance into it. Certainly they do not do so today. Or, does this apply only to those Jews who will be on earth at the time of the rapture, and who will then, it is to be inferred, enter without resurrection or change into the Messianic kingdom? These are questions which demand careful attention if this passage is to be taken literally; and Dr. Chafer has not made the application of the principle of literal interpretation clear in these respects.

In opposition to Dr. Chafer's literal interpretation of this passage and the application which he makes of it, the following points are especially to be noted: (a) Self-mutilation was strictly forbidden the Jews by the law of Moses. "Cuttings" for the dead and similar practices were heathenish (Lev. xix. 28, xxi. 5, Deut. xiv. 1). Physical perfection was highly desirable and in some cases indispensable (Lev. xxi. 17f.). The great scene on mount Carmel shows that self-mutilation is both pagan and futile (1 Kings xviii. 28). (*b*) In the case in question, the fact that only "one eye" or the "right eye" is to be plucked out implies quite clearly that the language is figurative. "The lust of the flesh and the lust of the eyes and the pride of life" can be ministered to by one eye almost if not quite as well as by two eyes. History knows of one-eyed men that were monsters of iniquity! (*c*) The Christian who is to have a perfect resurrection body is given, literally interpreted, far more drastic commands than is the Jew. Paul lays down the principle that if a man is a Christian, he has "crucified the flesh" (Gal. v. 24). He tells the Christian: "mortify [*nekroō*, literally, 'cause to die' or 'make corpses of'] your members which are upon the earth" (Col. iii. 5); and again, "if ye through the Spirit do mortify [*thanatoō*, literally, 'put to death'] the deeds of the body, ye shall live" (Rom. viii. 13). Taken literally, these passages mean that every Christian is to mutilate himself, even to the point of self-crucifixion, which is far worse than the sacrificing of an arm or a leg or even of an eye. Yet despite this self-mutilation the Christian is, as Dr. Chafer reminds us, to have a perfect resurrection body. (*d*) If the command in Matt. xviii. 8f. is to be taken with entire literalness, does the same apply to xix. 12? We know that Origen, whom Dispensationalists denounce as the great allegorizer, took it literally and later acknowledged his error.[2] All true Protestants regard the "mortifications of the flesh" which are practiced by various sects as forms of penance, *e.g.*, by the Flagellants, as distinctly contrary to the spirit of the New Testament.

What then is the conclusion which we must draw? It is this, that Dr. Chafer succeeds in finding in this passage evidence of a marked difference between the future state of the Jew and of the Christian only by an inconsistent application of the principle of literal interpretation, literal as regards the Jew, figurative as applied to the Christian; that his literal application of it to the Jew has as little warrant historically as a similar application to the Christian would have were he to draw it; and that the argument that the physical defects of the mortal body, even if limited to self-inflicted mutilations, must appear in the resurrection body and cannot, therefore, apply to the bodies of Christians who are to be raised in glory, is entirely unwarranted.

THE SCOFIELD REFERENCE BIBLE

THE fact that within a generation more than 2,000,000 copies of this Reference Bible have been printed in this country has made it a very influential factor in the religious world of today. There are thousands of Christians at the present time for whom it is their principal source of Biblical knowledge, as well as their final court of appeal. "The Scofield Bible says so!" That it is a Dispensational Bible and that it has been a potent factor in the dissemination of Dispensational doctrine has already been pointed out. The distinctively Dispensational notes and comments are of course an integral part of the system of interpretation which they represent and must stand or fall with it. Many of these notes have come up for consideration in our study of Dispensationalism. But there are others of a more general character which are of almost equal importance, because they throw light upon the methods employed in the preparation of this work and help to answer the important question whether it fully merits the immense popularity which it enjoys. Among these are the following:

Preface (*p. iv.*). "Chronological data have also been supplied." This is described as one of the "distinct improvements" to be found in the Revised Edition (1917). These data consist in little more than the insertion of what is very largely the Ussher Chronology in the page headings; and in occasional references to Ussher in some of the special introductions to the several books. This reverses a trend that has been quite noticeable in recent years. The Ussher chronology was first placed in the margin of editions of the AV in A.D. 1701; and it was widely used for about 200 years. Recently the tendency has been to omit it (as in the case of the ARV). Whether it is as unreliable as some would have us believe may be seriously questioned. But, to say the least, it contains

some features that are of decidedly questionable value. Scofield both accepts it and rejects it. Thus, he gives Ussher's
familiar date of creation (4004 B.C.), but intimates in a footnote that this is the date of a re-creation, and that the first
creation (Gen. i. 1) is to be referred to a "dateless past."
Scofield apparently agreed with Ussher that the genealogies
in Gen. v. and xi. furnish the basis for an exact chronology,
a position no longer held by many conservative scholars.
How fully his "chronological data" correspond with Ussher's
chronology is indicated by the fact that the marginal dates
given in the Book of Esther (B.C. 521-509) identify Ahasuerus
with Darius Hystaspis (cf. marginal dates of Haggai and Zechariah). Yet in the margin of Ezra iv. 6 it is positively stated
that Ahasuerus was Xerxes. In the case of the Epistle of
James, Scofield has given Ussher's date (A.D. 60), but has expressed complete agreement with Weston's opinion that
James was "the first Epistle to Christians," which would date
it at or before A.D. 54 (cf. RB, p. 1267). On the other hand,
in the case of Obadiah he changed Ussher's date (B.C. 587) to
B.C. 887, a date which readers unfamiliar with the reasons for
the divergence might easily regard as a misprint. Most remarkable of all, about the time when the decision was made
to place the Ussher chronology in the margin of RB, Scofield
adopted one of the most radical of the modifications of that
chronology proposed by Anstey. Such being the case, it would
have avoided confusion and misunderstanding had he simply
stated that, for the sake of convenience, he was restoring the
Ussher chronology in the margin of the text and at the same
time pointed out in what respects he deemed it unreliable and
in need of correction. This would not only have removed
the difficulties just mentioned, it would also have relieved
Scofield of direct responsibility for such dates as B.C. 1520
for Job, 1014 for the Song of Songs, 977 for Ecclesiastes, dates
which at best can only be approximate, but give the appearance of an accurate knowledge which no one can justly claim
to possess.

Gen. i. 1f. (p. 3). In adopting the theory of a timeless interval between vss. 1 and 2, in the course of which the pri-
mordial earth of vs. 1 became waste and void, Scofield was
apparently influenced by the theory that the earth was originally created to be the abode of Satan, and that the wrecking

of that wonderful earth was the consequence and punishment of his fall. This theory is based primarily, it would seem, on a literal interpretation of the highly figurative and ironical language of Ezek. xxviii. (*RB*, p. 871). The Bible is very reticent regarding such high mysteries. But it represents heaven as the proper abode of all angelic beings. Consequently, the words, "I will ascend into heaven" (Isa. xiv. 13), are appropriate to describe the arrogant pride of the king of Babylon and the words, "Thou hast been in Eden the garden of God" (Ezek. xxviii. 13) may be applied ironically to the king of Tyrus. But they are not applicable to Satan whose original abode was heaven and who is "the real prince of this world" (*RB*, p. 726) only in the sense that the fall of man made mankind the bond-servant of sin and of Satan. The heading inserted between the first and second verses, "Earth made waste and empty by judgment (Jer. iv. 23-26)," finds no support in the verse appealed to, which in its context clearly describes a vision of the future not the past. There is no convincing reason for changing the first "was" of Gen. i. 2 into "became." The most natural interpretation of this verse is, we believe, that it describes the state of created and unorganized matter, when God began to fashion the cosmos by the eight creative fiats of vss. 3-27. None of the passages appealed to by Scofield, if correctly interpreted, lend any real support to the "catastrophe" theory (Isa. xiv. 9-14, xxiv. 1, xlv. 18, Ezek. xxviii. 12-15). It is noteworthy that Bartoli in defending it makes large use of extra-Biblical literature, especially the Apocrypha and Pseudepigrapha (*The Biblical Story of Creation*, 1926), descriptions which are too vague, wild, and grotesque to commend themselves to the sober judgment of the careful student of the Bible.

Gen. ii. 4 (p. 7). "In His redemptive relation to man, Jehovah has seven compound names," etc. One of the best illustrations of that tendency to carry valid principles to unwarranted extremes, which is a marked weakness of Dispensational interpretation, is the exaggerated importance attached to the number *seven*. That seven is sometimes a significant number, no one will deny. But this fact does not justify us in attaching importance to every seven in the Bible or in making the quest of sevens an important principle of interpretation. Jehovah does not have only "seven compound names" in His "redemptive relation to man." If "the Lord is my shepherd" (Ps. xxiii. 1) is such a name, surely "the Lord is my Light" (Ps. xxvii. 1), and "the Lord is my helper" (Heb. xiii. 6) have a right to be included in the list. Ps. xviii. 1-2 contains at least eight such names.[3] Scofield would probably not have analyzed the Book of Ezekiel into "seven great prophetic strains, indicated by the expression, 'The hand of the Lord was upon me'" but for the fact that this phrase occurs seven times. To find three (or parts of three) of these great prophetic strains all in a single chapter (chap. iii.) is manifestly absurd, since it involves splitting up the account of Ezekiel's commission which is clearly a unit into three parts. By parity of reasoning the Book of Jeremiah could be divided into fourteen parts, because the words, "behold the days are coming," occur fourteen times (twice seven) in them.[4]

Gen. x. 2 (p. 18). "From these seven sons of Japheth are descended the goyim, or Gentile nations, translated 'heathen' 148 times in the AV." This note implies that the word "Gentiles" is used only of the Japhethites, and that the only other rendering of the Hebrew word goyim is "heathen." Such is not the case. In the AV, the text used by Scofield, goyim is rendered only 30 times by "Gentiles" (chiefly in Isaiah); elsewhere it is rendered "heathen" (142 times), "nations" (373 times), "people" (11 times). In Gen. x. it occurs six times, being rendered once by "Gentiles" (vs. 5), and five times by "nations" (vss. 5, 20, 31, 32 [twice]). In vs. 20 it is used of the Hamites, which shows that they are to be included among the "Gentile nations," an expression which would also include most of the Shemites as well.

Gen. xi. 9 (p. 19). Babel (Greek, Babylon) does not mean "confusion." It apparently means "gate of God" (bab-ili), and the city is given this name because the gate was the place of judgment and it was at Babel that the Lord judged the arrogance of the builders of the tower and pronounced upon them the judgment of the confusion of tongues. The discussion of the figurative meanings of Babel (RB, p. 724) is a very striking example of non-literal interpretation by a literalist!

Gen. xvii. 1 (p. 26). The explanation of "Almighty God" (El Shaddai) as "the breasted" is almost certainly wrong. It is contrary to the vocalization of the Hebrew text and is not supported by the ancient versions. Its origin may perhaps be traced to the use of the Latin word "uberrimus" to render it (cf. Kircher's *Concordentia* [1609], also Matt. Poole, *Synopsis* [1669]). But there is much uncertainty as to its "root, form, and meaning."[5] Scofield's explanation makes us think rather of the many-breasted Diana of Ephesus than of the God of Israel, who is "a Spirit and does not have a body like men."

Gen. xxxii. 28 (p. 48). Regarding Israel, the new name of Jacob, Scofield tells us: "When used *characteristically* 'Jacob' is the name for the natural posterity of Abraham, Isaac, and Jacob, 'Israel' for the spiritual part of the nation." This is, unfortunately, one of those simple and obvious explanations which seem very appropriate but tell us very little. For, when are these names used characteristically? It is true that divine names compounded with Israel are far more frequent than those compounded with Jacob. Thus "Lord God of Israel" occurs more than 150 times, while "God of Jacob" is comparatively rare (less than 20 times). But the fact that the latter does occur is significant. Furthermore, the name "Israel" is the special and distinctive, we might even say "characteristic" name of the Northern Kingdom as distinguished from Judah. This kingdom was *characterized* by apostasy, the worship of the golden calves, and was finally destroyed because of its stiff-necked (Jacob-like?) refusal to do the will of God. It is noteworthy that *RB* misinterprets Isa. ix. 8, to which it appeals as illustrating this explanation: "The Lord sent a word into Jacob, and it hath lighted upon Israel." The meaning is not that "The 'word' was sent to all the people, 'Jacob,' but it 'lighted upon Israel,' *i.e.*, was comprehended by the spiritual part of the people." The word "light upon" has nothing at all to do with spiritual illumination or receptivity. It is the archaic word for "alight." Here, as in Gen. xxiv. 64 and 2 Kgs. v. 21, it renders the Hebrew word "fall." The meaning is that the "word" of judgment uttered against Jacob (the people as a whole?), has fallen or rather will fall (prophetic perfect) upon Israel (the apostate Northern Kingdom), visiting it with disaster or destruction at the hands of Rezin and the Philistines. Judah which has seemed to be on the verge of destruction as a result of the "confederacy" between Rezin of Syria and Pekah, king of Israel, will not be involved in this tragedy. Had Scofield **consulted "good old Matthew Henry," who according to**

Gaebelein was "in darkness" as regards the interpretation of prophecy, he would not have made this rather serious blunder.

Num. xxxv. 6 (p. 213). "The cities of refuge are types of Christ sheltering the sinner from judgment." But the intent of this legislation, as is very carefully stated, was not to shelter the *sinner* but the *innocent,* that the man who had *not* committed a deed worthy of death might be saved from the wrath of the avenger of blood. The word for "refuge" *(miqlat)* used in this legislation is a technical term which is never used of "refuge" in the ordinary sense. The word used in this connection that does have typical meaning elsewhere in the OT and NT is "redeemer" *(goel),* which in these passages where the cities of refuge are referred to is properly rendered by "avenger" or "revenger" in AV.

Joshua (Introduction, p. 259). "The key-phrase [of Joshua] is 'Moses my servant is dead' (Josh. i. 2). Law, of which Moses was the representative, could never give a sinful people victory (Heb. vii. 19; Rom. vi. 14; viii. 2-4)." This comment is so completely contrary to what the Book of Joshua itself tells us, that it almost makes the thoughtful reader gasp in astonishment. Moses was dead. That is true. But Moses was only the lawgiver; he was not the law. The law was not dead. Chap. i., after referring to Moses' death, proceeds at once to tell us most emphatically that the keeping of the law which Moses had commanded was the one and only condition of successful conquest of the land. Joshua was to "observe to do according to all the law" that he might prosper. The "book of the law" was to be his constant meditation that he might have good success. The reason that Moses was not permitted to be the invasion-leader was not that he represented the law, but that he, the lawgiver, had himself broken the law (Deut. xxxii. 51f.), had transgressed the Third Commandment by arrogating to himself and Aaron the honor due to God only (Num. xx. 10f.). Since it was clearly the desire to bring out the typical element in the life of Joshua, and in so doing to set the gospel in sharp contrast with the law, which is responsible for this mistaken comment, it is to be remembered that it was precisely as lawgiver that Moses was the pre-eminent type of Christ. As lawgiver he was the unique OT prophet, declaring the will of God for the salvation and sanctification of men, and the type of the Prophet who was

to come (Deut. xviii. 15-19). Moses was far more definitely
a type of the Messiah than Joshua was, despite the fact that
the name Joshua has the same meaning as the name Jesus.

Josh. v. 2 (p. 263). Appealing to Ex. iv. 24f., *RB* suggests
that "during the later years of the Egyptian bondage, the
separating sign had been neglected." This explanation conflicts with Josh. v. 5 which expressly states that "all the people
that came out were circumcised." Moses' example cannot be
properly appealed to as proving the contrary since he had
been a sojourner in Midian for forty years and had married
the daughter of Jethro. It was during the Wanderings, not
while in Egypt, that the rite was neglected. It is much better
to find the explanation of the "reproach of Egypt" in Ex.
xxxii. 12. As a punishment for their apostasy at Kadesh
Barnea, of which their failure to practice the rite of circumcision during the 40 years of wandering was a sample, they
were compelled to remain outside the land until the generation of wrath had perished. This made them and their God
a reproach and derision in the eyes of Egypt. He had brought
them out, but had not brought them in. Cf., Ezek. xxxvi. 20.

1 Kgs. vi. 4 (p. 393). "In the holy of holies in the tabernacle
no light but the shekinah glory was provided. In many ways
Solomon's temple manifests the spiritual deterioration of the
people and Jehovah's condescension to it in grace." The first
statement quoted is based on 1 Kgs. vi. 4 which states, according to AV, "And for the house he made windows of narrow lights." The meaning is not perfectly clear. ARV renders by "windows of fixed lattice-work," giving as a marginal
paraphrase, "or *windows broad* within and *narrow* without."
Cf. Ezek. xl. 16, xli. 16, 26. The most probable explanation
of this difficult expression seems to be that these windows (in
the holy of holies?) were so constructed as to permit ventilation and at the same time secure perfect privacy, like the
lattices in an oriental harem. Since the temple differed from
the tabernacle in being a permanent structure, ventilation
was absolutely necessary; and it was apparently provided for
in this way. There is not one word in Kings or Chronicles
or anywhere else in Scripture to justify the claim made by
Scofield, on the basis apparently of his misunderstanding of
this verse, that the plan or the execution of the plan for the
construction of the temple included unlawful innovations,

that it was not made as God intended. It was the fulfilment of the most earnest desire of David, which the Lord prom-ised David should be carried out by his son (1 Chr. xxviii. 6, 11f.). The shekinah glory filled it at its dedication (1 Kgs. viii. 10f., 2 Chr. vii. 1f.) exactly as it had filled the tabernacle (Ex. xl. 34f.), which had been constructed in all respects "as the Lord commanded Moses."

1 Kgs. xviii. 3 (p. 412). It is not easy to see how a true and zealous servant of the Lord could have held office under Ahab and escaped the wrath of Jezebel. But it is noteworthy that, while the Biblical writer goes out of his way as it were (vss. 3f., cf. vs. 13) to speak a good word for Obadiah, Scofield goes out of his way to disparage and denounce him: by insert-ing the heading, "A believer out of touch with God," and by adding a decidedly derogatory marginal note.

Job xxxviii. 1 (p. 594). "Answered" occurs in its ordinary sense of "reply to" nearly 50 times in Job. There is not the slightest warrant for paraphrasing it in this one passage by "Jehovah answered *for* [or on behalf of] Job," in order, as it would seem, to turn a rebuke into a vindication. That the Lord is *answering* Job in this long discourse, and that there is in this answer not a little of reproof and rebuke is quite clear; and Job clearly so understood it, as is shown by xlii. 1-6. God first rebukes Job for presuming to know more than he did or could about God and the mysteries of His providential dealings with mankind and with himself in particular; and then He defends Job against the unjust accusations of his friends (xlii. 7f.) and rewards him.

Ezek. xxxviii. 2 (p. 883). "That the primary reference is to the Northern (European) powers headed up by Russia, all agree." In view of the meager amount of information given us in Scripture regarding Tubal and Meshech, the positiveness with which they are identified with Tobolsk and Moscow is quite unwarranted, because it lacks any adequate justification in fact.[6] It is by no means certain that Rosh, which AV renders "chief," is here a proper name, although nowhere else so used in the Bible. That as a proper name it stands for Russia is even more doubtful. Consequently, Scofield's "all agree" is a serious overstatement, unless it is taken to mean "all [Dis-pensationalists] agree."

Hos. i. 9 (p. 921). In commenting on the words "my people,"

Scofield says that this is "an expression used in the OT exclusively of Israel the nation. It is never used of the patriarchs, Abraham, Isaac, and Jacob. See Matt. ii. 6." This is a false antithesis. It is quite true that "my people" is not used of the patriarchs: Israel did not become a people until the sojourn in Egypt, when the seventy persons had multiplied many fold. But it is not true that this expression is used "exclusively of Israel the nation." It is used of *Egypt* in Isa. xix. 25. We might think that a *Reference Bible* which places the emphasis on prophetic and dispensational truth would attach great importance to this wonderful prophecy. Not only is no mention made of it here, but there is no marginal comment whatsoever on this verse in *RB*. That the distinctive title of Israel should be bestowed by an OT prophet on a Gentile nation does not fit into the Dispensational system of interpretation. It indicates too clearly that Isaiah foresaw the Church age when the distinction between Jew and Gentile should be done away. So this important prophecy is passed over in silence, as is also the similar prophecy in Ps. lxxxvii.

Mal. iii. 1 (p. 983). Here a "Summary of the OT revelation of Deity," based on the divine names which appear in it, is introduced. Three groups of names, each containing three names, are given: three "primary" names, three "compound (with El = God)," three "compound (with Jehovah = LORD)." The statement is made: "The Trinity is *suggested* by the three times repeated groups of threes. This is not an arbitrary arrangement, but inheres in the OT itself." That, on the contrary, the arrangement is purely arbitrary appears from such obvious facts as the following: (1) The primary names are reduced to three by treating *El, Elah* [*ie., Eloah*], and *Elohim* as one name, and by ignoring the fact that "Almighty" and "Most High" are more frequently used as primary names than in the compound forms, "Almighty God" and "God Most High." (2) The three names "compound with *El*" are "Almighty God," "Most High or most high God" and "everlasting God." The first two occur only seven or eight times each in the compound form, the third only twice. There are many other compound names in the OT. Why single out these three? Why should not "living God," "jealous God," and "God of Israel" be added to or substituted for these three? (3) In the third group, "LORD of hosts" is certainly an abbreviation of "LORD God of hosts." Why then should not "LORD God of Israel" be added to this group? The arrangement is decidedly arbitrary and very far-fetched.[7]

Matt. viii. 2 (p. 1005). The statement that *kurios* is used 663 times in the NT "as the divine title of Jesus, the Christ" is incorrect. The figure 663 is apparently the total given in Young's *Concordance* of all occurrences where the title is capitalized, because used of Deity. Consequently it includes the occurrences listed in *RB* under (1) and (2) as well as those under (3).

Lk. i. 3 (p. 1070). In the opening verses of his Gospel the evangelist Luke states definitely that he derived his information from *eyewitnesses,* and therefore had "perfect understanding of all things from the very first." The Greek word for "from the very first" is *anōthen.* It is used by John and by James in the sense of "from above." Scofield asserts that "In no other place is *anothen* translated 'from the very first.'" So he maintains that its use here by Luke "is an affirmation that his knowledge of these things . . . was confirmed by revelation." This amounts to saying that "from the very first" (AV) is faulty, and should be changed to "from above." There are two serious objections to this assertion: (1) Luke uses the word *anōthen* in only one other passage (Acts xxvi. 5). There the rendering is "from the beginning" (AV) which is a synonymous expression for "from the very first." Paul is speaking of his youthful career at Jerusalem as a matter of common knowledge to the Jews. In the context the idea of a confirmation by revelation is absolutely excluded. Paul's enemies did not need and certainly did not receive divine confirmation of the fact that he had been brought up a zealous Pharisee and had been a bitter persecutor of the faith for which he was now a prisoner. (2) Luke's appeal to *eyewitnesses* and his failure to mention any supernatural source of information indicates that Scofield has endeavored to read into the passage something that is not there.

Acts vii. 14 (p. 1157). Here Stephen refers to Jacob's "kindred" as 75 souls. The only thing which may be regarded as certain is that Stephen was following the LXX version, or a tradition represented by it, which gives this total in Gen. xlvi. 27, where the number of Joseph's descendants is given as nine instead of two (66 + 9 = 75), although only five are named in vs. 20. Scofield makes no mention of these important facts. Instead, perhaps following Sebastian Schmid (see Meyer), he declares the correct solution to be that the "kindred" included the wives of Jacob's sons. This solution is faced by two serious difficulties: (1) In the full list given in Gen. xlvi. not a single *wife* is included in the total. One daughter, Dinah (vs. 15), and a grand-daughter (vs. 17), are included; but no wives, either of Jacob or of his sons. (2) Jacob had four wives; and if each son had but one, the total would be 16. The deaths of only two are recorded: Jacob's wife Rachel and Judah's wife Shuah. Scofield's solution requires the death in Canaan, or the ignoring, of all the wives but five. It is a mere guess, not a solution.

Gal. i. 14 (p. 1242). Here the comment is made that the Greek words rendered "religion" (Acts xxvi. 5; Col. ii. 18; Jas. i. 26, 27) and "religious" (Jas. i. 26) are used in a "bad sense," except in Jas. i. 27, where they refer to "a believer's good works"; and the further statement is made that "It is never used as synonymous with salvation or spirituality." This is a mild statement of the claim made by some Dispensationalists, that Christianity is not a religion at all (cf., for example, the title of Gaebelein's book, *Christianity or Religion?*). This is a false and dangerous antithesis. As Trench has pointed out,[8] the word rendered "religion" *(threskeia)* refers to worship in its *external* manifestations (cf. *RB,* p. 1306); and James, in the spirit of Mic. vi. 8, is here pointing out the nature of those acts of service which are well-pleasing to God. These works are the fruit of salvation, the evidence of true spirituality; and when James tells us what "true religion" is, he is describing Christianity in its external workings and fruitage. To deny that Christianity is a religion (pre-eminently, *the* religion), would amount to saying that good works form no part of it (Tit. iii. 8).

"ROBBING" ISRAEL

SINCE Dispensationalists are so insistent, that Christians have "robbed" Israel of promises which are peculiarly and exclusively hers by interpreting the Old Testament kingdom promises as applying to and fulfilled in the Christian

Church, it may be well to consider this question somewhat more fully. We have already admitted that this accusation finds justification and support in the attitude of Christians toward the Jew in the course of the nineteen "Christian" centuries since Pentecost. The Church has not only appropriated the blessings to herself and pointedly applied to the Jew the curses which the prophets uttered regarding Israel. But what is far worse, she has often by sins of commission and of omission excluded the Jew from the Christian Church in which she professes to believe these promised blessings are exclusively to be found. The early Christians were instructed, in their proclamation of the gospel, to *begin at Jerusalem*. Both Peter and Paul began with the *Jew*. But the Christian Church has for centuries in her proclamation of the gospel begun with the Gentile, often completely ignored the Jew, and during long periods of time *never gotten to Jerusalem at all*. This is a tragic and lamentable fact. It is a sin to be confessed and repented of. If the great apostle of the Gentiles had great heaviness and continual sorrow in his heart because of Israel, if the "receiving" back of Israel will be "life from the dead," the conversion of the Jew should certainly figure very prominently in all plans and programs for world evangelization.

But while all this is true, it does not touch the main issue raised by the sharp distinction drawn by Dispensationalists between the kingdom and the Church. The question is not whether *excluding* the Jew from the Christian Church is a sin. That should not need to be argued about. The real issue is the *inclusion* of the Jew in that Church. Is it or is it not an injustice to the Jew to claim that the kingdom promises are being and to be fulfilled in the Christian Church, if the Jew is given an equal place and equal rights with the Gentile in that Church? It is at this point that definite issue must be taken with Dispensational doctrine. During the gospel age many thousands of Jews have become Christians. Not a few men of eminence in literature, art, science, finance, and philanthropy have left the Synagogue and entered the Church. We do not realize the full horror of the Nazi persecution of the Jew until we place it in relation with the fact, admitted by the *Jewish Lexicon*,[9] that during the 19th century alone approximately a quarter million Jews became members of existing Christian Churches. This fact makes the question unavoidable, Was this a gain for them or a loss? Centuries ago Paul gave a most definite answer to this question as it concerned him personally in Phil. iii. 1-9. And it is regarding such Jews as Paul that Gaebelein tells us that they "possess now something infinitely more glorious than the nation will possess when the Lord comes to restore His ancient people."[10] In saying this Gaebelein is expressing the view of Darby and, we believe, of most or all dispensational writers. Darby tells us that the failure of the Jews to accept their Messiah "only opened the way for a dispensation far more admirable, far more glorious."[11] The Church is, he tells us, "a higher thing than being God's people"; but he adds, "though both may be true at the same time."[12] Darby, Kelly, Scofield, the leading Dispensationalists of the past and of the present, cannot paint the glories of the Church in too brilliant colors. Gaebelein insists that "Christianity remains the highest possible revelation of God, and the Gospel the highest possible supernatural message. . . . Christianity is unconquerable, it is final and eternal."[13] Yet with singular inconsistency, Dispensationalists insist that in the coming age, an age which may be introduced "at any moment," the weak and beggarly elements of the OT law will be restored, that the middle wall of separation will again be raised up, and that after Jews have for hundreds of years been offered, and in thousands of individual instances accepted, membership in the glorious, heavenly, world-embracing Church, the Jewish nation will be placed in possession of an earthly kingdom, which on their own admission will be vastly inferior to the Church.

This is a great anomaly in Dispensational teaching. They paint the glories of the Church in most alluring colors. But they insist that they are not for the Jew, save as accepted individually and during this present age. They hold that the kingdom promises are earthly, vastly inferior to the heavenly promises to the Church; yet they insist that it is these earthly promises only which Israel the nation has any claim upon or may ever hope to receive, that the earthly kingdom and the heavenly Church can never become one. It is this attitude, we believe, that deserves to be characterized by the word "robbery." It robs Israel of her true destiny and glory by excluding her from the Church of God. By insisting that her heritage is earthly, it robs her of that better portion which is heavenly. Yet, as we have seen, Paul's great concern for Israel was not earthly, but heavenly. Whether Israel was to be restored to the land did not apparently interest or concern him. His great concern was that Israel might be saved. Is it not there that we should leave this question of the earthly promises? The hope of Israel is to be found in acceptance of that Gospel which Paul preached first to the Jew and then to the Gentile, and in inclusion in that Church in which this ancient distinction is unknown and forever done away. Whether, consistently with this all-important teaching, we may expect a literal restoration of the Jewish nation to Palestine, is a question of minor importance, if indeed it can be regarded as important at all.

How difficult it is to justify the sharp antithesis which is drawn by Dispensationalists between the Jewish Kingdom and the Christian Church is clearly illustrated by the complication which arises from the fact that individual Israelites have been and are being admitted into the Church during the Church age. Scofield, as we have seen, finds a reference to them in "the poor of the flock" (Zech. xi. 11) which is embarrassing because if these poor are "those Jews who did not wait for the manifestation of Christ in glory, but believed in Him at His first coming and since,"[14] this is a reference to Jews as Christians and therefore a prophecy of the Christian Church, which Scofield of course cannot consistently admit.

Especially noteworthy is Scofield's comment on Paul's words in which he describes himself, as "one born out of due time" (1 Cor. xv. 8).[15] The natural and obvious sense of this phrase, as indicated by the words which immediately precede, "and last of all he was seen of me also," is that Paul was not thinking of himself as a Jew but as an apostle. All who had been apostles before him had become disciples of Jesus during His earthly ministry and had also been eye-witnesses of His resurrection (Acts i. 21f.). To qualify Paul to be an apostle, a special post-ascension appearance of the Lord was necessary. As an apostle, then, Paul was "born out of due time." And the use of this expression suggests, on the one hand, a very special act of grace of which Paul was the recipient, on the other hand, perhaps, neglect on Paul's part to avail himself of the opportunity, which may well have been his, to know, accept, and serve Christ when He was on earth, as those who had been apostles before him had done. Scofield gives this expression a different rendering, "before the due time," and he tells us: "Paul thinks of himself here as an Israelite whose time to be born again had not come, nationally (cf. Matt. xxiii. 39), so that his conversion by the appearing of the Lord in glory (Acts ix. 3-6) was an illustration, or instance before the time, of the future conversion of Israel." This suggests quite plainly that there is an anomaly, an unnaturalness, in Paul's conversion and by inference in the conversion of every Jew who believes during the present dispensation. The "due time" for Jews is not yet! But, according to the Epistle to the Hebrews which was addressed especially to Jews, "today" is the only time to hear and be saved (iii. 7-19). And the Jew who accepts the gospel offer now does not receive God's second-best, because as one born before or out of the due time he is unworthy of God's best for the Jews, the earthly kingdom; but he receives something infinitely better as Dispensationalists themselves admit.

This, we repeat, is the anomaly. If the promises to the Church are so glorious that the individual Jew does not lose anything, but greatly benefits by accepting them, why should not this be equally true of the nation as a whole? Why should not the reception of the nation of Israel into the Church be as great a blessing to the nation proportionally as to the individual? For if it is robbery to deprive the Jews as a nation of their nationalistic expectations, then it follows inevitably that the Jews who believe during the Church age and become members of the Church are in a sense being penalized and punished. Their admission into the Church is a kind of second-best. They are for ever deprived of the kingdom blessings because their fathers rejected their Messiah and the time for the restoration of the kingdom is not yet; but as a matter of grace they are allowed membership in the Christian Church in which none of these earthly blessings are to be found. But, if the New Testament makes anything plain, it is that for the Jew as well as for the Gentile, for the Jew of the future quite as much as for the Jew of the present or the past, the greatest privilege and honor which can be his is to know Christ whom to know is everlasting life and to become a member of His glorious body, the Church of the living God.

WHO WILL PREACH THE GOSPEL WHEN THE CHURCH IS GONE?

THE issue we have been considering is presented in startling fashion by an advertisement bearing the above title which has recently been used, how extensively we cannot say, by the *American Board of Missions to the Jews*. The full text is as follows:

Who Will Preach the Gospel When the Church Is Gone?

If you are a well-taught child of God, you know the answer—the Jews, of course. We call them sometimes The Tribulation Jews. To them we must hand down our Torch of witness, that they may carry on, after we have heard the shout from heaven!

And if this is true, then do you not see the categorical imperative involved? It means that the true church must now evangelize Israel with a fervor and intensity never known before, to prepare that Remnant to take up the Testimony once the day of Grace is ended. This is the deeper meaning of the Jewish mission witness, and we are not asleep when it comes to an understanding of the inner workings and necessities of God's dispensational program.

If God leads you to fellowship with us in this divinely given task, we shall surely welcome your joining hands with us. *The Chosen People* is sent to contributors, and is proving a blessing to many of the Lord's people in opening their eyes to present day prophetic fulfillments and meanings.

AMERICAN BOARD OF MISSIONS TO THE JEWS, INC.
27 THROOP AVENUE   BROOKLYN 6 N. Y.
39 KING WILLIAM STREET
HAMILTON, ONTARIO   CANADA

Here two things are brought together which, on Biblical and Dispensational principles, are mutually exclusive and irreconcilable: first, that "the Jews," *i.e.,* the Jewish remnant of the tribulation period, are to "preach the gospel" after the rapture of the Church; secondly, that it is, therefore, now the imperative duty of the Church "to prepare that remnant to take up the testimony once the day of Grace is ended." This is an attempt to reconcile irreconcilables by ignoring the fact that they are irreconcilable. They are irreconcilable for a very simple and obvious reason. If the Church now proclaims to the Jews the "gospel of the grace of God," those Jews who accept it become at once Christian believers, members of the body of Christ, who will (if then living) be caught up with all other living believers to meet the Lord in the air. They cannot be left behind because they are *Jewish* believers. That would involve the building again of that "middle wall of partition" between Jew and Gentile which Paul definitely declares to have been broken down by Christ through His Cross, and which all Dispensationalists declare to have been abolished for the duration of the Church age. If then the believing Jewish remnant is no longer on earth, how can it preach the gospel to the Jews who are on earth? It cannot "take up the Testimony" after the Church has gone, for it will have gone with the Church. This seems to us so obvious that we cannot understand how the author or authors of the advertisement can have failed to perceive it.

There is as far as we can see only one possible loophole in the argument just stated. It results from the ambiguous use of language. What is "the Gospel" which the Church is now bound by a "categorical imperative" to preach to the Jews? We have seen that, according to Dispensationalists, the "gospel of the kingdom" differs from the "gospel of the grace of God." The one was preached to the Jews at the first advent, and its proclamation is to be resumed *after* the rapture of the Church. The other is the gospel for the whole of the Church age; and its proclamation is the solemn and imperative duty as well as the glorious privilege of the Church. This twofold use of the word "gospel" by Dispensationalists opens up two possibilities which must be explored: (1) That the Church by faithfully proclaiming the "gospel of the grace of God" to the Jews will succeed in preparing a remnant, which rejects that *heavenly* gospel, to proclaim the gospel of the *earthly* kingdom after the rapture of the Church. The difficulty with this solution lies in the simple fact that a remnant which rejects the "gospel of the grace of God" as proclaimed to it by the Church cannot possibly be envisaged as a "godly" or "pious" remnant. It will be composed of "despisers" (Acts xiii. 41) who have rejected the grace of God and merited for themselves the woes pronounced on obstinate unbelief by the prophet Isaiah (Acts xxviii. 25-28). Such a remnant cannot proclaim salvation to others when it has rejected it for itself. (2) That the Church, in order to conciliate and win the Jews and prepare them for the role the Dispensationalists assign them, might preach to them the "gospel of the kingdom" now. According to Scofield, this gospel concerns "a kingdom, political, spiritual, Israelitish, universal." It is earthly and holds out to the Jew the realization of his earthly hopes. It promises him world supremacy, rule over the nations as a chosen and peculiar people. It says nothing or next to nothing about the Cross which has been to the Jew a stumbling block for centuries. Such a gospel might be welcomed by many Jews. It would announce to them the speedy realization of all their fondest hopes. But the Church cannot preach such a gospel without being disloyal to her categorical imperative. Her duty is to declare to all men, Jew as well as Gentile, the gospel of the Cross, that salvation which leads a believing Jew to count all his earthly prerogatives as nothing and less than nothing and to know nothing among men save Jesus Christ and Him crucified. Were the Church, in order to win the Jews, to build again the wall of separation which the gospel committed to her was intended to break down and did break down, the Church would be false and disloyal to her Lord. Neither of these alternatives can be justified on Scriptural grounds. Yet we know of no other. Consequently, what greatly concerns us is lest the *American Board of Missions to the Jews* or any other Christian boards and agencies which are engaged especially in the great work of Jewish evangelization should fail to recognize it as their imperative duty and high privilege to preach the same gospel to the Jew as they would preach to the non-Jew, lest they should fail to magnify the Cross which is a stumbling block to the Jew, as the power of God unto salvation to *everyone* that believeth, lest they should offer the Jew a kingdom gospel which encourages him to cling to his earthly expectations as a Jew and to look for a glorious King yet to come, while rejecting the crucified and ascended Saviour, who has come and died upon a cross at Calvary, that whosoever believeth in him should not perish but have everlasting life.

NOTES

CHAPTER I (Pages 1-15)

1 "Millennial," from *mille* (thousand) and *annus* (year), is a more exact expression than "millenarian" from *millenarius* (thousand), of which "chiliad" and "chiliast" from *chilias* (thousand) are the equivalent. But all of these words and their derivatives are in current use and may be regarded as synonymous expressions.

2 An adequate account of the history and present state of the Millennial Question would require a volume of itself. Here the aim is simply to outline, logically rather than chronologically or historically, the main positions that have been advocated.

3 See E. B. Elliott, *Horae Apocalypticae*, vol. i., pp. 396f., vol. iv., p. 137. The belief that the world was to exist for 7000 years, *i.e.*, 6000 years of labor and 1000 years of rest (cf. Gen. i. and Ps. xc. 4), is found in the *Secrets of Enoch* (Chap. xxxii.) and is of pre-Christian origin. Augustine's identification of the millennium with what then remained of the sixth chiliad would make the seventh correspond with the eternal state.

4 Augustine followed the LXX chronology which adds nearly 1500 years to the length of the period from Adam to Abraham as it is given in the Hebrew text.

5 Since this coming, which was regarded as so imminent, was expected to be the Last Judgment, it struck terror into the hearts of multitudes as the year A.D. 1000 drew near. Cf. Richard H. Storrs, *Bernard of Clairvaux*, pp. 58ff. for a vivid description.

6 The fact that approximately a thousand years lay between the conversion of Constantine and the beginning of the Protestant Reformation made this view an attractive one, especially since the Reformers naturally found in the Book of Revelation the prediction of the rise and fall of the Papacy, as the great anti-Christian and persecuting power. Hengstenberg, writing in the last century, dated the beginning of the millennium from the crowning of Charlemagne in A.D. 800.

7 Whitby's insistence that the national conversion of the Jews must precede the millennium forced him to regard that age as still wholly future. In this respect his view differed radically from that form of the Augustinian view, which while regarding the millennium as already in progress looks forward to a climax, a glorious state of the Church yet to be attained.

8 *Die Offenbarung des Johannes*, iii, pp. 287ff.

9 *E.g.*, Gaebelein, *Listen! God Speaks*, p. 182. According to Albertus Pieters ("The Millennial Problem," in *Intelligencer Leader*, Mch. 5, 1943, p. 17), the term "amillennialism" originated with Abraham Kuyper. But whether this be so or not, the doctrine is old: "Saint Augustine was a true 'Amillenarian,' even though he did not call himself so." Among more or less recent writers the following may be classed as Amillenarians, since they are opposed both to Premillennialism and to Whitbyan Postmillennialism: L. Berkhof, R. R. Byrum, Th. Graebner, F. E. Hamilton,

D. Heagle, Hendriksen, A. Kuyper, Masselink, Mauro, W. Milligan, J. C. Rankin, T. P. Stafford, M. S. Terry, G. Vos, Wyngaarden. A word may be said about the view of Dr. B. B. Warfield as being of special interest. On the one hand, he held the recapitulation view regarding Rev. xx. 1-4 to be correct, but insisted that the 1000 years describe the heavenly bliss of the saints and have no reference to time on earth. The earthly scene he found described in the expressions "little season," 1260 days, 42 months, "a time, times and half a time," all designed to indicate the comparative brevity of the trial time of the church on earth. On the other hand, he held an optimistic view of the future of the Church on earth, basing it on Rev. xix. 11-21 and the "intimations" given in Rom. xi. and 1 Cor. xv. Consequently, Dr. Warfield was a Postmillenarian who looked for a future golden age of the Church on earth, but did not believe that Rev. xx. has anything to say about an earthly millennium.

10 Graebner, who takes the view that the 1000 years represent "the Gospel age," has recently declared that "the Church must stress today as never before its joyous expectancy of the Second Advent" (War in the Light of Prophecy, p. v).

11 Premillennial Essays (1879), p. 313.

12 The conclusion, so often drawn by Premillennialists, that because chiliastic views were more or less widely current in the Early Church, this teaching must be regarded as Apostolic and Biblical, as the pure because primitive faith of the NT Church, ignores the vitally important fact that chiliastic views were extensively circulated in the Early Church through such Jewish or Jewish-Christian writings as Enoch, 4 Esdras, Assumption of Moses, Ascension of Isaiah, Psalms of Solomon, Baruch, writings which neither Jews nor Christians regarded as canonical. Judaizing tendencies were very strong even in Apostolic times, as is made clear by the attitude of Jewish Christians to the Gentiles (e.g., Acts xv.), and especially by the Epistles to the Galatians and to the Hebrews. (Cf. Vos, The Pauline Eschatology, pp. 228-235.) Whether Chiliasm is Scriptural must, therefore, be determined solely by an appeal to the Scriptures.

13 Scofield Reference Bible (regularly abbreviated to RB), p. 5.

14 Dispensationalists recognize three important intervals or parentheses in Biblical history: (1) the interval in the first two verses of Gen. i.; (2) the Church or Mystery parenthesis between Pentecost and the rapture; and (3) the Jewish Remnant parenthesis, the interval of seven years between the rapture and the appearing. The first of these intervals has no direct bearing upon Dispensational teaching in general. But Scofield adopted it in RB. It was somewhat widely advocated about a century ago as a means of reconciling the Bible with modern geological theories. Darby apparently accepted it; and Kelly advocated it strongly. Like the Church parenthesis it is of quite indeterminate length, in rather striking contrast with the Jewish Remnant parenthesis which, while very important, is quite short.

15 Some readers may be disposed to insist that No. 3 should be included as characteristic of Premillennialism historically understood. That there will be an interval between the rapture of the saints and their return to earth with Christ, a period of time during which judgments will be poured out upon the nations, has been widely held. What is denied here

is that the recognition of this interval justifies any such distinction be-tween the rapture and the revelation or appearing as is drawn by Dis-pensationalists. (See the full discussion of this subject in Chapters VII and VIII.)

16 This has been strongly emphasized in two recent books which oppose Dispensationalism from diametrically opposite viewpoints. Alexander Reese (*The Approaching Advent of Christ,* 1940), writing in advocacy of historical Premillennialism, and Floyd E. Hamilton (*The Basis of Mil-lennial Faith,* 1942), writing as an Amillennialist, are heartily agreed that Modern Dispensationalism (the doctrine of Darby and Scofield) represents a radical departure from Premillennialism as that doctrine was taught and understood up to the time of the rise of the Brethren Movement. A serious defect, for example, in J. F. Silver's widely used book, *The Lord's Return,* is that it draws no adequate distinction between Premillennialism and Dispensationalism. Thus, Alford, Bickersteth, the Bonars, E. B. Elliott, Gresswell, Guinness, Tregelles, and Nathanael West were ardent Pre-millennialists. They were not Dispensationalists and some of them took up the cudgels and wielded them vigorously against what they considered to be the errors of this modern doctrine. To appeal to Augustine's words, "Distinguish the ages, and the Scriptures harmonize" (quoted *RB,* p. iii) as justifying "Dispensationalism" is entirely unwarranted. Augustine never heard of the distinctions which are characteristic of this modern system of interpretation. This proper and very necessary distinction between Dis-pensationalism and Premillennialism is also carefully drawn in the report made in 1944 to the General Assembly of the Presbyterian Church in the U.S. by its Ad Interim Committee *(Minutes,* p. 123f.). The Committee states that its condemnation of Dispensationalism as definitely un-Presby-terian is not to be regarded as applying to Premillennialism.

17 Darby published his article, "Considerations on the Nature and Unity of the Church of Christ," in 1828. The rise of Brethrenism is often dated from that event.

18 Darby was a voluminous writer. His best-known work is the *Synopsis of the Books of the Bible* (5 vols.), which was highly commended by Sco-field. His *Collected Writings* (32 vols.) deal with a wide range of subjects: *e.g.,* 4 with Prophecy, 4 with Ecclesiology, 7 with Exposition, etc. Several volumes of his *Letters* have been published. He made a new *Translation* of the Bible. He wrote a number of hymns. He traveled extensively and spent considerable time in Switzerland, Canada, and the U.S.A. [His writings can be secured from G. Morrish, Paternoster Square, London, the "official" publishers of the "Exclusive" or Darbyite branch of the Brethren.]

19 The sharp contrast between Paul and Peter, amounting almost to antithesis, developed in Brethrenism suggests the somewhat similar antith-esis in the teachings of the Tübingen School which arose in Germany at about the same time. But there appears to be no connection of any kind between them.

20 James Grant, *The Heresies of the Plymouth Brethren* (p. 2). This volume appeared originally as part of vol. ii. of *Religious Tendencies of the Times* (1869).

21 Ironside, *The Brethren Movement,* pp. 196ff.

22 These conferences were held annually during the years 1876-1899, most often at Niagara-on-the-Lake. Hence they are often called the Niagara Conferences. For a brief account, see Gaebelein, "The Story of the Scofield Reference Bible" [a series of articles published in *The Moody Monthly* Oct. 1942-Mch. 1943], pp. 203ff.

23 The use of initials is a characteristic of Brethren writers. Thus, J. N. D., C. S., W. K., C. H. M., are the well-known initials of Darby, Stanley, Kelly, and Mackintosh, respectively. W. E. Blackstone was a Methodist. But the "W. E. B." both suggests and indicates his familiarity with Brethren literature.

24 Cf. Gaebelein, "The Story of the Scofield Reference Bible" (pp. 65f.).

25 This issue was raised by B. W. Newton about 1840, in the first great controversy between the Brethren. While other questions were involved Newtonism represented a vigorous protest against the extremes of Dispensationalism, notably the any moment rapture and the Jewish remnant doctrines.

26 Like Darby, he was a prolific writer. According to the British *Who's Who* (1913), he was the author of "seventy-seven works." One of the best-known and most elaborate of these was *The Companion Bible*.

CHAPTER II (Pages 16-54)

1 The long-lost *Didache*, or *Teaching of the Twelve Apostles*, dating probably from about the beginning of the 2nd century, which was published in 1883, goes directly contrary to this claim. This was shown conclusively by Nathanael West in his brochures, *The Coming of the Lord in the Teaching of the Twelve Apostles* (1892) and *The Apostle Paul and the Any Moment Theory* (1893).

2 Scofield cautions his readers that "the mind should be freed, so far as possible, from mere theological conceptions and presuppositions" (*RB*, p. 989; cf. p. 1214). See also Gaebelein's diatribe against "man-made creeds, systems of theology, different kinds of orthodox statements" ("The Story of the Scofield Reference Bible," p. 401). Cf. heading to 2 Kgs. ii, 16f. in *RB*.

3 Scofield asserts regarding the Prophets, "This portion of the Bible, nearly one-fourth of the whole, has been closed to the reader by fanciful and allegorical schemes of interpretation" (*RB*, p. iii., No. VIII). Cf. also, for example, Savage, *The Scroll*, pp. 145ff. No one has emphasized this more than has William Kelly, perhaps the greatest scholar among the Brethren (*e.g.*, in his *Elements of Prophecy*, pp. 1-3). When Gaebelein says of Matthew Henry that he was "in darkness" as to the interpretation of prophecy, he is simply stating a fundamental of Dispensationalism.

4 Whether the word "hornet" (Ex. xxiii. 28) is to be taken literally or as a figurative reference to Egypt (cf. Isa. vii. 18) is a moot point with the commentators.

5 A familiar illustration of this literalism is the use of phylacteries by the Pharisees of NT times. This was based upon the literal interpretation

of Ex. xiii. 9, 16, Dt. vi. 8, xi. 18, and was denounced by Jesus as an example of formalism in worship (Matt. xii. 49f.). Cf., Matt. xvi. 6-12.

6 There is probably no more ardent literalist living today than A. C. Gaebelein. Yet Gaebelein holds that Dan. xii. 2 describes a *spiritual* resurrection of a *literal* Israel (*The Prophet Daniel*, p. 200).

7 For "The things represented have much more of reality and perfection in them than the things by which we represent them" (Angus-Green, *Cyclopedic Handbook*, p. 217). The words "This is my body" do not lose but gain in meaning when the literal sense is rejected as unscriptural.

8 In 1828 Alexander Keith published his *Evidences of the Truth of the Christian Religion Derived from the Literal Fulfilment of Prophecy*. This book was exceedingly popular (the 40th edition appeared in London in 1873). Yet Keith's literalism left much to be desired according to Brethren standards. For he found the fulfilment in the NT Church of many of the OT prophecies concerning Israel. A striking example of literal interpretation, as this method of interpretation is used today by a leading Dispensationalist, will be found in the Appendix (pp. 264-7).

9 *RB*, p. 721.

10 *RB*, p. 25. Scofield has inserted at xiii. 14 the heading, "*The Abrahamic Covenant; natural posterity promised* (vs. 16)," and at xv. 1 the corresponding heading, "*The Abrahamic Covenant confirmed; a spiritual seed promised* (vs. 5)." Cf., Wm. Lincoln, *Typical Foreshadowings in Genesis*, pp. 49f., 55; also Gaebelein, *World Prospects*, p. 31.

11 *E.g.*, Savage, *The Scroll*, p. 62, Feinberg, *Premillennialism*, p. 208, and many others.

12 L. S. Chafer, *The Kingdom in History and Prophecy*, p. 87. Chafer's elaborate article on "Dispensationalism," in the *Bibliotheca Sacra* (Oct.-Dec., 1936, pp. 390-499) may be regarded as an elaboration of this thesis: viz., that Israel and the Church are distinct and will continue distinct for ever.

13 That such a principle is hard to apply is illustrated by the following statement: "The interpretation of the prophecies is literal as to Israel, typical as to Christians" (*RB*, p. 198). This is not only quite arbitrary, but it amounts to an admission that the prophecies of the OT do apply to the NT Church.

14 *RB*, p. 34. There is no proof of this; and Eliezer as Abraham's *slave* was a decidedly unsuitable type of the Holy Spirit. An extreme example of this allegorical method as employed by Scofield is his typical use of Gen. i. 16, where he makes the "greater light" typify "Christ at His second advent" and the "lesser light" represent the Church "reflecting the light of the unseen sun." Not only is there not the slightest warrant for this in the words of Scripture themselves, but it involves the assumption that the sun and moon were not "made" on the fourth day but only made to appear, to "become visible" on that day, which is a hazardous interpretation to say the least. Scofield's analysis of Moses as a type (*RB*, p. 72) shows the same tendency to go beyond what is written. It is nowhere even hinted in the Bible that Moses' marriage with Zipporah was typical of Christ's relation to the Gentiles. His attempt to prove that "The transfiguration scene contains, in miniature, all the elements of the future kingdom in manifestation" (pp. 1022f.) is another impres-

sive example of a "typical" interpretation which does not differ from allegorizing. Cf. also *RB*, pp. 5, 53, 59, 62, 89, 103, 122, 261, 713, 840, 1114, 1133, 1139, 1312, 1331.

15 *E.g.*, I. M. Haldeman, *How to Study the Bible*, pp. 255-289. Haldeman's first statement is contrary to fact: "Joseph is the one and only character presented to us in the Bible without a flaw." The deception which Joseph practised on his brethren in the matter of the cup shows this quite plainly. Consequently, Joseph was not "a perfect type of our Lord Jesus Christ, the sinless man." The Bible knows nothing of sinless men and it gives us no perfect type of Christ. Joseph's character is singularly beautiful, but he was not perfect.

16 Walter Scott, *Bible Outlines*, p. 113 (1879, repub. 1930).

17 A good definition of allegory is a "narrative describing one subject under guise of another" (*The Pocket Oxford Dictionary*).

18 The fact that the widow of Zarephath was gathering "two sticks" does not, as some have supposed, make them a type of the Cross. It is clearly intended simply to give point to her statement that she had almost nothing to cook. No less hazardous is it to find in Gen. xiv. 18 the type of "the priestly work of Christ in *resurrection*, since Melchizedek presented only the memorials of sacrifice, bread and wine" (*RB*, p. 23).

19 *RB*, p. 4.

20 *RB*, p. 15. The etymology of Ararat (*id.*) and the typical meaning assigned have no warrant in fact and serve to illustrate how constantly "deep" meanings in Scripture are sought after by Dispensationalists. It is safe to say that Scofield did not consult Professor Sayce (see *RB*, p. iv) as to the correctness of this note.

21 Scofield declares that in the boards of the tabernacle the wood is "a fitting symbol of Christ in His humanity," while "the covering, gold, typifies Deity in manifestation, speaks of His divine glory" (*RB*, p. 103). Were this the true meaning, the fact that the mercy-seat was of pure gold would mean that it was only as God and not as man (the God-man) that Jesus suffered on the cross. Yet the object of the incarnation was that God the Son might "obey and suffer in our nature."

22 Cf. Darby, *Synopsis*, i. p. 287.

23 *RB*, pp. 8, 34, 59, 72, 315, 705, 1255.

24 *RB*, p. 970.

25 Fairbairn, *On Prophecy* (2nd Edinburgh ed.), p. 180.

26 *Collected Writings*, ii. p. 271.

27 *Maranatha*, p. 35.

28 This is a favorite expression with Gaebelein: *e.g.*, *The Prophet Daniel*, pp. 1, 166; cf. question 1, on p. 213, and the answer on p. 220. Also, *Christianity or Religion?*, p. 85, and various other of his writings.

29 The words "until Shiloh come" (Gen. xlix. 10) are so phrased that Shiloh may be either subject or accusative of destination, "until he come to Shiloh." Whether the identity of the enthroned ones of Rev. xx. 4 ("and they sat on them") is to be determined from the preceding or the following context has also been much discussed. Since the meaning of these and similar passages could easily have been made quite clear, we must infer that the ambiguity and obscurity is intentional. In such a passage as Gen. xxv. 23 the fact that the rendering "the elder [object]

shall the younger [subject] serve" is possible constituted this oracle a moral test for both Isaac and Rebekah, and may account for, although it does not excuse or justify, his determination to bless Esau. (Cf. article, "The Birth Oracle to Rebekah," in *The Evangelical Quarterly* (Edinburgh), Vol. xi., pp. 97-117).

30 The view of some scholars that these "evenings mornings" are 2300 half-days (1150 evenings and 1150 mornings = 1150 days) is improbable, but hardly deserves to be called an exegetical "monster" (Pusey). All students of prophecy are acquainted with the attempt of William Miller more than a century ago to prove that exactly 2300 prophetic years were to be counted between the edict of Artaxerxes and the year A.D. 1843, at which time (exactly 6000 years from Creation!) the Lord would come to earth to cleanse His temple. For a hundred years his followers have been maintaining that this took place as a heavenly event at that time.

31 Some commentators recognize two beginnings of this prophecy. *E.g.,* Bickersteth, in his *Practical Guide,* found one in the 4th year of Jehoiakim, the other in the 11th of Zedekiah. Cf. *RB*, p. 798.

32 That the fulfilment of a prophecy may be certain yet the nature of that fulfilment unpredictable is well illustrated by the incident in 2 Kgs. vii. The words "Behold, thou shalt see with thine eyes, but shalt not eat thereof" (vs. 2) were fulfilled to the letter (vs. 20). Yet no one probably suspected, least of all the king, that the post of honor assigned to the favorite would be the post of danger and death. The king may conceivably have hoped to falsify or frustrate the prediction by his act. The instructions given to Elijah at Sinai (1 Kgs. xix. 15f.) were precise and explicit. Yet, as far as the record goes, the fulfilment differed very greatly from what the terms of the command would lead us to expect. Elijah was given three things to do. He performed only one of them and that one in a symbolic way: he did not anoint Elisha, he cast his mantle over his shoulders. It was Elisha, not Elijah, who informed Hazael that he would become king over Syria; and we are not told that the prophet anointed him. Elisha did not himself anoint Jehu to be king of Israel; he sent one of the sons of the prophets to do this. Either Elijah carried out literally all of the instructions given to him (of this we have no record in Scripture), or Elijah was *providentially* (cf. 1 Kgs. xxi. 29) prevented from carrying out two of them and Elisha was *providentially* and *supernaturally* (2 Kgs. viii. 13, ix. 3, 6-10) instructed as to his duty in the matter. Yet there is not the slightest intimation that Elijah was neglectful of duty or disobedient. The narrative is an impressive warning against a too "wooden," if we may so call it, interpretation of prophecy.

33 J. M. Gray, *Prophecy and the Lord's Return,* p. 110f.; Scofield, *RB*, pp. 725, 1346f.

34 It is better, we believe, to hold with Fairbairn (*On Prophecy,* p. 55) that the prophecy regarding Babylon concerned the *people* not the *site,* and that the prophecy that ancient Babylon should be destroyed for ever has been fulfilled and might still be regarded as fulfilled, even though another city of the same name should be built on the ruins of that famous and infamous city of ancient times.

35 Darby calls it "an immense change" ("Hopes of the Christian Church" [1840], in *Collected Writings*, ii. p. 530).

36 *RB*, pp. 20, 250; cf. p. 95.

37 *RB*, p. 20.

38 Scofield declares that the law "was not *imposed* until it had been *proposed* and voluntarily accepted" (*RB*, p. 93). We cannot but wonder whether Dispensationalists seriously face the question as to what the result would have been, if Israel had refused this gracious offer of God on the ground—there was no other—that they did not wish to "obey" His voice.

39 *RB*, pp. 93, 95. Paul speaks of the "obedience of faith" (Rom. xvi. 26), on which Scofield comments: "Faith as a system, in contrast with law as a system," which certainly implies that faith has its rule of obedience no less than the law has (*RB*, p. 1210).

40 *RB*, pp. 20, 43. The comment on Ezek. xii. 25 (*RB*, p. 851) suggests the question whether, according to Dispensationalists, Ezekiel ought to have stayed in the land, or ought to have been there in order to be a thoroughly effective prophet. This out-of-place doctrine has been rather strikingly stated by A. H. Stewart in his booklet, *The Sure Word of Prophecy*. In discussing the question, "What is wrong with the world?" he declares: "There are four definite reasons why things are in such a dreadful condition." They are the following: "First, the Jew is in the wrong place altogether" (he should be in the land); "Second, the Church, too, is in the wrong place" (it belongs in heaven), and "This world never can have a millennium while the Church is here"; "Third, Satan also is out of his proper place" (he belongs in hell); "Fourth, the Lord Jesus is not in His proper and destined place. He is sitting on His Father's throne, instead of on the throne of David" (pp. 5-8). Here we have a strange confusion of ideas. To confine ourselves to only one of them, the claim that the presence of the Church is an actual hindrance to the establishing of "ideal" conditions on earth should give even the most thoroughgoing Dispensationalist cause for serious rethinking of his position and its logical implications.

41 *RB*, p. 65. The word of warning and encouragement given to Jacob as he was about to go down into Egypt is to be studied in connection with the command given to his father Isaac not to go thither (xxvi. 1-5). The warning is as definite as the command. Both were accompanied with the promise of blessing in terms of the Abrahamic covenant. That Jacob had no desire to disobey God is shown by the fact that, when he came to Beersheba, "he offered sacrifices unto the God of his father Isaac" (xlvi. 1). This may probably be taken to mean that he knew of or had recalled the injunction given to his father and desired definite guidance from God, over and above the providential sign that had been given to him in the advancement of Joseph in Egypt, before doing something that his father in somewhat similar circumstances had been definitely forbidden to do.

42 This necessitates a distinction between a state of *well-being* under the covenant and a state of suffering or chastisement, which only serves to show that the covenant blessings were dependent on obedience.

43 In his desire to distinguish sharply between the NT Church and

the OT Church, Scofield makes the following comment on Acts vii. 38: "Israel *in the land* is never called a church. *In the wilderness* Israel was a true church (Gr. *ecclesia* = called-out assembly), but in striking contrast to the NT *ecclesia* (Mt. xvi. 18 *note*)" (*RB*, p. 1158, cf. p. 1021). There is no warrant for the claim that Israel is only called a church (*ecclesia*) when out of the land. *Ecclesia* renders the Hebrew word *qahal* (assembly; AV, congregation) about 70 times in the LXX. It is used of Israel in the land (*e.g.*, 1 Kgs. viii. 14), out of the land (Num. xx. 4), and when in the land but under foreign rule (Ezra ii. 64). The fact that Stephen's reference to Israel as a church was to a time when she was out of the land is no warrant for asserting that he would have used another word in referring to her when in the land. The usage of the LXX definitely prohibits such an inference. Furthermore, this same word (church) is used in Heb. ii. 12 in a quotation from Ps. xxii. 22: "In the midst of the church (*ecclesia*) will I sing praise to thee." Scofield makes no attempt to prove that in their OT context these words describe Israel as out of the land. But he does say of them in their NT context that they refer to the *true Church (RB,* p. 1293g). This is an amazing statement to come from one who declares that "The church, corporately, is not in the vision of the OT prophet" (*RB*, p. 711). Scofield differs from Darby at this point. Darby declares that "the assembly [*i.e.*, the true Church] is not found in the Epistle to the Hebrews" except in an allusion in Chap. xii. (*Synopsis*, v. p. 241). At ii. 12 Darby seems to find a reference to the believing Jewish remnant as a part of the assembly, but not to the assembly *per se*. We agree with Scofield as against Darby, but we are surprised that he failed to recognize the utter inconsistency of his position.

44 When Scofield says: "The righteous man under law became righteous by doing righteously; under grace he does righteously because he has been made righteous" *(RB,* p. 1323) and appeals to Rom. iii. 22, x. 3, he ignores the words of Paul in Gal. ii. 16, "For by the works of the law shall no flesh be justified." The law was not a covenant of works. It was a preliminary form of the covenant of grace. Its function was to serve as a "schoolmaster" to bring men to Christ, typically set forth under the Mosaic law of atonement, by showing them their utter inability "perfectly to keep the commandments of God."

45 The NT counterpart of this is, "Be ye therefore perfect (*teleios*), even as your Father which is in heaven is perfect (*teleios*)." Scofield says: "The word implies full development, growth in maturity of godliness, not sinless perfection" (*RB*, p. 1001). That it does mean "sinless perfection" here is indicated by the words "as your Father which is in heaven is perfect." Sinless perfection is the goal after which every Christian should strive. The fact that it cannot be achieved in this life does not warrant us in lowering the standard. Cf. 1 Pet. i. 15f.

46 In his *Scottish Theology in Relation to Church History Since the Reformation* (1943, p. 31), Principal-emeritus John Macleod points out the importance which the question of Assurance acquired in the post-Reformation period and declares that "The outcome of the discussions that took place on the topic of Assurance we have in carefully guarded form in the chapter of the Westminster Confession that deals with it."

In 1872 R. L. Dabney vigorously attacked the teaching of the Brethren on this subject (*Discussions*, vol. i., pp. 169-213). He regarded it as having very dangerous antinomian tendencies. An excellent illustration of the importance attached to the doctrine of Assurance by the Puritan divines and to the practice of self-examination with a view to the enjoyment of this grace, is to be found in Charnock's sermon on "Self-Examination" based on 2 Cor. xiii. 5. The Brethren hold that the correct rendering of this verse is "if" not "whether," and that the meaning of Paul's words is that the members of the church at Corinth, proceeding on the assumption that they are Christians, are to satisfy themselves that what is true of themselves is also and more abundantly true of Paul, an *a fortiori* argument.

47 It could, however, easily be carried to dangerous extremes. Many of the Brethren held that a Christian should not hold public office. Bellett, one of the most attractive and lovable figures among them, did not take a daily newspaper. Captain Percy Hall resigned his commission in the army, regarding the life of a soldier as incompatible with Christian standards.

48 Scofield, *Rightly Dividing*, pp. 75f.

49 *RB*, p. 1253.

50 Teulon, *History and Teaching of the Plymouth Brethren* (1883), p. 108. That this book was regarded by the Brethren themselves as a very able criticism of their doctrines is indicated by the fact that Wm. Kelly, one of the leaders among the Brethren, discussed it chapter by chapter in successive issues of his organ, *The Bible Treasury*, vol. xiv. See also H. Bonar's chapter on "The New Life" in *God's Way of Holiness*.

51 Vol. ii, p. 155.

52 *RB*, p. 624.

53 *RB*, p. 1002. Haldeman refers to it as "the so-called 'Lord's Prayer,'" and describes it as "a prayer that has no more place in the Christian Church than the thunders of Sinai, or the offerings of Leviticus" (*How to Study the Bible*, p. 140). That this is not typical of the Premillennial view is illustrated by the fact that Edw. Bickersteth and Adolph Saphir have both written elaborate devotional commentaries on this Prayer as the model prayer for the Christian.

54 The Lord's Prayer is quoted almost verbatim in the *Didache*, and the rule is laid down that it be repeated three times a day. The petition to which Dispensationalists take especial exception, "Forgive us our debts as we forgive our debtors," is expressly quoted.

55 This was formerly the case in many, perhaps the majority, of Presbyterian Churches. In the Protestant Episcopal Church, the recitation of the Ten Commandments by the officiating priest, followed by a response on the part of the people, is a part of the Order of the Communion Service.

56 *RB*, p. 550.

57 *RB*, p. 1011.

58 Scofield's perfectly gratuitous comment on 1 Cor. vi. 15 illustrates his hostility to the law. It is true that Paul does not refer to the Seventh Commandment here. But he does refer to it in Rom. xiii. 9 and in a

way which does not abrogate it but stresses it by making its connection with Jesus' Second Commandment, "Thou shalt love thy neighbor as thyself," unmistakably plain.

59 Darby, article "Presbyterianism" in *Collected Writings,* xiv., p. 528. In the "Pacific Address" with which Herman Witsius introduced his *Economy of the Covenants* (1693), the author refers to the doctrine of the "threefold covenant of grace," which distinguishes, somewhat after the manner of Dispensationalists, between the promise, the law, and the gospel; and he asserts that "however those doctrines are explained, they are horrible to be mentioned and not to be defended without wresting the Scriptures." Since Witsius was a conspicuous advocate of the Covenant or Federal Theology, it is easy to understand Darby's intense aversion to it. Chafer deals with this question of the unconditional covenant at considerable length in his article on "Dispensationalism" (pp. 429-42). That he realizes that his position is out of harmony with the teachings of the Westminster Confession, which as a Presbyterian minister he has accepted "as containing the system of doctrine taught in the Holy Scriptures," is made clear by the attack which he makes on it early in this article (p. 396) and has renewed more recently in the same organ. It is highly significant that, in reporting to the 1944 General Assembly of the Presbyterian Church in the U.S. the Ad Interim Committee entrusted with the investigation of the question of the compatibility of Dispensationalism with the doctrinal Standards of the Presbyterian Church, stated its conclusions in part as follows: "It is the unanimous opinion of your Committee that Dispensationalism as defined and set forth above is out of accord with the system of the doctrine set forth in the Confession of Faith, not primarily or simply in the field of eschatology, but because it attacks the very heart of the Theology of our Church, which is unquestionably a Theology of one Covenant of Grace. As Dr. Chafer clearly recognizes, there are two schools of interpretation here which he rightly designates as 'Covenantism' as over against 'Dispensationalism'" *(Minutes,* p. 123f.). One of the members of this Committee, Prof. J. E. Bear of Union Theological Seminary, Richmond, has dealt with this question in a series of articles in *The Presbyterian of the South* (Mch.-April, 1941) and more fully in *The Union Seminary Review* (July, 1938, Oct., 1940, Jan., 1941). Needless to say, the findings of the Committee are fully in accord with the position taken by Prof. Bear.

60 Cf. "Judge" Rutherford's *Jehovah,* where this is frequently asserted.

61 *Maranatha,* p. 439.

62 *RB,* p. 990, cf. p. 1226.

63 *RB,* p. 1023.

64 See Waldegrave, *New Test. Millennarianism,* p. 7; E. B. Elliott. *Horae Apoc.,* iv. pp. 695f.; Edersheim, *Prophecy and History,* p. 368.

65 Fairbairn accurately described this viewpoint when he wrote many years ago as follows: "The late Mr. Irving only spoke out distinctly on this subject what is implied in many current interpretations, when he said, 'My idea is, that not the Old Testament, but the New Testament dispensation, hath an end; and then the other resumes its course under Christ and his bride, which is his church.' All who hold, that there is to be a return to the old sacrificial worship, must concur in this

opinion, whether they give expression to it or not" (*On Prophecy*, p. 158).

66 The Futurist interpretation is traced back to the Jesuit Ribera (A.D. 1580) whose aim was to disprove the claim of the Reformers that the Pope was Antichrist. Its acceptance by the Brethren was not due of course to any objection to the "Protestant" interpretation as such, but to the fact that their literal interpretation of prophecy and their refusal to admit that predicted events were to precede the rapture made their acceptance of this system of interpretation inevitable.

67 The Historical interpretation has been quite as acceptable to Pre-millennialists (*e.g.*, Mede, Bengel, Bickersteth, Elliott, Alford, Faussett, and Grattan Guinness) as to A- or Postmillennialists (*e.g.*, Augustine, Whitby, David Brown, Patrick Fairbairn, B. B. Warfield, Graebner, Hendriksen, and F. E. Hamilton).

68 *RB*, p. 971, cf. p. 154.

69 Biederwolf lists eleven as of more or less importance and several others that are "hardly to be taken seriously" (*Millennium Bible*, p. 218).

70 *The Romance of Bible Chronology*, pp. 277, 284.

71 *RB*, p. 754.

72 For an illustration of this we may well turn to Bauman's recent book, *Light from Bible Prophecy*. The chapter entitled "Why the End of the Age Must Be Very Near" begins as follows: "I believe that the *rapture of the Church must be very near, because I believe that the Lord Jesus will not break His word*. To do that would make Him a sinner like unto the first Adam; and this world, without a sinless Lamb, would have no Savior. I cannot help but wonder if supposedly Christian men know what they say when they speak their doubt as to the Incarnate God keeping His covenants inviolate, and His promises immutable" (p. 84). This statement is faced with a very obvious difficulty. A century ago Darby and his followers were quite as confident that the rapture must be "very near" as Bauman is today. But a century has elapsed· the coming is still future. What does this mean? As an earnest Christian Bauman would of course refuse to entertain the thought that the Lord Jesus Christ can have broken His word. Consequently, he resorts to the following explanation: "Now with all due respect to all those who did 'put on their white robes' [an allusion apparently to the Millerites] in days long past, I wish to affirm, without hesitation or equivocation, that *at no time* since our Lord uttered His great prophecies have any goodly number of the signs been present *contemporaneously,—* that is, at the same time. And contemporaneous they must be!" (p. 87). Then Bauman proceeds to state and discuss fifteen signs of the nearness of the coming. This can only mean that Bauman believes that the Dispensationalists of a hundred years ago were wrong in their interpretation of the signs and that his understanding of them is correct. Yet, as an ardent Dispensationalist, Bauman should agree with Darby and Scofield in holding that the rapture may take place at "any moment" and is therefore both timeless and signless. Apparently, he does hold to the "any moment" view of the coming. Yet this does not prevent him from giving fifteen signs of a coming which he holds to be signless. What we object to most in the statements which we have quoted is not that Bauman states his opinion with the confidence of deep conviction,

but that he has the irreverence to make the Lord Jesus Christ responsible for the correctness of his fallible opinion regarding the nearness of the coming. Jesus said Himself, "of that day and that hour knoweth no man." Bauman is not only sure that he knows, at least approximately. But he is ready to stake the reputation of his Lord on the correctness of his own fallible opinion.

73 Fairbairn, *On Prophecy*, p. 1.

74 This view is vigorously stated by F. C. Ottman in *God's Oath*, pp. 209f.

75 "Dr. Herman Bavinck very neatly turns this around. There is indeed, he says, a divine parenthesis in history, but it is not the church, it is Israel. From the beginning, for many centuries, until Abraham, redemption had a universal aspect. With him, and still more with the Sinaitic Covenant, under Moses, a parenthesis set in, which came to an end in Christ. Then redemptive history resumed the universal character which it had at the beginning" (Albertus Pieters, *Intelligencer-Leader*, March 19, 1943, p. 20).

CHAPTER III (Pages 55-89)

1 Scofield does not concern himself with the, for literalists, thorny question of Abraham's personal return to and possession of the land. He insists that his seed must possess it. But if Gen. xiii. 15 is to be taken with absolute literalness, Abraham himself and all his posterity, not merely his descendants of an age still future, must actually possess the land. Yet Hebrews tells us plainly that the patriarchs were seeking not an earthly but a heavenly country. If the promise is not to be taken literally as regards Abraham, why must it be taken literally as regards *some* of his descendants? If it is to be taken literally, then Abraham is to return to earth and possess the land of Canaan for ever. This raises a further question. How can Abraham possess the literal land of his sojourneyings, if the earth is to be consumed with fire and there are to be new heavens and a new earth?

2 Scofield says: "The gift of the land is modified by prophecies of three dispossessions and restorations (Gen. xv. 13, 14, 16; Jer. xxv. 11, 12; Deut. xxviii. 62-65; xxx. 1-3)" (*RB*, p. 25). He places Deut. xxx. 1-3 after Jer. xxv. 11f., because he regards it as referring to the second advent and therefore as skipping over the Babylonian captivity, although Jeremiah's prophecy might very properly be regarded as referring to a striking, though germinant or partial, fulfilment of that of Moses.

3 In Gal. iv. 24 Paul does, indeed, speak of the promise and the law as "two covenants" which are to be regarded as distinct and even as mutually exclusive. Yet he declares that the latter does not "disannul" the former, but was added "because of transgressions" (iii. 19). According to Paul, then, the law was a temporary modification or special form of that covenant of promise on which he based that gospel of free grace which he preached.

⁴ Although he distinguishes only seven dispensations, Scofield finds eight covenants recorded in the Bible. This is decidedly confusing. The first four covenants correspond with and introduce the first four dispensations: (1) the Edenic covenant (Gen. i. 28) governs the dispensation of innocence; (2) the Adamic (iii. 14), that of conscience; (3) the Noahic (viii. 20), that of civil government; (4) the Abrahamic (xii. 2), that of promise. Then the difficulty begins, for (5) the dispensation of law (Ex. xix. 8), which extends we are told to the Cross (Matt. xxvii. 35) is governed by three covenants, (5) the Mosaic (Ex. xix. 8), (6) the Palestinian (Deut. xxx.), and (7) the Davidic (2 Sam. vii.). This leaves two dispensations, (6) grace and (7) the kingdom, and one covenant, (8) the New. Apparently, the 8th covenant (the New) applies to the 6th dispensation (grace), while the 7th dispensation (the kingdom) will be governed by the covenants with Israel, viz., the Abrahamic, the Mosaic, the Palestinian, and the Davidic. How the Abrahamic covenant as unconditional and the other three as conditional will be related to one another, it is hard to see. Scofield tells us: "The Palestinian Covenant gives the conditions under which Israel entered the land of promise. It is important to see that the nation has never yet taken the land under the unconditional Abrahamic covenant, nor has it ever possessed the whole land (cf. Gen. xv. 18 with Num. xxxiv. 1-12)" (*RB*, p. 250). Here we find the words "condition" and "unconditional" both used with reference to Israel's possession of the land. This raises a difficult question. Having accepted the legal condition, "If ye will obey my voice" at Sinai, a condition that applies equally to the Mosaic, Palestinian, and Davidic covenants, how is Israel to be placed in a position to secure possession of the land under the unconditional Abrahamic covenant? Here it will suffice to observe that the Palestinian and Davidic covenants are only amplifications or applications of the Mosaic covenant (cf. Deut. xxix. 1 in the light of vs. 25). Darby and Savage, for example, apparently do not distinguish a Palestinian covenant

⁵ Of these psalms, Ps. cx. is ascribed to David by the heading (cf. Matt. xxii. 43f.); Ps. ii. is ascribed to David in Acts iv. 25; Ps. lxxii. is according to the heading either a psalm written by Solomon, or one written for him (by David, cf. vs. 20); Ps. xlv. is "by the sons of Korah" or "for" them. There is no sufficient reason for rejecting the view that all of these psalms date from the time of the United Monarchy. [The last three verses of Ps. lxxii. may properly be regarded as an integral part of that psalm. The benediction (vss. 18-19) is thoroughly appropriate, as is also the concluding statement or prayer (vs. 20). The proposal to make vs. 20 the colophon marking the end of a primary collection of "Davidic" psalms encounters the serious difficulty that "Davidic" psalms (18 of them) appear in the last three books of the Psalter.]

⁶ "The evangelists have clearly considered the two phrases as synonymous" (G. Dalman, *The Words of Jesus*, p. 93). Gresswell held the same opinion (*Parables*, i. p. 120). It is interesting to note that Bengel believed that Matthew used "heaven" instead of "God" "that he might cure the Jews, for whom he was writing, of the notion of an earthly kingdom" (*Gnomon*, on Matt. iii. 2). In *Parables and Metaphors of Our Lord* (1943), Campbell Morgan declares that the Sermon on the

Mount or Manifesto, as he calls it, is "the ultimate code of laws for the kingdom of God" (p. 18), which clearly indicates that he regards the two expressions as interchangeable. Compare especially the discussion in G. Vos, *The Kingdom and the Church*, pp. 25-37.

7 In the Sermon on the Mount, where "kingdom of heaven" occurs 7 times, "his kingdom and righteousness" occurs once (vi. 33). The only natural antecedent of "his" in the context is "Father" or "God"; and many manuscripts and versions read "kingdom of God and his righteousness." It is quite remarkable that Scofield not only accepted without demur the reading "kingdom of God" of the AV, but even attached his elaborate note on the topic "kingdom of God" to it. For, if "kingdom of God" were, as Scofield apparently believed, the correct reading, as we believe it to be unquestionably the legitimate paraphrase of the words "his kingdom," it would be very strong evidence that the two expressions are equivalent. It is almost incredible that, if there is any essential difference between "kingdom of heaven" and "kingdom of God," the latter would be referred to in this discourse, either expressly or by implication, without any explanation of the ("five" important) differences being given. The reference in Mt. xxi. 31f. to John's preaching (iii. 2) also implies the practical identity of the two expressions.

8 Compare also Matt. xi. 11 with Lk. vii. 28. Consequently, Darby is begging the whole question when he says that "it could not be said 'the kingdom of heaven is among you.'" Since the expression, "the kingdom of God is among you," occurs only in Luke (xvii. 21), we have no way of knowing how it would have been phrased had it appeared also in Matthew. The use of "kingdom of God" in Matt. xii. 28 is probably due to the fact that the phrase "Spirit of God" immediately precedes, which is a further strong indication that the two expressions are equivalent.

9 *RB*, p. 1003.

10 In an article published in the *Christian Witness* in 1834 entitled, "The Dispensation of the Kingdom of Heaven: Matthew xiii." (*Collected Writings*, ii. pp. 80-96; also published by G. Morrish, London, as a tract).

11 It is particularly stressed by Scofield (*RB*, p. 1003, cf. pp. 996, 1014f., 1029). Matthew's preference for the expression "kingdom of heaven" has been explained (*e.g.*, by G. Dalman, *The Words of Jesus*) as due to the fact that in NT times the Jews showed a certain hesitancy about using the name of God. They substituted "Lord" for the Memorial Name (Jehovah) in reading the OT and sometimes used "heaven" instead of "God" (*e.g.*, Lk. xv. 18, 21; cf. Matt. xxii. 25, Mk. xi. 30, Lk. xx. 4, Jn. iii. 27, also Mk. xiv. 61). Since Dispensationalists hold that Matthew is more "Jewish" than the other Gospels, we might expect them to find in this fact the explanation of his use of this expression. But the explanation is not entirely satisfactory in itself. The word "God" occurs quite frequently in Matthew and cannot be said to be studiously avoided (compare Matt. xxvi. 63 with Mk. xiv. 61, where Matt. has "Son of God" while Mk. has "Son of the Blessed"). It is significant that Matthew uses the expression "heavenly Father" or "Father in heaven" repeatedly (about a score of times). This may indicate that his special reason for using the phrase "kingdom of heaven" was to stress the heavenly origin and

nature of God's kingdom. The kingdom proclaimed by John and by Jesus was not to be an earthly but a heavenly kingdom.

12 *RB*, p. 996. Chafer, "Dispensationalism," p. 425.

13 *RB*, p. 1226.

14 *RB*, p. 1003.

15 The question asked by our Lord regarding the title "Son of David" was not intended to prove that He was David's Son, except inferentially, but rather that the Messiah, David's Son, must be more than a mere man.

16 The title which Jesus often applied to Himself, "Son of man," clearly has Messianic significance. It is used of Him as the coming heavenly Judge (cf. Dan. vii. 9-14 with Matt. xxvi. 64), as the ideal Man (Ps. viii.; cf. Heb. ii.) to whom the whole earth is to be a dominion, and probably also to point to His true humanity as God manifested in the *flesh*, "son of man" being simply the common Aramaic equivalent of "man." [Scofield's claim that, as used by Ezekiel, this designation implies "transcendence of mere Judaism" *(RB*, p. 841) is rather far-fetched, since Ezekiel is perhaps the most intensely nationalistic of all the prophets.]

17 It is in the light of these data (cf. also Lk. ix. 52, x. 33, xvii. 16) that such words as are found in Matt. x. 5, xv. 24 are to be interpreted. Scofield's comment on John xii. 23, "He did not receive these Gentiles. A Christ in the flesh, King of the Jews, could be no proper object of faith to the Gentiles, though the Jews should have believed on Him as such. For Gentiles the corn of wheat must fall into the ground and die; Christ must be lifted up on the cross and believed in as a sacrifice for sin, as Seed of Abraham, not David (vs. 24, 32; Gal. iii. 7-14; Eph. ii. 11-13)" is quite out of harmony with the entire spirit of the narrative *(RB*, p. 1132; cf. pp. 1008, 1012, 1020).

18 *RB*, p. 998.

19 There does not seem to be any substantial difference as far as the meaning is concerned between the two expressions for "was at hand": *eggus* (near) with the verb "to be," and *eggiken*, the perfect of the verb, *eggizō*, "to be or become near."

20 Edersheim points out that this interval of time might be a considerable one (*Life and Times of the Messiah*, ii. p. 129).

21 Scofield practically contradicts himself when he tells us on the one hand, "When Christ appeared to the Jewish people, the next thing in the order of revelation as it then stood should have been the setting up of the Davidic kingdom. In the knowledge of God, not yet disclosed, lay the rejection of the kingdom (and King)" *(RB*, p. 998), and elsewhere declares that, "The OT prophets saw in one blended vision the rejection and crucifixion of the King . . . and also His glory as David's Son" (p. 1015). The "order" of events as given by Scofield is determined solely by his definition of "at hand." The true order is indicated quite clearly in Isa. liii. which implies that travail and death are to precede glory (vs. 12) and is definitely stated by Jesus (Lk. xxiv. 26).

22 *Collected Writings*, xi. p. 577, in his reply to David Brown (p. 64 of the separate tract).

23 *Lectures on the Second Advent*, p. 113.

24 *RB*, pp. 1008g, 1132, cf. 1022 and 1012.

25 *Quiet Talks about Jesus;* cf. especially pp. 58f., 75, 111f., 124, 134f.

26 *RB,* p. 1011; cf. p. 996 where the word "virtual" is used.

27 According to Darby and Scofield, Peter offered the kingdom to the Jews in the discourse recorded in Acts iii. Commenting on Acts vii. 54 Scofield remarks, "It was the final trial of the nation" (*RB,* p. 1158a). This would imply that the rejection occurred at the time of the martyrdom of Stephen.

28 It may be noted that, while Scofield does not apparently use the word "unconditional" in speaking of the promised *kingdom* as he does in speaking of the Abrahamic *covenant,* he is quite as insistent that the one promise must be fulfilled unconditionally and literally as the other.

29 *RB,* p. 1014; cf. pp. 1018, 1022.

30 *Notes on the Parables,* p. 73; cf. also Plumptre's discussion in *A Bible Commentary,* edited by Ellicott, *in loco.*

31 The fact that OT Israel is often called the "house of Israel" makes the use of the word "build" quite appropriate, and also serves to bring out clearly the close connection between Christ's Church and Israel, the OT Church.

32 The word "church" does not appear at ii. 47 according to the best manuscripts.

33 Candlish, *The Kingdom of God,* pp. 205f.

34 According to Dr. Vos, "So far as extent of membership is concerned Jesus plainly leads us to identify the invisible church and the kingdom," to regard "the visible church as a veritable embodiment of the kingdom," and to recognize that the kingdom of God is "intended to pervade and control the whole of human life in all its forms of existence"; also to recognize that while the intimate union of state and church which subsisted under the Old Covenant is not to be perpetuated (Matt. xxii. 21, Jn. xviii. 36, xix. 11) and "While it is proper to separate between the visible church and such things as the Christian state, Christian art, Christian science, etc., these things, if they truly belong to the kingdom of God, grow up out of the regenerated life of the invisible church." (*The Teaching of Jesus Concerning the Kingdom of God and the Church,* pp. 158-165). "The thoroughgoing Protestants [of the time of the Reformation in Scotland] held that the Church in its visible embodiment is the outward Kingdom of its Lord and Head" (Macleod, *Scottish Theology,* p. 8; cf. pp. 31-40, where the importance which this doctrine assumed in the course of the struggle against the Erastianism of the Stuart kings is very clearly pictured). The *Westminster Confession of Faith* declares that the "visible Church . . . is the kingdom of the Lord Jesus Christ" (Chap. xxv., sec. ii.).

35 *RB,* p. 1011.

36 The fact that this exact phrase, "the mysteries of the kingdom of heaven," which occurs only once in Matt. xiii., is also found once in Mark (iv. 11) and once in Luke (viii. 10) in the form "the mysteries of the kingdom of God" is one of the clearest evidences that "kingdom of heaven" and "kingdom of God" are equivalent terms.

37 What could be more confusing than this: "In a word, he [Peter] had the power of command in the kingdom of God, this kingdom having now the character of kingdom of heaven, because its King was in heaven,

and would stamp his acts with its authority" (Darby, *Synopsis*, iii. p. 118f.)? The kingdom of heaven and the kingdom of God are distinct: but the kingdom of God now has the character of kingdom of heaven!

38 Schaff in discussing the Donatist controversy of the 4th and 5th centuries declares that the parables of the Tares and of the Net were "the chief ecclesiastical battle ground of the two parties" (*History of the Christian Church*, iii., p. 368). He states the issue as consisting in part in the claim that "the true church is not so much a school of holiness, as a society of those who are already holy." The Donatists insisted as do the Dispensationalists, that the Church consists only of true Christians, and that these parables are parables regarding the world or Christendom, and not regarding the Church.

39 Note also Scofield's interpretation of the Mustard Seed. The growth is, he tells us, "unsubstantial" and the refuge is "insecure." Dan. iv. 20-22 is appealed to for the key to its meaning. There we read that the tree, which here is interpreted as representing the "mystery form of the kingdom," is to be cut down.

40 *Synopsis*, iii. 94. All spiritually minded persons will admit that there is much of sin and sham and actual unbelief in the visible Church. But this is quite a different thing from saying that the entire professing church is apostate and unchristian. Darby, who left the Church of England very soon after he had accepted ordination at her hands, later gave as his reason for having done so: ". . . I found the system I was mixed up with *to be the world and not the Church of God at all*. This is a very different thing from worldly people being in the Church" (*Collected Writings*, xiv. pp. 267f.). This amounted to saying that a great religious body in which such men as Edward Bickersteth, William Wilberforce, and Reginald Heber were or had recently been active, being the "professing church," was not the "church of God" at all, but the "world." From such a worldly body, the true Church was quite distinct. Yet Scofield tells us definitely that the true Church is to be found "within" the sphere of Christian profession (*RB*, p. 1018, cf. p. 1017).

41 To appeal, as Scofield does (*RB*, p. 1016) to Gen. xix. 3 as proof that "Leaven as a symbolical or typical substance is always mentioned in the OT in an evil sense" is to read into this passage a meaning which, to say the least, is not the obvious one. In Gen. xviii. 6 as in xix. 3 unleavened cakes are served because the guests are *unexpected* (cf. 1 Sam. xxviii. 24). The only difference between these two passages is that the one states that the cakes were unleavened while the other clearly implies it.

42 Fairbairn, while holding that leaven "was commonly understood to symbolize malice and wickedness" and that this explains its exclusion from the symbolical offerings, declares that "there can be no doubt that leavened bread was used in ordinary life by the covenant people, without apparently suggesting any idea of corruption" and he also asserts that it "might be viewed simply with reference to its penetrating and expansive qualities" (*Typology*, ii. 312). It seems incredible that the Israelites would have been permitted to eat leavened bread 51 weeks of the year, if the symbolical meaning of leaven was always and solely evil. It would imply that except on special occasions they might quite

properly contaminate themselves with an "evil principle." Furthermore, it would be this *domestic* significance of leaven rather than the ecclesiastical or ritualistic which would most naturally suggest itself to Jesus' hearers and therefore be the more appropriate one for Him to use.

43 Jamieson, Fausset, and Brown, *Critical and Explanatory Commentary*, p. 90 (one-volume edition).

44 It is noteworthy that Trench makes no reference to the Donatists as having made use of the parable of the Leaven (nor does Schaff). He mentions only two now almost forgotten commentators "and also some little bands of modern separatists (whose motive, of course, is obvious)"; and he refers in a footnote to Darby's *Brief Exposition of Matthew xiii.* This and several other references to Darby show that Trench who was born in Dublin, an early center of Brethren teaching, was acquainted with this teaching and rejected it as erroneous.

45 *RB*, p. 1022. Broadly speaking this statement is correct. But certainly Philip opened the door to the Samaritans and then to the Ethiopian eunuch (Acts viii.); and if the Greeks mentioned in John xii. were still in Jerusalem on the day of Pentecost, they might well have applied Peter's quotation of Joel and exposition of it to themselves.

46 "The keys (however heaven sanctioned Simon's use of them) were, as we have seen, of the kingdom of heaven (not of the assembly); and that, the parable of the tares shows, was to be corrupted and spoiled, and this irremediably. Christ builds the Church, not Peter" (Darby, *Synopsis,* iii. p. 118, note). According to Scofield, "The predicted future of the visible Church is apostasy . . . of the true Church glory . . . *(RB*, p. 1276). Yet he has just said of this visible Church: "Within, for the most part, this 'historical Church' has existed the true Church."

·

CHAPTER IV (Pages 90-110)

1 This is usually understood as referring the readers of the epistle to the brief statements already made in i. 9f. and ii. 11-22. If so, it indicates how important Paul regarded a correct understanding of the mystery to be. Otherwise he would hardly direct the attention of his readers to statements made already in earlier paragraphs of this short epistle. But it is hard to believe that Paul is here referring to truths mentioned for the first time in this epistle. Paul had spent much time (two years or more) at Ephesus. He must have taught this doctrine during this period. Consequently, the words, "if ye have heard," may be equivalent to an emphatic "ye have certainly heard." On the other hand, if this epistle was an encyclical letter, intended for other churches besides Ephesus (*e.g.,* Laodicea, cf. Col. iv. 16), these words may be intended for those who actually have not had the opportunity to learn this important doctrine.

2 "Sons of men" seems to be used in a broad sense, to include mankind in general. Were it to be taken as referring to the Gentiles, it might

seem to suggest that the Jews did possess some information regarding the mystery, which Paul tells us was actually the case.

3 Cf. Rom. i. 2 where the writings of the prophets are referred to. That Paul is there referring to prophets of the NT Church, or even to himself and his epistles, seems very improbable. Darby draws a distinction between "prophetic writings" and "the writings of the prophets," declaring that "the epistles addressed to the Gentiles possessed this character" (*Synopsis*, iv. 203). Scofield is non-committal.

4 *RB*, p. 711. Cf. "The Secret of God" in *The Christian Witness*, Vol. i. pp. 435-460 [1834], which is one of the earliest statements of this doctrine.

5 *RB*, p. 989.

6 *RB*, p. 1252.

7 Savage lists 29 such prophecies, only one of which (Rom. xi. 23-27) is in the NT (*The Scroll*, p. 105).

8 To assert that such a statement is to be found in xi. 26 is decidedly precarious for several reasons: (1) Even if the earthly Sion is here meant. it by no means follows that all Israel will then be in the land of Canaan, since Messiah's kingdom is to be world-wide (Ps. lxxii.); (2) The Sion referred to may be the heavenly Sion of Heb. xii. 22 (cf. Rev. xiv. 1, which pictures the Lamb as standing on mount Sion and the 144,000 as standing around a throne which some regard as earthly, others as in heaven); (3) The words, "from Sion," in place of "to Sion" (the Hebrew could be rendered "to" or "for" [*i.e.*, "in the interest of"]) favor the view that the heavenly city is intended. At any rate it must be admitted that if Paul believed in the restoration of Israel to the land and considered this a matter of importance, he might well have expressed himself much more plainly here where such a statement would be most appropriate and pertinent.

9 *RB*, p. 970. "The fulfilment . . . will infinitely transcend the symbol."

10 How difficult it is to make the Church (or, assembly) a unique thing in the counsels of God, is illustrated by Darby's discussion of the Epistle to the Hebrews in the *Synopsis*. In commenting on this verse he tells us: "The Spirit does not here develop the entire extent of this 'better thing', because the assembly is not His subject. He presents the general thought to the Hebrews to encourage them, that believers of the present day have special privileges, which they enjoy by faith, but which did not belong even to the faith of believers in former days" (v. 336). This statement is quite contrary to the aim of the writer of the Epistle which is plainly to show that the patriarchs looked forward to the blessings of the Christian dispensation and laid hold on them by faith. Darby's aim is to make the privileges of the Church so "special" that "they did not belong even to the faith of believers in former days." It is significant that he has no comment to make on the words "they without us." For he regards the perfection of the Church as quite distinct from that of Israel.

11 This great question was fought out in the Puritan controversy of the 17th century in England, Holland, and the New England Colonies.

12 Scofield does not hesitate to insert the following heading between vss. 3 and 4: "The Holy Spirit forbids Paul to go to Jerusalem." At Acts xviii. 18 the heading is inserted: "The author of Rom. vi. 14; 2 Cor. iii.

7-14; and Gal. iii. 23-28 takes a Jewish vow." The tone of the statement suggests amazement and reproof. Compare Alexander on this passage who declares that "during the anomalous interval between the day of Pentecost and the downfall of Jerusalem, the observance of the ceremonial law, whether stated or occasional, was always lawful, sometimes necessary, often expedient, as a means of safety or conciliation" (*Commentary on Acts, in loco*). This is a necessary inference from the facts as they are placed before us in the NT.

13 Darby discusses this subject at considerable length in the *Synopsis*. The gist of it is that Paul meant well but was misled by his love for Israel ("for the moment Jerusalem intercepted his view"), and did not seek and follow the guidance of the Holy Spirit, for which the Lord chastened him, while also overruling it for good.

14 Yet Blackstone is less dogmatic than many others. For in speaking of the mystery he describes it as "but rarely, if at all, spoken of in the OT prophecies."

15 *RB*, p. 1252. Compare Darby's statement (*Synopsis*, iv. 404) where he refers to the mystery as "never made known in the past ages, but now revealed by the Spirit to the apostles and prophets." In saying this Darby ignores the words: "as it hath now been revealed."

16 *RB*, p. 1189.

17 Vol. iv, pp. 192ff.

CHAPTER V (Pages 111-133)

1 It was called "Jerusalem" and was anonymous as were nearly all the contributions to this organ.

2 See, for example, Alexander Keith's very popular works, *Evidence of the Truth of Christianity derived from the Literal Fulfilment of Prophecy* (1828) and *The Signs of the Times, Illustrated by the Fulfilment of Historical Predictions* (1832); also John Davison, *Discourses on Prophecy* (1824).

3 Darby resented, as an unwarranted ignoring of the teachings of the Brethren, the fact that Louis Gaussen in his *Daniel the Prophet* treated it "as an admitted truth, as an uncontested principle, namely that it is the Church which is in question in these prophecies." He wrote a scathing review of this book (*Collected Writings*, xi. pp. 95-165, see especially p. 116f.). Darby's summary statement of Gaussen's position is evidence of the general acceptance of that interpretation a hundred years ago.

4 Walter Scott, *Prophetic Scenes*, p. 36.

5 E. B. Elliott points out that Augustine regarded Dan. ix. 24-27 as fulfilled in the first advent, and declares that this seems to have been the view of Athanasius as of "the majority of his predecessors in the Ante-Constantinian age" (*Horae*, iv., pp. 326, 313). The "principal alternative interpretation" is, according to S. R. Driver, that one which dates the beginning of the 70 weeks in 587-6 B.C. and their termination in the Maccabean age, the 69th week ending with the murder of Onias III and

the 70th week extending from 171 to 164 B.C. *(The Book of Daniel* [1901], p. 146; cf. also J. A. Montgomery, *The Book of Daniel* [1926]). This interpretation is faced with the difficulty that the period from 587 to 171 B.C. is not 483 years but 416 years, about 67 years too few. When the Book of Daniel is assigned to the Maccabean period, the predictive element is largely or wholly eliminated and the prophecy of the 70 weeks becomes a *vaticinium post eventum*. To attain this result is the major objective of the rationalistic critic.

6 The reading is somewhat doubtful. The Hebrew text has "seal up"; but the margin *(Qeri)* has "finish" or "complete." Both expressions may be interpreted as referring to the Cross. On it sin was finally dealt with by God. In it sin reached its climax in man; the crucifixion was the supreme crime of human history.

7 According to Ussher, Prideaux, and others, the 70th week began with the appearance of John the Baptist, whose ministry lasted three and a half years and was followed by that of Jesus which covered a like period of time, making seven years in all: the crucifixion (the cutting off of the Anointed) came at the end of the week. But there is no sufficient warrant for giving so much time to the ministry of John, especially since it involves the assumption that there was an interval of three years and more between the baptism of Jesus and the beginning of His ministry. Hengstenberg, Pusey, and others, while accepting the view that the week began with the appearance of John, hold that the first half of the week represents the entire period of the combined ministries of John and of Jesus, that the "cutting off" came in the midst of the week, *i.e.*, at the end of the three and a half years, and that the last part of the week represents the period of the founding of the Church, the time when the gospel was preached "to the Jews only," ending with the stoning of Stephen, or with the destruction of Jerusalem.

8 It should be observed that Dispensationalists cannot take this prediction literally and find its fulfilment in the 70th week. For as will appear later, they regard the millennium, which is to follow the 70th week, as an age in which sin will still be present though controlled. They hold also that the millennium will be followed by the "little season," when evil will manifest itself to an almost unprecedented degree.

9 The Son of God could certainly be called a "prince" from His birth. Whether "Messiah" would be strictly appropriate before the baptism may be questioned (Hengstenberg denies it). If so, the angel used it proleptically (Lk. ii. 11).

10 Denny's "cancelled week" theory is a complicated one; for a brief statement of it, see Darby's *Synopsis*, ii. pp. 446f.

11 Scofield does not mention Anderson or any of the advocates of the parenthesis interpretation of this prophecy by name; and it is not clear from the notes in *RB* whether he accepted the claim that the triumphal entry formed the concluding event of the 69th week. He seems to have deprecated the attempt to be very exact in dealing with the chronological data, pointing out that prophecy is "so indeterminate as to give no satisfaction to mere curiosity." This looks a little like a slur on Anderson's mathematical calculation. But the words "mere curiosity" would certainly not apply to Anderson. Apparently, Scofield was uncertain as to

the details of interpretation. On several points, however, he was quite specific. According to the notes in *RB* the beginning of the period of the 70 weeks is to be counted from Artaxerxes' decree which was issued "between 454 and 444 B.C."; and in the first 7 weeks (49 years) "Jerusalem was to be rebuilt in 'troublous times.' This was fulfilled, as Ezra and Nehemiah record." 483 years (69 weeks) counted from 450 B.C. would extend to approximately 33 A.D. (Ussher's date for the crucifixion). But Scofield merely says that they bring us "to the time of Christ." On the two points which are characteristic of the Dispensational interpretation he is quite explicit: the crucifixion comes after the 69th week, and the entire 70th week is postponed and still future.

In the notes on this prophecy in *RB* we meet one of the most remarkable phenomena in this *Reference Bible*. In *What Do the Prophets Say?*, which appeared serially in 1916 and in book-form in 1918, Scofield asserts emphatically that the prophecy of the 70 weeks commences with the decree of Cyrus in 538 B.C. (pp. 142ff.); and he accepts Anstey's solution of the difficulty raised by this interpretation, viz., that the Ptolemaic chronology for the Persian period is *82 years too long*. Yet the notes on Dan. ix. 24-27 are exactly the same in the 1917 edition of *RB* as in the first edition where the 70 weeks are described as beginning with the decree of Artaxerxes. It is hard to reconcile these facts with the claim that the edition of 1917 represented an at all careful revision of the original edition. Somewhere between 1909 and 1917 Scofield evidently decided to print the Ussher chronology in the margin of the new edition. Somewhere between 1913 and 1916 he accepted, certainly in some important features, Anstey's system of chronology (*The Romance of Bible Chronology* appeared in 1913), which required a radical revision of the Ussher chronology. Yet no attempt is made to harmonize these differences, and the fact of their existence is not even referred to in *RB*. This is singular to say the least!

12 According to Dispensational principles, the Babylonian Captivity was to an almost unique degree "time out." Israel was not in the land; Israel was not governed by God. Yet this period was definitely defined prophetically as 70 years (Jer. xxv. 11). The same is true of the Egyptian Bondage which is described prophetically as 400 years (Gen. xv. 13) and historically more precisely as 430 years (Ex. xii. 40). If this theory were correct, these should be "uncounted" intervals. It may also be noted that Dispensationalists who, with Anstey, endeavor to explain the 480 years between the Exodus and the beginning of work on the temple (1 Kgs. vi. 1) by reckoning the periods of bondage during the time of the Judges as "time out," do not treat the "40 years" of wandering, when Israel was both outside the land and rejected by God as also representing such an uncounted period. This is both inconsistent and arbitrary; and it shows the weakness of this "Jewish time" theory.

13 Since this is an important matter and one the significance of which is not appreciated it would seem by Dispensationalists, the following very lucid statement from Savage's *Scroll* may well be quoted in full, it being remembered that *The Scroll* is an explanation of the prophetic chart which he has drawn up: "The narrow red line that runs through the three dispensations C, D, and H,—*i.e.*, from the call of Abram to the

Captivity, where it is broken off, and resumed again in the millennium,—
is intended to represent the history of the Israelites as a *nation,* under
the special and direct government of God, during which He could say
of them, 'Ye are My people.' After the Captivity, more than two thousand
years ago, they ceased to be a nation of God's people, and they have
ever since continued in the 'Loammi' position of 'Not My people,' having
been cast off for their repeated rebellions. Hence the break or discontinuance of the red line at epoch 5. But they will be restored again
as a nation to God's favour, and to their own land, as stated in Hosea
i. 10,—'In the place where it was said unto them, Ye are not My people,
there it shall be said unto them, Ye are the sons of the living God.'
Therefore the red line is again resumed, and continued through the
millennial dispensation" (p. 3). Cf. also *RB,* p. 535. This means that
the entire scope of the prediction of the 70 weeks, a prophecy which
concerns Israel the nation and is definitely chronological, that is to say,
counts time for Israel, lies within the period when God has no direct
dealings with Israel the nation. It belongs to the Loammi period; yet
it is definitely chronological. Kelly speaks of it as a parenthesis within
a parenthesis, declaring that "as the calling of the church is a heavenly
parenthesis, so also are 'the times of the Gentiles' a still wider earthly
one, which fills the blank in the earth's history since God governed in
the midst of His people under law, as He will by-and-by when they
are under the new covenant" (William Kelly, *Elements of Prophecy,* p.
173). This is interesting as an illustration of the adroitness of one who
may be regarded as the ablest exegete among the Brethren. But it does
not really explain how the clock can both stop and run during a considerable part of the times of the Gentiles. Certainly the "times of the
Gentiles" cannot be regarded as "Jewish time" (*RB,* p. 1106) Yet the
clock runs with great accuracy during part of it!

14 *E.g.,* Savage, *The Scroll,* p. 69.

15 Dispensationalists are not agreed as to the number of the actors of
the time of the end whom they find described in the Book of Daniel.
Darby distinguished: (1) a Roman king, the "little horn of Dan. vii. and
ix."; (2) an Eastern (Grecian) king (Chap. viii.); and (3) a Jewish apostate
king (Chap. xi.), who is not to be identified with either 'the king of the
north (Assyria) or "the king of the south" (Egypt). The "little horn"
he identified with the first Beast of Rev. xiii., the apostate king with the
second Beast. This is substantially the view of Gaebelein and Savage,
except that they identify the king of Dan. viii. with the "king of the
north," the Assyrian of Isaiah and of Micah. Scofield, on the other hand,
apparently finds only one king described in Dan. vii.-xii. This king he regards as "the last civil head," *i.e.,* the Beast of Rev. xiii. 1-8 (*RB,* p. 1343),
holding that the words "the God of his fathers" (xi. 37) imply that the
king of vs. 36 is an apostate, not from Judaism, but from Christianity,
i.e., is a Gentile (*RB,* p. 918). The decision of this question, if indeed
it can be decided, has no important bearing upon the subject under
discussion.

16 This is the usual meaning of the verb (*e.g.,* Gen. vii. 19f.). The
causative form occurs only here and in Ps. xii. 4.

17 Cf. Dan. vii. 12 which implies that each of the first three kingdoms

continued to exist in a sense after its overthrow by the one which succeeded it.

18 *E.g., RB,* p. 902.

19 The symbolism which is used in the description of the image is a *natural* symbolism. Since the image has a human form, it will naturally have two legs, two feet, and ten toes. The question whether special significance attaches to these details is not easy to answer. It has often been asserted that the two legs represent the division of the Roman Empire into two parts, Eastern and Western. But the words in the original for *legs* and *feet* clearly imply that the fourth kingdom did not include the loins but began with the knees or perhaps at the hips. The loins belonged to the third kingdom. Hence the legs cannot represent the two divisions of the Empire, since these divisions did not arise until centuries after the Roman Empire attained to world dominion. Nothing is said in the interpretation about there being *two* legs; and there is as little warrant for attaching special significance to the *ten* toes. These features do not figure in the interpretation at all.

20 This does not necessarily mean that the number ten is absolutely literal. The symbolism of the description must be taken into account.

21 This can be accounted for most naturally by the fact that the vision in Chap. ii. is restricted to one side of the picture only, the destruction of the world power by the stone. The strength and weakness of the fourth kingdom are described, but only with a view to exhibiting the fragility of the image and the certainty of its complete overthrow. In Chap. vii. we are shown something which is only hinted at in Chap. ii. It is the opposition of the world power as concentrated in the little horn which is stressed in Chap. vii. There is nothing in Chap. ii. to correspond to the wearing out of the saints (vii. 25). In this respect the one vision is the converse of the other.

22 Since most, if not all, advocates of the "Protestant" interpretation regard the Papacy and any individual pope as only a type of the final Antichrist who is yet to appear, the issue between them and the Dispensationalists is not as to whether the Antichrist has come or is still to come, but whether he will come during this dispensation or after it is ended. In other words it concerns the question whether the Church will or will not be on earth when the Antichrist appears and when the great tribulation which he brings about takes place.

23 Gaebelein, *The Prophet Daniel,* p. 50f.

24 It is to be noted that the word "end" (*qets*) is used in viii. 17, 19; also ix. 26, xi. 6, 27, 35, 40, 45, xii. 4, 6, 9, 13. A different word (*soph*) is used in Dan. iv. 11, 22 of territory, vi. 26, vii. 26 of time, vii. 28 of prediction or interpretation. The "end" of Chap. viii. would seem to be defined by the words "and in the latter time of their kingdom" (vs. 23), *i.e.,* the four kingdoms into which Alexander's was divided.

25 *RB,* p. 912.

26 Alexander, *Commentary on Isaiah,* i., p. xxxv.

27 John Davison in his *Discourses on Prophecy* (1824) frequently uses the word "Christian" in referring to prophecies in the OT. He holds it to be "clear and explicit" that the prophets "foretold the establishment of a new dispensation of things, to be effected by the advent of an

extraordinary Person, for ends of a religious nature, particularly of Mercy and Redemption, which is the complex account of the Gospel Dispensation." And he says more specifically: "For what less have we in the single book of Isaiah, than the *scheme* of the Gospel, and the *establishment* of it unfolded?" (edition of 1870, pp. 73, 198f.). The same position is taken by Alexander in his *Commentary on Isaiah* (1846-47).

28 Kelly accuses the Church, in adopting this interpretation, of "coveting" for herself "the earthly place of power and dignity in store for converted Israel in the future" and of "straining after it by force or fraud" (*Minor Prophets*, 1874, pp. 1-3). Gaebelein speaks of this interpretation as making the Church "a thief stealing Israel's promises to enrich herself" (*World Prospects*, p. 60). Savage describes it as "both selfish and unfair, as well as unscriptural" (*The Scroll*, p. 147) and quotes from J. Wilkinson's *Israel, My Glory*, to support his statement.

29 *RB*, p. 747. Cf. Isa. xlix. 8f., where, according to Scofield, "The Lord Jesus and the believing [Jewish] remnant are here joined" (*RB*, p. 757).

30 *Synopsis*, ii., p. 315.

31 *RB*, p. 723. The Assyrian of Mic. v. 4 is naturally to be regarded as an eschatological person or people. But if this is the correct interpretation, as Scofield held it to be (*RB*, p. 949) what has become of the principle of literal interpretation of prophecy? If Israel must be the literal Israel, must not Assyria be the literal Assyria? Yet the literal Assyria passed away centuries ago!

32 *RB*, p. 975. Scofield has apparently followed Darby closely here (*Synopsis*, ii. p. 565).

33 Zech. xii-xiv is another good illustration of the futurist emphasis of Dispensationalists. We could not expect them, of course, to admit that Jerome (see Pusey) was right in finding numerous fulfilments of this prophecy in the course of the history of the Christian Church. But we might expect them to recognize that in part at least it has already been fulfilled in the history of Israel. C. H. H. Wright, for example, argues that xii. 1-9 was fulfilled in the days of the Maccabees. But Scofield does not hesitate to make the whole refer to the end time, the Jewish remnant, the Beast, and Armageddon. That is, it skips over the Church age completely.

34 *Synopsis*, ii., p. 45. Thus he says of Ps. li.: "Psalm li. is the true remnant's confession. They have fully entered into the mind of God." In vs. 14 we have "the dreadful crime of Christ's death owned." David's name appears only once in nearly two pages of exposition (*Synopsis*, ii. pp. 154f.).

35 *RB*, p. 599.

36 See Appendix, pp. 277-281.

CHAPTER VI (Pages 134-166)

1 It is not to be forgotten that we are told in vs. 3 that during a period of forty days Jesus had been speaking to His disciples of "the things pertaining to the kingdom of God." Obviously, this was with a view to preparing them for their apostolic mission. The nature of this kingdom has been already discussed. That it would be an Israelitish kingdom the disciples apparently still regarded as self-evident. Scofield shares the same view, for he tells us: "One point was left untouched, viz., the *time* when He would restore the kingdom to Israel." Obviously not a word has been said about Israel in vss. 1-5. Hence the question in vs. 6. Scofield implies that Jesus gives only one answer to the question, viz., that "the *time* was God's secret." As a matter of fact He gives two, and the second is the one which is especially important to us in this connection: "ye shall receive power . . . ye shall be witnesses unto me . . . in Samaria and unto the uttermost part of the earth." The kingdom to be proclaimed under the terms of the Great Commission was "the kingdom of God." It was not to be Israelitish: it was to be world-embracing. This was the answer to the question as it related to Israel.

2 There is quite general agreement that the rendering "when" of the AV is incorrect. Darby and Scofield render by "that."

3 In his lectures on *New Test. Millennarianism* Waldegrave entitled Lecture VIII. "The True Burden of Old Testament Prophecy." In it he aimed to show that there is Scriptural ground for believing that "the Israel which is, next to the Messiah himself, their most prominent subject, is not the nation of the Jews, but the whole mystical Church of Gospel times, including both Jew and Gentile alike within its pale" (p. 405). For this lecture he chose as his text Acts iii. 24, "Yea, and all the prophets from Samuel and those that follow after, as many as have spoken, have likewise foretold of these days."

4 The word "raised up" is ambiguous. If it refers to the resurrection of Christ, the "sending" must be an invisible coming through the Holy Spirit. If it refers to the first appearance of the Messiah on earth, the reference is to the significance of the fact that He came as a Jew to Israel. Alexander holds that both ideas may be present (*Commentary on Acts*). In either case the relative order, Jew first, is clearly implied. In the one, the thought of rejection is prominent; in the other, the present offer of amnesty and blessing.

5 Cf. *What Do the Prophets Say?*, pp. 106f. and *RB*, p. 1153. The warrant for this distinction must be found, if it can be found at all, in their interpretation of vss. 19-21. For in many ways the two addresses are strikingly similar. In both Peter addresses his auditors as Israelites (ii. 22, 36; iii. 12), as brethren (ii. 29; iii. 17), as heirs of the promise (ii. 39; iii. 25). Yet in both it is the universal sweep of the promise that is stressed (ii. 39, cf. ii. 17, 21; iii. 25). The words "church" and "kingdom" are absent from both. But the outpouring of the Spirit is represented

in ii. 33 as due to an act of Jesus who is now exalted to the right hand of power.

6 *Synopsis*, iv. 11. This suggests only one condition. But note the *three* "untils" stated by Scofield (*RB*, p. 1032).

7 *RB*, p. 1343. In *What Do the Prophets Say?*, Scofield refers to this as the "great final appeal to the Jews." How could there be such a final appeal, if the kingdom offer had been definitely and finally withdrawn by the Lord during the course of His earthly ministry? Scofield uses the words "virtually rejected" (p. 996), "morally rejected" (p. 1011) with reference to the incident in Matt. xi. He even tells us that the "final official rejection" came in Matt. xxvii. 31-37. Yet he speaks of Acts vii. 54 as "the final trial of the nation." All this serves to show the difficulties which the postponement theory encounters when it is faced with the facts of Scripture.

8 *RB*, p. 1169. Yet Scofield does not include it among the chapters which he describes as pivotal: "The pivotal chapters, taking prophecy as a whole, are, Deut. xxviii., xxix., xxx.; Psa. ii.; Dan. ii., vii." There are, however, frequent references to it in *RB*, e.g., 250, 476, 711, 721, 723, 727, 765, 795, 881, 961, 977, 990, 1334. He calls it "the great dispensational passage" (p. 765).

9 The word "tabernacle" in Isa. xvi. 5 is not the same as the one used by Amos. It is the ordinary word for "tent" (*ohel*); and it does not necessarily suggest, as does the word "booth," the lowly estate to which the glorious house of David had been reduced.

10 The words "I will return and gather you" (Deut. xxx. 3) are treated as an express prediction of the second advent. In fact they are made the first link in a long chain of references to that event which is carried as far as Acts i. 9-11; and this passage is referred to a number of times. Yet it is a well-known fact that "return and (do something)" is frequently in Scripture an idiom for "(do it) again." It is rendered by "again" 49 times in the AV, e.g., in vs. 9 of this very chapter in the phrase "the LORD will again rejoice over thee for good." Darby apparently attached no such meaning to this verse as Scofield has found in it.

11 *Synopsis*, iii. p. 93.

12 Philip Mauro has made these words the title of a book, *The Hope of Israel*, in which he has ably defended the position we are advocating.

13 *RB*, p. 1297f.

14 *Synopsis*, v., p. 285f.

15 *RB*, pp. 1289, 1291.

16 *RB*, p. 1289.

17 *RB*, p. 998.

18 A. J. Mason, in *The Bible Commentary*, edited by Bishop Ellicott.

19 *History and Teaching of the Plymouth Brethren*, p. 171.

20 *RB*, p. 989.

21 *How to Enjoy the Bible*, p. 147.

22 It may be noted, however, that Bullinger held the same view regarding the interpretation of Acts xv. as Darby and Scofield did.

23 *The Mystery*, p. 40 (quoted from A. J. Pollock, *An Examination of Dr. E. W. Bullinger's Bible Teaching*, pp. 50f.).

24 *How to Enjoy*, p. 142. Pollock points out that according to Bullinger,

"The public preaching of the kingdom ends with Acts xix. 20" (*An Examination*, p. 45). There is no warrant for this as Pollock clearly shows. It simply exposes the difficulty of Bullinger's position.

25 *How to Enjoy*, p. 144.

26 Scofield undoubtedly had this erroneous teaching in mind when he said in commenting on this passage: "Verses 30, 31 are quoted from Gen. ii. 23, 24, and exclude the interpretation that the reference is to the church merely as the body of Christ. Eve taken from Adam's body, was truly 'bone of his bone and flesh of his flesh,' but she was also his wife, united to him in a relation which makes of 'twain . . . one flesh' (Matt. xix. 5, 6), and so a clear type of the church as bride of Christ (see 2 Cor. xi. 2, 3)." This, in some respects, admirable note illustrates the disadvantage under which Darby's followers labor in their attempts to refute Bullingerism. Scofield writes here as if Eve as the sinful wife of Adam could be a true type of the Church as the bride of Christ. Yet elsewhere he is very insistent that the wife and the bride must be quite distinct types, that the wife of Jehovah is Israel, while the bride of the Lamb is the Church (*RB*, p. 922).

27 *How to Enjoy*, pp. 128-138.

28 What has been said regarding Bullingerism is based largely on Bullinger's book, *How to Enjoy the Bible* (2nd edition, 1910, London). Attacks on his writings by Dispensationalist writers are somewhat numerous: *e.g.*, William Hoste, *Bullingerism, or, Ultra Dispensationalism Exposed;* A. J. Pollock, *An Examination of Dr. E. W. Bullinger's Bible Teaching;* A. H. Stewart, *Bullingerism Exploded;* H. A. Ironside, *Wrongly Dividing the Word of Truth;* W. R. Newell, *Revelation* (Appendix iv.). Two replies to their opponents by American Bullingerites are worthy of mention: *Forgotten Truths Re-affirmed*, published by the Philadelphia Bible Testimony (P.O. box 4709, Philadelphia), and Harold P. Morgan, *The Revolt Against the Distinctive Ministry of the Apostle Paul.* Morgan's brochure is a reply to Ironside, and in it, as well as in *Forgotten Truths*, it is made clear that leading Dispensationalists teach doctrines which are either identical with or closely approximate teachings which, as advocated by Bullinger, they so strongly denounce.

29 *Wrongly Dividing*, p. 41.

30 The *Westminster Confession of Faith*, pp. 40, 43.

CHAPTER VII (Pages 167-191)

1 Jonathan Edwards wrote in 1747 with enthusiasm of the glorious task of the Church in preparing the way for the millennium which he expected to begin more than two hundred years later, *i.e.*, about A.D. 2000 (see his *An Humble Appeal*). Brookes quotes in *Maranatha* a striking testimony from John Ker; and H. W. Frost points out that "many postmillennial Christians in effect, do look for the second coming" (*Matthew xxiv. and the Revelation*, p. 282).

2 This is the main thesis of *Maranatha,* nine of the twenty-one chapters being devoted to establishing it.

3 Some Premillennialists seek to express the distinction by using the word "impending" instead of "imminent," as conveying the idea of possible remoteness. Both of these words, as distinguished from "threatening," involve the idea of certainty of occurrence.

4 The completion of the number of the elect of the Church age is of course regarded by them as a precondition. But since that number is known to God alone, as far as men are concerned it is assumed that it may be completed at any moment and therefore is not to be regarded as an "event" which must delay the rapture; and the thought that they may help to complete or actually complete the number and so remove this sole hindrance to the coming, is undoubtedly a great incentive to many to be active in Christian service. But the command of the Lord was to "preach the gospel to every creature." This would imply that at least world evangelization must precede the coming. Are Dispensationalists prepared to assert that the world has now been evangelized, that the gospel has been preached to all the nations for a witness? If so, are they prepared to assert that such was the case a century and more ago when the modern missionary movement had little more than begun, at which time Irving and the Brethren announced and proclaimed this any moment doctrine with the utmost positiveness and conviction?

5 *Maranatha,* p. 73.

6 The words, "now is our salvation nearer than when we believed" (Rom. xiii. 11), may certainly have this sense. According to Charles Hodge what is referred to here is ". . . the consummation of the work of Christ in their deliverance from this present evil world, and introduction into the purity and blessedness of heaven. Eternity is just at hand, is the solemn consideration that Paul urges on his readers as a motive for devotion and diligence" (*Commentary on Romans, in loco*). In other words, whether his life on earth is terminated by death or by the rapture is in its eternal issues a matter of indifference to the Christian. In either event, he will be with Christ and the time of his probation and suffering will be ended.

7 Darby, *Lectures on the Second Advent,* p. 3.

8 "Has arrived" or "impends" (*ephestēken*).

9 Scofield, *What Do the Prophets Say?,* p. 97.

10 Bauman, *Light from Bible Prophecy* (1940). The discussion of these signs occupies fifty pages or approximately one-third of the book. Some years ago L. S. Chafer published a little book entitled *Seven Signs of the Times.* In no respect is the inconsistency of Dispensationalists more glaringly apparent, than in their persistent efforts to discover *signs* of the nearness of an event which they emphatically declare to be *signless.* Savage appeals to such events, but refuses to call them signs. This shows that he recognized the inconsistency of attempting to prove by *signs* the nearness of an event which is held to be sign*less* (*The Scroll,* p. 201).

11 *RB,* pp. 1226f. In *What Do the Prophets Say?* Scofield speaks of the interval between the 69th and 70th weeks of Daniel ix. as "the period during which the two great divine secrets—the outcalling of the church

and the mysteries of the kingdom of heaven, run their course"; and he adds, "Both seem well-nigh complete" (p. 143). Cf. also *RB*, p. 1017, n. 3.

12 "The counting of time belongs entirely to the Jews . . . It is a perfect riddle how people who profess to receive Scripture have invented all sorts of notions as to the course of events connected with Christianity in this world. The moment I come to Scripture they are all gone" (*Lectures on the Second Coming*, pp. 171, 177).

13 *Synopsis*, iii., pp. 480f.

14 *Rightly Dividing the Word of Truth*, p. 36. Scofield declares that the prophecies concerning the return of the Lord were not fulfilled by the descent of the Holy Spirit at Pentecost (p. 32). Certainly they were not all fulfilled nor were they entirely fulfilled in it. But he should not have ignored the fact that the presence of Christ with His people through the Holy Spirit is described in John xiv. 16 as a coming.

15 *On Prophecy*, p. 445.

16 The rendering of these words in the ARV is followed since it is more uniform than that of the AV. Thus *apokalupsis* is rendered in the AV by "revealed" (2 Thess. i. 7; 1 Pet. iv. 13), "appearing" (1 Pet. i. 7), "revelation" (1 Pet. i. 13), "coming" (1 Cor. i. 7). Such variety is unnecessary and confusing.

17 1 Cor. xv. 23, 1 Thess. ii. 19, iii. 13, iv. 15, v. 23, 2 Thess. ii. 1, 8, 9. In 2 Thess ii. 9 it is used of Antichrist.

18 Rom. ii. 5, viii. 19, xvi. 25, 1 Cor. i. 7, xiv. 2, 26, 2 Cor. xii. 1, 7, Gal. i. 12, ii. 2, Eph. i. 17, iii. 3, 2 Thess. i. 7.

19 "The Rapture" (*Collected Writings*, xi., p. 233).

20 What Is the Church?" (*Collected Writings*, iii. p. 602).

21 *Premillennialism or Amillennialism?*, p. 207. It is rather significant, therefore, that Scofield has only a brief comment on these three words (*RB*, p. 1212).

22 Heb. xii. 22f. is a difficult passage. Whether "general assembly and church of the first-born" refers to angels or to men or to both has been much debated. "To the spirits of just men made perfect" clearly refers to men. Here the word "spirits" may refer to them as disembodied spirits. But however it be understood, this passage does not speak of a coming of Christ. It does speak of the redeemed in heaven. But if these redeemed are referred to as (disembodied) spirits, the rapture cannot yet have taken place.

23 Cf. George Duffield, *Dissertation on the Prophecies* (1842), pp. 164f., for a summary statement of the Millenarian doctrine current in his day.

24 Cf. "What Saints will be in the Tribulation?" (p. 15 of tract published by Loizeaux Brothers; also "The Rapture of the Saints," p. 50 [as cited by Teulon, *Plymouth Brethren*, p. 189]).

25 *RB*, p. 1349. Cf. Acts ii. 20 and Matt xxiv.

26 *RB*, pp. 1212, 1271f.

27 Were this distinction correctly drawn, it would necessitate a further distinction between the "day of the Lord" and the "day of God." For in 2 Pet. iii. 12 Christians are described as expecting (whether hopefully or fearfully) and hastening (to) the coming of the day of God. "Hastening" according to some scholars, means that Christians can make possible, by zealous carrying out of the Great Commission, the more speedy coming

of the day; according to others, it describes Christians as "hastening to" in the sense of earnestly desiring its coming, thinking of it as near at hand. Now if this "day of God" is a day of terror, Christians cannot, according to Dispensational principles, desire or long for its coming. Yet Scofield, who distinguishes between the "day of the Lord" and the "day of Christ" finds himself obliged to identify this "day of God" for which the Christian longs with the terrible "day of the Lord" (*RB*, p. 1349). The description of it in the immediate context makes this inescapable.

28 *RB*, p. 868.

29 For example in the widely read novels of Sydney Watson. In *In the Twinkling of an Eye*, he illustrates the suddenness and secrecy of the rapture by telling how a drunken husband rushes at his wife, determined to kill her. She vanishes (is raptured) and he dashes his brains out against the wall in front of which she has just been standing.

30 R. V. Bingham points this out very clearly in *Matthew the Publican— His Gospel*, p. 16.

31 Wimberley describes the former as the "invisible coming" (*Behold the Morning*, pp. 100ff., 145ff.).

32 Reese (*The Approaching Advent*, p. 147) hardly speaks too strongly when he says: "Admitting the principle of secrecy is selling the pass of the Pre-Millennial position." For those who interpret 1 Thess iv. 15f. as describing a *secret* rapture are at a decided disadvantage when it comes to insisting that Rev. xix, 11f. *must* describe a *visible* appearing.

CHAPTER VIII (Pages 192-217)

1 This is illustrated by the fact that James H. Brookes in *I Am Coming* (7th ed., Pickering and Inglis, London) gives as the first of seven reasons for believing that there will be an interval between the rapture and the appearing, the fact that it is "essential" to the "any moment" doctrine of the coming. Louis S. Bauman declares in *Light from Bible Prophecy* (1940): "The longer I live and the more I meditate upon the revelation of God to man, the more I am convinced of the correctness of that interpretation of the Scriptures which sets forth two distinct phases in the return of our Lord from heaven" (p. 138). It must be perfectly obvious to anyone who will study the question carefully that, as Brookes declares, the interval interpretation is absolutely indispensable to the any moment theory of the coming. The basic question must be, therefore, whether this theory of the coming is true.

2 The difficulties are obvious. The word *genea* (vs. 34) may of course mean "race," as Scofield points out (*RB*, p. 1034). But that meaning seems decidedly inappropriate here. The Jewish race had already existed for nearly 2000 years. Neither Pharaoh, nor Haman, nor Antiochus Epiphanes had succeeded in destroying it. There were millions of Jews in Palestine and of the Diaspora, when Jesus spoke these words. The statement that this race would still be in existence when He would return sounds very strange in a prediction which seems to stress the

imminence of that event. On the other hand, it is hard to believe that "all these things" (vs. 34) were fulfilled when Titus destroyed Jerusalem. The only probable solution seems to be the one adopted by very many expositors that this chapter refers to both events and stresses especially that which would be characteristic of both, the suddenness with which they would come upon an unprepared and unexpecting world.

3 *RB*, p. 1033.

4 The *Didache* quotes Matt. xxiv. 31 twice and both times substitutes the word "church" for "elect." This and other features make it surprising that Dispensationalists (*e.g.*, Chafer and Gaebelein) have appealed to the *Didache* as supporting their claim that Dispensationalism represents the faith of the Early Church. William Kelly saw its significance more clearly. So he spoke of it as "meagre and incorrect" and declared that "it serves to manifest the melancholy and rapid decline of the second century from revealed truth" (*Bible Treasury*, xix, pp. 95f.).

5 According to the Dispensational view, the words "one shall be taken" (vs. 40) must refer to the (pious) Jewish remnant, who are to be gathered together on earth (vs. 31) at the appearing of Christ with His saints. The usual interpretation is that the reference is to the Christian believers (*i.e.*, to the true Church).

6 The statement that two men shall be working in the field and two women grinding meal has been taken to mean that these things will be going on at the same time, which normally belong to different periods of the twenty-four hours. So it has been inferred that Jesus was anticipating modern knowledge that the earth is round and revolves on its axis (*Maranatha*, p. 532). It seems much more probable that He was simply illustrating the fact that the coming might take place at any hour of day or night (cf. Lk. xii. 37).

7 The Greek word is *enestēken*. Since the perf. participle is repeatedly used of the "present" age, some insist that the rendering should be "*now* (or, *already*) present." The expression seems to be a stronger one than the more usual "near" or "at hand." The rendering of ARV, "just at hand," seems preferable. In 1851 William Kelly sent E. B. Elliott an article he had written on 1 & 2 Thess. in which the Brethren doctrine was set forth that the Thess. Christians were distressed because they believed the day of the Lord had already set in and they had not had a part in the rapture which was to precede it. Elliott in a brief personal note, clearly not meant for publication, suggested as a sufficient objection to this view the fact that it would involve belief on their part that the apostle Paul had also been "overlooked" when the rapture took place. (See Kelly, *Elements of Prophecy*, pp. 249f.) B. B. Warfield refers to the rendering "is now present" or "had already come" as a "curious misinterpretation" which is almost ludicrously inappropriate in the context (*Biblical Doctrines*, p. 607).

8 The Historical interpretation has two main forms: the Continuist, which regards the series of visions as historically consecutive, and the Synchronous, which regards them as more or less contemporaneous, *i.e.*, as all covering practically the entire inter-adventual period.

9 Kelly admits that "the Thessalonians had no adequate light up to

this on the relative order of these events" (*Elements*, pp. 254f.). If this be so, we fail to see that 2 Thess. cleared up the matter. It says nothing about the rapture, but only assures them that the day of the Lord is not as near as they had supposed. According to Scofield, 2 Thess. "had more in view . . . the 'day of the Lord' " (*RB*, p. 1271).

10 It is of course true that many of the redeemed, the whole body of OT saints as well as many Church saints, were already in heaven when John saw this vision. Many NT saints, perhaps most of them, possibly nearly all of them, are now in heaven. But this is quite in harmony with the view that the "living" Church was then and is now to be regarded as still on earth.

11 *RB*, p. 1334.

12 The rendering "beast" (AV) is both inappropriate and confusing. The word used to describe these four beings is "living creature" *(zōon)*; and it is to be compared with the similar word which is frequently applied to the cherubim in Ezekiel. This word, which is only rarely used of any but heavenly beings, is used 20 times in Revelation of the four that stand before the throne of God. "Beast" *(thērion)*, properly "wild beast," is used in Rev. 39 times, and almost always of the great eschatological enemies of God and of His Christ.

13 In *RB*, Scofield repeatedly gives a cross-reference at the word "elder" to Acts xi. 30, where the elders of the NT church are first mentioned. This seems to justify the conclusion that the 24 elders stand for the Church. In *Will the Church Pass Through the Great Tribulation?* he defends this interpretation in some detail.

14 Govett, for example, denies that the elders are human beings. He regards them as "the rulers of the angelic sons of God, who kept their government and their abode, when others left it" (*The Apocalypse*, abridged edition of 1929, p. 107).

15 This is a most attractive and suitable interpretation and it is favored by the reference to "the song of Moses and of the Lamb" (xv. 3) and especially by the fact that the gates of the heavenly Jerusalem bear the names of the twelve tribes of Israel, while the foundations of the wall bear the names of the twelve apostles of the Lamb (xxi. 12, 14).

16 The better view is, we believe, that the woman signifies, not the literal Israel, but that Israel which represents the Church of all ages, that Jerusalem which is the mother of us all. Her eminent and preeminent Seed is the "man child"; and "the remnant of her seed" (vs. 17) represents those Christians who are still on earth and, therefore, exposed to the furious hate of the dragon.

17 The fact that in the case of the bride the linen is said to be "bright and pure," while in the case of the armies it is called "white and pure" can hardly have any special significance. "White" is used of the elders (iv. 4), of the martyrs (vi. 11), of the innumerable multitude (vii. 9, 13).

18 This would not be remarkable were it not that "bride" is also used by the Revelator. The Greek word "wife" *(gunē)* like the corresponding Hebrew word means of course both "woman" and "wife" (cf. Gen. xxiv. 39 and 1 Cor. vii. 34) and may be used in a proleptic sense of a woman who is shortly to become a wife.

19 In his eagerness to make as sharp a distinction as possible between OT Israel and the NT Church, Scofield says, in commenting on Hos. ii. 2: "That Israel is the wife of Jehovah (see vss. 16-23), now disowned but yet to be restored, is the clear teaching of the passages . . . The NT speaks of the Church as a virgin espoused to one husband (2 Cor. xi. 1, 2); which could never be said of an adulterous wife, restored by grace" (*RB*, p. 922). The falsity of this statement is proved by the very passage in Hosea to which Scofield appeals. In vss. 19-20, the word "betroth" is used three times (for emphasis) of the restoration of the erring "wife" of Jehovah. This word is used elsewhere of the betrothal of a *virgin*. The word "virgin" is also used repeatedly by the OT prophets in speaking of apostate Israel (*e.g.*, Jer. xiv. 17). "Virgin," "wife," "widow," "whore" are epithets all of which are applied to Israel. It is the glory of the grace of God, as shown alike to Israel and to the Church, that it wipes the slate so clean, that the adulterous wife is looked upon as a pure virgin, and treated as if she had never sinned. "Though your sins be as scarlet, they shall be as white as snow; and though they be red like crimson, they shall be as wool"—this is the heart of the "gospel of the grace of God"; and it is declared so plainly by Isaiah that he is justly called "the evangelical prophet." The "virgins" of Rev. xiv. 8 are not men and women who have never sinned; they are "redeemed" from among men; they have "washed their robes and made them white in the blood of the Lamb" (cf. 1 Cor. vi. 11). Every believer, whether of Israel or of the Church, should be able to say with the hymnist, "His blood can make the vilest clean. His blood availed for me." For "there is no difference," as the apostle reminds us; *all* have sinned and come short of the glory of God.

20 Reese (*The Approaching Advent*, pp. 142f.) is most emphatic that 1 Thess. iv. 14ff. and Rev. xix. 11ff. refer to the same event, the premillennial advent of Christ. He considers this a very important and distinctive difference between Premillennialism, in the ordinary and proper sense of the word, and Modern Dispensationalism (*id.*, p. 17f.).

21 Neatby, W. B., *A History of the Plymouth Brethren*, p. 105.

22 Darby, "Hopes of the Christian Church" (*Collected Writings*, ii. 521, cf. 502f.).

23 Darby, *Collected Writings*, xi. 167ff. Cf. Savage, *The Scroll*, p. 80.

24 This verse and vs. 9 must be interpreted consistently. If "Jacob" must mean the Twelve Tribes, then "David" must mean the literal son of Jesse, who is again to reign in Jerusalem as he did centuries ago. If, on the other hand, "David" means the Messiah, then a higher and typical meaning may properly be assigned to the word "Jacob" also. Biederwolf finds here an "incontrovertible argument that '*the time of Jacob's trouble*' looks primarily to a period prior to the appearance [first advent?] of the Messiah" (*Millennium Bible*, p. 156).

25 *RB*, pp. 1331f.

26 Cf. "C. S." (Charles Stanley), "The Revelation of Jesus Christ" (p. 32); A. C. Gaebelein, *World Prospects* (p. 176f.). According to R. V. Bingham, the latest view is that "the last three are contemporaneous" (*Matthew the Publican*, p. 112).

27 Scofield, *What Do the Prophets Say?*, p. 97, cf. pp. 78, 124.

28 *RB*, p. 1331.

29 *What Do the Prophets Say?*, p. 143.

30 The most natural explanation is that the symbolism of the number 12 as representative of *all* Israel was so important that one tribe was omitted to preserve it. To omit Levi would have been unfortunate and might have had dangerous implications. So Dan, of which little good is recorded in Scripture, is left out, just as Simeon is omitted in Deut. xxxiii.

31 The use of *four* descriptive nouns together with the word "all" (cf. also vii. 9, x. 11, xiv. 6) is clearly intended to emphasize the world-embracing character of redemption; and this is contrasted with the almost equal extent of the kingdom of evil (xi. 9, xiii. 7, xvii. 15). This is brought out clearly in the description of the heavenly city which is four-square and has gates on every side.

32 It is then that "the enormous majority of mankind will be saved" (*RB*, p. 977). It is then that "the Gospel wins its greatest triumphs in salvation" (*What Do the Prophets Say?*, p. 173).

33 *Practical Guide*, p. 204. According to West, the any moment doctrine of Pretribulationism "snatches away the Church from the Tribulation which Paul declares her highest honor on earth, 2 Thess. i. 5" (*The Apostle Paul and the "Any Moment" Theory*, p. 9). Both Bickersteth and West were, it is to be remembered, very ardent Premillennialists.

34 "The Story of the Scofield Reference Bible," pp. 233, 277f. The man, "who was considered an outstanding biblical and ecclesiastical scholar (as he undoubtedly was)," whom Gaebelein holds largely responsible for this dissention was apparently Nathanael West. In a historical sketch of events which took place a generation ago we might expect plain speaking. But Gaebelein seems to be very unwilling to mention West by name as a conspicuous opponent of the position which he has been advocating so vigorously for half a century.

35 Gordon is often quoted as a great admirer of the Plymouth Brethren. But at least as early as 1890 he had forsaken the Futurist position and refused to dogmatize on the question of a secret rapture before the epiphany (*Ecce Venit*, pp. vi. 211). Shortly before his death he expressed agreement with the views stated in a forthcoming book by Robert Cameron, who was a vigorous opponent of Pretribulationism.

36 See Scofield's tract, *Will the Church Pass Through the Great Tribulation? Eighteen Reasons which Prove that It Will Not* (Philadelphia School of the Bible) p. 36.

37 W. J. Erdman, *Notes on the Book of Revelation*, edited by Charles R. Erdman, [1930] p. 47. The editor does not state when this radical change in his father's position on this important matter took place. But the fact that Gaebelein does not mention him as having supported Scofield in the controversy over Pretribulationism indicates quite clearly that it dates from about that time, the late nineties. In justice to Scofield it is to be noted that in *RB* he refers only to Erdman's analysis and not to his interpretation of Chaps. iii.-xix.

CHAPTER IX (Pages 218-235)

1 This committee consisted of A. A. Bonar, McCheyne, Keith, and Black. Their *Narrative* was published in 1842, the year of the Disruption. In 1840 John ("Rabbi") Duncan was sent to Pesth to work among the Jews. His brief ministry of about 3 years was wonderfully fruitful. Alfred Edersheim and Adolph Saphir were among his converts.

2 *Horae*, iv., p. 207. Elliott points out that Origen, Jerome, Tertullian and Ephrem Syrus believed in the conversion of the Jews but not in their restoration to Palestine.

3 *RB*, p. 711.

4 *RB*, pp. 989, 1189.

5 *What Do the Prophets Say?*, p. 161.

6 Among the advocates of this teaching are Seiss, Govett, Pember, Peters, Campbell Morgan, Panton, J. Q. Adams.

7 *The Brethren*, p. 151. Darby puts it concisely: "When I say 'saints,' I mean all the saints, those of the Old Testament, as well as those under the New Testament dispensation" (*Lectures on the Second Coming*, p. 56).

8 Scofield insists that a person is referred to here, and that "this Person can be no other than the Holy Spirit in the church" (*RB*, p. 1272). Cf. Darby, *Synopsis*, v., p. 122. Yet, while they insist that the Holy Spirit will be removed from the earth with the Church, Dispensationalists must hold, on the basis of such prophecies as Isa. xxxii. 15, Ezek. xxxvii., and Joel ii. 28, that there will be an outpouring of the Spirit on Israel after the rapture of the Church (cf. *RB*, p. 982). But this activity will be different and apparently inferior to that during the Church age. Gaebelein remarks: "The Holy Spirit will nevertheless act in a certain way in connection with the believing Jewish remnant, which will be called and sealed by Him" (*As It Was—So Shall It Be*, p. 164.).

9 *RB*, p. 1205; cf. pp. 975, 1033.

10 *RB*, p. 1337. According to Savage, there will be "a godly remnant in their midst" (*The Scroll*, p. 70).

11 *Collected Writings*, xi., p. 182.

12 *Ibid.*, p. 185.

13 Compare Acts xx. 24f. where "the gospel of the grace of God" and the "kingdom of God" are similarly identified.

14 *RB*, p. 975.

15 *Collected Writings*, vol. xix, p. 11.

16 The three classes of sufferings distinguished by Darby were the following: (1) "During His whole life, even up to death itself, He suffered from man for righteousness' sake." These sufferings were not atoning. (2) "Besides this, on the cross He suffered for sin, drank the cup of wrath for sin, the cup His Father had given Him to drink." These sufferings were atoning; and He suffered them for all the redeemed. (3) ". . . He bore in His soul, at the close of His life (we may say from after the paschal supper), all the distress and affliction under which the Jews will come through the government of God—not condemnation, but still the consequence of sin" (*Synopsis*, ii. p. 54). These "third class"

sufferings were non-atoning. Jesus suffered them "to sympathize with the Jews in their afflictions, which they come into through their integrity and yet in their sins." In these last words the difficulty of Darby's position clearly appears. The remnant in Israel is "characterized by integrity of heart," it is godly; yet it is also sinful. Darby recognized that the atonement applied to all the redeemed. Yet he insisted that, in these sufferings, Jesus' "place" was "association with Israel in their Israelitish condition" (*Collected Writings*, xv. pp. 236f.), that Jesus associated Himself non-atoningly with this pious remnant in Israel. This means either that the Holy One associated or identified Himself non-atoningly with sinners in their sinful remoteness from God (this was the error for which Darby so unmercifully denounced B. W. Newton); or else that the remnant was not in such a sense sinful as that the Holy One could not sympathetically identify Himself with it non-atoningly. The latter seems clearly to have been Darby's position. If such was the case, could it not very easily be claimed that this godly remnant did not need atonement, did not need the Cross, or at least did not need it as other men did? Ironside believes that Hall, Dorman, and Newberry (old and ardent friends and admirers of Darby, who accused him of heresy and separated from him on this issue) completely misunderstood him, and that the same applies to Henry Groves (*Darbyism*, 2nd ed., pp. 66-84) and others who did not belong to the Exclusive (Darbyite) group of the Brethren and opposed him on other grounds as well. Ironside believes that Darby was seeking to develop precious truth taught in Scripture. But he admits that Darby's language was "most ambiguous, so that it is difficult for another to make clear exactly what he really did teach" (*A Historical Sketch of the Brethren Movement*, pp. 77f.) Unfortunately, this obscurity and ambiguity of statement is by no means rare in Darby's writings. It has often been alluded to by those of Darby's critics who have made an earnest endeavor to ascertain what he really taught on a number of important subjects. [This teaching regarding a "third-class" of sufferings did not originate in Brethren circles, neither with Newton nor with Darby. Witsius devoted a chapter in his *Economy of the Covenants* [1693] to the question, "What Sufferings of Christ were Satisfactory?" and opposed among other things the claim that only the sufferings during the three hours of darkness were "satisfactory," *i.e.*, atoning.]

17 *Lectures on the Second Advent*, p. 113.

18 *RB*, p. 973.

19 *RB*, p. 1343.

20 *RB*, p. 977.

21 *RB*, p. 1000; cf. *What Do the Prophets Say?*, p. 75. This must mean that the "constitution" as given here is not a complete one. For animal sacrifice will, according to Scofield, be revived in the millennium, though only as a memorial. But these statements show plainly that the constitution for the millennium does not require or involve the Cross. It is to be a reign of law not grace.

22 *RB*, p. 1008, cf. p. 1132 and also *Rightly Dividing*, p. 5. This sharp distinction is also illustrated by the comment on Acts xix. 2 (*RB*, p. 1175) where with reference to the answer given by Apollos's Ephesian con-

verts, Scofield says: "Their answer brought out the fact that they were Jewish proselytes, disciples of John the Baptist, looking forward to a coming King, not Christians looking backward to an accomplished redemption." This ignores the fact that John pointed to Jesus as "the Lamb of God, which taketh away the sin of the world." This sharp distinction between the King and the Saviour, and the attempt to refer these closely related offices of Christ to two distinct dispensations, is one of the most serious errors of the Dispensational system.

CHAPTER X (Pages 236-255)

1 *RB*, p. 977. Waldegrave describes it as "a convertible term for such general, such unmixed, such long continued terrestrial blessedness, as the world has certainly never yet beheld" (*New Test. Millenn.*, p. 312).

2 The interpretation of Heb. xii. 27f. is difficult. Many commentators hold that the "shaking" which is referred to with the words "yet once more" is future and will take place when the new heavens and new earth are brought into being at the second advent. Others (*e.g.*, Owen, Lindsay, Moses Stuart) hold that this shaking took place when the Christian dispensation was first introduced and the Jewish economy abolished (having perhaps especial reference to the destruction of Jerusalem and the temple by Titus). But so much at least seems to be clear, that the "unshakeable kingdom" is the Christian dispensation. The great aim of the epistle is to show the vast difference between it and the Jewish; and one of the most important of these differences consists in the fact that the one was shakeable while the other is not (Dan. ii. 44; vii. 14, 18). To attempt to find here any reference to or room for a future *Jewish* millennial kingdom which is to supplant the Church would therefore be manifestly absurd. It would contradict the whole aim of the writer of the epistle.

3 This point was stressed by J. Agar Beet in the British Weekly Debate of 1887 on the subject, "The Second Advent: Will It Be Premillennial?" "Nowhere," he tells us, "in the Book of Daniel, or throughout the Bible except Rev. xx. 1-7, have we one word about the millennium, *i.e.*, about a limited though long period of peace followed by insurrection. The visions of Daniel refer always to the eternal glory. And we have no right to assume that the splendid visions of Isaiah refer to the limited period of the millennium. Indeed, the vision of the New Earth and Heaven in Rev. xxi. 1 reproduces Isaiah lxv. 17 and lxvi. 22, as does Rev. xxi. 4 the words of Isaiah xxv. 8. There is nothing to prevent us from reading the glorious visions of the prophets as descriptions of the final glory. Certainly there is no shadow of hint that the splendors there described are to be followed by further conflict. Consequently the prophets afford no support to the premillennial theory" (pp. 33f. of the pamphlet). See also Moule, *Outline of Christian Doctrine*, p. 108.

4 The most recent attempt to avoid this difficulty was made at the Congress on Prophecy held in New York, Nov. 1-8, 1942. It shows quite clearly that basic principles of literalistic interpretation must be sur-

rendered if this prediction is to be brought into harmony with the prophetic chart of Dispensationalists (cf. the report given in *The Sure Word of Prophecy*, edited by John W. Bradbury, 1943).

5 *The Second Coming*, Part I, Chap. IV, especially pp. 64-81.

6 *Collected Writings*, xi., p. 534. See also Kelly, *Lectures on the Book of Revelation*, p. 432.

7 *Maranatha*, p. 490. Cf. Webb-Peploe, *He Cometh*, pp. 103f., Scofield, *What Do the Prophets Say?*, pp. 56f., Savage, *The Scroll*, pp. 163f., 181f.

8 This statement may seem to ignore the fact that Dispensationalists find many references to the millennium in the NT. According to Kelly, "The following are but a selection of NT scriptures which apply to the millennial day rather than to any other: Mt. xix. 28, Lk. i. 70-79, Acts xvii. 31, Rom. viii. 19, 23, xi. 26-31, I Cor. vi. 2, 3, Eph. i. 10, Phil. ii. 10, 11, Col. i. 20, 2 Thess. i. 5-10, 2 Tim. ii. 12, iv. 1, Heb. ii. 5-8." But when we examine these passages we find that, even if it be admitted for the sake of argument that they refer to this period, they tell us almost nothing about it, except that it is to be a time of blessing for the saints who will reign with Christ, of judgment for the wicked, and of the fulfilment of God's covenant promises.

9 *Practical Guide*, pp. 41, 111.

10 It is to be recognized, of course, that Dispensationalists insist that the Church saints will reign with Christ in the coming kingdom. This might suggest that the millennium will be a distinctively Christian age; and many Premillennialists have so regarded it. But Dispensationalists must hold this doctrine in strict accord with two great principles of their system of interpretation: (1) The Church and Israel are quite distinct, the one a heavenly, the other an earthly, people; (2) The earthly people is a Jewish people, and the kingdom promises made to it are to be fulfilled literally in terms of the OT economy: Christ will sit on the throne of David. Consequently, to regard this earthly kingdom as dominated by a Church which can recognize no difference and distinction between Jew and Gentile would lead to the utmost confusion.

11 See the excellent discussion of the results of "literal" interpretation by Hamilton in *The Basis of Millennial Faith*, pp. 38-59.

12 *RB*, p. 890. Cf. Walter Scott, *Prophetic Scenes*, pp. 74f.; Savage, *The Scroll*, pp. 173f.

13 It is very significant that it was this fact apparently which was responsible for the radical change in the views of Principal Fairbairn. This is brought out clearly in the little volume, *The Prophetic Prospects of the Jews; or Fairbairn vs. Fairbairn* (1930). Here Albertus Pieters has brought together a Lecture delivered by Fairbairn before 1840 and a chapter from his elaborate work on *Prophecy* published nearly twenty years later. A comparison of these two carefully argued discussions shows that it was his inability on literalistic principles to solve the problem raised by Ezekiel's statements regarding the restoration of sacrifice in the millennium, which caused Fairbairn to forsake the view, advocated in the Lecture, that Israel will be restored to the literal land of Canaan. In a lengthy footnote to the Lecture he states the problem thus: (1) Ezekiel xl.-xlviii. must refer to the future and "to events which are to have an exact and literal fulfilment." (2) "And yet it is just as impossible, on the

other hand, to understand how, seeing the events did not take place at any period during the Jewish dispensation, they can do so during any period of the Christian." (3) "They [the sacrifices] are plainly described as expiatory," and cannot be regarded as memorial. The conclusion at which Fairbairn arrived from these premises was that, "Our only wisdom appears to be to leave this portion of Scripture out of the discussion which we now hold concerning the future prospects of Israel." But Fairbairn could not be content to leave this problem in Ezekiel unsolved. So a decade later in his *Ezekiel* (1851) he gives us that "Christian spiritual" interpretation of Chaps. xl-xlviii. which, employing that typical method of interpretation which is set forth in his *Typology* (1854) and applied in his work on *Prophecy* (1856), regards the vision of Ezekiel as "a grand complicated symbol of the good God had in reserve for his Church, especially under the coming dispensation of the Gospel" *(Ezekiel*, 4th ed., p. 435). To this vitally important question David Brown devotes an entire chapter *(The Second Advent*, pp. 357-79). Brookes in *Maranatha* mentions it but does not discuss it.

14 The "parenthesis" interpretation of Dan. ix. 24-27 involves this dangerous error. According to the "traditional" view, Jesus caused the oblation and sacrifice of the temple worship to cease through His atoning death, which was the fulfilment of these typical sacrifices and alone gave them value and efficacy. According to Dispensationalists the temple must be rebuilt at Jerusalem by the Jews after the rapture of the Church as a result of a covenant with Antichrist, in order that "in the midst of the week" he may break the covenant and abolish the OT sacrificial worship which had been restored in it. This temple is to be destroyed and a fifth, Ezekiel's kingdom temple, is to be built for the worship of the millennial age. This means that the temple at Jerusalem is to be rebuilt twice: the first time by virtue of a covenant with Antichrist, the second time by divine command. The former will according to Scofield be used by "unbelieving Jews" *(RB*, p. 963). According to Savage, on the other hand, the temple services are "partly restored by the pious Jews in Jerusalem, and to a certain extent owned by God." In the latter case he tells us "this movement will be approved and owned by God" *(The Scroll*, p. 89, cf. pp. 70, 74, 173f.).

15 Literally interpreted, this must take place at or after the visible return of Christ to the earth to set up the millennial kingdom. If so, the great missionary work, the result of which is described in Rev. vii., the conversion of the multitude that no man could number, must be carried out by the "godly" remnant of Israel before the Jews as a nation have confessed the guilt of slaying their Messiah.

16 Chafer, "Dispensationalism," p. 413.

17 Cf. the report of the conference in Pettingill, *Light on Prophecy*, p. 32.

18 In this statement Scofield goes directly counter to the teaching of 2 Pet. iii. 8f. There the apostle definitely affirms that the apparent delay in the coming of Christ is due to God's being "unwilling that any should perish, but that all should come to repentance." By "any" and "all" Peter clearly means what Scofield calls "humanity"; and he definitely places the time of repentance, the day of salvation as it is

called in 2 Cor. vi. 2, before the coming of Christ. Scofield definitely asserts the opposite: the hope of humanity is in the coming of Christ; the day of salvation in a pre-eminent sense, the period of mass-salvation, will follow the advent.

19 *Wrongly Dividing the Word of Truth,* pp. 17f.

20 Vol. iii., p. 195.

APPENDIX (Pages 264-284)

1 That Dr. Chafer attaches no little importance to this passage is indicated by the fact that he refers to it again, near the close of the article, listing it as the 12th among 22 illustrations of the "insuperable conflicts" which arise if Dispensational distinctions are not properly observed.

2 Scholars differ as to Origen's motive. Whether Fairweather is correct in holding that his "deepest motive for self-sacrifice probably lay in the literalistic interpretation of Holy Scripture which at this period commended itself to him" *(Origen and Greek Patristic Theology,* p. 42) or other reasons figured more prominently, it is hard to avoid the conclusion that the fact that this false step could find Scriptural warrant only on the basis of a strictly literal interpretation, may well have influenced him in his swing to the opposite extreme of a highly allegorical method of interpretation.

3 John Newton in the beautiful hymn, "How sweet the name of Jesus sounds in a believer's ear," gathers together more than a dozen such descriptive names.

4 The number seven figures in the analysis of fifteen books of the Bible as given by Scofield (Deut., Judg., 1 & 2 Kgs., Esth., Job, Isa., Ezek., Lk., Jn., Rom., Gal., Col., 1 Jn., Rev.). In most of these cases the analysis is more or less arbitrary. Cf. especially pp. 287, 1262f. Note also: 7 dispensations (p. 5), 7 judgments (pp. 1133, 1351), 7 events in the Day of the Lord (p. 1349), 7 distinct periods in Israel's history (p. 257), Christ's 7-fold relation to the law (p. 1000), the believer's 7-fold position (p. 1313), 7 parts of the Abrahamic covenant (p. 24), of the Palestinian covenant (p. 250), 7 features of the dispensation of the fulness of times (p. 1250), *etc.*

5 Cf. R. D. Wilson, "The Names of God in the Old Testament" *(Princeton* Theol. Rev., vol. xxii., p. 113; also vol. xviii., p. 480f.).

6 *RB,* p. 883. This claim has recently been quite conclusively refuted by Th. Graebner *(War in the Light of Prophecy,* pp. 81ff.).

7 Cf. R. D. Wilson (Princeton Theol. Rev., vol. xviii., pp. 466f.). Dr. Wilson lists seven names as "simple," *i.e.,* primary.

8 Trench, *New Testament Synonyms,* p. 165.

9 See Wyngaarden, *The Future of the Kingdom,* p. 185. Darby recognized that "thousands . . . have repented as individuals" ("Restoration," p. 27).

10 *Unsearchable Riches,* p. 30; cf., *Christianity or Religion?,* pp. 146f., 149.

11 "The Purpose of God" (1839) in *Collected Writings,* ii., p. 410. Elsewhere he speaks of it as "a far deeper and more glorious economy" *(ibid.,* pp. 191f.), as an "immense change" (p. 530).

12 "What is the Church?" (1849) in *Collected Writings*, iii., p. 555.
13 *Christianity or Religion?*, p. 149.
14 *RB*, p. 975.
15 *RB*, p. 1226.

ADDENDA (Pages 267-277)

Ex. ii. 13-14 (p. 73). The heading, "The revelation of the name Jehovah," is misleading and dangerous. It implies that this name was first known and used in the time of Moses (cf. Gen. xiv. 17, "The revelation of God as *El Elyon,*" *RB*, p. 23). The critics have long maintained that Ex. iii. 13-15 (E) and vi. 3 (P) must mean just what this heading implies, and that they flatly contradict Gen. iv. 26 (J) which declares that the worship of God as Jehovah was introduced centuries earlier. That Scofield did not accept the critical view is indicated by his note on Gen. ii. 4. But the statement there, "The first distinct *revelation* of Himself by His name Jehovah was in connection with the redemption of the covenant people out of Egypt (Ex. iii. 13-17)," is by no means adequate and concedes far too much to the critics. How did men in the days of Enosh come to "call on the name of Jehovah" or to swear by the name of Jehovah in the time of Abraham (Gen. xiv. 22), unless He had distinctly revealed Himself to them by that name? The use of the name Jehovah in the pre-Mosaic period may have been rare, the name may have been almost forgotten. But it was not a new name. It was an old name, the *meaning* of which and the *preciousness* of which was to be made clear, or at least very much clearer, by the mighty acts of the deliverance from Egypt. The words, "Jehovah, the God of your fathers" (Ex. iii. 15, *ARV*) conflict sharply with the heading, "The revelation of the name Jehovah" in *RB*. Furthermore, it is hard to understand why Scofield favored the rendering "to call themselves by the name of Jehovah" (Gen. iv. 26) instead of "to call on the name of Jehovah." Exactly the same phrase occurs in xii. 8 and xxvi. 25. The words, "*Contra* xii. 8; xxvi. 25" (*RB*, p. 12c), seem to mean that the rendering, "to call themselves by," which is an impossible rendering of the Hebrew, is to be insisted on despite these two passages where the usual rendering is accepted without comment or correction.

1 Cor. x. 8 (p. 1220). In the Hebrew Bible, numbers are always spelled out, just as in the English translations (e.g., Gen. v. 27). This may have been with a view to prevent errors in the transmission of the text, since words would be less easily misread than signs or figures. The statement that "the Hebrews used letters in the place of numerals" is a sweeping assertion which should have been carefully guarded. Whether this usage goes farther back than Maccabean times is doubtful. Whether it was ever employed in the writing or copying of manuscripts of the OT is still more doubtful. Several other explanations of the variation discussed in this note are at least worthy of consideration. To represent this doubtful one as the correct one and to draw the sweeping inference, "Error in transcription of Hebrew numbers thus becomes easy, preservation of numerical accuracy difficult," is not only unwarranted but highly detrimental to the very aim which Scofield had constantly in view, the defense of the trustworthiness of the Biblical record.

INDEX

TEXTS

330

AUTHORS

SUBJECTS